# Full-Stack React, TypeScript, and Node

Build cloud-ready web applications using React 17 with Hooks and GraphQL

**David Choi**

BIRMINGHAM—MUMBAI

# Full-Stack React, TypeScript, and Node

**Commissioning Editor**: Pavan Ramchandani
**Acquisition Editor**: Ashitosh Gupta
**Senior Editor**: Hayden Edwards
**Content Development Editor**: Divya Vijayan
**Technical Editor**: Deepesh Patel and Saurabh Kadave
**Copy Editor**: Safis Editing
**Project Coordinator**: Kinjal Bari
**Proofreader**: Safis Editing
**Indexer**: Pratik Shirodkar
**Production Designer**: Jyoti Chauhan

First published: December 2020

Production reference: 1181220

Published by Packt Publishing Ltd.
Livery Place
35 Livery Street
Birmingham
B3 2PB, UK.

ISBN 978-1-83921-993-1

www.packt.com

*To my beautiful wife, Eun. Thank you for your faith and love.*
*I made it because of you.*

*– David Choi*

Packt.com

Subscribe to our online digital library for full access to over 7,000 books and videos, as well as industry leading tools to help you plan your personal development and advance your career. For more information, please visit our website.

## Why subscribe?

- Spend less time learning and more time coding with practical eBooks and videos from over 4,000 industry professionals

- Improve your learning with Skill Plans built especially for you

- Get a free eBook or video every month

- Fully searchable for easy access to vital information

- Copy and paste, print, and bookmark content

Did you know that Packt offers eBook versions of every book published, with PDF and ePub files available? You can upgrade to the eBook version at packt.com and, as a print book customer, you are entitled to a discount on the eBook copy. Get in touch with us at customercare@packtpub.com for more details.

At www.packt.com, you can also read a collection of free technical articles, sign up for a range of free newsletters, and receive exclusive discounts and offers on Packt books and eBooks.

# Contributors

## About the author

**David Choi** is a developer with over 10 years' experience in building enterprise-class applications using a variety of frameworks and languages. Most of his professional development experience has involved working in finance for companies such as JPMorgan, CSFB, and Franklin Templeton. He currently works at his own start-up, DzHaven, building an application to help devs help other devs.

You can find David on YouTube at the David Choi channel, or on Twitter at jsoneaday.

*I would like to thank the good people at Packt, and Mike Rourke, without whose help this book would not have been possible.*

## About the reviewer

**Mike Rourke** is a software engineer based in Chicago who works primarily with web technologies and the Node.js ecosystem. He has been writing code for over 10 years. Mike started out writing VB and switched to JavaScript about 2 years ago. He loves all aspects of programming and spends most of his free time learning new technologies and improving his skills.

## Packt is searching for authors like you

If you're interested in becoming an author for Packt, please visit `authors.packtpub.com` and apply today. We have worked with thousands of developers and tech professionals, just like you, to help them share their insight with the global tech community. You can make a general application, apply for a specific hot topic that we are recruiting an author for, or submit your own idea.

# Table of Contents

## Section 2:
## Learning Single-Page Application Development Using React

# 4

## Learning Single-Page Application Concepts and How React Enables Them

# 5
# React Development with Hooks

# 6
# Setting Up Our Project Using create-react-app and Testing with Jest

# 7
# Learning Redux and React Router

# Section 3: Understanding Web Service Development Using Express and GraphQL

## 8

## Learning Server-Side Development with Node.js and Express

## 9

## What is GraphQL?

## 10

## Setting Up an Express Project with TypeScript and GraphQL Dependencies

# 11

## What We Will Learn – Online Forum Application

# 12

## Building the React Client for Our Online Forum Application

# 13

## Set Up a Session State Using Express and Redis

# 14

## Setting Up Postgres and a Repository Layer with TypeORM

# 15

## Adding GraphQL Schema Part I

# 16

## Adding a GraphQL Schema – Part II

# 17

## Deploying an Application to AWS

## Other Books You May Enjoy

## Index

# Preface

According to GitHub, the largest repository for open source software, JavaScript is still the most popular programming language in the world. More projects are written in JavaScript than any other language. Even projects normally not associated with the web, such as machine learning and crypto currencies, often use JavaScript.

The JavaScript programming language is enormously powerful and capable, but in addition to the language, there are frameworks, including React and Node, that add to the language's capabilities, making it even better. On top of this, TypeScript has now become the standard for doing large JavaScript projects. It provides language features that make coding with JavaScript more productive and better suited for large applications.

Modern web development has advanced tremendously over the years. In the past, client code generally meant static HTML and CSS, with perhaps a tiny bit of JavaScript. And the backend was usually written in a completely different language, such as PHP or CGI scripts. However, it is now common to write the entire application, from client to server, using only JavaScript and its related frameworks. This ability to write our applications using only a single language provides enormous benefits during development. Furthermore, the robust and mature frameworks that are available make full stack programming in JavaScript competitive with any other platform.

In this book, we will learn to use the power of JavaScript to build complete full stack web applications. We will augment this power with TypeScript, another powerful top-ten language. Then, using frameworks such as React, Redux, Node, Express, and GraphQL, we will build a realistic, fully functional best-practices web application that will give you all the knowledge you need in order to build modern full stack web applications. And once our application is complete, we'll deploy it to AWS cloud services, the world's most popular and feature-rich cloud services provider.

## Who this book is for

The book is for web developers who want to go beyond front-end web development and enter the world of full-stack web development by learning about modern web technologies and how they come together. A good understanding of JavaScript programming is required before getting started with this web development book.

# What this book covers

*Chapter 1, Understanding TypeScript*, explains what TypeScript is and what makes it ideal for use in large application development.

*Chapter 2, Exploring TypeScript*, dives deep into TypeScript. We'll explore its features, including static typing, and why these features are an improvement over JavaScript. We'll also look at application design with object-oriented programming and how TypeScript features enable this important programming paradigm.

*Chapter 3, Building Better Apps with ES6+ Features*, reviews the important features of JavaScript that every developer needs to know. We'll focus on the latest features added in ES6 and beyond.

*Chapter 4, Learning Single-Page Application Concepts and How React Enables Them*, explains how websites are built and focuses on single-page application-style apps. We'll then introduce React and how React is used to create a single-page application.

*Chapter 5, React Development with Hooks*, dives deep into React. We'll learn about the limitations of the older class style of writing React applications, as well as learn about Hooks and functional components and how they are an improvement on the older class style.

*Chapter 6, Setting Up Our Project Using create-react-app and Testing with Jest*, describes the modern methods used for developing React applications. This includes the standard for creating React projects, `create-react-app`, and client-side testing with Jest and testing-library.

*Chapter 7, Learning Redux and React Router*, covers Redux and React Router to help us build our React application. These two frameworks have been the go-to frameworks for managing state and routing almost since React's inception.

*Chapter 8, Learning Server-Side Development with Node.js and Express*, covers Node and Express. Node is the underlying runtime that makes JavaScript server apps possible. Express is the framework around Node that makes it easy to build powerful server-side apps using Node.

*Chapter 9, What is GraphQL?*, reviews what GraphQL is and how it uses data schemas to help build a web API.

*Chapter 10, Setting Up an Express Project with TypeScript and GraphQL Dependencies*, explains how to create a production quality, server-side project using TypeScript, Express, GraphQL, and Jest for testing.

*Chapter 11, What We Will Learn – Online Forum Application*, discusses the application we will be building. We will review its features and how building such an app will help us learn about web development in more detail.

*Chapter 12, Building the React Client for Our Online Forum Application*, explains how to start coding the client side of our application with React. We will use functional components, Hooks, and Redux to begin building our screens.

*Chapter 13, Setting Up Session State Using Express and Redis*, explores what session state is and how to create a session for our server using Redis, the world's most powerful in-memory datastore. We also begin coding our server using Express.

*Chapter 14, Setting Up Postgres and Repository Layer with TypeORM*, explains how to create a database for our application in Postgres and how to access it using a powerful design technique called Repository Layer.

*Chapter 15, Adding a GraphQL Schema – Part I*, begins the integration of GraphQL into our application. We will build our schema and add our queries and mutations. We will also begin adding our GraphQL Hooks to our React frontend.

*Chapter 16, Adding a GraphQL Schema – Part II*, completes our application by finishing the work of integrating GraphQL into both our client and server.

*Chapter 17, Deploying an Application to AWS*, takes our finished application and deploys it to AWS cloud services. We will use Ubuntu Linux and NGINX to host our server and client code.

# To get the most out of this book

You should have a year or more of programming experience in at least one modern language, along with some basic knowledge of building applications, although this does not have to be for the web.

| Software/hardware covered in the book | OS requirements |
| --- | --- |
| React 17 (all code is compatible with React 16.x) | Windows, macOS X, and Linux (any) |
| TypeScript 3.7 or greater | |
| A modern browser: Chrome, Safari, or Firefox | |
| Node 12 or greater | |

This book will provide step-by-step instructions on using or installing these dependencies. However, this list does give some idea of what will be needed. Application source code will be for the final completed version of the application. The book will include any intermediate code.

**If you are using the digital version of this book, we advise you to type the code yourself or access the code via the GitHub repository (link available in the next section). Doing so will help you avoid any potential errors related to the copying and pasting of code.**

Ideally, you should always endeavor to type the code yourself as it will help you remember both the code and give you experience of what to do when things go wrong.

# Download the example code files

You can download the example code files for this book from GitHub at `https://github.com/PacktPublishing/Full-Stack-React-TypeScript-and-Node`. In case there's an update to the code, it will be updated on the existing GitHub repository.

We also have other code bundles from our rich catalog of books and videos available at `https://github.com/PacktPublishing/`. Check them out!

# Conventions used

There are a number of text conventions used throughout this book.

`Code in text`: Indicates code words in text, database table names, folder names, filenames, file extensions, pathnames, dummy URLs, user input, and Twitter handles. Here is an example: "Create a new file in the `src` folder called `Home.tsx` and add the following code."

A block of code is set as follows:

```
let a = 5;
let b = '6';
console.log(a + b);
```

When we wish to draw your attention to a particular part of a code block, the relevant lines or items are set in bold:

```
[default]
exten => s,1,Dial(Zap/1|30)
exten => s,2,Voicemail(u100)
exten => s,102,Voicemail(b100)
exten => i,1,Voicemail(s0)
```

Any command-line input or output is written as follows:

```
npm install typescript
```

**Bold**: Indicates a new term, an important word, or words that you see on screen. For example, words in menus or dialog boxes appear in the text like this. Here is an example: "Select **System info** from the **Administration** panel."

> **Tips or important notes**
> Appear like this.

# Get in touch

Feedback from our readers is always welcome.

**General feedback**: If you have questions about any aspect of this book, mention the book title in the subject of your message and email us at customercare@packtpub.com.

**Errata**: Although we have taken every care to ensure the accuracy of our content, mistakes do happen. If you have found a mistake in this book, we would be grateful if you would report this to us. Please visit www.packtpub.com/support/errata, selecting your book, clicking on the Errata Submission Form link, and entering the details.

**Piracy**: If you come across any illegal copies of our works in any form on the internet, we would be grateful if you would provide us with the location address or website name. Please contact us at copyright@packt.com with a link to the material.

**If you are interested in becoming an author**: If there is a topic that you have expertise in, and you are interested in either writing or contributing to a book, please visit authors.packtpub.com.

# Reviews

Please leave a review. Once you have read and used this book, why not leave a review on the site that you purchased it from? Potential readers can then see and use your unbiased opinion to make purchase decisions, we at Packt can understand what you think about our products, and our authors can see your feedback on their book. Thank you!

For more information about Packt, please visit packt.com.

# Section 1: Understanding TypeScript and How It Can Improve Your JavaScript

This section gives you an overview of the benefits of TypeScript and its most important language features. We will also cover what the most important features of ES6 are, and how we can improve code quality and readability.

This section comprises of the following chapters:

- *Chapter 1, Understanding TypeScript*
- *Chapter 2, Exploring TypeScript*
- *Chapter 3, Building Better Apps with ES6+ Features*

# 1
# Understanding TypeScript

JavaScript is an enormously popular and powerful language. According to GitHub, it is the most popular language in the world (yes, used even more than Python), and the new features in ES6+ continue to add useful capabilities. However, for large application development, its feature set is considered to be incomplete. This is why TypeScript was created.

In this chapter, we'll learn about the TypeScript language, why it was created, and what value it provides to JavaScript developers. We'll learn about the design philosophy Microsoft used in creating TypeScript and why these design decisions added important support in the language for large application development.

We'll also see how TypeScript enhances and improves upon JavaScript. We'll compare and contrast the JavaScript way of writing code with TypeScript. TypeScript has a wealth of cutting-edge features to benefit developers. Chief among them are static typing and **Object-Oriented Programming (OOP)** capabilities. These features can make for code that is higher quality and easier to maintain.

By the end of this chapter, you will understand some of the limitations of JavaScript that make it difficult to use in large projects. You will also understand how TypeScript fills in some of those gaps and makes writing large, complex applications easier and less prone to error.

In this chapter, we're going to cover the following main topics:

- What is TypeScript?
- Why is TypeScript necessary?

# Technical requirements

In order to take full advantage of this chapter, you should have a basic understanding of JavaScript version ES5 or higher and some experience with building web applications with a JavaScript framework. You'll also need to install Node and a JavaScript code editor, such as **Visual Studio Code** (**VSCode**).

You can find the GitHub repository for this chapter at `https://github.com/ PacktPublishing/Full-Stack-React-TypeScript-and-Node`. Use the code in the `Chap1` folder.

# What is TypeScript?

TypeScript is actually two distinct but related technologies – a language and a compiler:

- The language is a feature-rich, statically typed programming language that adds true object-oriented capabilities to JavaScript.
- The compiler converts TypeScript code into native JavaScript, but also provides the programmer with assistance in writing code with fewer errors.

TypeScript enables the developer to design software that's of a higher quality. The combination of the language and the compiler enhances the developer's capabilities. By using TypeScript, a developer can write code that is easier to understand and refactor and contains fewer bugs. Additionally, it adds discipline to the development workflow by forcing errors to be fixed while still in development.

TypeScript is a development-time technology. There is no runtime component and no TypeScript code ever runs on any machine. Instead, the TypeScript compiler converts TypeScript into JavaScript and that code is then deployed and run on browsers or servers. It's possible that Microsoft considered developing a runtime for TypeScript. However, unlike the operating system market, Microsoft does not control the ECMAScript standards body (the group that decides what will be in each version of JavaScript). So, getting buy-in from that group would have been difficult and time-consuming. Instead, Microsoft decided to create a tool that enhances a JavaScript developer's productivity and code quality.

So then, if TypeScript has no runtime, how do developers get running code? TypeScript uses a process called transpilation. **Transpilation** is a method where code from one language is "compiled" or converted into another language. What this means is that all TypeScript code ultimately is converted into JavaScript code before it is finally deployed and run.

In this section, we've learned what TypeScript is and how it works. In the next section, we'll learn about why these features are necessary for building large, complex applications.

# Why is TypeScript necessary?

The JavaScript programming language was created by Brendan Eich and was added to the Netscape browser in 1995. Since that time, JavaScript has enjoyed enormous success and is now used to build server and desktop apps as well. However, this popularity and ubiquity have turned out to be a problem as well as a benefit. As larger and larger apps have been created, developers have started to notice the limitations of the language.

Large application development has greater needs than the browser development JavaScript was first created for. At a high level, almost all large application development languages, such as Java, C++, C#, and so on, provide static typing and OOP capabilities. In this section, we'll go over the advantages of static typing over JavaScript's dynamic typing. We'll also learn about OOP and why JavaScript's method of doing OOP is too limited to use for large apps.

But first, we'll need to install a few packages and programs to allow our examples. To do this, follow these instructions:

1. Let's install Node first. You can download Node from here: `https://nodejs.org/`. Node gives us npm, which is a JavaScript dependency manager that will allow us to install TypeScript. We'll dive deep into Node in *Chapter 8, Learning Server-Side Development with Node.js and Express.*

2. Install VSCode. It is a free code editor and its high-quality and rich features have quickly made it the standard development application for writing JavaScript code on any platform. You can use any code editor you like, but I will use VSCode extensively in this book.

3. Create a folder in your personal directory called `HandsOnTypeScript`. We'll save all our project code into this folder.

> **Important Note**
>
> If you don't want to type the code yourself, you can download the full source code as mentioned in the *Technical requirements* section.

4.  Inside `HandsOnTypeScript`, create another folder called `Chap1`.

5.  Open VSCode and go to **File | Open**, and then open the **Chap1** folder you just created. Then, select **View | Terminal** and enable the terminal window within your VSCode window.

6.  Type the following command into the terminal. This command will initialize your project so that it can accept npm package dependencies. You'll need this because TypeScript is downloaded as an npm package:

```
npm init
```

You should see a screen like this:

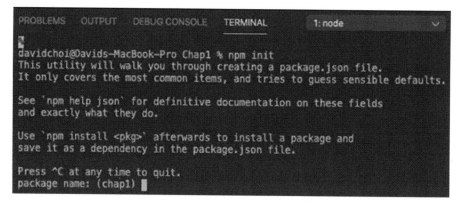

Figure 1.1 – npm init screen

You can accept the defaults for all the prompts as we will only install TypeScript for now.

7.  Install TypeScript with the following command:

```
npm install typescript
```

After all the items have been installed, your VSCode screen should look like this:

Figure 1.2 – VSCode after setup is complete

We've finished installing and setting up our environment. Now, we can take a look at some examples that will help us better understand the benefits of TypeScript.

# Dynamic versus static typing

Every programming language has and makes use of types. A type is simply a set of rules that describe an object and can be reused. JavaScript is a dynamically typed language. In JavaScript, new variables do not need to declare their type and even after they are set, they can be reset to a different type. This feature adds awesome flexibility to the language, but it is also the source of many bugs.

TypeScript uses a better alternative called **static typing**. Static typing forces the developer to indicate the type of a variable up front, when they create it. This removes ambiguity and eliminates many conversion errors between types. In the following steps, we'll take a look at some examples of the pitfalls of dynamic typing and how TypeScript's static typing can eliminate them:

1. On the root of the `Chap1` folder, let's create a file called `string-vs-number.ts`. The `.ts` file extension is a TypeScript specific extension and allows the TypeScript compiler to recognize the file and transpile it into JavaScript. Next, enter the following code into the file and save it:

```
let a = 5;
let b = '6';

console.log(a + b);
```

2. Now, in the terminal, type the following:

```
tsc string-vs-number.ts
```

`tsc` is the command to execute the TypeScript compiler, and the filename is telling the compiler to check and transpile the file into JavaScript.

3. Once you run the `tsc` command, you should see a new file, `string-vs-number.js`, in the same folder. Let's run this file:

```
node string-vs-number.js
```

The `node` command acts as a runtime environment for the JavaScript file to run. The reason why this works is that Node uses Google's Chrome browser engine, V8, to run JavaScript code. So, once you have run this script, you should see this:

```
56
```

Obviously, if we add two numbers together normally, we want a sum to happen, not a string concatenation. However, since the JavaScript runtime has no way of knowing this, it guesses the desired intent and converts the a number variable into a string and appends it to variable b. This situation may seem unlikely in real-world code but if left unchecked it could occur, because in web development, most inputs coming in from HTML come in as strings—even if the user types a number.

4.  Now, let's introduce TypeScript's static typing into this code and see what happens. First, let's delete the `.js` file, as the TypeScript compiler may consider there to be two copies of the a and b variables. Take a look at this code:

```
let a: number = 5;
let b: number = '6';


console.log(a + b);
```

5.  If you run the `tsc` compiler on this code, you will get the error `Type "'6'" is not assignable to the type 'number'`. This is exactly what we want. The compiler tells us that there is an error in our code and prevents the compilation from successfully compiling. Since we indicated that both variables are supposed to be numbers, the compiler checks for that and complains when it finds it not to be true. So, if we fix this code and set b to be a number, let's see what happens:

```
let a: number = 5;
let b: number = 6;


console.log(a + b);
```

6.  Now, if you run the compiler, it will complete successfully, and running the JavaScript will result in the value `11`:

```
davidchoi@Davids-MacBook-Pro Chap1 % tsc string-vs-number.ts
davidchoi@Davids-MacBook-Pro Chap1 % node string-vs-number.js
11
davidchoi@Davids-MacBook-Pro Chap1 %
```

Figure 1.3 – Valid numbers addition

Great, when we set b incorrectly, TypeScript caught our error and prevented it from being used at runtime.

Let's look at another more complex example, as it's like what you might see in larger app code:

1.  Let's create a new `.ts` file called `test-age.ts` and add the following code to it:

```
function canDrive(usr) {
    console.log("user is", usr.name);


    if(usr.age >= 16) {
```

```
            console.log("allow to drive");
        } else {
            console.log("do not allow to drive");
        }
}

const tom = {
    name: "tom"
}

canDrive (tom);
```

As you can see, the code has a function that checks the age of a user and determines, based on that age, whether they are allowed to drive. After the function definition, we see that a user is created, but with no age property. Let's pretend that the developer wanted to fill that in later based on user input. Now, below that user creation, the canDrive function is called and it claims the user is not allowed to drive. If it turned out that user tom was over 16 years old and this function triggered another action to be taken based on the user's age, obviously this could lead to a whole host of issues.

There are ways in JavaScript to deal with this problem, or at least partially. We could use a for loop to iterate through all of the property key names of the user object and check for an age name. Then, we could throw an exception or have some other error handler to deal with this issue. However, if we had to do this on every function, it would become inefficient and onerous very quickly. Additionally, we would be doing these checks while the code is running. Obviously, for these errors, we would prefer catching them before they make it out to users. TypeScript provides a simple solution to this issue and catches the error before the code even makes it into production. Take a look at the following updated code:

```
interface User {
    name: string;
    age: number;
}

function canDrive(usr: User) {
    console.log("user is", usr.name);
```

```
    if(usr.age >= 16) {
        console.log("allow to drive");
    } else {
        console.log("do not allow to drive");
    }
}

const tom = {
    name: "tom"
}

canDrive (tom);
```

Let's go through this updated code. At the top, we see something called an interface and it is given a name of User. An interface is one possible kind of type in TypeScript. I'll detail interfaces and other types in later chapters, but for now, let's just take a look at this example. The User interface has the two fields that we need: name and age. Now, below that, we see that our canDrive function's usr parameter has a colon and the User type on it. This is called a type annotation and it means that we are telling the compiler only to allow parameters of the User type to be given to canDrive. Therefore, when I try and compile this code with TypeScript, the compiler complains that when canDrive is called, age is missing from the passed-in parameter, because our tom object does not have that property:

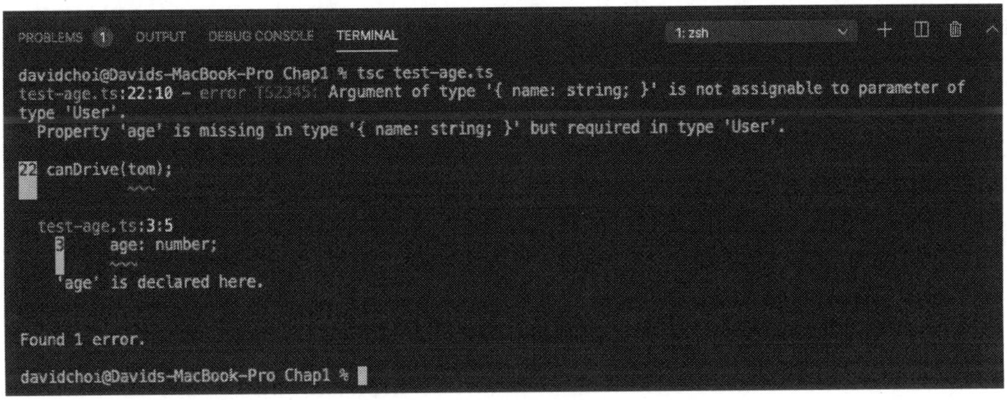

Figure 1.4 – canDrive error

2.  So, once again, the compiler has caught our error. Let's fix this issue by giving `tom` a type:

```
const tom: User = {
    name: "tom"
}
```

3.  If we give `tom` a type of `User`, but do not add the required `age` property, we get the following error:

```
Property 'age' is missing in type '{ name: string; }' but
required in type 'User'.ts(2741)
```

However, if we add the missing `age` property, the error goes away and our `canDrive` function works as it should. Here's the final working code:

```
interface User {
    name: string;
    age: number;
}

function canDrive(usr: User) {
    console.log("user is", usr.name);

    if(usr.age >= 16) {
        console.log("allow to drive");
    } else {
        console.log("do not allow to drive");
    }
}

// let's pretend sometime later someone else uses the
//function canDrive
const tom: User = {
    name: "tom",
```

```
        age: 25
    }

    canDrive (tom);
```

This code provides the required `age` property in the `tom` variable so that when `canDrive` is executed, the check for `usr.age` is done correctly and the appropriate code is then run.

Here's a screenshot of the output once this fix is made and the code is run again:

```
davidchoi@Davids-MacBook-Pro Chap1 % tsc test-age.ts
davidchoi@Davids-MacBook-Pro Chap1 % node test-age
user is tom
allow to drive
davidchoi@Davids-MacBook-Pro Chap1 %
```

Figure 1.5 – canDrive successful result

In this section, we learned about some of the pitfalls of dynamic typing and how static typing can help remove and protect against those issues. Static typing removes ambiguity from code, both to the compiler and other developers. This clarity can reduce errors and make for higher-quality code.

# Object-oriented programming

JavaScript is known as an OOP language. It does have some of the capabilities of other OOP languages, such as inheritance. However, JavaScript's implementation is limited both in terms of available language features and design. In this section, we'll take a look at how JavaScript does OOP and how TypeScript improves upon JavaScript's capabilities.

First, let's define what OOP is. There are four major principles of OOP:

- Encapsulation
- Abstraction
- Inheritance
- Polymorphism

Let's review each one.

## Encapsulation

A shorter way of saying encapsulation is information hiding. In every program, you will have data and functions that allow you to do something with that data. When we use encapsulation, we are taking that data and putting it into a container of sorts. This container is known as a class in most programming languages and basically, it protects that data so that nothing outside of the container can modify or view it. Instead, if you want to make use of the data, it must be done through functions that are controlled by the container object. This method of working with object data allows strict control of what happens to that data from a single place in code, instead of being dispersed through many locations across a large application—which can be unwieldy and difficult to maintain.

There are some interpretations of encapsulation that focus mainly on the grouping of members inside a common container. However, in the strict sense of encapsulation, information hiding, JavaScript does not have this capability built in. For most OOP languages, encapsulation requires the ability to explicitly hide a member via a language facility. For example, in TypeScript, you can use the `private` keyword so that a property cannot be seen or modified outside of its class. Now, it is possible in JavaScript to simulate member privacy through various workarounds, but again this is not part of the native code and adds additional complexity. TypeScript supports encapsulation with access modifiers such as `private` natively.

> **Important Note**
> Privacy for class fields will be supported in ECMAScript 2020. However, as this is a newer feature, it is not supported across all browsers at the time of writing.

## Abstraction

Abstraction is related to encapsulation. When using abstraction, you hide the internal implementation of how data is managed and provide a more simplified interface to the outside code. Primarily, this is done to cause "loose coupling." This means that it is desirable for code that is responsible for one set of data to be independent and separated from other code. In this way, it is possible to change the code in one part of the application without adversely affecting the code in another part.

Abstraction for most OOP languages requires the use of a mechanism to provide simplified access to an object, without revealing that object's internal workings. For most languages, this is either an interface or an abstract class. We'll review interfaces more deeply in a later chapter, but for now, interfaces are like classes whose members have no actual working code. You can consider them a shell that only reveals the names and types of object members, but hides how they work. This capability is extremely important in producing the "loose coupling" mentioned previously and allowing code to be more easily modified and maintained. JavaScript does not support interfaces or abstract classes, while TypeScript supports both features.

## Inheritance

Inheritance is about code reuse. For example, if you needed to create objects for several types of vehicles—car, truck, and boat—it would be inefficient to write distinct code for each vehicle type. It would be better to create a base type that has the core attributes of all vehicles, and then reuse that code in each specific vehicle type. This way, we write some of the needed code only once and share it across each vehicle type.

Both JavaScript and TypeScript support classes and inheritance. If you're not familiar with classes, a class is a kind of type that stores a related set of fields and also may have functions that can act on those fields. JavaScript supports inheritance by using a system called prototypical inheritance. Basically, what this means is that in JavaScript, every object instance of a specific type shares the same instance of a single core object. This core object is the prototype, and whatever fields or functions are created on the prototype, they are accessible across the various object instances. This is a good way of saving resources, such as memory, but it does not have the level of flexibility or sophistication of the inheritance model in TypeScript.

In TypeScript, classes can inherit from other classes but they can also inherit from interfaces and abstract classes. Since JavaScript does not have these features, in comparison, its prototypical inheritance is limited. Additionally, JavaScript has no ability to inherit from multiple classes directly, which is another method of doing code reuse called multiple inheritance. But TypeScript does allow multiple inheritance using mixins. We'll dive deep into all these features later, but basically, the point is that TypeScript has a more capable inheritance model that allows for more kinds of inheritance and therefore more ways to reuse code.

## Polymorphism

Polymorphism is related to inheritance. In polymorphism, it is possible to create an object that can be set to one of any number of possible types that inherit from the same base lineage. This capability is useful for scenarios where the type needed is not immediately knowable but can be set at runtime once the appropriate circumstances have arisen.

This feature is used less often in OOP code than some of the other features, but nevertheless can be useful. In the case of JavaScript, there is no direct language support for polymorphism, but due to its dynamic typing, it can be simulated reasonably well (some JavaScript enthusiasts will strongly disagree with this statement, but please hear me out).

Let's look at an example. It is possible to use JavaScript class inheritance to create a base class and have multiple classes that inherit from this one parent base class. Then, by using standard JavaScript variable declaration, which does not indicate the type, we can set the type instance at runtime to whichever inheriting class is appropriate. The issue I find is that there is no way to force the variable to be of a specific base type since there is no way to declare types in JavaScript, therefore there is no way of enforcing only classes that inherit from the one base type during development. So, again, you have to resort to workarounds such as using the `instanceof` keyword in order to test for certain types at runtime, to try and enforce type safety.

In the case of TypeScript, static typing is on by default and forces type declaration when the variable is first created. Additionally, TypeScript supports interfaces, which can be implemented by classes. Therefore, declaring a variable to be of a specific interface type forces all classes instantiated to that variable to be inheritors of the same interface. Again, this is all done at development time before code is deployed. This system is more explicit, enforceable, and reliable than the one in JavaScript.

In this section, we have learned about OOP and its importance in large application development. We've also understood why TypeScript's OOP capabilities are significantly better and more feature-rich than JavaScript's.

# Summary

In this chapter, we introduced TypeScript and learned why it was created. We learned why type safety and OOP capabilities can be so important for building large apps. Then, we saw some examples comparing dynamic typing and static typing and saw why static typing might be a better way of writing code. Finally, we compared the styles of OOP between the two languages and learned why TypeScript has the better and more capable system. The information in this chapter has given us a good high-level conceptual understanding of the benefits of TypeScript.

In the next chapter, we'll do a deeper dive into the TypeScript language. We'll learn more about types and investigate some of the most important features of TypeScript, such as classes, interfaces, and generics. This chapter should give you a strong foundation for using the various frameworks and libraries in the JavaScript ecosystem.

# 2

# Exploring TypeScript

In this chapter, we'll dive deeper into the TypeScript language. We'll learn about TypeScript's explicit type declaration syntax, as well as about the many built-in types in TypeScript and their purpose.

We'll also learn how to create our own types and build applications adhering to object-oriented principles. Finally, we'll review some of the latest features added to the language, such as optional chaining and nullish coalescing.

By the end of this chapter, you will have a strong understanding of the TypeScript language, which will allow you to read and understand existing TypeScript code with ease. You will also know enough about the language to produce high-quality code that achieves your application goals and is reliable.

In this chapter, we're going to cover the following main topics:

- What are types?
- Exploring TypeScript types
- Understanding classes and interfaces
- Understanding inheritance
- Learning generics
- Learning the latest features and configuring the compiler

# Technical requirements

The requirements for this chapter are the same as in *Chapter 1, Understanding TypeScript.* You should have a basic understanding of JavaScript and web technologies. You will once again be using Node and **Visual Studio Code** (**VSCode**).

The GitHub repository is again at `https://github.com/PacktPublishing/ Full-Stack-React-TypeScript-and-Node`. Use the code in the `Chap2` folder.

Before continuing, let's set up for this chapter:

1.  Go to your `HandsOnTypeScript` folder and create a new folder called `Chap2`.

2.  Open VSCode and go to **File | Open**, and then open the `Chap2` folder you just created. Then, select **View | Terminal** and enable the terminal window within your VSCode window.

3.  Type the `npm init` command, as in *Chapter 1, Understanding TypeScript*, to initialize the project for `npm`, and accept all the defaults.

4.  Type the `npm install typescript` command, as in *Chapter 1, Understanding TypeScript*, to install TypeScript.

Now we're ready to get started.

# What are types?

A **type** is a reusable set of rules. A type may include properties and functions (capabilities). It can also be shared and reused over and over again. When you reuse a type, you are creating an **instance** of it. This means that you are creating an example of your type that has specific values for properties. In TypeScript, as the name implies, types are very important. They're the main reason why the language was created in the first place. Let's take a look at how types work in TypeScript.

## How do types work?

As mentioned previously, JavaScript does have types. Number, string, Boolean, array, and so on are all types in JavaScript. However, those types are not explicitly set during declaration; they are only inferred at runtime. In TypeScript, types are normally set during declaration. It is possible to allow the compiler to infer your type. However, the type the compiler chooses may not be the one you desire since it isn't always obvious. In addition to the types supported by JavaScript, TypeScript has its own unique types and also allows you to create your own types.

The first thing to realize about types in TypeScript is that they are handled by their shape and not by their type name. This means the name of a type is not that important for the TypeScript compiler, but the properties it has and their types are important.

Let's look at an example:

1.  Create a file called `shape.ts` and add the following code:

```typescript
class Person {
    name: string;
}
const jill: { name: string } = {
    name: "jill"
};
const person: Person = jill;
console.log(person);
```

The first thing you should notice is that we have a class called `Person` with a property called `name`. Below that, you see that we have a variable called `jill` that is of the `{ name: string }` type. This is a little weird because, as you can see, this type declaration is not an actual type name; it's more like a type definition. But the compiler has no issues with it and does not complain. In TypeScript, it is possible to define and declare a type at the same time. Additionally, below that, you can see that we have another variable called `person` of the `Person` type and we set that to `jill`. Again, the compiler does not complain, and everything seems OK.

2.  Let's compile this code and run it to see what happens. Type the following lines in the terminal:

```
tsc shape
node shape
```

Once you've run the commands, you should see the following:

```
PROBLEMS    OUTPUT    DEBUG CONSOLE    TERMINAL

davidchoi@Davids-MacBook-Pro Chap2 % tsc shape
davidchoi@Davids-MacBook-Pro Chap2 % node shape
{ name: 'jill' }
davidchoi@Davids-MacBook-Pro Chap2 %
```

Figure 2.1 – The shape.ts output

As you can see, the code compiles and runs without issue. This demonstrates that in TypeScript, the compiler looks at the shape of a type and is not concerned with its name at all. You will see in later chapters, as we dig more deeply into TypeScript types, why it is so important to be aware of this behavior.

# Exploring TypeScript types

In this section, we'll look at some of the core types available in TypeScript. Using these types will give you error checking and compiler warnings that can help improve your code. They will also provide information about your intent to other developers that may be on your team. So, let's continue and see how these types work.

## The any type

The any type is a dynamic type that can be set to any other type. If you declare a variable to be of the any type, this means that you can set it to anything and reset it to anything else later as well. It is in effect no type because the compiler will not check it on your behalf. This is the key fact to remember about any – the compiler will not intercede and warn you of issues at development time. Therefore, if possible, using the any type should be avoided. It may seem weird that a language that was built to be statically typed would have such a feature, but it is a necessity under certain circumstances.

In a large application, it is not always possible for a developer to control the types that come into their code. For example, if a developer is relying on a web service API call to get data, that data's type may be controlled by some other team or even a different company entirely. This is also true during interop, when code relies on data from a different programming language – for example, when a company maintains a legacy system in another language while building out its new system in a different language. Situations like these require type flexibility and an escape hatch from the type system.

It is important not to abuse the any type. You should be careful to only use it when you know you have no other alternative – for example, when type information is not clear or can change. There are a few alternatives to using the any type, however. Depending on the circumstance, you may be able to use interfaces, generics, unions, or the unknown type instead. We'll cover the rest of these possibilities later, but for now, let's go over the unknown type next.

# The unknown type

The unknown type is a type released in TypeScript version 3. It is similar to any in that once a variable of this type is declared, a value of any type can be set to it. That value can subsequently be changed to any other type. So, I could start by setting my variable to a string type and then later set it to number. However, you cannot call any of its members or set the variable as a value to another variable without first checking what its type really is. I'll show an example of this as follows. The only time you can set unknown to something else without first checking its type is when you set an unknown type to another unknown or an any type.

Let's take a look at an example of any and then we'll see why the unknown type is preferable to using the any type (it is in fact recommended by the TypeScript team over using any):

1.  First, let's take a look at an example of the issue with using any. Go to VSCode and create a file called any.ts, and then type the following code:

```
let val: any = 22;
val = "string value";
val = new Array();
val.push(33);

console.log(val);
```

    If you run this code using the following commands, you will see the following result:

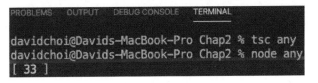

Figure 2.2 – any run result

2.  Since val is of the any type, we can set it to whatever we like and later call push into it since push is a method of Array. However, this is obvious only because we, as developers, are aware that Array has a method called push in it. What if we accidentally called something that does not exist on Array? Replace the previous code with the following code:

```
let val: any = 22;
val = "string value";
val = new Array();
```

```
val.doesnotexist(33);


console.log(val);
```

3.  Now, run the TypeScript compiler again:

```
tsc any
```

You will see that unfortunately, the compiler succeeds, since again making something of the any type causes the compiler to no longer check the type. Additionally, we also lost IntelliSense, the VSCode development time code highlighter and error checker. Only when we try and run the code do we get any indication that there is a problem, which is never what we want. If we now try and run the code, as shown next, it fails immediately:

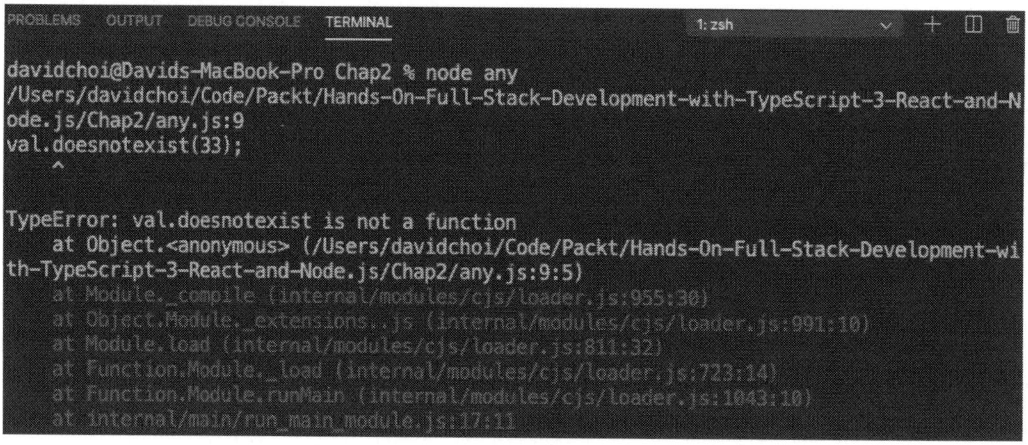

Figure 2.3 – any failing

For this simple example, this error is unlikely, but in a large application, it is an easy error to make, even if the mistake is simply to mistype something.

Let's see a similar example using unknown:

1.  First, comment out your code inside of any.ts and delete the any.js file (as we will use the same variable names, if you do not, it will cause conflict errors).

---

**Important Note**

We'll learn about something called namespaces later that can eliminate these sorts of conflicts, but it's a little too soon to introduce them now.

---

2. Now, create a new file called unknown.ts and add the following code to it:

```
let val: unknown = 22;
val = "string value";
val = new Array();
val.push(33);

console.log(val);
```

You will notice that VSCode gives you an error, immediately complaining about the push function. This is weird since obviously, Array has a method called push in it. This behavior shows how the unknown type works. You can consider the unknown type to be sort of like a label more than a type, and underneath that label is the actual type. However, the compiler cannot figure out the type on its own, so we need to explicitly prove the type to the compiler ourselves.

3. We use type guards to prove that val is of a certain type:

```
let val: unknown = 22;
val = "string value";
val = new Array();
if (val instanceof Array) {
    val.push(33);
}

console.log(val);
```

As you can see, we've wrapped our push call with a test to see whether val is an instance of Array.

4. Once we have established this to be true, the call to push can proceed without error, as shown here:

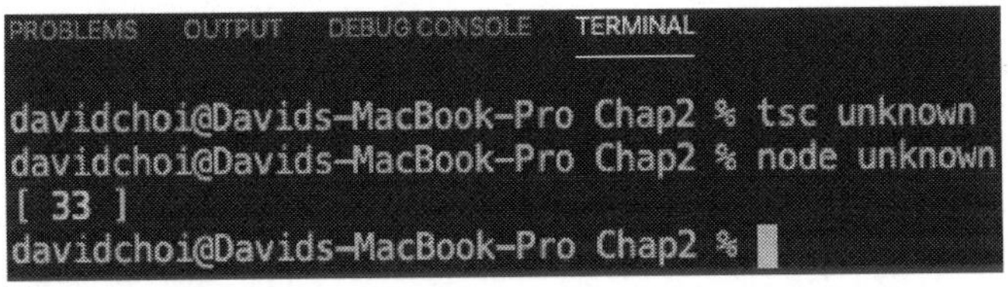

Figure 2.4 – unknown

This mechanism is a bit cumbersome since we always have to test the type before calling members. However, it is still preferable instead of using the `any` type and a lot safer since it is checked by the compiler.

## Intersection and union types

Remember when we started this section by saying that the TypeScript compiler focuses on type shape and not the name? This mechanism allows TypeScript to support what's called **intersection** types. This means that TypeScript allows the developer to "create types" by merging multiple distinct types together. This is hard to imagine, so let me give you an example. If you look at the following code, you can see a variable called `obj` that has two types associated with it. You will recall that in TypeScript, we can not only declare named types as a variable's type but also dynamically define and declare a type at the same time. In the following code, each type is a distinct type, but the `&` keyword is used to merge the two into a single type:

```typescript
let obj: { name: string } & { age: number } = {
    name: 'tom',
    age: 25
}
```

Let's try running this code and displaying the result on the console. Create a new file called `intersection.ts` and add the following code to it:

```typescript
let obj: { name: string } & { age: number } = {
    name: 'tom',
    age: 25
}
console.log(obj);
```

If you compile and run this code, you will see an object that contains both the name and age properties together:

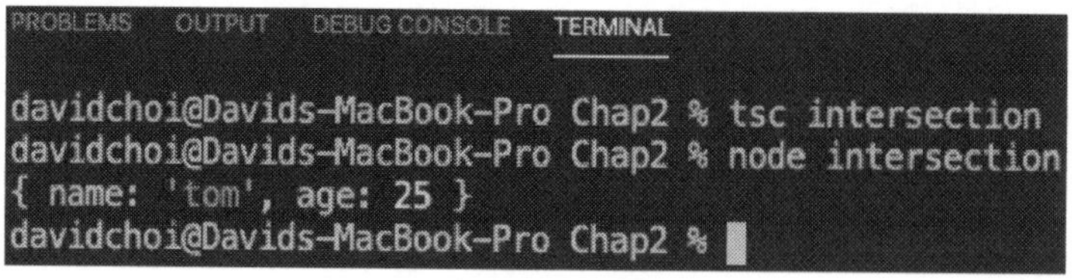

Figure 2.5 – Intersection result

As you can see, both IntelliSense and the compiler accept the code and the final object has both properties. This is an intersection type.

The other type is similar and is called the `union` type. In the case of unions, instead of merging types, we are using them in an "or" fashion, where it's one type or another. Let's look at an example. Create a new file called `union.ts` and add the following code to it:

```
let unionObj: null | { name: string } = null;
unionObj = { name: 'jon' };


console.log(unionObj);
```

The `unionObj` variable is declared to be of the null type or `{ name: string }`, by the use of the `|` character. If you compile and run this code, you'll see that it accepts both type values. This means that the type value can be either null or an object of the `{ name: string }` type.

## Literal types

**Literal** types are similar to union types, but they use a set of hardcoded string or number values. Here's a simple example of string literals that is fairly self-explanatory. As you can see, we have a bunch of hardcoded strings as the type. This means that only values that are the same as any of these strings will be accepted for the literal variable:

```
let literal: "tom" | "linda" | "jeff" | "sue" = "linda";
literal = "sue";


console.log(literal);
```

As you can see, the compiler is happy to receive any of the values on the list and even reset them. However, it will not allow the setting of a value that is not on the list. This will give a compile error. Let's see an example of this. Update the code as shown by resetting the literal variable to `john`:

```
let literal: "tom" | "linda" | "jeff" | "sue" = "linda";
literal = "sue";
literal = "john";
console.log(literal);
```

Here, we set the literal variable to john, and compiling gives the following error:

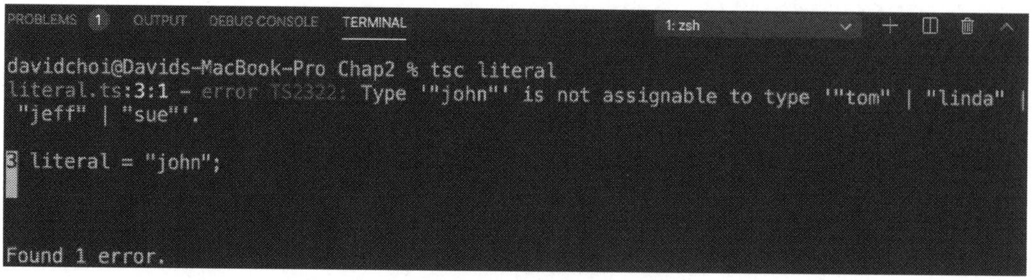

Figure 2.6 – A literal error

A numeric literal is also possible in the same way, but the values are made of numbers instead of strings.

## Type aliases

Type aliases are used very frequently in TypeScript. This is simply a method to give a different name to a type and most of the time it is used to provide a shorter simpler name to some complex type. For example, here's one possible usage:

```
type Points = 20 | 30 | 40 | 50;
let score: Points = 20;


console.log(score);
```

In this code, we take a long numeric literal type and give it a shorter name of Points. Then, we declare score as the Points type and give it a value of 20, which is one of the possible values for Points. And of course, if we tried to set score to, let's say, 99, compilation would fail.

Another example of aliases would be for object literal type declarations:

```
type ComplexPerson = {
    name: string,
    age: number,
    birthday: Date,
    married: boolean,
    address: string
}
```

Since the type declaration is very long and does not have a name, as, for example, a class would, we use an alias instead. Type aliasing can be used for just about any type in TypeScript, including things such as functions and generics, which we'll explore further later in the chapter.

## Function return types

For completeness' sake, I wanted to show one example of a function return declaration. It's quite similar to a typical variable declaration. Create a new file called `functionReturn.ts` and add this into it:

```
function runMore(distance: number): number {
    return distance + 10;
}
```

The `runMore` function takes a parameter of the `number` type and returns a number. The parameter declaration is just like any variable declaration, but the function return comes after the parentheses and indicates what type is returned by the function. If a function returns nothing, then you can either not declare any type for the return or you can declare `void` to be more explicit.

Let's look at an example of returning `void`. Comment out the `runMore` function and console log, and then compile and run this code:

```
function eat(calories: number) {
    console.log("I ate " + calories + " calories");
}


function sleepIn(hours: number): void {
    console.log("I slept " + hours + " hours");
}


let ate = eat(100);
console.log(ate);
let slept = sleepIn(10);
console.log(slept);
```

The two functions return nothing but write their given parameters to the console, as shown here:

Figure 2.7 – Function void results

As you can see, their internal `console.log` statements do run. However, trying to grab a return value results in `undefined` since nothing is being returned.

So, function return type declaration is quite similar to variable declarations. Now, let's take a look at using functions as types.

## Functions as types

It may seem a bit odd but in TypeScript, a type can also be an entire function signature. That is to say that in the previous section, we saw how functions can accept parameters based on types and also return a type. Well, this definition is also known as a function signature. In TypeScript, this signature can also act as a type for an object's properties.

Let's take a look at an example of this. Create a new file called `functionSignature. ts` and add the following code into it:

```typescript
type Run = (miles: number) => boolean;
let runner: Run = function (miles: number): boolean {
    if(miles > 10){
        return true;
    }
    return false;
}
console.log(runner(9));
```

The first line shows us a function type that we will be using in this code. The Run type alias is only there to make it easier to reuse the long function signature. The actual function type is `(miles: number) => boolean`. This looks odd, but it's nothing more than a slimmed-down function signature. So, the only things needed then are the parentheses to indicate parameters, the `=>` symbol, which indicates that this is a function, and then the return type.

In the code after the function definition line, you have the declaration of the `runner` variable as the Run type, which is again a function. This function simply checks whether the person has run more than 10 miles, and returns `true` if they have and `false` if they have not. Then, at the bottom of the code, the `console.log` statement writes out the result of the function call. You should see this once compiled and run:

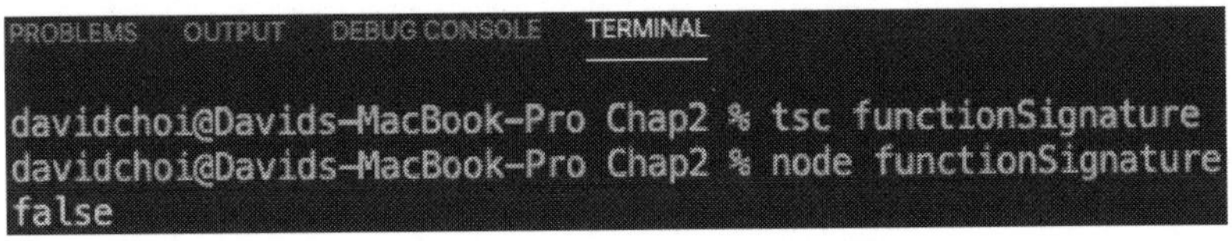

Figure 2.8 – Function type result

As you can see, calling `runner` with a parameter of 9 would make the function return `false`, which is correct. With static typing, it is important to be able to type all the ways we can return data, which means not only variables but also functions.

## The never type

This type is going to sound quite strange at first. A `never` type is used to indicate a function that never returns (completes), or a variable that is not set to anything, not even `null`. At first glance, this sounds like the `void` type. However, they are not at all the same. In `void`, a function does return, in the complete sense of the word, it just does not return any value (it returns `undefined`, which is no value). In the case of `never`, the function does not finish at all. Now, this seems totally useless but it's actually quite useful for indicating intent.

Again, let's look at an example. Create a file called `never.ts` and add the following code:

```
function oldEnough(age: number): never | boolean {
    if(age > 59) {
        throw Error("Too old!");
    }
    if(age <=18){
        return false;
    }
```

```
        return true;
    }
```

As you can see, this function returns a `union` type that is either `never` or a Boolean. Now, we could have only indicated the Boolean and the code would still work. However, in this function, we are throwing an error if the person is over a certain age, indicating that this is an unexpected `age` value. So, since encapsulation is a high-level principle for writing good-quality code, it is beneficial to indicate explicitly that a failure of the function to return could occur without needing the developer to know about the internals of how the function works. `never` provides that communication.

In this section, we learned about the many built-in types in TypeScript. We were able to see why using these types can improve our code quality and help us catch errors early on in the coding cycle. In the next section, we'll learn about how we can use TypeScript to create our own types, and also follow object-oriented programming principles.

# Understanding classes and interfaces

We've already briefly looked at classes and interfaces in previous sections. Let's take a deeper look, in this section, and see why these types can help us write better code. Once we complete this section, we will be better prepared to write more readable, reusable code with fewer bugs.

## Classes

At a base level, classes in TypeScript look just like classes in JavaScript. They are a container for a related set of fields and methods that can be instantiated and reused. However, classes in TypeScript support extra features for encapsulation that JavaScript does not. Let's take a look at an example.

Create a new file called `classes.ts` and enter the following code:

```
class Person {
    constructor() {}
    msg: string;
    speak() {
        console.log(this.msg);
    }
}
```

```
const tom = new Person();
tom.msg = "hello";
tom.speak();
```

As you can see, this example shows a simple class that, with the exception of the static typing, is just like what you might see in JavaScript. Firstly, you have a name for the class so that it can be reused. Next, you have a constructor, which is used to initialize any fields that the class might have and do any other setup for the class instance (again, an instance is just a specific example of our class with its own unique values for fields). Then, you have a single variable called msg declared and a function called speak that writes the msg value to the console. We then create an instance of our class. Finally, we set the msg field to a value of hello and call the speak method. Now, let's look at how classes differ between TypeScript and JavaScript.

## Access modifiers

We stated previously that one of the main principles of object-oriented development is encapsulation, or information hiding. Well, if we take a look at the code again clearly, we are not hiding the msg variable as it is exposed and editable outside of the class. So, let's see what TypeScript allows us to do about this. Let's update the code like this:

```
class Person {
    constructor(private msg: string) {}

    speak() {
        console.log(this.msg);
    }
}

const tom = new Person("hello");
// tom.msg = "hello";
tom.speak();
```

As you can see, we updated the constructor with a keyword called `private`. This method of declaring a constructor parameter and also adding an access modifier is doing several things in one line. Firstly, it is telling the compiler that the class has a field called `msg` of the `string` type that should be `private`. Normally, this sort of declaration is done in a line above or below the constructor separately, which is totally valid to do, but TypeScript allows us to use a shortcut by adding it to the constructor parameter. Additionally, by adding this to the constructor, you can see that it allows our `msg` field to be set at instantiation time with the `new Person("hello")` call.

Now, what does setting something to `private` actually do? By setting the field to `private`, we make it inaccessible from outside of the class. The result of this is that `tom. msg = "hello"` no longer works and causes an error. Try removing the comments and compile again. You should see this message:

```
PROBLEMS 1    OUTPUT    DEBUG CONSOLE    TERMINAL                           1: zsh
davidchoi@Davids-MacBook-Pro Chap2 % tsc classes
classes.ts:12:5 - error TS2341: Property 'msg' is private and only accessible within clas
s 'Person'.

12  tom.msg = "hello";


Found 1 error.
```

Figure 2.9 – Classes error

As you can see, it complains that a private member, `msg`, cannot be accessed from outside of the class. Now, we only applied our modifier to a field, but note that access modifiers can be applied to any member field or function.

> **Important Note**
>
> As mentioned previously, ECMAScript 2020 will support private fields via the # symbol. However, only fields are supported, and it is such a new standard that browser support is limited as of the time of writing.

Now, let's learn about the `readonly` modifier. This one is relatively straightforward; it causes a field to become read-only after it has been set one time in the constructor. So, update the code as follows and add `readonly` to the declaration of the `msg` field:

```
class Person {
    constructor(private readonly msg: string) {}

    speak () {
        this.msg = "speak " + this.msg;
```

```
            console.log(this.msg);
    }
}

const tom = new Person("hello");
// tom.msg = "hello";
tom.speak();
```

If you do this, IntelliSense complains because, in the `speak` function, we are attempting to change the value of `msg` even though it has already been set once through the constructor.

The `private` and `readonly` access modifiers are not the only modifiers available in TypeScript. There are several other types of access modifiers. However, they will make more sense if we explain them in the context of inheritance later.

## Getters and setters

Another feature of classes is actually available in both TypeScript and JavaScript: **getters** and **setters**:

- **Getter**: A property that allows modification or validation of a related field before returning it

- **Setter**: A property that allows modification or computation of a value before setting to a related field

In some other languages, these types of properties are known as computed properties. Let's look at an example. Create another file called `getSet.ts` and add the following code:

```
class Speaker {
    private message: string;
    constructor(private name: string) {}

    get Message() {
        if(!this.message.includes(this.name)){
            throw Error("message is missing speaker's name");
        }
        return this.message;
    }
```

```typescript
    set Message(val: string) {
        let tmpMessage = val;
        if (!val.includes(this.name)) {
            tmpMessage = this.name + " " + val;
        }
        this.message = tmpMessage;
    }
}

const speaker = new Speaker("john");
speaker.Message = "hello";
console.log(speaker.Message);
```

There's a fair amount happening here, so let's go over it before compiling and running. First, you can see that our message field is not available in the constructor but is a private field, and therefore not accessible directly from outside our class. The only initializer the constructor takes is our name field. After that, you can see the Message property is a getter because its name is prefixed with the get keyword. In the getter, we test to see whether our message field value has the speaker's name in it, and if it does not, we throw an exception to indicate an unwanted situation. The setter, also called Message, is indicated by the set keyword and this property receives a string and adds the speaker's name if needed by checking whether it is missing from the message field. Note that although both getter and setter look like functions, they are not. When they are called later in code, they are called just like a field would be called without the parentheses. So then, toward the end of the code, the speaker object is instantiated to a new speaker with a name of john and its Message property is set to hello. Thereafter, the message is written to the console.

Now, we want to compile this code so that we can run it, but we need to do something a bit differently this time. The TypeScript compiler has options that it can take in order to customize its behavior. In the case of this example, getters and setters and the includes function are only available in ES5 and ES6, respectively. If you're not familiar with it, the includes function checks whether a string is a substring of a larger string. So, let's tell the TypeScript compiler that it needs to compile to a newer JavaScript target than ES3, which is the default.

Here's the new compile command you'll need (we'll go over the `tsc` compiler options in more depth later, including using a configuration file):

```
tsc --target "ES6" getSet
```

Now, you can run the command. Once again, it's as follows:

```
node getSet
```

So, you now get the following output:

```
davidchoi@Davids-MacBook-Pro Chap2 % node getSet
john hello
```

Figure 2.10 – getSet output

To drive the point home further, let's try switching the `speaker.Message = "hello"` line to `speaker.message = "hello"`. If you compile, you should see this error:

```
davidchoi@Davids-MacBook-Pro Chap2 % tsc --target "ES6" getSet
getSet.ts:24:9 - error TS2341: Property 'message' is private and only accessible within class 'Speaker
'.

24  speaker.message = "hello";



Found 1 error.
```

Figure 2.11 – Message field error

Can you guess why this failed? Yes, this occurred because `message` is a `private` field and cannot be accessed from outside our class.

You may be wondering why I mentioned `getters` and `setters` here when they are available in regular JavaScript too. If you look at the example, you can see that the `message` field is `private` and the `getter` and `setter` properties are `public` (note that when you are not explicitly declaring access modifiers, the default is `public`). So, to allow good encapsulation, it is a best practice to hide our field and only expose it when needed via a getter and/or setter or some function that allows modification of the field. Also remember, when deciding on an access level to your members, that you want to start with the most restrictive capabilities first and then become less restrictive as needed. Additionally, by allowing field access via accessors, we can do all sorts of checks and modifications, as we've done in our example, so that we have ultimate control over what comes in and out of our class.

## Static properties and methods

Finally, let's discuss **static** properties and methods. When you mark something as static inside of a class, you are saying that this member is a member of the class type and not of the class instance. Therefore, it can be accessed without needing to create an instance of a class, but instead by prefixing with the class name.

Let's look at an example. Create a new file called `staticMember.ts` and add the following code:

```
class ClassA {
    static typeName: string;

    constructor(){}

    static getFullName() {
        return "ClassA " + ClassA.typeName;
    }
}

const a = new ClassA();
console.log(a.typeName);
```

If you attempt to compile this code, it will fail, stating that `typeName` is a static member of the `ClassA` type. Again, static members must be called using the class name. Here are the fixed versions of the code:

```
class ClassA {
    static typeName: string;

    constructor(){}

    static getFullName() {
        return "ClassA " + ClassA.typeName;
    }
}

const a = new ClassA();
console.log(ClassA.typeName);
```

As you can see, we reference typeName with the class name. So then, the question is why might I want to use a static member instead of an instance member? Under certain circumstances, it may be useful to share data across class instances. For example, I might want to do something like this:

```
class Runner {
    static lastRunTypeName: string;

    constructor(private typeName: string) {}

    run() {
        Runner.lastRunTypeName = this.typeName;
    }
}

const a = new Runner("a");
const b = new Runner("b");

b.run();
a.run();

console.log(Runner.lastRunTypeName);
```

In the case of this example, I am trying to determine the last class instance that has called the run function at any given time. This can be straightforward by using a static member. Another point to be aware of is that inside a class, static members can be called by both static members and instance members. However, static members cannot call instance members.

Now we have learned about classes and their features in this section. This will help us design our code for encapsulation, which will enhance its quality. Next, we will learn about interfaces and contract-based coding.

# Interfaces

In object-oriented programming design, another important principle is abstraction. The goal of abstraction is to reduce complexity and the tight coupling of code by not exposing the internal implementation (we've already covered abstraction in *Chapter 1, Understanding TypeScript*). One way of doing this is to use **interfaces** to show only the signature of a type, as opposed to its internal workings. An interface is also sometimes called a contract, since having specific types for parameters and return types enforces certain expectations between both the user and the creator of the interface. So, another way of thinking about interfaces is as strict rules about what can come out of and go into a type instance.

Now, interfaces are just a set of rules. In order to have working code, we need an implementation of those rules to get any work done. So, let's show an example of an interface with implementation to get started. Create a new file called `interfaces.ts` and add the following interface definition:

```
interface Employee {
    name: string;
    id: number;
    isManager: boolean;
    getUniqueId: () => string;
}
```

This interface defines an `Employee` type that we will create instances for later. As you can see, there is no implementation of the `getUniqueId` function, just its signature. The implementation comes later when we define it.

Now, add the implementation to the `interfaces.ts` file. Insert the following code, which creates two instances of the `Employee` interface:

```
const linda: Employee = {
    name: "linda",
    id: 2,
    isManager: false,
    getUniqueId: (): string => {
        let uniqueId = linda.id + "-" + linda.name;
        if(!linda.isManager) {
            return "emp-" + uniqueId;
        }
        return uniqueId;
```

```
        }
    }
}
console.log(linda.getUniqueId());
const pam: Employee = {
    name: "pam",
    id: 1,
    isManager: true,
    getUniqueId: (): string => {
        let uniqueId = pam.id + "-" + pam.name;
        if(pam.isManager) {
            return "mgr-" + uniqueId;
        }
        return uniqueId;
    }
}
console.log(pam.getUniqueId());
```

So, we create an instance by instantiating an object literal called linda, setting the two field names – name and id – and then implementing the getUniqueId function. Later, we console log the linda.getUniqueId call. After that, we create another object, called pam, based on the same interface. However, not only does it have different field values, but its implementation of getUniqueId is also different than the linda object. This is the main use of interfaces: to allow for a single structure across objects but to enable different implementations. In this way, we provide strict rules about what the type structure is, but also allow some flexibility in terms of how functions go about doing their work. Here's the output of our code:

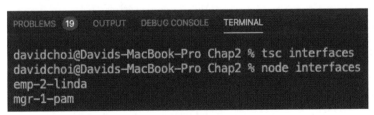

Figure 2.12 – Employee interface results

Another possible use of interfaces is when using third-party APIs. Sometimes, the type information is not well documented and all you're getting back is untyped JSON or the object type is extremely large and has many fields you will never use. It is quite tempting, under these circumstances, to just use any as the type and be done with it. However, you should prefer providing a type declaration if at all possible.

What you can do under these circumstances is to create an interface that has only the fields that you know and care about. Then, you can declare your data type to be of this type. At development time, TypeScript will not be able to check the type since for API network call's data will be coming in at runtime. But regardless, since TypeScript only cares about the shape of any given type, it will ignore the fields not mentioned in your type declaration and as long as the data comes in with the fields you defined in your interface, the runtime will not complain and you will maintain development time type safety. However, please do be careful to handle null or undefined fields appropriately, by allowing them to use unions or testing for those types.

In this section, we learned about interfaces and the differences between interfaces and classes. We will be able to use interfaces to abstract away the implementation details of a class and therefore produce loose coupling between our code and therefore better code quality. In the next section, we will learn about how classes and interfaces allow us to perform inheritance and therefore code reuse.

# Understanding inheritance

In this section, we'll learn about **inheritance**. Inheritance in object-oriented programming is a method for doing code reuse. This will shrink our application code size and make it more readable. Also, generally, shorter code tends to have fewer bugs. So, all these factors will improve our app quality once we get started building.

As stated, inheritance is primarily about allowing code reuse. Inheritance is also conceptually designed to be like real-life inheritance so that the logical flow of inheritance relationships can be intuitive and easier to understand. Let's look at an example of this now. Create a file called classInheritance.ts and add the following code:

```
class Vehicle {
    constructor(private wheelCount: number) {}

    showNumberOfWheels() {
        console.log(`moved ${this.wheelCount} miles`);
    }
}
```

```
class Motorcycle extends Vehicle {
    constructor() {
        super(2);
    }
}
class Automobile extends Vehicle {
    constructor() {
        super(4);
    }
}
const motorCycle = new Motorcycle();
motorCycle.showNumberOfWheels();
const autoMobile = new Automobile();
autoMobile.showNumberOfWheels();
```

> **Important Note**
> Quick note if you've never seen back ticks, ` `` `, and $ { } before. It's called string
> interpolation and is simply a quick and easy way to insert string values inside
> strings by embedding objects.

As you can see, there is a base class, also known as a parent, called Vehicle. This class
acts as the main container for source code that is being reused later by whatever classes
inherit from it, also known as children. The child classes inherit from Vehicle by using
the extends keyword. One thing to notice that's important is that in the constructor
for each child class, you see that the first line of code is the call to super. super is the
name of the instance of the parent class that a child is inheriting from. So, in this case,
that would be the Vehicle class. Now, as you can see, each child is passing a different
number of wheels to the parent's wheelCount variable via the parent's constructor.
Then, at the end of the code, an instance of each child, Motorcycle and Automobile,
is created and the showNumberOfWheels function is called. If we compile and run this
code, we get the following:

```
davidchoi@Davids-MacBook-Pro Chap2 % tsc classInheritance
davidchoi@Davids-MacBook-Pro Chap2 % node classInheritance
moved 2 miles
moved 4 miles
```

Figure 2.13 – The classInheritance result

So then, each child provides a different number of wheels to the parent `wheelCount`
variable, although they cannot access the variable directly. Now, let's say that there was a
reason why the child classes would want to access the `wheelCount` variable of the parent
directly. For example, let's say that if a flat tire occurred, an updated wheel count would be
necessary. What could we do? Well, let's try creating a function unique to each child class
that tries to update `wheelCount`. Let's see what happens. Update the code by adding a
new function, `updateWheelCount`, to the `Motorcycle` class:

```typescript
class Vehicle {
    constructor(private wheelCount: number) {}

    showNumberOfWheels() {
        console.log(`moved ${this.wheelCount} miles`);
    }
}
class Motorcycle extends Vehicle {
    constructor() {
        super(2);
    }
    updateWheelCount(newWheelCount: number) {
        this.wheelCount = newWheelCount;
    }
}
class Automobile extends Vehicle {
    constructor() {
        super(4);
    }
}
const motorCycle = new Motorcycle();
motorCycle.showNumberOfWheels();
const autoMobile = new Automobile();
autoMobile.showNumberOfWheels();
```

As a test, if we update only the `Motorcycle` class and add an `updateWheelCount` function as shown, we get an error. Can you guess why? It's because we are trying to access a private member of the parent class. So, therefore, even when child classes inherit their members from a parent, they still do not have access to that parent's `private` members. This is the right behavior, again to promote encapsulation. So then, what do we do? Well, let's try editing the code again to allow this:

```
class Vehicle {
    constructor(protected wheelCount: number) {}

    showNumberOfWheels() {
        console.log(`moved ${this.wheelCount} miles`);
    }
}
class Motorcycle extends Vehicle {
    constructor() {
        super(2);
    }
    updateWheelCount(newWheelCount: number) {
        this.wheelCount = newWheelCount;
    }
}
class Automobile extends Vehicle {
    constructor() {
        super(4);
    }
}
const motorCycle = new Motorcycle();
motorCycle.showNumberOfWheels();
const autoMobile = new Automobile();
autoMobile.showNumberOfWheels();
```

Do you see the small change we made? That's right, we changed the `wheelCount` parameter on the `Vehicle` parent class constructor to be of the `protected` accessor type. `protected` allows the class and any inheriting classes to have access to the member.

Before we move on to the next topic, let's introduce the concept of **namespaces** so that we can create scoping containers and separate one set of code from another. Providing scope with namespaces hides whatever is inside one namespace from the outside of it. In that sense, it's sort of like a class, but it is capable of containing any number of classes, functions, variables, or any other types. Here's a simple example of using namespaces. Create a new file called `namespaces.ts` and add the following code:

```
namespace A {
    class FirstClass {}
}

namespace B {
    class SecondClass {}
    const test = new FirstClass();
}
```

As you can see from this code, even before compiling, VSCode IntelliSense is already complaining that `FirstClass` cannot be found. This is because it is hidden from `namespace B`, since it is only defined in `namespace A`. This is the purpose of namespaces, to hide information within one scope, away from other scopes.

In this section, we learned about inheriting from classes. Class inheritance is a very important tool for reusing code. In the next section, we'll look at using abstract classes, which is a more flexible way of doing inheritance.

## Abstract classes

As mentioned previously, interfaces can be useful for defining contracts, but they have no implementation for working code themselves. Classes have working implementations, but sometimes only a signature is required. It is possible, for certain situations, that we may want to have both in one object type. For these types of scenarios, you would use an **abstract class** instead of either a class or an interface. Let's create a new file called `abstractClass.ts` and copy and paste our code from our `classInheritance.ts` file into it. If you do this, you might get some errors, since the two files both have the same class and variable names.

So, in our new `abstractClass.ts` file, we are going to update it with namespaces and modify the `Vehicle` class to be abstract. Add the namespace and update the `Vehicle` class like this:

```
namespace AbstractNamespace {
    abstract class Vehicle {
        constructor(protected wheelCount: number) {}

        abstract updateWheelCount(newWheelCount: number): void;

        showNumberOfWheels() {
            console.log(`moved ${this.wheelCount} miles`);
        }
    }
```

So, to start, we've obviously wrapped all the code within a bracket called `namespace AbstractNamespace` (note that a namespace can have any name; it does not need `namespace` in the name). Again, this is merely a container that allows us to control scoping so that the members of our `abstractClass.ts` file do not bleed out into the global scope, and thereby affect other files.

If you look at the new `Vehicle` code, we have a new keyword before the class called `abstract`. This is what indicates that the class will be an abstract one. You can also see that we have a new function called `updateWheelCount`. This function has an `abstract` keyword in front of it, which indicates that it will have no implementation within the `Vehicle` class and needs to be implemented by an inheriting class.

Now, after the `Vehicle abstract` class, we want our child classes that are inheriting from it. So, add the `Motorcycle` and `Automobile` classes below the `Vehicle` class:

```
    class Motorcycle extends Vehicle {
        constructor() {
            super(2);
        }
        updateWheelCount(newWheelCount: number) {
            this.wheelCount = newWheelCount;
            console.log(`Motorcycle has ${this.wheelCount}`);
        }
    }
    class Automobile extends Vehicle {
```

```
    constructor() {
        super(4);
    }
    updateWheelCount(newWheelCount: number){
        this.wheelCount = newWheelCount;
        console.log(`Automobile has ${this.wheelCount}`);
    }
    showNumberOfWheels() {
        console.log(`moved ${this.wheelCount} miles`);
    }
}
```

After adding the classes, we instantiate them and call their respective
updateWheelCount methods, as shown:

```
    const motorCycle = new Motorcycle();
    motorCycle.updateWheelCount(1);
    const autoMobile = new Automobile();
    autoMobile.updateWheelCount(3);
}
```

As you can see, the implementation of the abstract member updateWheelCount is
in the child classes. This is the capability that an abstract class provides. An abstract class
can act both as a regular class, providing member implementations, and as an interface,
providing only the rules for implementation for a child class. Note that since an abstract
class can have abstract members, you cannot instantiate an abstract class.

Furthermore, if you look at the Automobile class, you can see that it has its own
implementation of showNumberOfWheels, even though this function is not abstract.
This demonstrates something called **overriding**, which is the ability of a child's member to
create a unique implementation of the parent's member.

In this section, we learned about the different kinds of class-based inheritance. Learning
about inheritance will allow us to reuse more of our code, reducing both code size and
potential bugs. In the next section, we'll learn about doing inheritance with interfaces and
how it's different from class-based inheritance.

# Interface

As explained earlier, **interfaces** are a way of setting agreed-upon rules for a type. They will allow us to separate implementation from definition and therefore provide abstraction, which again is a powerful object-oriented programming principle that will give us higher-quality code. Let's learn about how to use interfaces to inherit explicitly and in a well-structured way.

TypeScript interfaces provide a set of type signatures for an interface's members but have no implementation themselves. Now, we did show some examples of using standalone interfaces, but this time, let's see how we can use interfaces as a means of doing inheritance and code reuse. Create a new file called `interfaceInheritance.ts` and add the following code:

```
namespace InterfaceNamespace {
    interface Thing {
        name: string;
        getFullName: () => string;
    }


    interface Vehicle extends Thing {
        wheelCount: number;
        updateWheelCount: (newWheelCount: number) => void;
        showNumberOfWheels: () => void;
    }
```

After the namespace, you can see that there is an interface called `Thing`, and after that, the `Vehicle` interface is defined and it inherits from `Thing` using the `extends` keyword. I put this into the example to show that interfaces can also inherit from other interfaces. The `Thing` interface has two members – `name` and `getFullName` – and as you can see, although `Vehicle` extends `Thing`, there is no mention of those members anywhere inside of `Vehicle`. This is because `Vehicle` is an interface and therefore cannot have any implementation. However, if you look at the following code, at the `Motorcycle` class, you can see that, since this class extends `Vehicle`, the implementations are there:

```
    class Motorcycle implements Vehicle {
        name: string;
        wheelCount: number;
        constructor(name: string) {
            // no super for interfaces
```

```
        this.name = name;
    }
    updateWheelCount(newWheelCount: number){
        this.wheelCount = newWheelCount;
        console.log(`Automobile has ${this.wheelCount}`);
    }
    showNumberOfWheels() {
        console.log(`moved Automobile ${this.wheelCount}
        miles`);
    }
    getFullName() {
        return "MC-" + this.name;
    }
}

const moto = new Motorcycle("beginner-cycle");
console.log(moto.getFullName());
}
```

So, if we compile and run this code, we get the following:

Figure 2.14 – The interfaceInheritance result

Interfaces do not provide a means to do code reuse directly, as they have no implementation. However, it is still advantageous for code reuse because the structure of interfaces provides definite expectations around what code will receive and return. Hiding the implementation behind an interface is also beneficial in terms of doing encapsulation and abstraction, which are also important principles of object-oriented programming.

> **Important Note**
>
> When using TypeScript, take full advantage of inheritance models from object-oriented programming that are available to you in TypeScript. Use interfaces to abstract implementation details. Use `private` and `protected` to help encapsulate data. Remember, when the time comes to compile and convert your code into JavaScript, the TypeScript compiler will do any translation work for you to get things back into the prototypical style. But while in development mode, you should take advantage of all the capabilities that TypeScript provides to enhance your development experience.

In this section, we learned about inheritance and how it can be used for code reuse. We learned about how to do inheritance with the three major container types: classes, abstract classes, and interfaces. You will see, once we begin coding our app, why being able to do code reuse is such a critical element in large application development. In the next section, we will cover generics, which will use the types that we learned about in this section.

# Learning generics

**Generics** allows a type definition to include an associated type that can be chosen by the user of the generic type, instead of being dictated by the type creator. In this way, there are structures and rules, but still some amount of flexibility. Generics will definitely come into play later when we code with React, so let's learn about them here.

Generics can be used for functions, classes, and interfaces. Let's look at an example of generics with functions. Create a file called `functionGeneric.ts` and add the following code:

```
function getLength<T>(arg: T): number {
    if(arg.hasOwnProperty("length")) {
        return arg["length"];
    }
    return 0;
}


console.log(getLength<number>(22));
console.log(getLength("Hello world."));
```

If we start at the top, we see a function called getLength<T>. This function is using a generic that tells the compiler that wherever it sees the T symbol, it can expect any possible type. Now, internally, our function implementation checks to see whether the arg parameter has a field called length and then tries to grab it. If it does not, it just returns 0. Finally, toward the bottom, you can see that the getLength function is called two times: once for a number and another time for a string. Additionally, you can see that for number, it explicitly has the <number> type indicator, whereas for string, it does not. This is there only to show that you can be explicit, but the compiler can usually figure out which type you meant based on the usage.

The thing with this example is that there's extra code in order to check for the length field. This makes the code busy and longer than it needs to be. Let's update this code to prevent calls of this function if an argument does not have a length property. First, comment out the code we just wrote and add the following new code below it:

```
interface HasLength {
    length: number;
}

function getLength<T extends HasLength>(arg: T): number {
    return arg.length;
}

console.log(getLength<number>(22));
console.log(getLength("Hello world."));
```

This code is quite similar except we use an HasLength interface to constrain what types are allowed. Constraining generic types is done with the extends keyword. By writing T extends HasLength, we are telling the compiler that whatever T is, it must inherit from or be of the HasLength type, which effectively means that it must have the length property. Therefore, when the two previous calls are made, it fails for number types, since they don't have a length property, but works for string.

Now, let's look at an example that uses interfaces and classes. Let's create a file called classGeneric.ts and add the following code to it:

```
namespace GenericNamespace {
    interface Wheels {
        count: number;
        diameter: number;
    }
```

```
interface Vehicle<T> {
    getName(): string;
    getWheelCount: () => T;
}
```

So, we can see that we have an interface called `Wheels`, which provides wheel information. We can also see that the `Vehicle` interface takes a generic of type `T`, meaning any specific type.

Subsequently, we see that the `Automobile` class implements the `Vehicle` interface with the generic as the `Wheel` type, which associates `Wheel` to `Automobile`. Then, finally, we see that the `Chevy` class extends `Automobile`, providing some default values:

```
class Automobile implements Vehicle<Wheels> {
    constructor(private name: string, private wheels:
        Wheels){}

    getName(): string {
        return this.name;
    }

    getWheelCount(): Wheels {
        return this.wheels;
    }
}

class Chevy extends Automobile {
    constructor() {
        super("Chevy", { count: 4, diameter: 18 });
    }
}
```

After all these types are defined, we create one instance of the `Chevy` class and log some output from it:

```
const chevy = new Chevy();
console.log("car name ", chevy.getName());
console.log("wheels ", chevy.getWheelCount());
}
```

This code compiles and runs successfully and gives the following result:

```
Davids-MacBook-Pro:Chap2 davidchoi$ tsc classGeneric
Davids-MacBook-Pro:Chap2 davidchoi$ node classGeneric
car name  Chevy
wheels  { count: 4, diameter: 18 }
```

Figure 2.15 – The classGeneric.ts result

You can see that our inheritance hierarchy is several levels deep, but our code is able to successfully return a valid result. Although specific details in real-world code may be different, nevertheless, the multi-level type hierarchy shown here is something that can happen quite frequently in object-oriented programming design.

In this section, we learned about using generics on both functions and class types. Generics are commonly used in React development, as well as some Node packages. So, they will be of use once we start coding in later chapters. In the next section, we'll take a look at several miscellaneous items to round out this chapter.

# Learning the latest features and configuring the compiler

In this section, we will learn about some newer features in TypeScript, as well as how to configure the TypeScript compiler. By learning about these newer features, we will be able to write cleaner and easier-to-read code, which, of course, will be beneficial for working with the app in a team. By using the configuration options of TypeScript, we can have the compiler work in the way we think is best for our project.

## Optional chaining

Let's take a look at **optional chaining**. This feature will allow us to write simpler code, but also prevent a small class of errors having to do with null objects. Let's create a file called optionalChaining.ts and add the following code to it:

```
namespace OptionalChainingNS {
    interface Wheels {
        count?: number;
    }

    interface Vehicle {
        wheels?: Wheels;
    }
```

```
class Automobile implements Vehicle {
    constructor(public wheels?: Wheels) {}
}

const car: Automobile | null = new Automobile({
    count: undefined
});
console.log("car ", car);
console.log("wheels ", car?.wheels);
console.log("count ", car?.wheels?.count);
}
```

If we look at this code, we can see that there are several types being used together. car has a property of wheels, and wheels has a property of count. So, later when we log, you can see that calls are being chained together. For example, the last console.log line refers to car?.wheels?.count. This is called optional chaining. The question mark indicates that the object could possibly be null or undefined. If it is null or undefined, then the code will end at that object, returning whichever value the object or property is, and not continue to the rest of the properties, but without causing an error.

So, if we wrote the bottom console code the old way, we would have to do a great deal of code testing in order to make sure that we would not cause an error by calling something that is potentially undefined. We would use the ternary operation and it could look something like this:

```
const count = !car ? 0
    : !car.wheels ? 0
    : !car.wheels.count ? 0
    : car.wheels.count;
```

Obviously, this is both difficult to write and read. So then, by using optional chaining, we allow the compiler to stop as soon as null or undefined is found and just pass that back. This saves us from writing a bunch of verbose, potentially error-prone code.

# Nullish coalescing

Nullish coalescing is simply a shortcut of the ternary operator. So, it's pretty straightforward and it looks like this:

```
const val1 = undefined;
const val2 = 10;
const result = val1 ?? val2;
console.log(result);
```

The double question marks work from left to right. The statement means if `val1` is not `null` or `undefined` and has an actual value, then return that value. However, if `val1` does not have a value, return `val2`. So, in this case, compiling and running would result in `10` being written to the console.

You may be wondering whether this is the same thing as the `||` operator. It's somewhat similar but more constrained. The logical or operator, when it is used in this manner, is checking for "truthyness." In JavaScript, this is a concept where a large set of possible values can be considered "truthy" or "falsey." For example, `0`, `true` or `false`, `undefined`, and `""` all have true or false equivalency in JavaScript. However, in the case of nullish coalescing, only `null` or `undefined` specifically are being checked.

# TypeScript configuration

TypeScript configurations can be passed in via the command line or, more commonly, through a file called `tsconfig.json`. If you use the command line, then call the compiler like this:

```
tsc tsfile.ts -lib 'es5, dom'
```

This tells TypeScript to ignore any `tsconfig.json` file and just use the command-line options – in this case, the `-lib` option, which states which version of JavaScript is being used during development, and compiles only this one file. If you just put `tsc` onto the command line, TypeScript will look for a `tsconfig.json` file and use that configuration and compile all `ts` files it finds.

There are many options, so we won't cover all of them here. However, let's review a few of the most important ones (when we start coding, I'll provide a sample `tsconfig.json` file to use):

- `--lib`: This is used to indicate which JavaScript version you will use during development.
- `--target`: This indicates which version of JavaScript you want to emit out into `.js` files.
- `--noImplicitAny`: Does not allow the `any` type, without explicitly declaring it.
- `--outDir`: This is the directory where JavaScript files will be saved to.
- `--outFile`: This is the final JavaScript filename.
- `--rootDirs`: This is an array that stores the `.ts` file source code.
- `--exclude`: This is an array of folders and files to exclude from compilation.
- `--include`: This is an array of folders and files to include in compilation.

This section provided just a brief overview of some newer features of TypeScript, as well as some configuration-related information. Nevertheless, these newer features and the ability to configure TypeScript are very important and will be used extensively once we start writing code in later chapters.

# Summary

In this chapter, we learned about the TypeScript language. We learned about the many different types that exist in the language and also how to create our own types. We also learned about how to use TypeScript to create object-oriented code. It was a large and complex chapter but will be absolutely necessary knowledge for when we begin building our app.

In the next chapter, we will review some of the most important features in traditional JavaScript. We will also learn about some of the newer features in the latest versions of the language. Since TypeScript is a true superset of JavaScript, it is important to have an up-to-date understanding of JavaScript in order to make maximal usage of TypeScript.

# 3
# Building Better Apps with ES6+ Features

In this chapter, we'll review certain important features of JavaScript in its latest ES6+ form (I've added the plus sign to indicate ES6 and beyond). It is important to understand that although this book uses TypeScript, the two languages are complementary. In other words, TypeScript does not replace JavaScript. It augments and enhances JavaScript, adding features that make it better. Therefore, we'll do a review of some of the most important features in the JavaScript language. We'll review variable scoping and the new `const` and `let` keywords. Also, we'll dive deeper into the `this` keyword and how we can switch it if needed. We'll also learn about the many new features in JavaScript, such as the new array functions and `async await`. This knowledge will give us a solid foundation upon which we can code in TypeScript.

In this chapter, we're going to cover the following main topics:

- Learning about ES6 variable types and JavaScript scoping
- Learning about arrow functions
- Changing the `this` context
- Learning about spread, de-structuring, and rest

- Learning about new array functions
- Learning about new collection types
- Learning about `async await`

# Technical requirements

The requirements for this chapter are the same as for *Chapter 2, Exploring TypeScript*. You should have a basic understanding of JavaScript and web technologies. You will once again be using Node and **Visual Studio Code** (**VSCode**).

The GitHub repository is at `https://github.com/PacktPublishing/Full-Stack-React-TypeScript-and-Node`. Use the code in the `Chap3` folder.

Let's set up this chapter's code folder:

1. Go to your `HandsOnTypescript` folder and create a new folder called `Chap3`.
2. Open VSCode and go to **File | Open**, and then open the `Chap3` folder you just created. Then, select **View | Terminal** and enable the terminal window within your VSCode window.
3. Type the `npm init` command, as in the previous chapter, to initialize the project for npm, and accept all the defaults (you can also use `npm init -y` to accept all defaults automatically).
4. Type the `npm install typescript` command, as in the previous chapter, to install TypeScript.

Now we're ready to get started.

# Learning about ES6 variable types and JavaScript scoping

In this section, we will learn about JavaScript's scoping rules and some new variable types that help to clarify and improve upon some issues regarding these scope rules. This information is valuable since you will be creating variables constantly throughout your career as a software developer, and it is important to understand under what scope a variable can be accessed and under what circumstances it may be changed.

In most other languages, variable scoping happens within any arbitrary set of brackets or *begin end* scope statements. However, scope in JavaScript is handled by the body of a function, which means when a variable is declared inside a function body using the `var` keyword, that variable is only accessible within that body. Let's take a look at an example of this. Create a new file called `functionBody.ts` and add the following code to it:

```
if (true) {
    var val1 = 1;
}

function go() {
    var val2 = 2;
}

console.log(val1);
console.log(val2);
```

In VSCode, you should see an error indication on the call to `console.log(val2)`, whereas the call to `console.log(val1)` works just fine. You might have thought that since `val1` is declared within the brackets of the `if` statement, it would not be accessible later. However, clearly it is. But on the other hand, `val2` scoped by the `go` function is not accessible outside of it. This shows that as far as variable declaration using `var` is concerned, it is functions that act as scoping containers.

This feature is actually the source of much confusion in JavaScript. So, in ES6, a new set of variable declaration prefixes have been created: `const` and `let`. Let's review them here.

`const` variables support something called block-level scoping. Block-level scoping is scoping between any squiggly brackets. For example, in our previous example, that would be the `if` statement. In addition, as the name implies, `const` creates a constant variable value that, once set, cannot be reset to something else. However, what this means is a little bit different from some other languages. In JavaScript, this means that the variable's assignment cannot be changed. However, the variable itself can be edited. This is hard to imagine, so let's look at some examples. Create a new file called `const.ts` and add the following code:

```
namespace constants {
    const val1 = 1;
    val1 = 2;

    const val2 = [];
```

```
        val2.push('hello');
}
```

In VSCode, this code will show an error for `val1 = 2`, but it will be OK for `val2.push('hello')`. The reason for this is that in the case of `val1`, the variable is actually being reset into an entirely new value, which is not allowed. However, for `val2`, the array value remains the same and a new element is being added to it. So, this is allowed.

Now, let's look at the `let` keyword. `let` variables are, like `const` variables, also block-scoped. However, they can be set and reset at will (of course, in TypeScript, the type needs to stay the same). Let's show an example of `let`. Create a file called `let.ts` and add the following code:

```
namespace lets {
    let val1 = 1;
    val1 = 2;

    if(true) {
        let val2 = 3;
        val2 = 3;
    }

    console.log(val1);
    console.log(val2);
}
```

So, here, we have two sets of `let` variables. `val1` is not scoped in a block, but `val2` is scoped in an `if` block. As you can see, only the call to `console.log(val2)` is failing, since `val2` only exists inside the `if` block.

So then, which variable declaration method do you use? The current best practice in the community is to prefer using `const`, as immutability is a beneficial attribute and also, using constants adds a tiny performance benefit. However, if you know that you need to be able to reset the variable later, then use `let` instead. Finally, avoid using `var`.

We've learned about scoping and the new `const` and `let` variable types in ES6. Understanding scoping and knowing when to use `const` versus `let` is an important skill for doing modern JavaScript development. In newer JavaScript code, you'll see these keywords often. Next, we'll review the `this` context and arrow functions.

# Learning about arrow functions

Arrow functions were a new addition to ES6. Basically, they serve two main purposes:

- They shorten the syntax for writing functions.
- They also automatically make the immediate scope parent, the `this` object, the arrow function's parent.

Let me explain `this` a bit more before continuing as it's critical knowledge for JavaScript developers.

In JavaScript, the `this` object, the owner object instance that member properties and methods belong to, can change based on the context of a call. So, when a function is called directly—for example, `MyFunction()`—the parent `this` would be the caller of the function; that is to say, the current scope's `this` object. For browsers, that would usually be the `window` object. However, in JavaScript, functions can also be used as object constructors—for example, `new MyFunction()`. In this case, the `this` object inside the function would be the object instance that was created from the `new MyFunction` constructor.

Let's look at an example to clarify as this is a really important feature of JavaScript. Create a new file called `testThis.ts` and add the following code:

```
function MyFunction () {
    console.log(this);
}


MyFunction();
let test = new MyFunction();
```

If you compile and then run this code, you will see the following result:

```
davidchoi@Davids-MacBook-Pro Chap2 % tsc testThis
davidchoi@Davids-MacBook-Pro Chap2 % node testThis
Object [global] {
  global: [Circular],
  clearInterval: [Function: clearInterval],
  clearTimeout: [Function: clearTimeout],
  setInterval: [Function: setInterval],
  setTimeout: [Function: setTimeout] { [Symbol(util.promisify.custom)]: [Function] },
  queueMicrotask: [Function: queueMicrotask],
  clearImmediate: [Function: clearImmediate],
  setImmediate: [Function: setImmediate] {
    [Symbol(util.promisify.custom)]: [Function]
  }
}
MyFunction {}
```

Figure 3.1 – testThis result

So, when `MyFunction` is called directly, the immediate scope parent is going to be Node's global object, since we are not running in a browser. Next, if we create a new object from `MyFunction` using `new MyFunction()`, the `this` object becomes its own object instance since the function was used to create an object as opposed to being run directly.

Now that we have that out of the way, let's see what an arrow function looks like. Create the `arrowFunction.ts` file and add the following code:

```
const myFunc = (message: string): void => {
    console.log(message);
}


myFunc('hello');
```

If you compile and run this code, you'll see that `hello` is printed out. The syntax is very similar to a function type; however, they are not the same. If we look at the code, you can see a colon after the parameter parentheses and then the void type after the parameter parentheses. This is the return type of the function. In the case of function types, the return type is indicated after the `=>` symbol.

Here are some additional things to note about arrow functions. All non-arrow functions in JavaScript have access to a collection called `arguments`. This is a collection of all the parameters given to the function. Arrow functions do not have their own `arguments` collection. However, they do have access to the immediate function parent's `arguments` collection.

The arrow function has several body styles. Here are examples of the three styles:

```
const func = () => console.log('func');
const func1 = () => ({ name: 'dave' });
const func2 = () => {
    const val = 20;
    return val;
}
console.log(func());
console.log(func1());
console.log(func2());
```

Let's look at each of the three styles:

- The first function, `func`, shows the case where only a single line of code is used in the function body, and nothing is returned, as you can see that the body has no closing braces or parentheses.

- The second function, `func1`, shows when there is only a single line, but something is returned. In this case, the `return` keyword is not needed, and parentheses are needed only if an object is returned.

- The final case is `func2`. In this case, squiggly brackets are needed because it is a multi-line statement (regardless of whether it returns or not).

We covered arrow functions in this section. Arrow functions are used a great deal in modern JavaScript and TypeScript code, so it's beneficial to know about this feature in depth.

# Changing the this context

We already discussed the `this` context object in the previous section. As mentioned, in JavaScript, functions have access to an internal object called `this` that represents the caller of the function. Now, the confusing part of using `this` is that the value of `this` can change depending on how the function is called. So, JavaScript provides helpers that allow you to reset the `this` object of a function to the one you want, instead of the one given to you. There are several methods, including `apply` and `call`, but the most important one for us to learn is the `bind` keyword. This is important for us to know because `bind` is used often in React class-based components. It's a bit early to show a full-blown React example. So, let's start with something a little easier. Create a new file called `bind.ts` and add the following code to it:

```
class A {
    name: string = 'A';
    go() {
        console.log(this.name);
    }
}

class B {
    name: string = 'B';
    go() {
        console.log(this.name);
```

```
        }
    }

const a = new A();
a.go();
const b = new B();
b.go = b.go.bind(a);
b.go();
```

As you can see from this code, there are two distinct classes: A and B. Both of these classes have a go function that writes the specific class name to the log. Now, when we reset the this object's bind of our b object's go function to be the a object, it switches the console.log(this.name) statement to use a as the this object. So, if we compile and run, we get this:

```
Davids-MacBook-Pro:Chap3 davidchoi$ tsc bind
Davids-MacBook-Pro:Chap3 davidchoi$ node bind
A
A
```

Figure 3.2 – bind

As you can see, a.go() writes A but b.go() also writes A, instead of B, since we switched this to be a instead of b. Note that also, in addition to taking the this argument, bind can also take any number of parameters thereafter.

You may be wondering what the difference between using bind, call, and apply is. bind is used to make the this context change and later, when the function is called, it will have the changed this object. However, call and apply are used at the time the function is called and immediately replace the this context at the time of calling. The difference between call and apply is that call takes an indeterminate number of parameters and apply takes an array of parameters. Let's look at some examples. Create a file called call.js and add the following code to it:

```
const callerObj = {
    name: 'jon'
}

function checkMyThis(age) {
    console.log(`What is this ${this}`)
    console.log(`Do I have a name? ${this.name}`)
    this.age = age;
```

```
        console.log(`What is my age ${this.age}`);
}

checkMyThis();
checkMyThis.call(callerObj, 25);
```

First, we are creating a new object called `callerObj` that has a field called name, which is jon. After that, we declare a checkMyThis function, which tests what this is currently and whether it has a name. Finally, we run both calls. Note that the second call looks weird but `checkMyThis.call` is an actual execution of the checkMyThis function. If we run this code, we will see something interesting. Run the following command:

```
node call
```

You will see the following result:

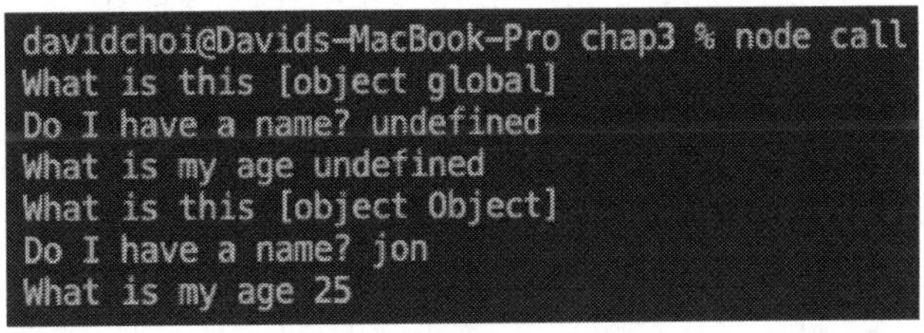

```
davidchoi@Davids-MacBook-Pro chap3 % node call
What is this [object global]
Do I have a name? undefined
What is my age undefined
What is this [object Object]
Do I have a name? jon
What is my age 25
```

Figure 3.3 – node call

The first execution of the checkMyThis function uses the global object by default, since it was not overridden. Again, for Node, it's Node's global object, but for browsers, it's the window object. We also see that the name and age fields are undefined, since Node's global object does not have the name field and the age was not passed as a parameter to checkMyThis. However, on the second execution of the function, the one that uses call, we see that the object has changed to a standard object type and it has a name of jon, which is the name field for callerObj, and an age field equal to 25, which is the parameter we passed into call. You should note the order of the parameters list for call follows the order of the parameters list of the function being called. The usage of apply would be identical; however, it takes parameters as an array.

In this section, we learned about the difficulties of working with the `this` context and how to deal with this using `bind`. We will use `bind` extensively later once we start creating React components. But even beyond that specific use case, you will find that your code will sometimes need the ability to change the `this` context and possibly some parameters for your functions. So, this ability is a very useful feature to have.

# Learning about spread, destructuring, and rest

In ES6+, there are new methods for handling object copying and displaying variables and parameters. These capabilities go a long way in making JavaScript code both shorter and easier to read. These features have become standard practice in modern JavaScript, so it is important that we know about them and use them properly.

## Spread, Object.assign, and Array.concat

The **spread**, `Object.assign`, and `Array.concat` JavaScript features are fairly similar. Basically, you are appending multiple objects or arrays together into one object or array. However, strictly speaking, there are some differences.

In the case of objects, there are two ways of merging or concatenating objects:

- Spread—for example, { ... `obja`, ...`objb` }: You are creating a non-modified copy of these two objects and then creating a brand-new object. Note that spread can handle more than just two objects.

- `Object.assign`—(`obja`, `objb`): You are adding the properties from `objb` into `obja` and returning `obja`. Therefore, `obja` is being modified. Here's an example. Create a new file called `spreadObj.ts` and add the following code:

```
namespace NamespaceA {
    class A {
        aname: string = 'A';
    }
    class B {
        bname: string = 'B';
    }

    const a = new A();
    const b = new B();
```

```
    const c = { ...a, ...b }
    const d = Object.assign(a, b);
    console.log(c);
    console.log(d);


    a.aname = 'a1';
    console.log(c);
    console.log(d);
}
```

First, we create a new object, c, which is set using the spread operator, .... After that, we create d from the Object.assign call. Let's try running this code. You'll need to target ES6 since Object.assign is only available on that version of JavaScript. Let's compile and then run with the following commands:

```
tsc spreadObj -target 'es6'
node spreadObj
```

Once these commands run, you will see the following:

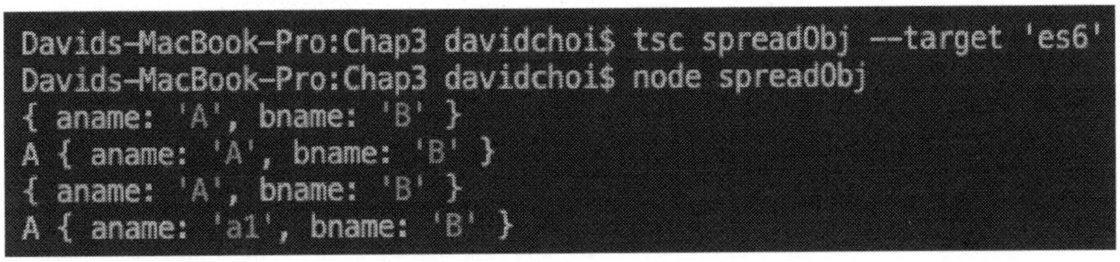

```
Davids-MacBook-Pro:Chap3 davidchoi$ tsc spreadObj --target 'es6'
Davids-MacBook-Pro:Chap3 davidchoi$ node spreadObj
{ aname: 'A', bname: 'B' }
A { aname: 'A', bname: 'B' }
{ aname: 'A', bname: 'B' }
A { aname: 'a1', bname: 'B' }
```

Figure 3.4 – spreadObj

As you can see, c has both aname and bname properties but is a unique object unto itself. However, d is actually object a with the properties of object b, which is demonstrated by the aname variable being equal to a1 after a.aname = 'a1' was set.

Now, for merging or concatenating arrays, you also have two methods:

- The spread operator: Like spread for objects, it merges the arrays and returns a single new array. Original arrays are not modified.

- Array.concat: Creates a new array by merging the two source arrays into a single array. Original arrays are not modified.

Let's take a look at an example using both methods. Create a file called `spreadArray.ts` and add the following code:

```
namespace SpreadArray {
    const a = [1,2,3];
    const b = [4,5,6];

    const c = [...a, ...b];
    const d = a.concat(b);
    console.log('c before', c);
    console.log('d before', d);

    a.push(10);
    console.log('a', a);
    console.log('c after', c);
    console.log('d after', d);
}
```

As you can see, array c is created using spread from two arrays: a and b. Then, array d is created using a.concat(b). In this case, both resulting arrays are unique and do not refer to any of the original arrays. Let's compile and run this code as we did before and see what we get:

```
Davids-MacBook-Pro:Chap3 davidchoi$ tsc spreadArray —target 'es5'
Davids-MacBook-Pro:Chap3 davidchoi$ node spreadArray
c before [ 1, 2, 3, 4, 5, 6 ]
d before [ 1, 2, 3, 4, 5, 6 ]
a [ 1, 2, 3, 10 ]
c after [ 1, 2, 3, 4, 5, 6 ]
d after [ 1, 2, 3, 4, 5, 6 ]
```

Figure 3.5 – spreadArray

You will see that a.push(10) has no effect on the console.log('d after', d) statement even though array d was created from array a. This shows that both spread and concat for arrays create new arrays.

## Destructuring

**Destructuring** is the ability to display and directly use the internal properties of an object instead of relying on the object name alone. I'll explain this later with an example, but please be aware that this is a very frequently used feature in modern JavaScript development, especially in React hooks, so we need to be comfortable with it.

Let's look at an example of object destructuring. For this example, let's just use a JavaScript file, as the example will be clearer that way. Create a new file called `destructuring.js` and add the following code to it:

```
function getEmployee(id) {

    return {
        name: 'John',
        age: 35,
        address: '123 St',
        country: 'United States'
    }
}

const { name: fullName, age } = getEmployee(22);
console.log('employee', fullName, age);
```

Let's pretend for a moment that the `getEmployee` function goes to a server and retrieves the information of an employee by `id`. Now, as you can see, the `employee` object has lots of fields and perhaps not every caller of the function will need every field. So, we use object destructuring to select only the fields we care about. Note, in addition, that we also give the field name an alias of `fullName` by using the colon.

Destructuring is also possible for arrays. Let's add the following code to this file:

```
function getEmployeeWorkInfo(id) {
    return [
        id,
        'Office St',
        'France'
    ]
}

const [id, officeAddress] = getEmployeeWorkInfo(33);
console.log('employee', id, officeAddress);
```

In the case of this example, the getEmployeeWorkInfo function returns an array of facts about the employee's work location; but it returns it as an array. So, we can also destructure an array as well, but note that the order of the elements does matter at destructure time. Let's look at the results for both functions. Note that we only need to call Node since this is a JavaScript file. Run the following command:

```
node destructuring.js
```

You will see the following results for both functions:

```
Davids-MacBook-Pro:Chap3 davidchoi$ node deconstruction
employee John 35
employee 33 Office St
```

Figure 3.6 – Destructuring

As you can see, both functions have returned the correct relative data.

## Rest

**Rest** is a feature that allows you to refer to an indefinite set of parameters with one keyword, the ... keyword. Any rest parameters are arrays and therefore have access to all array functions. The rest keyword refers to "the rest of the items" and not "pause" or "stop." This keyword allows more flexibility when creating your function signature, as it allows the caller to determine how many parameters they want to pass. Please note that only the last parameter can be a rest parameter. Here's an example of using rest. Create a file called rest.js and add the following code:

```
function doSomething(a, ...others) {
    console.log(a, others, others[others.length - 1]);
}

doSomething(1,2,3,4,5,6,7);
```

As you can see, ...others refers to the rest of the parameters after a. This indicates that rest parameters do not have to be the only parameters for a function. So, if you run this code, you get the following:

```
Davids-MacBook-Pro:Chap3 davidchoi$ node rest
1 [ 2, 3, 4, 5, 6, 7 ] 7
```

Figure 3.7 – Rest

The doSomething function receives two parameters: the a variable and the **rest** parameter. It then writes a log entry where the a parameter, the rest parameter (which again is an array of parameters), and the last element of the rest parameter are written. Rest is not as frequently used as spread and destructuring. Nevertheless, you will see it, so you should be aware of it.

In this section, we learned about JavaScript features that make code shorter and easier to read. The usage of these features is very common in modern JavaScript programming, so you'll benefit greatly from learning how to use these capabilities. In the next section, we'll learn about some very important array manipulation techniques that streamline dealing with arrays and are also very popularly used.

# Learning about new array functions

In this section, we will review the many methods added for manipulating arrays in ES6. It is a very important section as you will have to deal with arrays frequently in JavaScript programming, and using these performance-optimized methods is preferable over creating your own. The use of these standard methods also makes code more consistent and readable by other developers on your team. We will take advantage of these methods extensively in both our React and Node development. Let's get started.

## find

The find keyword allows you to grab the first instance of an element from an array that matches your search criteria. Let's look at a simple example. Create find.ts and add the following code:

```
const items = [
    { name: 'jon', age: 20 },
    { name: 'linda', age: 22 },
    { name: 'jon', age: 40}
]

const jon = items.find((item) => {
    return item.name === 'jon'
});
console.log(jon);
```

If you look at the code for `find`, you can see that it takes a function as the parameter and the function is looking for an item with the name of `jon`. The function does a truth check to see whether the item's name is equal to `jon`. If the item truth check is true, `find` will return that item. However, you can also see that there are two `jon` items in the array. Let's compile and run this code and see which one returns. Run the following commands:

```
tsc find -target 'es6'
node find
```

After compiling and running the preceding commands, you should see the following result:

```
Davids-MacBook-Pro:Chap3 davidchoi$ tsc find --target 'es6'
Davids-MacBook-Pro:Chap3 davidchoi$ node find
{ name: 'jon', age: 20 }
```

Figure 3.8 – find

You can see in the output that the first `jon` item found is returned. This is how `find` works; it always gives back only one item—the first one found in the array.

## filter

`filter` is similar to `find` except it returns all items that match a search criterion. Let's create a new file called `filter.ts` and add the following code:

```
const filterItems = [
    { name: 'jon', age: 20 },
    { name: 'linda', age: 22 },
    { name: 'jon', age: 40}
]

const results = filterItems.filter((item, index) => {
    return item.name === 'jon'
});
console.log(results);
```

As you can see, the `filter` function can also take an optional second parameter for the index number of the item in the array. But moving on, internally, it looks identical to how `find` works in that there is a truth check to see whether a certain match is found. However, for `filter`, all matches get returned, as shown here:

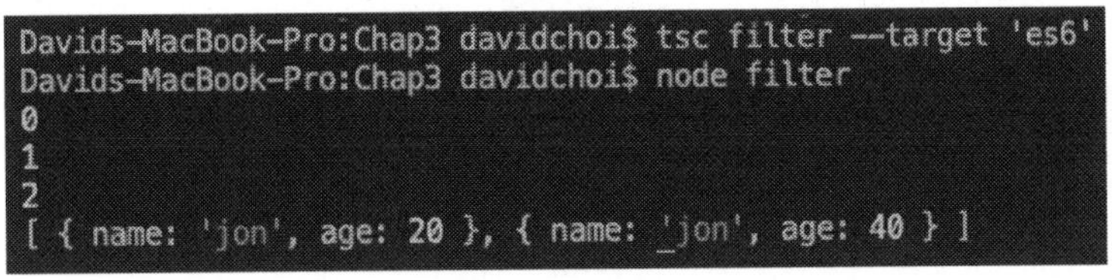

```
Davids-MacBook-Pro:Chap3 davidchoi$ tsc filter --target 'es6'
Davids-MacBook-Pro:Chap3 davidchoi$ node filter
0
1
2
[ { name: 'jon', age: 20 }, { name: 'jon', age: 40 } ]
```

Figure 3.9 – filter

As you can see, for `filter`, all items that meet the filter criteria are returned, which in this sample case is both `jon` items.

## map

The `map` function is one of the more important array functions to know about for ES6 style coding. It appears frequently in React component creation in order to create a collection of component elements from an array of data. Note that the `map` function is different from the `Map` collection, which we'll cover later in this chapter. Create a new file called `map.ts` and add the following code:

```
const employees = [
    { name: 'tim', id: 1 },
    { name: 'cindy', id: 2 },
    { name: 'rob', id: 3 },
]

const elements = employees.map((item, index) => {
    return `<div>${item.id} - ${item.name}</div>`;
});

console.log(elements);
```

As you can see, the map function has two parameters, item and index (you can call them whatever you like, but the order matters), and it maps custom return values to each array element. To be clear, return means to return each item back into a new array. It does not mean to return and stop running the iteration. If we run the code, it results in the following DOM string:

```
Davids-MacBook-Pro:Chap3 davidchoi$ tsc map --target 'es6'
Davids-MacBook-Pro:Chap3 davidchoi$ node map
[ '<div>1 - tim</div>', '<div>2 - cindy</div>', '<div>3 - rob</div>' ]
```

Figure 3.10 – map

This function may in fact be the most common ES6 array function, so it is very important that you understand how it works. Try modifying the code and practice using it with different array item types.

## reduce

The reduce function is an aggregator that takes each element in an array and, based on custom logic, creates a single final value. Let's look at an example. Create a reduce.js file—again, we'll use a JavaScript file to remove some noise from the TypeScript compiler and focus—and add the following code:

```
const allTrucks = [
    2,5,7,10
]

const initialCapacity = 0;
const allTonnage = allTrucks.reduce((totalCapacity,
    currentCapacity) => {
    totalCapacity = totalCapacity + currentCapacity;

    return totalCapacity;
}, initialCapacity);

console.log(allTonnage);
```

In this example, let's imagine we need to calculate the total tonnage capacity a trucking company can carry with all its trucks. So then, `allTrucks` lists out the tonnage of each of its trucks. Then, we use `allTrucks.reduce` to get the total capacity of all trucks. The `initialCapacity` variable is used only to have some starting point, which is currently set at 0. Then, when we log out the final value, we see the following:

Figure 3.11 – reduce

The total capacity of all the trucks is 24 since the sum of each truck's capacity is 24. Notice the logic of the reducer can be anything; it does not have to be a sum. It could be a subtraction or any other logic that you may need. The core point is that at the end, you will have only a single value or object result. This is why it is called `reduce`.

## some and every

These functions are designed to test for certain criteria. So, they only return `true` or `false`. `some` tests to see whether *any* element in an array meets certain criteria and `every` tests whether *all* elements meet a certain criteria. Let's take a look at both. Create a file called `someEvery.js` and add the following code:

```
const widgets = [
    { id: 1, color: 'blue' },
    { id: 2, color: 'yellow' },
    { id: 3, color: 'orange' },
    { id: 4, color: 'blue' },
]

console.log('some are blue', widgets.some(item => {
    return item.color === 'blue';
}));

console.log('every one is blue', widgets.every(item => {
    return item.color === 'blue';
}));
```

The code is pretty straightforward and both conditions of some and every are tested. If you run this code, you'll see the following result:

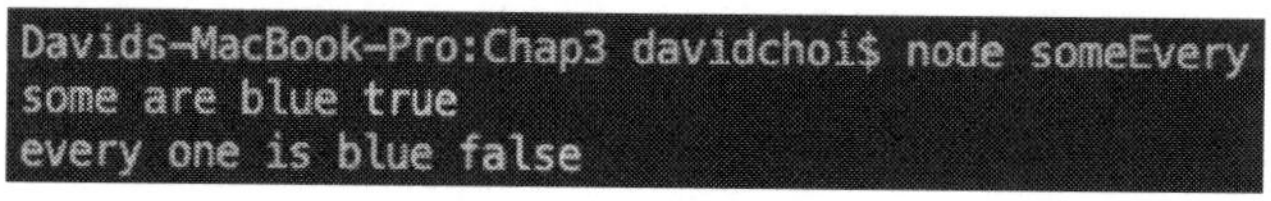

```
Davids-MacBook-Pro:Chap3 davidchoi$ node someEvery
some are blue true
every one is blue false
```

Figure 3.12 – someEvery

As you can see, the results are valid for each test.

In this section, we learned about the many new functions added to ES6 that help us deal with and use arrays in JavaScript more efficiently. You will definitely be using many of these functions in your own code later when we build our app. Next, we'll learn about some new collection types that can be used instead of arrays.

# Learning about new collection types

ES6 has two new collection types, Set and Map, which can be useful for certain specific scenarios. In this section, we will learn about these two types and how to write code for them so that we can use them later when we start building our app.

## Set

Set is a collection of unique values or objects. This is a good function to use when you simply want to see whether an item is contained in a large complex list. Let's see an example. Create a new file called set.js and add the following code:

```
const userIds = [
    1,2,1,3
]

const uniqueIds = new Set(userIds);
console.log(uniqueIds);

uniqueIds.add(10);
console.log('add 10', uniqueIds);

console.log('has', uniqueIds.has(3));

console.log('size', uniqueIds.size);
```

```
for (let item of uniqueIds) {
    console.log('iterate', item);
}
```

There are many members for the Set object, but these are some of its most important features. As you can see, Set has a constructor that can take an array, which makes that array a unique set.

> **Important Note**
> In regard to sets, size is used to check quantity not length.

At the bottom, notice how iterating Set is different from the normal way of using array indexes. Running this file will result in the following:

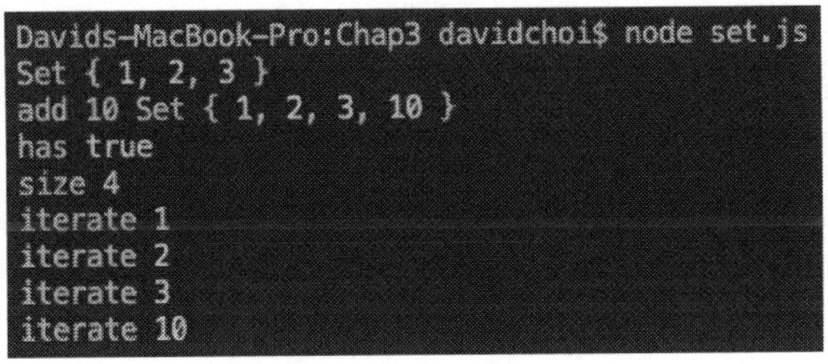

```
Davids-MacBook-Pro:Chap3 davidchoi$ node set.js
Set { 1, 2, 3 }
add 10 Set { 1, 2, 3, 10 }
has true
size 4
iterate 1
iterate 2
iterate 3
iterate 10
```

Figure 3.13 – Set

Conceptually, it is still quite similar to an array but is optimized for unique collections.

# Map

Map is a collection of key-value pairs. In other words, it's a dictionary. Every member of Map has a unique key. Let's create a sample Map object. Create a new file called mapCollection.js and add the following code:

```
const mappedEmp = new Map();
mappedEmp.set('linda', { fullName: 'Linda Johnson', id: 1 });
mappedEmp.set('jim', { fullName: 'Jim Thomson', id: 2 });
mappedEmp.set('pam', { fullName: 'Pam Dryer', id: 4 });

console.log(mappedEmp);
console.log('get', mappedEmp.get('jim'));
console.log('size', mappedEmp.size);
```

```
for(let [key, val] of mappedEmp) {
    console.log('iterate', key, val);
}
```

As you can see, some of the calls are quite similar to Set. One difference, however, is the iteration loop at the bottom, which uses an array to indicate the key and value. Running this file results in the following output:

```
Davids-MacBook-Pro:Chap3 davidchoi$ node mapCollection
Map {
  'linda' => { fullName: 'Linda Johnson', id: 1 },
  'jim' => { fullName: 'Jim Thomson', id: 2 },
  'pam' => { fullName: 'Pam Dryer', id: 4 }
}
get { fullName: 'Jim Thomson', id: 2 }
size 3
iterate linda { fullName: 'Linda Johnson', id: 1 }
iterate jim { fullName: 'Jim Thomson', id: 2 }
iterate pam { fullName: 'Pam Dryer', id: 4 }
```

Figure 3.14 – mapCollection

It's pretty straightforward. First, a list of all Map objects is logged. Then, we get the jim item by using its key value with get. Next is size, and then finally an iteration over all elements.

This section showed the two new collection types in ES6. These types are not used that frequently but can come in handy should you have the needs that these collections address. In the next section, we'll discuss async await, which is an ES7 feature. async await has seen very rapid adoption by the JavaScript developer community because it makes difficult-to-read asynchronous code much more readable and makes it appear as if it is synchronous.

# Learning about async await

Before explaining async and await, let's explain what asynchronous code is. In most languages, code is usually synchronous, which means that statements run one after another. If you have statements A, B, and C, statement B cannot run until statement A is completed and statement C cannot run until statement B is completed. However, in asynchronous programming, if statement A is asynchronous, it will start but then immediately after that, statement B will start. So then, statement B never waits for A to complete before it runs. This is great for performance but makes code harder to read and fix. async await in JavaScript attempts to address some of these difficulties.

So, asynchronous programming provides faster performance because statements can run simultaneously without having to wait for each other. However, in order to understand asynchronous programming, we need to first understand callbacks. Callbacks are a core feature of Node.js programming since its inception, so it is important to understand. Let's look at an example of callbacks. Create a new file called `callback.js` and enter the following code:

```
function letMeKnowWhenComplete(size, callback) {
    var reducer = 0;
    for (var i = 1; i < size; i++) {
        reducer = Math.sin(reducer * i);
    }
    callback();
}
letMeKnowWhenComplete(100000000, function () { console.
log('Great it completed.'); });
```

If we look at this code, we can see that the `letMeKnowWhenComplete` function has two parameters. The first one indicates the size of an iteration to do a math calculation and the second one is the actual callback. As you can see from the code, `callback` is a function that is executed once the math work is complete, hence the name. To be precise, technically a callback is not actually asynchronous. However, it does provide capabilities that are effectively the same in that secondary work, the callback, is done exactly once the primary is complete without needing to wait or poll. So now, let's look at JavaScript's first method for doing asynchronous completion.

The first capability JavaScript received to do asynchronous execution was with the `setTimeout` and `setInterval` functions. These functions are simple; they take a callback that is executed once a certain specified time completes. In the case of `setInterval`, the only difference is that it repeats. The reason why these functions are truly asynchronous is that when a timer runs, it runs outside of the current **callstack**. A callstack is simply the sequence of code and data running for the current thread. In the case of JavaScript, it is single-threaded, so timers generally are run by the browser engine on behalf of JavaScript and then the result comes back to the main JavaScript thread—again, the callstack. Let's look at a simple example. Create a new file called `setTimer.js` and enter the following code:

```
// 1
console.log('Let's begin.');

// 2
```

```
setTimeout(() => {
    console.log('I waited and am done now.');
}, 3000);


// 3
console.log('Did I finish yet?');
```

Let's review this code. I've added comments to separate out the main sections. First, under comment 1, we have a log message indicating that this code is starting. Then, under comment 2, we have setTimeout, which will execute our arrow function callback after waiting 3 seconds. When the callback runs, it will log that it finished. After setTimeout, we see another log message, under comment 3, asking whether the timer has finished yet. Now, when you run this code, a strange thing will happen, as shown in the following figure:

```
davidchoi@Davids-MacBook-Pro Chap3 % node setTimer
Let's begin.
Did I finish yet?
I waited and am done now.
```

Figure 3.15 – setTimer

The last log message asking Did I finish yet? will run first, and then the log for I waited and am done now.' will complete. Why is that? SetTimeout is an asynchronous function, so when it executes, it allows whatever code was written after it to execute immediately (even though setTimeout is not done yet). That means in this case, the log in comment 3 actually runs before the callback in comment 2. So then, if we imagine that comment 3 had some important code that needed to run right away, without waiting for comment 2, we can see how using an asynchronous call would be helpful for performance. Now, let's combine our understanding of callbacks and asynchronous calls and take a look at Promises.

Before async await, asynchronous code was handled using Promises. A Promise is an object with a delayed completion at some indeterminate future time. An example of Promise code would be something like this. Create a file called promise.js and add the following code:

```
const myPromise = new Promise((resolve, reject) => {
    setTimeout(() => {
        //resolve('I completed successfully');
        reject('I failed');
    }, 500);
```

```
});

myPromise
.then(done => {
    console.log(done);
})
.catch(err => {
    console.log(err);
});
```

In this code, we first create a `Promise` object and internally, we use an asynchronous timer to execute a statement after 500 milliseconds. On the first try, we are deliberately failing the timer by calling `reject` and this causes the code below the `Promise` definition to go to the `catch` handler. Now, if we comment out `reject` and then uncomment `resolve`, the bottom code will then go to the `then` handler. Clearly, this code works, but if you imagine a much more complex `Promise`, having many `then` statements, or even many Promises, things become increasingly complex to read and understand.

This is where `async await` can help. It does two main things: it cleans up the code and makes it simpler and smaller and it also makes the code easier to follow as it *looks* like synchronous code. Let's view an example. Create a new file called `async.js` and add the following code:

```
async function delayedResult() {
    return new Promise((resolve, reject) => {
        setTimeout(() => {
            resolve('I completed successfully');
        }, 500);
    });
}

(async function execAsyncFunc() {
    const result = await delayedResult();
    console.log(result);
})();
```

This code has a function called `delayedResult`, which, as you can see, has the `async` prefix in front of it. Prefixing a function with `async` tells the runtime that this function will return a `Promise` and therefore should be handled asynchronously. After `delayedResult`, we see a function called `execAsyncFunc` that is both declared and executed simultaneously. If you are not familiar with it, this capability is called an **Immediately Invoked Function Expression (IIFE)**. We'll learn about IIFE later, but for now, let's continue. The `execAsyncFunc` function is also `async`-capable and as you can see, internally, it uses the `await` keyword. The `await` keyword tells the runtime that we are about to execute an asynchronous function, so it should wait on our behalf, and then, once the statement completes, give us the actual return value instead. If we run this code, we see the following:

```
Davids-MacBook-Pro:Chap3 davidchoi$ node async
I completed successfully
```

Figure 3.16 – async

As you can see, the `result` variable contains the `I completed successfully` string instead of the `Promise` that `delayedResult` normally returns. This syntax is clearly much shorter and easier to read than having many nested `Promise then` statements. Please note that `async` and `await` have taken over asynchronous development in the JavaScript community. You must understand it well in order to succeed with modern JavaScript. We'll look at one more example to further our understanding.

> **Important Note**
>
> We had to use an IIFE for the `execAsyncFunc` function because in current JavaScript, top-level `await` is not allowed. Top-level `await` basically means being able to run a call to await a function that is not inside of another `async` function. In the ECMAScript 2020 version of JavaScript, this is enabled, but as of the time of writing, it is not yet completely supported across all browsers.

Because `async await` is so important, let's look at one more example. Let's make a call to a network resource to get some data. We'll use the `fetch` API, but since Node does not support it natively, we'll need to install one more npm package first. Here are the steps:

1.  Run the following command in your terminal to install `fetch`:

```
npm i node-fetch
```

2.  Create a file called `fetch.js` and enter the following code:

```
const fetch = require('node-fetch');

(async function getData() {
    const response = await fetch('https://pokeapi.co/api/v2/
    pokemon/ditto/');
    if(response.ok) {
        const result = await response.json();
        console.log(result);
    } else {
        console.log('Failed to get anything');
    }
})();
```

Notice, in this example, the easy-to-read and natural flow of the code. As you can see, we are using the `fetch` API, which allows us to make asynchronous network calls. After importing `fetch`, we again create an `async` wrapper function to execute `await` calls to our `fetch` function. If you're wondering, the URL is a public API for Pokémon characters that requires no authentication. The first call to `await` is for the actual network call itself. Once that call completes, a check for success is made using `response.ok`. If successful, another call to `await` is made to convert the data into JSON format. Each call to `await` blocks the code at that point until the function completes and returns.

We are *awaiting* because we cannot continue without this data from the network API and therefore we have no choice but to wait. If you run this code, you will see the following data:

```
PROBLEMS    OUTPUT    DEBUG CONSOLE    TERMINAL

    name: 'ditto',
    order: 197,
    species: {
      name: 'ditto',
      url: 'https://pokeapi.co/api/v2/pokemon-species/132/'
    },
    sprites: {
      back_default: 'https://raw.githubusercontent.com/PokeAPI/sprites/master/sprites/pokemon/back/132.png',
      back_female: null,
      back_shiny: 'https://raw.githubusercontent.com/PokeAPI/sprites/master/sprites/pokemon/back/shiny/132.png',
      back_shiny_female: null,
      front_default: 'https://raw.githubusercontent.com/PokeAPI/sprites/master/sprites/pokemon/132.png',
      front_female: null,
      front_shiny: 'https://raw.githubusercontent.com/PokeAPI/sprites/master/sprites/pokemon/shiny/132.png',
      front_shiny_female: null
    },
    stats: [
      { base_stat: 48, effort: 0, stat: [Object] },
      { base_stat: 48, effort: 0, stat: [Object] },
      { base_stat: 48, effort: 0, stat: [Object] },
      { base_stat: 48, effort: 0, stat: [Object] },
      { base_stat: 48, effort: 0, stat: [Object] },
      { base_stat: 48, effort: 1, stat: [Object] }
    ],
    types: [ { slot: 1, type: [Object] } ],
    weight: 40
}
davidchoi@Davids-MacBook-Pro Chap3 %
```

Figure 3.17 – fetch

When this code ran, you probably noticed a small delay before the code completed. This shows the code needed to wait until the network call for the data to complete.

In this section, we learned what asynchronous programming is. We also discussed both Promises, the foundation of asynchronous programming in JavaScript, and `async await`, which provides us with a means to streamline our asynchronous code. You will see `async await` used heavily in both React and Node development.

# Summary

In this chapter, we looked at a lot of the newer, cutting-edge features of JavaScript programming, such as methods for merging objects and arrays with **spread**, new and improved ways of handling arrays, and, of course, `async await`, a new and very popular way of working with asynchronous code. It is very important to understand these features as they are extensively used in modern JavaScript and React development.

In the next section, we will begin digging into single-page application development using React. We will start using many of the features that we learned about in this chapter.

# Section 2: Learning Single-Page Application Development Using React

In this section, we will learn how to set up and build a React web application.

This section comprises of the following chapters:

# 4

# Learning Single-Page Application Concepts and How React Enables Them

In this chapter, we'll learn about **Single-Page Applications (SPAs)**. This style of programming web applications is relatively new in the history of web development but has caught on strongly in recent years. Its use is now common practice for building large complex web applications that need to feel like native desktop or mobile apps.

We will review the former methods of building web apps and why SPA-style apps were created. We'll then learn how React can help us build this style of application in a performant and efficient way.

In this chapter, we're going to cover the following main topics:

- Understanding how websites were built in the past

- Understanding SPA benefits and attributes

- Understanding how React helps build SPA applications

# Technical requirements

The requirements for this chapter are similar to the ones for *Chapter 3*, *Building Better Apps with ES6+ Features*. You should have a basic understanding of JavaScript as well as HTML and CSS. We will once again be using Node.js and **Visual Studio Code** (**VSCode**).

The GitHub repository is again at `https://github.com/PacktPublishing/Full-Stack-React-TypeScript-and-Node`. Use the code in the `Chap4` folder.

To set up this chapter's code folder, go to your `HandsOnTypescript` folder and create a new folder called `Chap4`.

# Understanding how websites were built in the past

In this section, we will investigate the reasons for the creation of SPA-style programming by reviewing the original methods for designing and writing web pages. Having this knowledge will help us understand the reason for the shift to SPAs.

Originally, when the web was getting started, there was no JavaScript language. Initially, it was all just static HTML pages created to share documents among scientists. Once this document format and the internet became more popular, people realized that these documents needed improved styling methods to enhance communication. So, CSS was created and it became a standard for styling and the layout of HTML documents. Then, finally, the Netscape browser company decided the web needed a scripting language to make page content more dynamic, and they created JavaScript.

Despite these features, the original web was still very static in nature. When you entered a URL into your browser, you got back a single document—that is, an actual file on the server—and this would be the case for every URL you entered. CSS and JavaScript did help to make the web look better and be more dynamic, but it did not change the page-focused model of the web.

As websites became more and more sophisticated, many web developers wanted to have better control over their web documents. They wanted to dynamically control the layout and content of web pages. This resulted in **Common Gateway Interface** (**CGI**) being created. CGI was an early attempt at doing **Server-Side Rendering** (**SSR**). This basically means that requests from browsers were received by web servers, but instead of returning static HTML pages, the server would run a processor that would dynamically generate a page on the fly based on parameters and logic and then send that back.

Whether the website used a static HTML page that did not change or rendered its pages on a server using server-side logic, in the past, the emphasis was on sending to browsers complete HTML pages as files. This was how websites worked in general.

This single-file or page-based model is not at all like how native apps work, either on desktops or mobile devices. The native app model is different in that the entire app is downloaded and installed onto the user's device. When the user opens the app, it is ready to use in its entirety at that moment. Any controls that need to be drawn on the screen are done so from the code that is already there, and no additional calls to a backend server are necessary (other than calls to send or get data). This makes apps feel noticeably more responsive and faster than classic web applications, which constantly required a page refresh to show new content in the old model.

The impetus of SPA applications was to make web apps feel much more like native device applications, in order to give them the same sense of speed and responsiveness. Therefore, the SPA style uses various techniques and libraries to make web applications function and feel more like native applications.

In this section, we reviewed how websites were built in the early days of the web. Back then, the focus was on generating and serving individual HTML document files. We saw how there are limitations with this style of programming, especially when compared with native applications, and that SPA-style applications are an attempt to address those limitations and make web apps seem like native apps. In the next section, you will see what SPA apps are and how they may improve upon the page-focused model of the original web.

# Understanding SPA benefits and attributes

In this section, we will learn about what the benefits and attributes of SPA applications are. By learning about these attributes, they will help us understand some of the architectural decisions that were made during React's creation, as well as some of the related libraries and components used in creating React apps.

As mentioned earlier, the impetus for using SPA-style application building is to make our web app look and feel more like a native application. By using SPA application methods, we will make our program respond and look like it was installed on the device. Classic-style web apps can seem sluggish since any changes to the page require a call back to the server to get a new screen. However, SPA-style apps redraw portions of the screen immediately without waiting for a new file to come back from the server. Therefore, as far as the user can tell, a SPA application is a native device application.

Building SPA applications is quite complex, with many components and libraries that need to be used. However, whether we're using Angular, Vue, React, or some other framework, there are certain features and requirements that will always be common across SPA applications.

Let's understand some of the requirements:

- As the name suggests, the entire app lives on one HTML page only. Unlike standard HTML apps, which use separate pages to show different screens, the first page is the only page that ever loads on a SPA application.

- Instead of static HTML files, JavaScript renders the screen dynamically. Therefore, the HTML page that is first downloaded is actually almost entirely empty of content. But what it will have is a root element inside of the body tag that becomes the container for the entire application, which again is rendered live as the user interacts with the application.

- All scripts and files needed to run the application are generally downloaded in the beginning, when retrieving the main HTML file. However, this method is changing and more applications are downloading only a base-level script file and then downloading other scripts on-demand as needed. We'll review how to use these techniques later, as they can enhance the user experience by reducing screen wait times.

- URL routing is handled differently for SPAs. In SPA applications, there is some mechanism used, depending on the framework you choose, in order to create **virtual routing**. Virtual routing simply means that although it appears to the user that different calls to different server-side URLs are being made, in reality, all the "routing" is only happening on the client browser in order to make logical transitions to different screens. In other words, no calls to servers are made and URL routing becomes a means to logically separate an app into different screens. For example, when a user types a URL into their browser, they must then press *Enter* for the submission to be posted back to the server that is the destination of the URL. However, in the case of routing happening in a SPA app, there is no actual server path indicated by the URL. It does not exist. Therefore, the postback is never triggered. Instead, the application uses the URL as a sort of container for sections of the application and also to trigger certain behaviors when certain URLs are given. Having said this, URL routing is still a useful feature to have, as routing is an expected capability by most users and it allows them to bookmark screens.

In this section, we have learned about the attributes that make up a SPA. We covered the different methods to deal with having only a single file for our entire application and the methodologies used for building these kinds of applications. In the next section, we will drill into details about how React enables SPAs and the decisions that were made by the React team for creating this style of application.

# Understanding how React helps build SPAs

In this section, we'll learn about React at a high level. This understanding will help us build better React-based applications as we'll understand how React operates internally.

As mentioned previously, a website is primarily just an HTML file, which is a text-based document. This file contains code that the browser uses to create a logical tree called the **Document Object Model** (**DOM**). This tree represents all of the HTML elements within the file according to their order and relative to other elements in the structure. All websites have a DOM structure on their pages, whether they use the SPA style or not. However, React takes advantage of the DOM in unique ways in order to help build apps.

React has two main constructs:

- React maintains its own virtual DOM at runtime. This virtual DOM is distinct from the browser's DOM. It is React's own unique copy of the DOM that it creates and maintains based on the instructions from our code. This virtual DOM is created and edited as needed based on a reconciliation process that the React service does internally. The reconciliation process is a comparison process where React looks at the browser DOM and contrasts that with its own virtual DOM. This reconciliation process is generally known as the **render phase**. When differences are found—for example, the virtual DOM contains an element not contained in the browser DOM—React will send instructions to the browser DOM to create that element so that the browser DOM and the virtual DOM match. This process of adding, editing, or removing elements is known as the **commit phase**.

- The other main attribute of React development is that it is state-driven. In React, an application is made up of many components, and in each component, there may be some local state (that is, data). If this data changes for any reason, React will trigger its reconciliation process and make changes in the DOM if needed.

To make these concepts more concrete, we should take a look at an example of a simple React application. But before we do that, let's review what a React application is "made of."

# Attributes of a React application

At its core, a modern React application will need a few base features to function. We'll need npm to help us manage the application's dependencies. As you've seen from our previous exercises, npm is a repository that allows us to download open source dependencies from a central store and use them in our application. We'll also need a tool for doing what's called bundling. A bundling system is a service that aggregates all of our script files and assets, such as CSS files, and minifies them into a single set of files. The minification process removes whitespace and other unneeded text from our scripts so that the files that ultimately get downloaded onto user browsers are as small as possible. This smaller payload size improves app startup time and improves user experience. The bundling system we'll use is called webpack, and we've selected it because it's the industry standard for bundling React applications. In addition, we can use npm's built-in script system and create scripts to automate some of our work. For example, we can create scripts that will start up our test server, run our tests, and build the final production version of our app.

If we use the create-react-app npm package, we can get all of the previously mentioned dependencies, as well as common dependencies for doing React development and some built-in scripts to manage our app. Let's use this package and create our first app:

1. On your terminal or command line, go to the HandsOnTypescript/Chap4 folder and run the following command:

```
npx create-react-app try-react --template typescript
```

We are using npx, instead of npm i -g, so that you don't have to install create-react-app locally.

2. Once this command completes, open VSCode and open the newly created folder, try-react, which we created at the start of this chapter.

3. Open the terminal in VSCode and run the following command:

```
npm run build
```

This command will create a production build of our app and put it into a folder called build. After the build completes, you should see the following structure from VSCode:

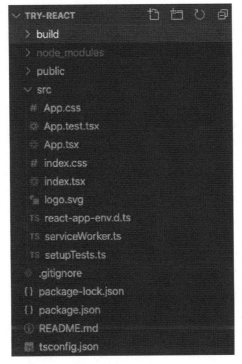

Figure 4.1 – try-react

Let's take a look at what `create-react-app` gives us, starting from the top:

- The `build` folder is the destination of all of our bundled and minified final production files. They have been shrunken down to be as small as possible and debug information has also been removed in order to enhance performance.

- Next, we have the `node_modules` folder, which contains all of our dependencies that we download from the npm repository.

- Then, we have the `public` folder, which is a folder for static assets, such as the `index.html` file, which will be used to build out our final app.

- Next, we have what is perhaps the most important folder, called `src`. As the shortened name implies, this is the folder that contains all of our source scripts. Any files with a `.tsx` extension indicate a React component. `.ts` files are just plain TypeScript files. Finally, `.css` files have our styling attributes (and there can be more than one). `d.ts` files are files that contain TypeScript typing information that the compiler uses to determine static type checks it needs to do.

- Next is the `.gitignore` file. This file is for use with the GitHub code repository we are using to save this book's source code. As the name implies, with this file, we are telling our `git` system to not upload certain files and folders, but to ignore them.

- The `package.json` and `package-lock.json` files are for configuring and setting our dependencies. Additionally, they can store configurations for our build, test, and run scripts, as well as configurations for the Jest testing framework.

- Finally, we have our `tsconfig.json` file, which we discussed in *Chapter 2, Exploring TypeScript*. It will configure the TypeScript compiler. Please notice that by default, strict mode is turned on, and therefore we cannot use implicit `any` or `undefined`.

Now that we've done this quick inventory of our project, let's take a look at the contents of some of our files. First, we'll start with the `package.json` file. There are many sections to the `package.json` file, but let's look at some of the most important ones:

- The `dependencies` section contains the libraries that our app will be using for certain pieces of functionality. These dependencies include React, as well as TypeScript and Jest libraries for doing testing. The `@types` dependencies contain the TypeScript definition files. TypeScript definition files store static typing information for frameworks that are written in JavaScript. In other words, this file tells the TypeScript compiler the shape of the types being used by a framework so that type declarations and checking can be done.

- There is another dependencies section, called `devDependencies`—although it's not used here—which normally stores development time dependencies (as opposed to the `dependencies` section, which normally only stores the runtime dependencies). For whatever reason, the React team decided to merge the two into `dependencies`. Having said that, you should be aware of it as you'll see this section in many projects.

- The scripts section is for storing scripts that manage the application. For example, the `start` script is used by calling `npm run start`, or `npm start` for short. This script is used to start our application using a development server. We can also add our own scripts, as we'll do later, for doing things such as deploying production files to a server.

Be aware that the projects created by `create-react-app` have been highly modified by the React team. They have been optimized by the team and have hidden scripts and configurations that are not readily visible—for example, base webpack configurations and scripts. If you're curious, you can run `npm run eject` to see what all these configurations and scripts are. However, please note that this is not reversible. So, you will not be able to undo it. We will not be using an ejected project, as there's little benefit in doing so.

Now, let's look at some of the scripts. Open the `index.tsx` file from the `src` folder and you'll see the following:

```tsx
import React from 'react';
import ReactDOM from 'react-dom';
import './index.css';
import App from './App';
import * as serviceWorker from './serviceWorker';

ReactDOM.render(
  <React.StrictMode>
    <App />
  </React.StrictMode>,
  document.getElementById('root')
);

// If you want your app to work offline and load faster, you
  // can change
// unregister() to register() below. Note this comes with some
  // pitfalls.
// Learn more about service workers: https://bit.ly/CRA-PWA
serviceWorker.unregister();
```

> **Service workers**
>
> Service workers are a way of doing simple threading in JavaScript. We will not be using this feature, but it comes as part of the `create-react-app` project, so I have left it for completeness.

Again, any file containing a React component that returns JSX will have a .tsx file extension. We are starting with this file because this is React's entry point for the application. It's where React starts its runtime build process. Now, if we start from the top, we can see that ES6 syntax for importing dependencies is being used. React and related modules are being imported, including the core App module, which we'll explore shortly. After the imports, we can see that ReactDOM.render is called, which ultimately "writes out" the HTML of all our components combined. It takes two arguments. One is the lowest - level React component from which rendering will start and the other is the HTML element used to contain the rendered content. As you can see, the App component is wrapped with a component called React.StrictMode. This component is simply an aid to development. When compiling in production mode, it has no effect and does not impact performance. However, in development mode, it provides extra information about potential issues in our code. This may change over time, but here is a list of the current help it provides:

- Identifying components with unsafe life cycles: It will show you if you are using unsafe life cycle calls, such as componentWillMount, componentWillReceiveProps, and componentWillUpdate. When coding with Hooks, these issues don't apply, but it is good to be aware of them for legacy class-based components.

- Warning about legacy string ref APIs: The older way of creating a reference to an HTML element, as opposed to a React component, was to use a string—for example, <div ref="myDiv">{content}</div>. Because this method uses a string, it has issues and now the preferred method is to use React.createRef instead. We'll discuss why you might use a ref in later chapters.

- Warning about deprecated findDOMNode usage: findDOMNode is now deprecated because it broke abstraction principles. Specifically, it allowed parent components, in a component tree, to code for specific child components. This tie-in to code implementation means that it becomes difficult to change code later because the parent now depends on something existing in its component tree. We discussed object-oriented programming principles, including abstraction, in *Chapter 2, Exploring TypeScript*.

- Detecting unexpected side effects: Side-effects are unintended consequences of our code. For example, if my class component initializes its state in the constructor from some other function or property, it would not be acceptable if that state sometimes received different values for every initialization. In order to help catch these kinds of issues, React.StrictMode will run certain life cycle calls, such as, for example, the constructor or getDerivedStateFromProps, twice to try and show whether this type of thing is happening. Note that this only happens during development.

- Detecting the legacy context API: The context API is a React feature that provides a global state across all components of an application. There is a newer version of the API and the older one is now deprecated. This checks that you are not using the older one.

Most of the checks being done revolve around the older class-based component style. However, since the vast majority of existing code that you will probably have to maintain is still written in the older style with classes, it's still important to know.

Next, let's take a look at the App.tsx file:

```tsx
import React from 'react';
import logo from './logo.svg';
import './App.css';
function App() {
  return (
    <div className="App">
      <header className="App-header">
        <img src={logo} className="App-logo" alt="logo" />
        <p>
          Edit <code>src/App.tsx</code> and save to reload.
        </p>
        <a
          className="App-link"
          href="https://reactjs.org"
          target="_blank"
          rel="noopener noreferrer"
        >
          Learn React
        </a>
      </header>
    </div>
  );
}
export default App;
```

> **Important note**
>
> Please note that the JSX syntax, as shown here, is not actually HTML. It is custom JavaScript. Therefore, any time there is a potential conflict with JavaScript keywords, React uses another name. For example, `class` is a reserved keyword in JavaScript. So, React uses `className` instead to represent CSS classes.

Although the `index.tsx` file is the main starting point for React, the actual components that we will build for our app start in the `App.tsx` file. So, this is a very important file for us.

Let's discuss some items in this code:

- First, we are importing React from the React npm dependency. If you look inside of the npm_modules folder, you will find a subfolder called `react`, and that folder is what this `import` statement is referring to. Any code imports we did not create ourselves will be in the `node_modules` folder.

- Next is the `logo` import. Image assets are imported into a JavaScript variable—in this case, the `logo` variable. Also, as you can see, since this is not an npm module, it requires a dot reference. npm modules do not require a relative path because the system is aware of which folder to start looking in, npm_modules.

- Next, we import `App.css`. This file is the styles file and therefore does not have an associated JavaScript variable to it. Since it is not an `npm` package, it also requires a relative path.

- The `App` component is a functional component, as shown by its syntax. The `App` component is the root parent component for the entire application. This component has no state of its own and just renders out content. So, the `return` statement is the rendered content and it is using **JSX**.

- We'll go into much more detail about what JSX is in later chapters; however, for now, JSX is HTML-like syntax written in JavaScript. It was created by the React team to make it easier and clearer to create HTML content with React components. The main thing to note is that although it looks almost identical to HTML, it is not really HTML and therefore there are some differences in the way it works.

- The style reference to CSS classes, which is normally set as `class`, is set as `className`, as shown in the code. This is because `class` is a JavaScript keyword and so cannot be used here.

- Squiggly brackets indicate code is being passed, not strings. For example, the `img` tag's `src` attribute takes a JavaScript variable, `logo`, as its value, and also that value is inside of squiggly brackets. To pass strings, use quotes.

Let's start our app in development mode to see what this basic screen looks like. Run the following command:

```
npm start
```

Once you run the previous command, you should see the following screen in your browser:

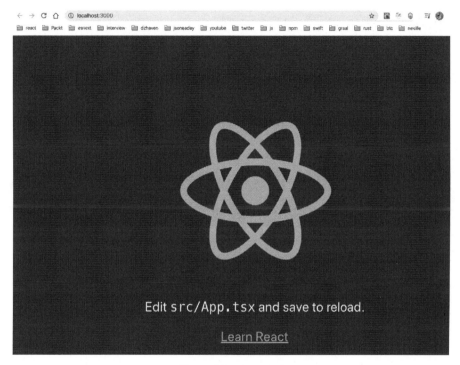

Figure 4.2 – App start

As you can see, the text and logo from our App.tsx file is showing up, since this is the main starting component of our application. Once we start coding, we will leave this server running, and when we save any script files, the page will automatically update, allowing us to see our changes in real time.

To get a better feel for building components in React, as well as how React routing works, let's create our first simple component:

1. Create a new file in the src folder called Home.tsx and add the following code:

```
import React, { FC } from "react";

const Home: FC = () => {
```

```
    return <div>Hello World! Home</div>;
};

export default Home;
```

2. Now, as you can see, we are creating a component called Home that returns a div tag with the words Hello World!. You should also notice that we are using the FC, functional component, declaration to type our component. Functional components are the only way of creating components when using React Hooks, as opposed to the older class style. This is because the React team believes composition works better as a means of doing code reuse than inheritance. But do notice that the importance of having code reuse, whatever the method, is still there.

3. Now, in order to get our component to show on the screen, we need to add it to our App.tsx file. But let's also add routing to our app and explore that as well. First, update the index.tsx file like this:

```
import React from 'react';
import ReactDOM from 'react-dom';
import './index.css';
import App from './App';
import * as serviceWorker from './serviceWorker';
import { BrowserRouter } from "react-router-dom";

ReactDOM.render(
  <React.StrictMode>
    <BrowserRouter>
    <App />
    </BrowserRouter>
  </React.StrictMode>,
    document.getElementById('root')
);

// If you want your app to work offline and load faster,
// you can change
// unregister() to register() below. Note this comes with
// some pitfalls.
```

```
// Learn more about service workers:
    // https://bit.ly/CRA-PWA
serviceWorker.unregister();
```

The index.tsx file now has a component called BrowserRouter. This component is part of React Router and is the base component that allows routing to happen across the application. Since it wraps our App component, and the rest of the application lives inside of this App component, it means routing services are being provided for the entire application.

4.  Since we will be using React Router, let's also create a component for a second route, called AnotherScreen:

```
import React, { FC } from "react";


const AnotherScreen: FC = () => {
    return <div>Hello World! Another Screen</div>;
};


export default AnotherScreen;
```

5.  Now, update the App.tsx file like this:

```
import React from "react";
import "./App.css";
import Home from "./Home";
import AnotherScreen from './AnotherScreen';
import { Switch, Route } from "react-router";


function App() {
  return (
    <div className="App">
      <header className="App-header">
        <Switch>
          <Route exact={true} path="/"
            component={Home}></Route>
          <Route path="/another"
            component={AnotherScreen}></Route>
        </Switch>
      </header>
```

```
        </div>
    );
}

export default App;
```

As you can see, the header contents have been replaced. In this file, you can see that among the tags, you have a component called `Switch`. This component acts a lot like a switch statement. It tells React Router which component to display when a certain route, URL path, is given. Inside of the `Switch` component, we can see two `Route` components. The first one is for the default root route, as indicated by `path` being equal to `"/"`. For this route, React Router will display the `Home` component (note that using `exact` just means the URL should be an exact match). The second route is for the `"/another"` path. So, when this path is in the URL box, the `AnotherScreen` component will be loaded.

6.  If you left `npm start` running, you should see **Hello World!** Home, as follows:

Figure 4.3 – Home

7.  If you look at the URL, you can see that it is on the root of the site. Let's try switching the URL to `http://localhost:3000/another`:

Figure 4.4 – Another screen

As you can see, it loaded the AnotherScreen component, as per our instructions to load that component for this specific URL.

Additionally, if you open your Chrome browser debugger, you will see that no network calls to that specific path were actually made. Again, this confirms that React Router is not doing any postbacks for these paths and they only exist on the browser locally:

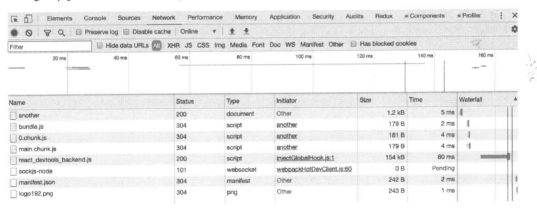

Figure 4.5 – Chrome debugger

This was just a quick example of building a React app and components just to get us started.

In this section, we learned how React works internally and how to set up a React project. This knowledge will be valuable in the coming chapters as we begin to build out our application.

## Summary

In this chapter, we learned about how websites were built in the early days of the web. We also learned about some of the limitations of the older style of web development and how SPA applications attempt to overcome them. We saw how a SPA application's main driver is to make web apps behave more like native applications. Finally, we got an introduction to React development and building components.

In the next chapter, we'll build upon this knowledge and go into React component building in more depth. We'll look at class-based components and compare and contrast them to the newer Hook-style components. The things we've learned so far about web development and React-based web development will help us to better understand this next chapter.

# 5
# React Development with Hooks

In this chapter, we'll learn about development with React Hooks. We'll compare and contrast Hook development with the older class-based style and see why development with Hooks is a better way of developing in React. We'll also learn about best practices when coding with Hooks so that we can have the best quality code.

In this chapter, we're going to cover the following main topics:

- Understanding the limitations of class-style components
- Learning about React Hooks and understanding the benefits
- Comparing and contrasting the class-style and the Hooks style

## Technical requirements

You should have a basic understanding of web development and the SPA style of coding. We will once again be using Node and Visual Studio Code.

The GitHub repository is at `https://github.com/PacktPublishing/Full-Stack-React-TypeScript-and-Node`. Use the code in the `Chap5` folder.

To set up the *Chapter 5* code folder, go to your `HandsOnTypescript` folder and create a new folder called `Chap5`.

# Understanding the limitations and issues with the old class-style components

In this section, we'll review what class-style components are. We'll see why inheritance-style code reuse and lifecycle methods, although well intentioned, ultimately did not provide good code reuse and component structure capabilities. Although we will not write our code with class components, it is very important to understand class-based components because most existing React code uses classes, since Hooks are still somewhat new. So, as a professional developer, you will have to read and maintain this code base until it uses Hooks.

In order to understand the limitations of class-style components, we first need to review what they are. A React application is made up of many individual structures called components. When using a class-based style, these components are JavaScript ES6 classes that inherit from `React.Component`. A component is basically a machine that may contain data, called state, and the component will emit HTML via a language called JSX based upon changes to this data. Although components can become quite complex, at a basic level this is what they are.

A class component usually has state of its own, although this is not a requirement. In addition, a class-based component can have child components. Child components are simply other React components that have been embedded into the render function of a parent component and therefore will be rendered out when the parent is rendered.

A class component must inherit from the `React.Component` object. By doing this, it receives all the capabilities of a React component, including the lifecycle functions. These functions are event handlers that React provides that allow developers to hook into events that occur at specific times during the lifetime of a React component. In other words, these functions allow us as developers to inject our own code and logic into a React component at the desired time.

# State

We touched upon state in *Chapter 4, Learning Single-Page Application Concepts and How React Enables Them*. Let's dive a little deeper before we learn more about React components. React uses JSX to render HTML to the browser. However, the thing that triggers these renders is component state or, more accurately, any change to component state. So, what is component state? In a React class component, there is a single field called state. This field is an object that can contain any number of properties that describe the associated component. Functions should not be applied to state, but you can have as many functions as you require as members of your class component.

As mentioned, changing state causes the React system to re-render your component. State changes are what drive renders in React and components contain only the UI elements for themselves, which is a good way of maintaining a separation of concerns and clean coding practices. State changes in class-based components are triggered by the setState function. This function takes a parameter that is your new state and React will later asynchronously update your state. This means the actual state change does not happen immediately but is controlled by the React system.

In addition to state there is the ability to share the state of a component using props. Props are state properties that have been passed down to child components of a component. Just like when state changes, if props change, a re-render on the child is also triggered. A re-render of a parent will also trigger a re-render to a child. Note that a re-render does not mean the entire UI is updated. The reconciliation process will still run and will only change what is needed based upon what state has changed and what is already on the screen.

# Lifecycle methods

The following image is a good overview of the lifecycle calls in a class-based React component. As you can see, it's quite complicated. In addition, there are also several deprecated functions that are not mentioned in the diagram, such as `componentWillReceiveProps`, which have been completely eliminated as they were causing issues such as unwanted renders and infinite loops:

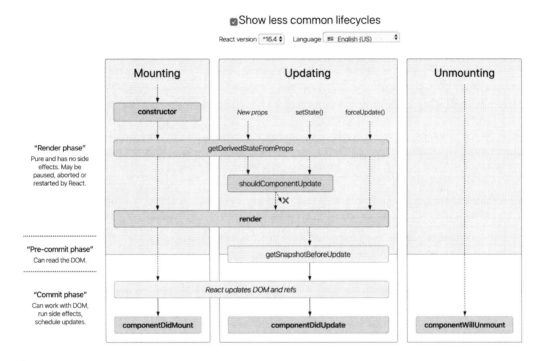

Figure 5.1 – React class component lifecycle

Image source: `http://projects.wojtekmaj.pl/react-lifecycle-methods-diagram/`

Let's review this diagram starting at a high level. First off, you can see we have **Mounting**, **Updating**, and **Unmounting**. Mounting is simply the instantiation and initialization of a component, and then the addition of the initialized component into the virtual React DOM. We discussed the virtual DOM that React uses to reconcile components between itself and the real browser DOM in *Chapter 4, Learning Single-Page Application Concepts and How React Enables Them*. Updating refers to re-renders. That is when state changes and the UI must be updated. Unmounting is when a component is no longer used and is to be removed from the DOM.

Now we'll go over the lifecycle methods. Since there are many, let's list them.

## Mounting

Under mounting, we have the following methods:

- `Constructor`: This is not a lifecycle method but the built-in class constructor. It is traditionally used to initialize state and bind any custom event functions. You may recall from *Chapter 3, Building Better Apps with ES6+ Features*, `bind` is used to switch the `this` object of a function. This is done in the constructor.

- `getDerivedStateFromProps(props, state)`: If you are basing your local state on props from a parent you would use this function. This is a static function. It should be used sparingly as it triggers additional renders. It can also be used in updates.

- `render`: This can also run during updating for re-renders. This function is what triggers the reconciliation process for React. It should only render out JSX, which could also be inside arrays or plain text. If due to state or props you decide there is nothing to render you should return `null`. It is possible to return a boolean, but outside of testing I see little value in doing this.

- `componentDidMount`: This function is triggered after a component is finished mounting (being initialized). You can place network API calls here. You can also add event handler subscriptions here, but you must remember to unsubscribe them in the `componentWillUnmount` function or it can cause a memory leak. You can call `setState` to change local state data here, but you are then triggering a second call to render so it should be used sparingly. `SetState` is used to update local state.

- `UNSAFE` deprecated methods (do not use) are `UNSAFE_componentWillMount`, `UNSAFE_componentWillReceiveProps`, and `UNSAFE_componentWillUpdate`.

## Updating

Let's look at the methods under updating:

- `shouldComponentUpdate(nextProps, nextState)`: This is used to decide whether a re-render should be done or not. It usually compares the previous props to the current props.

- `getSnapshotBeforeUpdate(prevProps, prevState)`: This runs immediately before the render to DOM occurs so you can capture the DOM state just before React changes it. If you return something from this function, it is given as a parameter to the `componentDidUpdate` function.

- `componentDidUpdate(prevProps, prevState, snapshot)`: This function runs immediately after a re-render is complete. You can make changes to the finished DOM here, or you can call to `setState`, but you must have a condition so that you do not cause an infinite loop error. The snapshot state comes from the `getSnapshotBeforeUpdate` function.

## Unmounting

The following method is used at this level:

- `componentWillUnmount`: This is similar to `dispose` functions in languages such as C# and can be used to do cleanup work, for example, removing event listeners or other subscriptions.

The main concern in dealing with any of these lifecycle methods is to prevent unnecessary or unwanted re-renders. We must select the one that is less likely to trigger unnecessary re-renders, or if we need to use a specific method so our code runs at a specific time, we should add prop and state checks in order to reduce unneeded re-renders. It is paramount that you get renders until control or your user experience will suffer because of a slow and buggy application.

Let's go over some of the main calls. Let's start with `getDerivedStateFromProps`. In general, it is a good idea to avoid using this function, or just use it sparingly. From experience, it makes it very difficult to figure out when a component will re-render. In general, it tends to trigger unwanted re-renders, which can cause unintended behavior that's again difficult to track down.

The React team recommends some alternatives, and we should always prefer these as they are almost always easier to reason about and more consistent in behavior:

- When you need to trigger behavior based upon a prop value that changed. For example, getting network data or triggering some other action. Use `componentDidUpdate` instead. It is less likely to trigger an infinite loop as long as you do a check before causing anything that changes state. For example, you can use the `prevProps` parameter and compare it to your local state values before calling `setState` to change your state data.

- Use the `memoization` technique (note this idea is not a part of React necessarily; it's just a programming technique). `Memoization` is basically like caching, except instead of having a cache expiration you would use a variable change to update the cache. So, in React, this simply means use a property or function that first checks whether a props value is different from last time, and only if it is different does it trigger a state update.

  There is a built-in component wrapper in React called `React.memo`. It will trigger a re-render only when a child's props change, not when the parent component re-renders.

- Make your component fully controlled, which simply means that it will have no state of its own and will render under the direction of its parent whenever props change or the parent renders. Facebook also recommends using uncontrolled components as well by changing their key (a key is a unique identifier for the component), which then triggers a re-render. However, I disagree with this suggestion. As you recall, we discussed encapsulation and abstraction in *Chapter 1, Understanding TypeScript*, and this means that the uncontrolled component's behavior should be unknown to the parent. This also means that it is not entirely controllable by the parent, and it shouldn't be. Therefore to get an uncontrolled component to do what the parent wants may make it tempting to add implementation changes inside that component, which will then tie it more closely to the parent. At times this may be unavoidable, but if it can be avoided it should be.

- If your component's rendered state depends on network data you can use `componentDidMount` to make your network call there, and then update state (assuming you need this data only once on load). Note `componentDidMount` only runs once on the component's first load. Also, if you use this function you will be doing one additional render, but that's still better than the potential for causing additional unwanted renders.

- `ComponentDidUpdate` can be used to handle scenarios where state needs to change due to prop changes. Since this method is called after the render, it is less likely to cause infinite render loops as long as you compare your props to state before triggering any state changes. Having said that, it is better to avoid derived state entirely if at all possible and keep your state in a single parent root component and share that state via props. To be honest, this is tedious work as you will need to pass down your state via props to children that may be several layers deep. It also means you need to structure your state schema well so that you can cleanly separate state bound for a specific child. When we use Hooks later, you'll see that this is much easier to do with Hooks than with a single state object. Nevertheless, having as little local component state as possible is a best practice for React development.

Let's create a small project where we can try out a class component and discuss its features:

1. Switch your command line or terminal to the `Chap5` folder.

2. Run the following command within that folder:

```
npx create-react-app class-components --template
typescript
```

3. Now open Visual Studio in the folder you just created, `class-components`, and also open a terminal or command line in that same folder. Let's create a new file called `Greeting.tsx` in the `src` folder. It should look like this:

```
import React from "react";
interface GreetingProps {
    name?: string
}
interface GreetingState {
    message: string
}
export default class Greeting extends React.
  Component<GreetingProps, GreetingState> {
    constructor(props: GreetingProps){
        super(props);
        this.state = {
            message: `Hello from, ${props.name}`
        }
    }
```

```
    render() {
        if(!this.props.name) {
            return <div>no name given</div>;
        }
        return <div>
            {this.state.message}
        </div>;
    }
}
```

If you look at this file, first you notice that the file extension is tsx. When using TypeScript and creating a React component you must use tsx as your file's extension. Next, when we look at the code we see the import of React, which provides not only the Component to inherit from but also access to JSX syntax. Next, we see two new interfaces: GreetingProps and GreetingState. Again, because we are using TypeScript and want type safety we are creating the expected types for both any props that come into our component and the state that is being used inside of our component. Also take note that the name field in the GreetingProps interface is optional, which means it can also be set to undefined, as we'll use it later. Again, avoid having local state in your non-parent non-root components when possible. I am doing this for example purposes here.

4.  When we create our class we also need to remember to export it so that it can be accessed by whatever component will be using it. This is done with the **export** keyword. In addition, we use the **default** keyword to indicate that this is the main export of this module, and therefore when importing this module we do not need to use brackets. I'll show an example of importing this module later. In the class definition signature, we see that it extends React. Component<GreetingProps>. This type declaration is indicating not only that this class is a React component but also that it takes a prop of the GreetingProps type. Once the declaration is set we define the constructor, which takes a prop of the same type, GreetingProps.

> **Important Note**
>
> If your component takes props, it is important that the first call you make inside the constructor is the call to the base class constructor, `super(props)`. This ensures that React is aware of your incoming props and so can react when props change (no pun intended). Inside the constructor, we don't need to use `this.props` to reference the `props` object since it is being passed in as a constructor parameter. Anywhere else, `this.props` is required.

5. Next, we see that `state` is instantiated in `constructor`, and the variable and its type are declared in the line below as being the `GreetingState` type. Then, finally, we have our `render` function, which declares JSX that will eventually be converted into HTML. Notice that the `render` function has a logical `if/else` statement to show a different UI depending on the value of `this.props.name`. `render` functions should try and control the proper UI and not render anything when there is no reason to. This can improve performance and memory when done consistently. Just return `null` if there is nothing to `render`, as React understands this value is indicating not to render anything.

6. Now all we need to do is update the `App.tsx` file so that it includes our `Greeting.tsx` component. Open the `App.tsx` file and update it like this:

```tsx
import React from 'react';
import logo from './logo.svg';
import './App.css';
import Greeting from "./Greeting";

function App() {
  return (
    <div className="App">
      <header className="App-header">
        <img src={logo} className="App-logo" alt="logo" />
        <Greeting />
      </header>
    </div>
  );
```

```
}
```

```
export default App;
```

First, notice that we are importing the `Greeting` class. Since our `Greeting` class is the default export of the `Greeting.tsx` module file (we don't need to indicate the extension) we need not use { } in between `import` and `from`. If the `Greeting` class was not the default export, for example, if we had many exports in the same module file, then we would need to use this syntax: `import { Greeting } from "./Greeting"`.

7.  As you can see, we used the `Greeting` component to replace some of the JSX that was already there. Notice that we did not pass the `name` property to `Greeting`. Let's see what happens when we run the app. Execute this command in your terminal, making sure you are in the `class-components` folder:

```
npm start
```

You should see this screen:

Figure 5.2 – Application first load

This message appeared because we had not passed a `name` property to our `Greeting` component. As we saw, it was possible to leave this property empty because of the `?` next to the field's type definition.

8.  Now let's go to our `App.tsx` file and update `Greeting` to add a name value. Replace the `Greeting` component inside `App.tsx` with this:

```
import React from 'react';
import logo from './logo.svg';
import './App.css';
import Greeting from "./Greeting";

function App() {
```

```
    return (
      <div className="App">
        <header className="App-header">
          <img src={logo} className="App-logo" alt="logo"
            />
          <Greeting name="Dave Choi" />
        </header>
      </div>
    );
  }

export default App;
```

Notice that we added a property called name with a value of my own name. Feel free to enter your name instead and then save the file. Since React includes an auto-updating test server, the browser page should update with your new code automatically. You should see your name like this on the screen:

Hello from, Dave Choi

Figure 5.3 – Updated screen

OK, so we've created a simple class-based component. Let's now start making use of some of the lifecycle methods and see how they work:

1.  Update Greeting.tsx to include the getDerivedStateFromProps function:

```
import React from "react";
interface GreetingProps {
    name?: string
}
interface GreetingState {
    message: string
}
export default class Greeting extends
```

```
React.Component<GreetingProps> {
    constructor(props: GreetingProps){
        super(props);
        this.state = {
            message: `Hello from, ${props.name}`
        }
    }
    state: GreetingState;
```

2.  The code is virtually identical except we will now add the
    getDerivedStateFromProps function just above the render function:

```
static getDerivedStateFromProps(props: GreetingProps,
    state:GreetingState) {
        console.log(props, state);
        return state;
}
render() {
        console.log("rendering Greeting")
        if(!this.props.name) {
            return <div>no name given</div>;
        }
        return <div>
            {this.state.message}
        </div>;
    }
}
```

As you can see this is a static function, a function that is associated with the class
and not a class instance. This function takes the current props and state values and
passes them in for the component to use to update its state if needed. Right now, we
do not update our local state. We only log the props and state and just return the
state (this function must always return a state object, whether it has been updated
or not). Also notice in the render function we are console logging the fact that the
render function was called.

3.  Let's leave this code as is for now and update our App.tsx file so that it can accept an input, which takes the name of the current user:

```
import React from 'react';
import logo from './logo.svg';
import './App.css';
import Greeting from "./Greeting";
class App extends React.Component {
  constructor(props:any) {
    super(props);

    this.state = {
      enteredName: ""
    }
    this.onChangeName = this.onChangeName.bind(this);
  }

  state: { enteredName: string }
  onChangeName(e: React.ChangeEvent<HTMLInputElement>) {
    this.setState({
      enteredName: e.target.value
    });
  }
```

In order to accept input and hold onto it so it can be used later, we create a state object with a field called enteredName. We also create a new function called onChangeName and bind it to the current this class instance, like we learned in *Chapter 3, Building Better Apps with ES6+ Features*.

4.  In onChangeName, we are then setting the state property enteredName to the value of the user input by using the setState function. You must never modify state in your class components without using this function or else your state will lose synchronization with the React runtime:

```
render() {
  console.log("rendering App");

  return (
    <div className="App">
```

```
      <header className="App-header">
        <img src={logo} className="App-logo" alt="logo"
        />
        <input value={this.state.enteredName}
          onChange={this.onChangeName} />
        <Greeting name={this.state.enteredName} />
      </header>
    </div>
    )
  }
}
export default App;
```

5.  Next, we have added a `console.log` statement to see when the `App.tsx`
    render function is called. Also, we have defined a new `input` control whose
    value is `this.state.enteredName` and its `onChange` event is tied to our
    `onChangeName` function. If you save this code and open the Chrome dev tools,
    you will see this:

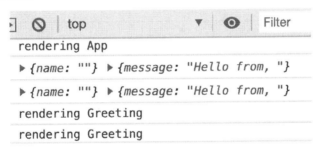

Figure 5.4 – Rendering Greeting

You can see our render logging messages and also the `Greeting` name prop and
`message` state values. Additionally, since we did not enter a value in the `input`,
the `name` prop is blank and therefore the `name` property of our `Greeting`
component and the end of the `message` string are also blank. You're probably
wondering why the logs for `Greeting` run twice. It's because we are running in
StrictMode for development purposes.

6.  Let's quickly remove that so we don't get confused. Go to your `index.tsx` file and replace the code with this:

```
import React from 'react';
import ReactDOM from 'react-dom';
import './index.css';
import App from './App';
import * as serviceWorker from './serviceWorker';

ReactDOM.render(
  <React.Fragment>
    <App />
  </React.Fragment>,
  document.getElementById('root')
);

// If you want your app to work offline and load faster,
// you can change
// unregister() to register() below. Note this comes with
// some pitfalls.
// Learn more about service workers:
// https://bit.ly/CRA-PWA
serviceWorker.unregister();
```

We replaced `StrictMode` with `Fragment`. We don't actually need `Fragment` as it's only used to wrap a set of JSX elements that don't have a parent wrapping element such as `div`, but it's fine for our testing, and I want to leave a placeholder to put back the `StrictMode` tags.

7.  If you save and look at your browser debug console, you will see this:

Figure 5.5 – Browser debug console

The rationale for all this work is to show what specifically can trigger calls to render and how we can be more careful about this.

8.  Now let's type our name into the input, and you'll see this:

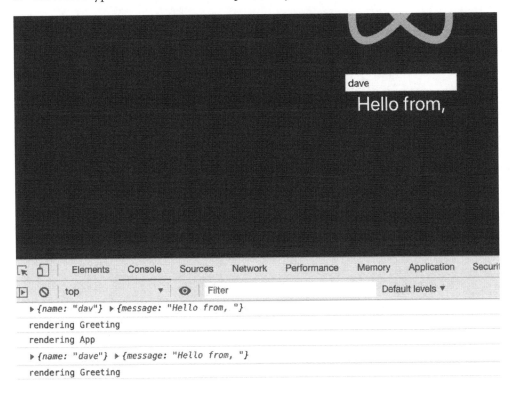

Figure 5.6 – App.tsx input

9.  The question is, why does my message end with "Hello from, "? If you look at the code in `Greeting`, you can see that we only set the `message` state property once during the constructor run (which is effectively like using `componentDidMount`). So, since this event runs only once when the screen first loads, at that time `this.props.name` is blank as we've not entered a value yet. So, what can we do? Well, let's try using the `getDerivedStateFromProps` function and see what happens:

```
export default class Greeting extends React.
  Component<GreetingProps> {
    constructor(props: GreetingProps){
      super(props);

      this.state = {
        message: Greeting.getNewMessage(props.name)
      }
```

```
    }
    state: GreetingState;
```

10. I'm only showing the `Greeting` class as that's the only thing I want to change for this example. So, in the following code, take a look at the updated `getDerivedStateFromProps`:

```
static getDerivedStateFromProps(props: GreetingProps,
    state:GreetingState) {
    console.log(props, state);
    if(props.name && props.name !== state.message) {
        const newState = {...state};
        newState.message =
            Greeting.getNewMessage(props.name);
        return newState;
    }
    return state;
}

static getNewMessage(name: string = "") {
    return `Hello from, ${name}`;
}

render() {
    console.log("rendering Greeting")
    if(!this.props.name) {
        return <div>no name given</div>;
    }
    return <div>
        {this.state.message}
    </div>;
}
}
```

As you can see, that function has now become more complex and I am doing a comparison against the new prop and our existing state. Then we clone our `state` object. It is very important to make sure you do this so that you do not accidentally edit your state directly. Then we update the `state.message` value using a new static function, `getNewMessage` (since I'm setting the message in multiple places). Now let's try adding our name. If you do this, you'll see that our name gets added to the message, but also we get a `Greeting` and `App` render for each letter we type. Right now this isn't too bad as we don't have much code, but you can imagine if we keep adding new properties to our local state on our `Greeting` component and we have a much more complex application, things can get very difficult.

Let's refactor this code and see if we can improve things a bit:

1. Update `App.tsx`:

```tsx
class App extends React.Component {
  constructor(props:any) {
    super(props);

    this.state = {
      enteredName: "",
      message: ""
    }

    this.onChangeName = this.onChangeName.bind(this);
  }

  state: { enteredName: string, message: string }

  onChangeName(e: React.ChangeEvent<HTMLInputElement>) {
    this.setState({
      enteredName: e.target.value,
      message: `Hello from, ${e.target.value}`
    });
  }
```

I'm only showing the App class since that's all we're changing. As you can see, we add a new property to our state object called message (we'll be removing message from Greeting shortly) and we update it whenever the user enters a new username into the input element:

```
render() {
    console.log("rendering App");

    return (
    <div className="App">
      <header className="App-header">
        <img src={logo} className="App-logo" alt="logo"
        />
        <input value={this.state.enteredName}
          onChange={this.onChangeName} />
        <Greeting message={this.state.message} />
      </header>
    </div>
    )
  }
}
```

Then we send this message state property to our Greeting component as a prop.

2.  Now we'll look at our Greeting component, but to keep things clean, let's create a new file called GreetingFunctional.tsx and put the following code inside it:

```
import React from "react";

interface GreetingProps {
    message: string
}

export default function Greeting(props: GreetingProps) {
    console.log("rendering Greeting")

    return (<div>
            {props.message}
```

```
        </div>);
    }
```

3.  Once you have added this file, you'll also need to update your `App.tsx` file import of `Greeting` to refer to this file like this:

```
import Greeting from "./GreetingFunctional";
```

As you can see, `Greeting` has been drastically shortened and made simpler. It is now a functional component because it is a best practice to make components that have no local state to be functions instead of classes. We weren't able to reduce the re-renders, since changing the message necessarily triggers a re-render, but even this shortening and reducing of code is worth this change. Also, even though we moved some code into `App.tsx`, you'll notice that this code is also less involved than the code that was in our original `Greeting` component.

There is one issue with this style of component building, where most of the state is inside a single parent component and child components get props passed down to them, which is that for complex multi-level component hierarchies there can be a lot of boilerplate code to pass the props through multiple levels of components. It is for these scenarios that we could use React Context to bypass the hierarchy and send parent state directly to a child. However, I don't like using Context because bypassing the natural component hierarchy to arbitrarily inject state to some component feels like an anti-pattern (a design method you should not be using). It's bound to cause confusion and make it more difficult to refactor code later. I'll get into Context more later in *Chapter 7, Learning Redux and React Router*.

In this section, we learned about class-based React components. Since Hooks are still relatively new, most existing React apps are still using class-based components, therefore having an understanding of this style of coding is still important. In the next section, we will explore Hook-based components and then later compare the two styles.

# Learning React Hooks and understanding how it is an improvement over class-style components

In this section, we will learn about React Hooks. We'll take a look at an example project and see how it works. Since this book is primarily about Hooks, at least with regard to React, it will help us write our code later.

Let's discuss some of the reasons for Hooks. We saw in the class components section that classes have lifecycle methods that allow you to handle certain events that occur while a component is alive. With React Hooks, we don't have those lifecycle methods, because with Hooks all components are functional components. We created a functional component in the class-components sample app called `GreetingFunctional` in the previous section. A functional component is a component that is a JavaScript function and returns JSX. The reason for this change is that the entire design is attempting to move away from **Object Oriented Programming (OOP)** inheritance models and instead use composition as its primary code reuse model. We covered OOP inheritance models in *Chapter 2, Exploring TypeScript*, but composition means that instead of receiving functionality as an inheritance from some parent class we are simply combining functional components, sort of like Lego pieces, to design our screens.

Along with these functional components we have Hooks. Hooks are just JavaScript functions that provide certain capabilities to the component. These include the creation of state, access to network data, and just about anything else a component needs. Additionally, Hooks are not component specific, and therefore any Hook can be used in any component—assuming it's useful and makes sense. If you look back at our class-component project, you will see that there's really no way of sharing the logic in our lifecycle event methods. We cannot easily extract it out and then reuse it in some other class component. This is one of the primary reasons for the creation of the Hooks model in React. Therefore, these two pieces, functional components and reusable functions (Hooks), are the key to understanding React Hooks.

To start, let's list some of the more important Hooks that we will be using in our code. We will give examples of their use in code soon, but for now, we'll discuss them at a high level:

- `useState`: This function is the bread and butter of development with Hooks. It replaces the `state` and `setState` calls within class components. `useState` takes a value as a parameter that represents the initial state of the state property it is trying to represent. It also returns an array. The first item is the actual state property and the second is a function that can update that property. In general, it is used to update a single value, as opposed to a more complex object that has multiple properties. A better Hook for that type of state may be `useReducer`, which is explained later.

- `useEffect`: This function triggers after components have finished being drawn on the screen. It is similar to `componentDidMount` and `componentDidUpdate`. However, they run before drawing onto the screen happens. It is intended to be used to update state objects. So if, for example, you need to get network data and then update state, you can do it here. You can also subscribe to events here, but you should also unsubscribe by returning a function that does the unsubscribing.

You can have multiple separate implementations of useEffect, each responsible for doing something unique. This function usually runs after every completed screen draw. So, if any component state or props change, this will run. You can force it to run only once, like componentDidMount, by passing an empty array as a parameter. You can also force it to run only when specific props or state changes by passing those as arrays into the useEffect array parameter.

This function runs asynchronously, but if you need to know some element values on the screen, such as scroll position, you may need to use useLayoutEffect. This function runs synchronously, allowing you to get certain element values as they currently are on the screen and then do something with them in a synchronous manner. But, of course, this blocks your UI, so you need to only do things that are very fast or the user experience will suffer.

- useCallback: This function will create an instance of a function once a set of parameters has been changed. This function exists to try and save memory, because otherwise an instance of the function would be recreated on each render. It takes a handler function as its first parameter and then an array of items that may change as its second. If the items don't change, the callback doesn't get a new instance. Therefore any properties used inside this function will be the prior values. When I first learned about this function, I found it difficult to understand, so I'll give an example of it later.

- useMemo: This function is intended to save the result of a long-running task. It's a bit like caching, but it only runs if the array of parameters has changed, so in this sense it's similar to useCallback. However, useMemo returns a value that is the result of some heavy computation.

- useReducer: This function works similarly to React Redux. It takes two parameters, reducer and initial state, and returns two objects: a state object that will be updated by the reducer and a dispatcher that receives updated state data, called an action, and passes it to the reducer. The reducer acts as a filtering mechanism and determines how action data will be used to update the state. We will show an example later in code. This method works well when you want to have a single complex state object with multiple properties that may need to be updated.

- useContext: This function is a way of having global state data that can be shared across components. It is better to use it sparingly as it gives the ability to arbitrarily inject state into any child without regard to hierarchy. We will use React Redux rather than Context, but it is good to know it exists.

- `useRef`: This can be used to hold any value in its current property. This value does not trigger a re-render if it changes, and the value lives as long as the component it was created in lives. It's a way of holding state that has no effect on renders. One of its use cases is to hold a DOM element. You may want to do this because under certain circumstances it is necessary to opt out of the standard state-driven React model and access HTML elements directly. For this purpose, `useRef` is used to access an instance of an element.

There are, of course, many other Hooks out there, both from the React team and third parties. But once you are comfortable, you'll be able to see what else you may need or, even better, be able to create your own Hooks. We will also be creating our own Hooks for our project as well.

Let's take a look at some examples of using Hooks. We'll create a new project in `Chap5` to get started:

1. Switch your command line or terminal to the `Chap5` folder and run the following command within that folder:

```
npx create-react-app hooks-components –template
typescript
```

2. In the last example for the class-components project, we created a class component called `Greeting.tsx` that had its own state. For demonstration purposes, let's create the same component as a React Hooks functional component. In the `src` folder of your `hooks-components` project, create a new file called `Greeting.tsx` and add this code:

```tsx
import React, { FC, useState, useEffect } from 'react';

interface GreetingProps {
    name?: string
}
const Greeting: FC<GreetingProps> =
({name}:GreetingProps) => {
    const [message, setMessage] = useState("");
    useEffect(() => {
        if(name) {
            setMessage(`Hello from, ${name}`);
        }
    }, [name])
```

```
    if(!name) {
        return <div>no name given</div>;
    }
    return <div>
        {message}
    </div>;
}


export default Greeting;
```

This is the version of the code where we get a name as a prop and have our own local state. We should try and avoid local state, but I'm doing this for demonstration purposes. As you can see, it's way shorter than the class version. In addition, we have no lifecycle functions to override. We are using an arrow function because it's shorter than using a regular function and we don't need a function's features. As you can see, we do have a declaration for the Greeting component. It uses FC, **Functional Component**, and it is a generic associated with the GreetingProps interface. The state is stored in the message property by using the useState function, which is a small one-line statement with no constructor since this is a function and not a class. Note GreetingProps next to the parameter is not necessary; I only included it for completeness. Notice also that we are using parameter deconstruction by passing { name } instead of props.

Next, we have our useEffect function. As stated, this is sort of similar to componentDidMount or componentDidUpdate, but runs after drawing to the screen finishes. It will update the message state property whenever our name prop updates because we pass it as a parameter to the useEffect function. Since this is not a class, we have no render function. The return value of the function is the call to render.

3.  Now we'll refactor a bit by placing our state into the App.tsx component. Let's make GreetingFunctional.tsx like we did in the class version of our component:

```
import React from "react";


interface GreetingProps {
    message: string
}
```

```
export default function Greeting(props: GreetingProps) {
    console.log("rendering Greeting")


    return (<div>
            {props.message}
        </div>);
}
```

4.  Now let's refactor App.tsx as a functional component and use the useReducer Hook we learned about in this section. We'll leave out the imports since they're the same:

```
const reducer = (state: any, action: any) => {
    console.log("enteredNameReducer");
    switch(action.type) {
      case "enteredName":
        if(state.enteredName === action.payload) {
          return state;
        }
        return { ...state, enteredName: action.payload}
      case "message":
        return { ...state, message: `Hello, ${action.
          payload}` }
      default:
        throw new Error("Invalid action type " + action.
          type);
    }
}


const initialState = {
  enteredName: "",
  message: "",
};
```

We define our reducer and an initial state object called `initialState`. The default signature for reducers is parameters of the `any` type because both the state and action objects can technically be of any type. If you look at the `reducer` function, you'll notice it tries to handle different types of actions by returning a new state object and an appropriate updated member (again, it is very important you do not modify the original state object directly. Copy it and then do your update on the new object and return that). So, this is the intended usage of `useReducer`. If your state objects are complex and the logic to change the properties is complex, you would use a `useReducer` function. You can think of it as a form of containment for related logic on your state object. Next, you can see the actual call to `useReducer` in the App component:

```
function App() {
    const [{ message, enteredName }, dispatch] =
      useReducer(reducer, initialState);


    const onChangeName = (e: React.
      ChangeEvent<HTMLInputElement>)
      => {
        dispatch ({ type: "enteredName", payload: e.target.
        value
        });
        dispatch ({ type: "message", payload: e.target.
        value });
    }


    return (
    <div className="App">
      <header className="App-header">
        <img src={logo} className="App-logo" alt="logo"
        />
          <input value={enteredName}
          onChange={onChangeName} />
          <Greeting message={message} />
        </header>
    </div>
    )
    }
    export default App;
```

As you can see, this function returns an object and a `dispatch` function. The object is the entire state object after the reducer runs, but in our case we do deconstruction so we can directly call the `message` and `enteredName` properties. So after this setup, the `onChangeName` event is defined, which, when triggered, runs the `useReducer` dispatcher, `dispatch`, to trigger the actual change by sending over the appropriate action. If you run this code, you'll see it runs as before.

Now the nice thing about all this is that, as you can see, we can take our `reducer` function and reuse it in other functional components. We can also take our dispatcher and pass it down to child components so that the child can trigger updates to our state as well. Let's try that out:

1. Let's update our `GreetingFunctional.tsx` component with this code:

```tsx
import React from "react";

interface GreetingProps {
    enteredName: string;
    message: string;
    greetingDispatcher: React.Dispatch<{ type: string,
    payload: string }>;
}

export default function Greeting(props: GreetingProps) {
    console.log("rendering Greeting")

    const onChangeName = (e: React.
      ChangeEvent<HTMLInputElement>) => {
        props. greetingDispatcher ({ type: "enteredName",
          payload: e.target.value });
        props. greetingDispatcher ({ type: "message",
          payload: e.target.value });
    }

    return (<div>
        <input value={props.enteredName} onChange=
        {onChangeName} />
        <div>
            {props.message}
```

```
            </div>
        </div>);
    }
```

As you can see, we have passed down `enteredName` and `greetingDispatcher` to our `Greeting` component as props. Then we also brought over the `input` and `onChangeName` events in order to use them in our component.

2. Now, let's update our `App.tsx` file like this:

```
function App() {
  const [{ message, enteredName }, dispatch] =
  useReducer(reducer, initialState);

    return (
    <div className="App">
      <header className="App-header">
        <img src={logo} className="App-logo" alt="logo" />

        <Greeting
          message={message}
          enteredName={enteredName}
          greetingDispatcher={ dispatch } />
      </header>
    </div>
    )
  }
```

As you can see, we have removed `onChangeName` and the input so that we can use it in our `GreetingFunctional.tsx` component. We are also passing `enteredName`, `message`, and `dispatch` as parameters to the `Greeting` component. If you run this you should see that it is our child `GreetingFunctional.tsx` that is triggering the `reducer` updates.

3. Next, let's look at the `useCallback` function. Update `App.tsx` like this:

```
function App() {
  const [{ message, enteredName }, dispatch] =
  useReducer(reducer, initialState);
    const [startCount, setStartCount] = useState(0);
    const [count, setCount] = useState(0);
```

```
const setCountCallback = useCallback(() => {
  const inc = count + 1 > startCount ? count + 1 :
    Number(count + 1) + startCount;
  setCount(inc);
}, [count, startCount]);
const onWelcomeBtnClick = () => {
  setCountCallback();
}


const onChangeStartCount = (e:
  React.ChangeEvent<HTMLInputElement>) => {
  setStartCount(Number(e.target.value));
}
```

What we're doing is having an input that will take the user's initial number value, using startCount. Then we will increment that number by clicking setCountCallback. But make note of how useCallback is having the count state as a parameter. This means that when count changes, setCountCallback will be reinitialized with current values. The remaining code is returning the desired JSX that will generate the final HTML:

```
console.log("App.tsx render");
return (
<div className="App">
  <header className="App-header">
    <img src={logo} className="App-logo" alt="logo" />

    <Greeting
      message={message}
      enteredName={enteredName}
      greetingDispatcher={dispatch} />

    <div style={{marginTop: '10px'}}>
      <label>Enter a number and we'll increment
        it</label>
      <br/>
      <input value={startCount}
        onChange={onChangeStartCount}
```

```
                style={{width: '.75rem'}} /> 
        <label>{count}</label>
        <br/>
        <button onClick={onWelcomeBtnClick}>Increment
            count</button>
    </div>
  </header>
</div>
)
}
```

The return is providing the UI for this incrementation ability.

If you run this code and click the **Increment count** button, you will see that it increments, as shown here:

Figure 5.7 – Increment count clicked 8 times

However, try changing the passed-in array, `[count, startCount]`, and remove the `count` variable so it just says `[startCount]`. Now, it does not keep incrementing because there is no dependency on `count`. It only counts once, on the first run, no matter how many times we click:

Figure 5.8 – After removing count

Therefore, even if you click many times, it will always be incremented by one, since the function is cached in memory and it always runs with the same initial value of `count`.

Let's look at one more example for performance. We'll use the memo wrapper on this example to reduce re-renders. It's not a Hook, but it is a new capability added recently to React. Let's look at the steps:

1.  Create a new file called `ListCreator.tsx` and add this code:

```
import React, { FC, useEffect, useRef } from 'react';

export interface ListItem {
    id: number;
}
export interface ListItems {
    listItems?: Array<ListItem>;
}
const ListCreator: FC<ListItems> =
({listItems}:ListItems) => {
    let renderItems = useRef<Array<JSX.Element> |
        undefined>();
    useEffect(() => {
        console.log("listItems updated");
```

```
        renderItems.current = listItems?.map((item,
          index) => {
            return <div key={item.id}>
                {item.id}
              </div>;
          });
    }, [listItems]);

    console.log("ListCreator render");
    return (
        <React.Fragment>
        {renderItems.current}
        </React.Fragment>
      );
}
export default ListCreator;
```

This component will take a list of items and render them as a list.

2.  Now, let's update our App.tsx file to send new list items based on the increment count. Again, I've only included the App function. Please note there is a new import called ListCreator that is needed as well:

```
function App() {
  const [{ message, enteredName }, dispatch] =
  useReducer(reducer, initialState);
    const [startCount, setStartCount] = useState(0);
    const [count, setCount] = useState(0);
    const setCountCallback = useCallback(() => {
        const inc = count + 1 > startCount ? count + 1 :
        Number(count
          + 1) + startCount;
        setCount(inc);
    }, [count, startCount]);
    const [listItems, setListItems] =
      useState<Array<ListItem>>();

    useEffect(() => {
        const li = [];
```

```
   for(let i = 0; i < count; i++) {
      li.push({ id: i });
   }
   setListItems(li);
}, [count]);
```

As you can see, we have a list of `listItems` and a new `useEffect` function to populate that list. The list is updated any time `count` is updated:

```
const onWelcomeBtnClick = () => {
  setCountCallback();
}

const onChangeStartCount = (e:
  React.ChangeEvent<HTMLInputElement>) => {
    setStartCount(Number(e.target.value));
}
console.log("App.tsx render");
return (
<div className="App">
  <header className="App-header">
    <img src={logo} className="App-logo" alt="logo" />
    <Greeting
      message={message}
      enteredName={enteredName}
      greetingDispatcher={ dispatch } />
    <div style={{marginTop: '10px'}}>
      <label>Enter a number and we'll increment
        it</label>
      <br/>
      <input value={startCount}
        onChange={onChangeStartCount}
        style={{width: '.75rem'}} /> 
      <label>{count}</label>
      <br/>
      <button onClick={onWelcomeBtnClick}>Increment
        count</button>
    </div>
    <div>
```

```
        <ListCreator listItems={listItems} />
    </div>
  </header>
</div>
)
}
```

If you run this example, you will see that not only do we get new list item elements when we increment the number, but we also get them when we type our name. This is because whenever the parent component renders, as its state was updated, so do any children.

3.  Let's do a small update to `ListCreator` to reduce our renders:

```
const ListCreator: FC<ListItems> =
  React.memo(({listItems}:ListItems) => {
    let renderItems = useRef<Array<JSX.Element> |
      undefined>();
    useEffect(() => {
        console.log("listItems updated");
        renderItems.current = listItems?.map((item,
            index) => {
            return <div key={item.id}>
                {item.id}
            </div>;
        });
    }, [listItems]);

    console.log("ListCreator render");
    return (
        <React.Fragment>
        {renderItems.current}
        </React.Fragment>
    );
});
```

I only showed the `ListCreator` component, but as you can see we added a wrapper called `React.memo`. This wrapper only allows component updates if the props passed in have changed. Therefore we get a small performance benefit. If this was a complex object with lots of elements it could make a big difference.

As you can see throughout these examples, for any given Hook, we can reuse that same Hook in different components and with different parameters. This is the key takeaway of Hooks. Code reuse is now much easier.

Please note `useState` and `useReducer` are just reusable functions that allow you to use functions across multiple components. So using `useState` in component A and then `useState` in component B will not allow you to share the state across both components, even if the state names are the same. You're just reusing capability, that's all.

In this section, we learned about React Hooks. We reviewed some of the main Hooks available in the library as well as how to use some of them. We will cover more Hooks later and also begin building our app in future chapters. This coverage of Hooks is going to help us to start building our components later.

# Comparing and contrasting the class way versus the Hooks way

In this section, we will discuss some of the differences between the class way and the Hooks way of writing code in React. We will see why the React team decided Hooks was the way forward. Learning these details will give us confidence in using Hooks in our own code.

## Code reuse

If you look at the class-based lifecycle methods, not only are there many to remember and understand, you can also see that for each class component you would have a pretty much unique implementation of lifecycle functions. This makes code reuse difficult to do with classes. With Hooks, we also have many different built-in Hooks we can use and need to know. However, they are not component specific and can be reused for different components at will. This is the key motivator for using Hooks. Code reuse is much easier because the Hooks are not tied to any specific class. Each Hook is focused on providing a specific capability or functionality, regardless of where it's used. Additionally, if we do the work of building our own Hooks, we can reuse them when appropriate as well.

Take a look at Greeting in the class-component project. How could we reuse the code in this component? Even if we could do this, it adds no real value or benefit. In addition to this, getDerivedStateFromProps adds complexity that may trigger a re-render. And we haven't even used any of the other lifecycle methods at all.

Hook components and React in general prioritize componentization over inheritance. In fact, the React team states that it is a best practice to use components within other components as a means of sharing code instead of inheritance.

So, to reiterate, lifecycle components are generally tied to a specific component, but Hooks can be used across components with a little work to properly generalize them.

## Simplicity

Do you recall how large Greeting became once we added the getDerivedStateFromProps call into it? In addition, we always need a constructor to instantiate our state and use bind for all of our components. Since our components are simple, it didn't matter. But for production code, you'll see components with many functions that will all need bind calls put on them.

Greeting in the hooks-component project was much simpler. Even when that component grows, the Hooks being called will mostly repeat, additionally making code easier to read.

## Summary

This chapter covered a very large amount of information. We learned about class-based components and what makes them difficult to work with. We also learned about Hook-based components, which are simpler and easier to reuse.

We now know the fundamentals of React programming. We can now create our own React components and begin building our application!

In the next chapter, we'll learn about the tooling around React. We'll combine the knowledge we gained here with the tooling information, and it will help us write clean, responsive code.

# 6

# Setting Up Our Project Using create-react-app and Testing with Jest

In this chapter, we'll learn about the tools that help us build React applications. High-level, professional application development, regardless of the language or framework, always involves using tooling to help build applications faster and with higher code quality. The React development ecosystem is no different. A community has gathered around certain tooling and coding methodologies and we will go over those in this chapter. These sophisticated tools and methods will help us code better applications and help us refactor our code to adapt it to new requirements.

In this chapter, we're going to cover the following main topics:

- Learning React development methods and about the build system
- Understanding client-side testing for React
- Learning common tools and practices for React development

# Technical requirements

You should have a basic understanding of web development and the SPA style of coding that we've been learning in the previous chapters. We will once again be using Node (npm) and VS Code.

The GitHub repository is at `https://github.com/PacktPublishing/Full-Stack-React-TypeScript-and-Node`. Use the code in folder `Chap6`.

To set up the Chapter 6 code folder on your own machine, go to your `HandsOnTypescript` folder and create a new folder called `Chap6`.

# Learning React development methods and about the build system

In this section, we will learn about the tools and practices used for coding and building React applications. Many of these methods are used in general for modern JavaScript development, even in competing frameworks such as Angular and Vue.

In order to build large, complex applications, we need tools – lots and lots of tools. Some of these tools will help us write better quality code, some will help us share and manage our code, and still others will exist only to enhance developer productivity and make it easier to debug and test our code. Therefore, by learning the tooling used to build modern React apps, we will ensure our application works as it should with minimal issues.

## Project tools

As we've seen from the prior chapters, modern React development uses many components to build a final application. For project structure and base dependencies, most developers will use `create-react-app`, which is based on the development tools first created for Node development (npm). We've already seen what `create-react-app` can do, but in this section, we'll take a deeper look.

But first, we need to understand how we arrived at using the current state of the art in tools and coding. This knowledge will help us better understand why a shift to this current style was made and what the benefits are.

## How it was done before tooling

The web is actually a hodgepodge of different technologies. HTML came first, to create text sharing capabilities. Then CSS, for better styling and document structure. And then finally, JavaScript, to add some event-driven capabilities and programmatic control. So, it's no wonder that sometimes integrating these technologies into a single coherent application can feel awkward and even difficult. Let's look at some examples of bringing these pieces together without using much tooling:

1.  Open your terminal or command line to the Chap6 folder. Create a new folder called OldStyleWebApp.

2.  Using VS Code create an HTML file called index.html and add this code into it. We'll create a simple input and display:

```html
<html lang="en">
<head>
  <meta charset="utf-8">

  <title>Learn React</title>

   <link rel="stylesheet" href="core.css">
</head>

<body>
<label>Enter your name</label>
<input id="userName" />
<p id="welcomeMsg"></p>
    <script src="script.js"></script>
</body>
</html>
```

3.  Create a .css file called core.css in the same folder.

4.  Create a .js file called script.js in the same folder.

Now, we'll fill in the CSS and JS files later, but immediately we have an issue. How do I run this app? In other words, how do I see it run so I can check whether it's working? Let's see what we can do:

1.  In your VS Code, right-click on the index.html file and copy its path like this:

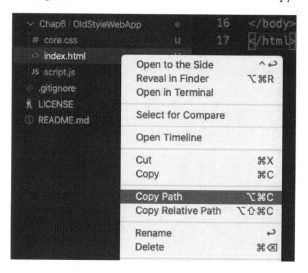

Figure 6.1 – Copy index.html

2.  Now, open your browser and paste this file path into the URL. You should see the following:

Figure 6.2 – index.html in the browser

You may not have already known this, but you do not need an HTTP server in order to view HTML files in your browser. However, you can see this process isn't the most efficient and it would be better if it could be automated, including auto-refreshing when I make changes to any related files.

3. Now, let's fill in our CSS file:

```css
label {
    color: blue;
}


p {
    font-size: 2rem;
}
```

You'll notice that even if I save this file, the `label` element on the web browser does not automatically update. I have to refresh my browser and then it will update. What if I have dozens of files that get updated during my development session? Having to manually refresh each time would not be a good experience.

4. Next, let's add some code to `script.js`:

```javascript
const inputEl = document.querySelector("#userName");
console.log("input", doesnotexist);
```

We want to read this code carefully as there are multiple issues with it. Let's see what those issues are. If we save this file, open the browser debugger tools, and then refresh the browser, you can see that it fails immediately with this error in the **Console** tab:

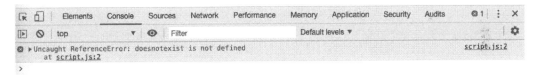

Figure 6.3 – script.js first error

This type of error, an undefined variable, will usually be caught by the `create-react-app` project tooling. `create-react-app` projects have what's called a linter. A linter is a code checker tool that runs in the background as you're writing your code. It will check for common errors, such as the one we just saw, so that it they do not end up in your production code. There's a lot more functionality to linters, but we will explore them more deeply later. The point here is we want to avoid these types of errors before running the app. And `create-react-app`, or in this case some of the built-in tooling, can help us do that.

5.  Let's try adding the correct variable name and try reloading the browser again. Update the `script.js` file like this, save it, and then reload the browser:

```
const inputEl = document.querySelector("#userName");
console.log("input", inputEl);
```

As you can see in the debugger console, the log statement does not find the `inputEl`, as it returns `null`. This is happening because we mistyped the `id` of the `input` element as `"userNam"` instead of `"userName"`. Now, again, with the `create-react-app` project running, this sort of error is simply not possible, because the vast majority of React code does not attempt to query or look for elements in our HTML page. Instead, we use React components directly and therefore we can avoid this class of error altogether. Admittedly it is possible to opt out of this behavior and use a reference to HTML elements via `useRef`. However, this is something that should be done sparingly, as you are deliberately exiting out of the normal React ecosystem behavior by using this Hook and therefore losing its benefits.

6.  Let's fix our `script.js` file and complete it. Update it like so:

```
const inputEl = document.querySelector("#userName");
console.log("input", inputEl);
const parEl = document.querySelector("#welcomeMsg");

inputEl.addEventListener("change", (e) => {
    parEl.innerHTML = "Welcome " + e.target.value;
});
```

If you run this code by refreshing the browser, you will see that if you type your name into the input box and then click out of the input element, a message will display like this:

Figure 6.4 – Welcome display

So, this code does work to display a welcome message. However, it's easy to make mistakes, and not have any help indicating why. In addition to this, notice that we have no TypeScript since browsers don't run TypeScript; they can only run JavaScript. This means we are also missing the type indicators that are also helpful in avoiding bugs related to incorrect types.

So, we've seen some of the issues around doing things in the original web way. But the reality is we haven't even scratched the surface of issues with doing development in this manner. For example, having script tags embedded in our HTML is a reasonable thing to do when we have only a few scripts to deal with. But what about when our dependencies grow? For larger apps, it is quite possible to have hundreds of dependencies. Managing that many script tags would be very difficult. And not only that – a lot of JavaScript dependencies no longer provide a URL from which they can be called.

Having said all this, perhaps one of the biggest issues is the highly free-form nature of the code. If you look at the `script.js` file again, you can see there is no pattern or structure to the code. Sure, it is likely your team could come up with a pattern on its own, but what about new programmers joining the team? They would have to learn a unique way of structuring the code that is specific to your team.

So, the point is tooling, frameworks, and structure provide consistent, repeatable ways of writing and maintaining code. You can consider it a sort of culture of programming, where everyone has accepted the norms and practices of the culture and therefore knows what to do and how to behave. This makes code easier to write, share, and refactor. Now that we've taken a look at free-form coding, let's start looking at `create-react-app` more deeply.

## create-react-app

In prior chapters, such as *Chapter 4, Learning Single-Page Application Concepts and How React Enables Them*, and *Chapter 5, React Development with Hooks*, we used `create-react-app` to set up our base application project. Let's look more closely at what is inside a `create-react-app` project. To better understand the parts that make up a `create-react-app` project, we need to `eject` it first. Here, eject simply means that we will reveal all of the internal dependencies and scripts that make `create-react-app` work, as normally these are hidden.

> **Warning: Ejection is a non-reversable action**
>
> In the vast majority of cases, you will not eject a `create-react-app` project, as there is little value in doing so. We are doing it here only to gain more insights into how this project works.

Let's look at the steps:

1.  Create a new project inside of the Chap6 folder by executing the following command from inside that folder:

    ```
    npx create-react-app ejected-app --template typescript
    ```

    Once this command completes, you should see a new project created in Chap6 called ejected-app.

2.  Now let's eject the project. Change directories in your command line to the new ejected-app folder and run this command:

    ```
    npm run eject
    ```

Then enter y at the prompt to continue.

Let's take a look at this project from the top of the VS Code explorer menu:

*   config

    This folder contains most of the configuration files and scripts that the project uses to set itself up. The main thing to note is that the React team by default uses **Jest** for testing and **Webpack** for the bundling and minification of JavaScript files. We'll discuss Jest in the *Understanding client-side testing for React* section, and Webpack is discussed later in this section.

*   node_modules

    As you know, this folder contains our project's dependencies. As you can see, even before we add our own dependencies, the default set of dependencies is vast. It would be quite difficult to try and use HTML script tags to list out these dependencies. And in most cases, these dependencies don't support script tag references.

*   public

    This folder contains static assets that are used in generating our single-page application. This includes our one HTML file called index.html, the manifest.json file that is needed if we are building a PWA application. It is also possible to add additional files such as image files for deployment.

- `scripts`

  The `scripts` folder contains scripts that are used to manage the project, for example, scripts that build, start, or kick off tests of the application. Actual test files should not be added here. We'll cover testing later, in the *Understanding client-side testing for React section.*

- `src`

  This is, of course, the folder that contains the source files of our project.

- `.gitignore`

  `.gitignore` is a file that tells the Git source code repository system which files and folders not to track. We will dive deeper into Git later in this section.

- `package.json`

  As mentioned in prior chapters, npm is the dependency management system originally created for use with the Node server framework. The capabilities and popularity of this dependency manager eventually made it a standard for client-side development as well. So, the React team uses npm as its base system for project creation and dependency management.

  On top of listing dependencies for projects, it can also list scripts that can be run to manage a project.

  It also has configuration capabilities for things such as Jest, ESLint, and Babel.

- `Package-lock.json`

  This is a related file that helps maintain a proper set of dependencies and sub-dependencies regardless of their order of installation. We don't need to work with this file directly, but knowing that this helps prevent issues when different developers update their `npm_modules` folder at different times with a different set of existing dependencies is good knowledge to have.

- `tsconfig.json`

  We already reviewed this file in *Chapter 2, Exploring TypeScript,* and as mentioned in that chapter, it contains the settings for the TypeScript compiler to use. Note that, in general, the React team prefers stricter compilation settings. Also notice that the target JavaScript version is ES5. This is because some browsers are not compatible with ES6 yet.

`create-react-app` also contains two very important tools that enable some of its functionality: Webpack and ESLint. Webpack is a bundling and minification tool that automates the task of gathering all of the files that make up a project, removing any extraneous, unused pieces, and consolidating them into a few files. By removing extraneous pieces, such as white spaces and unused files or scripts, it can drastically lower the file sizes that must be downloaded by user browsers. This, of course, enhances the user experience. In addition to this core functionality, it provides a "hot reloading" development server, which can allow certain script changes to automatically show in the browser without needing a page refresh (although most changes do seem to trigger browser refreshes, but at least those are automated).

ESLint is also an important tool. Since JavaScript is a scripting language and not a compiled language, it does not have a compiler that will check syntax and code validity (obviously, TypeScript does but the TypeScript compiler focuses primarily on typing issues). So, ESLint provides development-time code checking to make sure it is valid JavaScript syntax. And in addition, it allows for the creation of custom code-formatting rules. These rules are generally used to ensure that everyone on the team is coding using the same style; for example, variable naming conventions and bracket indentation. Once rules are set up, the ESLint service will enforce these rules with warning messages.

The rules are not just specific to JavaScript, but they can also be rules around how to write code for frameworks such as React. So, for example, in a `create-react-app` project, the ESLint setting is `react-app`, as shown in `package.json`, which is a set of coding rules specific to React development. So, many of the messages we will see are not necessarily JavaScript errors but rules around best practices for coding React apps.

Webpack, although extremely powerful, is also enormously difficult to set up. And creating custom rules for ESLint can take a very long time to do. So, fortunately, another benefit of using `create-react-app` is that it provides us with good default configurations for both of these tools.

## Transpilation

We introduced transpilation in *Chapter 1, Understanding TypeScript*. However, we should cover it a little more deeply in this chapter since `create-react-app` depends on transpilation for much of its code generation. `create-react-app` allows us to use TypeScript or Babel so that we can develop code in one language or language version and emit code as a different language or language version. Here's a simple diagram showing the flow of code during the transpilation of TypeScript:

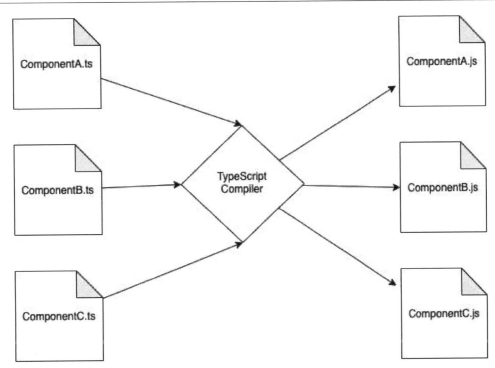

Figure 6.5 – Transpilation from TypeScript to JavaScript

The TypeScript compiler will search your project and find all the `ts` or `tsx` files inside of the root code folder, usually `src`. If there are errors, it will stop and let us know, otherwise, it will parse and convert the TypeScript into pure JavaScript as `js` files and that is what is run on systems. Notice in the diagram we are also changing the JavaScript version as well. So, transpilation is a lot like compilation. Code is checked for validity and some classes of bugs, but instead of being converted into byte code that can be run directly, it is converted into a different language or language version. Babel is also capable of emitting JavaScript and working with TypeScript developer code. However, I prefer to use the original TypeScript compiler, as it is made by the same team that designs TypeScript and is usually more up to date.

Choosing transpilation as the method of compilation has multiple important benefits. For one, developers do not need to worry whether their code will run on a browser, or whether the user would need to either upgrade or install a bunch of dependencies on that machine first. The TypeScript compiler emits web standard ECMAScript (ES3, ES5, ES6, and so on) and therefore the code can be set to run on any modern browser.

Transpilation also allows developers to take advantage of newer versions of JavaScript before their final release. Since JavaScript is on an almost annual update cycle, this feature can be extremely useful in terms of taking advantage of new language features or performance capabilities; for example, when a new feature of JavaScript is being considered. The ECMA foundation, the standards body that maintains the JavaScript language, goes through several stages before accepting changes into an official version of JavaScript. But the TypeScript and Babel teams will sometimes accept new JavaScript features when they are still in one of these earlier stages. This is how many JavaScript developers were able to use async-await in their code before it became an official standard.

## Code repositories

A code repository is a system that allows the sharing of source code among multiple developers. Code can be updated, copied, and merged. For large teams, this tool is absolutely necessary for building complex applications. The most popular modern source code control and repository is Git. And the most popular online repository host is GitHub.

Although thoroughly learning Git is beyond the scope of this book, it is important to understand some of the basic concepts and commands, as you will need them when interacting with other developers and maintaining your own projects.

One of the more important concepts of any code repository is that of branching. This means the ability to indicate multiple versions of a project. For example, these branches could be for the version numbers of a project, such as 1.0.0, 1.0.1, and so on. It could also be for creating separate versions of an app where perhaps some experimental or high-risk code is being tried out. It would not be a good idea to place such code into the main branch. Here's an example of the React GitHub page and its many versions:

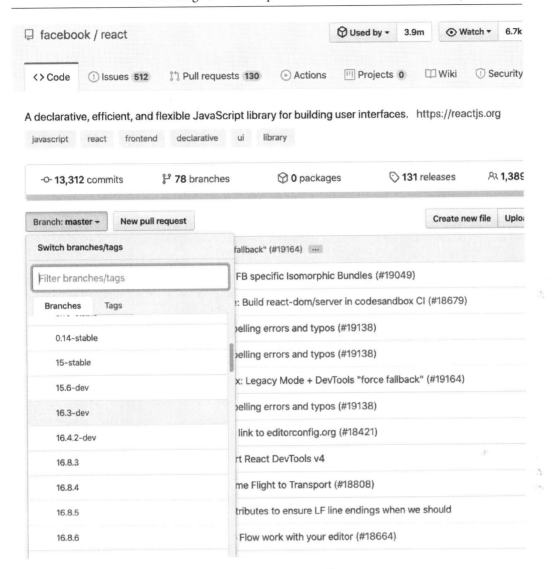

Figure 6.6 – React GitHub

As you can see, there are many branches. The current stable branch, although not visible in this screenshot, is usually called the master.

Again, learning Git well would require a book of its own, so here I'll just go over some of the main commands that you would use daily:

- `git`: This command is the Git **CLI** (**command-line interface**). It must start any Git commands you want to execute. When working with the `git` command, you are working on a local copy of the repository; you are not directly working on the online repository or affecting your teammates' repositories until you push your changes onto the server.

- `clone`: This command allows you to copy a repository onto your local machine. Note that when you clone, generally, you will default to the master branch. Here's an example:

```
git clone https://github.com/facebook/react.git
```

- `checkout`: This subcommand allows you to change your working branch to a different desired branch. So, if you wanted to work in another branch other than the master, you would use this command. Here's an example:

```
git checkout <branch-name>
```

- `add`: This subcommand adds the files you recently changed as needing to be tracked, which indicates you will later commit them into the repository. You can do all your changed files in one shot by using `.` after `add` or indicate the files explicitly:

```
git add <file name>
```

- `commit`: This subcommand indicates that you will eventually update your working branch with the files that you just added locally. If you add the `-m` parameter, you can add a label inline to describe your commit. This command helps team members track which changes were done in each commit:

```
git commit -m "My change to xyz"
```

- `push`: This subcommand does the actual moving of local committed files into the remote repository:

```
git push origin <branch name>
```

In this section, we covered some of the core project tools available for React developers. `create-react-app`, ESLint, Webpack, and npm provide invaluable features that make development more efficient and less error-prone. We also covered transpilation, to understand how we can take advantage of newer language versions, without compromising compatibility, on end user devices.

Additionally, we took a quick look at Git. Currently, it is the most popular code-sharing repository. As a professional developer, you will most certainly end up using it for projects.

Now that we have some important core tools knowledge, we'll continue in the next section by discussing testing. Modern development practices make heavy use of testing and test frameworks. Fortunately, JavaScript has great testing frameworks to help us write good-quality tests.

# Understanding client-side testing for React

Unit testing is a very important part of development. These days, no large projects will be written without some level of unit testing. The purpose of tests is to ensure that your code is always working correctly and doing the expected things. This is especially true when code is modified, that is, refactored. In fact, it is probably more difficult to change existing complex code than it is to create brand-new code. Unit testing can prevent breaking existing code during refactoring. But if code does break, it can also help pinpoint the exact place where code no longer works so it can be fixed quickly.

In React, previously, there were two main testing libraries that were commonly used: **Jest** and **Enzyme**. Jest is the main testing library that provides base calls such as assertions to check for specific values and wrapper functions to help set up tests. Enzyme has a set of helpers that allows the testing of React components in concert with Jest. It has features targeted at testing the output of React components. However, these days, a library called **testing-library**, and its related versions, has basically taken the place of Enzyme. And it is the default component testing library built into `create-react-app`. So, for this book, we will be learning about Jest and testing-library.

All unit tests work in the same way. This is true not only for React and JavaScript tests, but tests in any language will work in the same manner. So then, what is a unit test? A unit test attempts to test one specific portion of code and it attempts to assert that something about it is true. That's basically it. To put it another way, it means that the test is checking to see whether something expected is indeed the case. If it is not, then the test should fail. Although this goal is simple, creating high-quality tests is not. So, we'll go over some examples here, but please keep in mind that large-application testing can be as complicated if not more so than the actual code for creating the app. So, it will take some time for you to become proficient in writing tests.

To make things clearer, let's take a look at a simple test. Do the following:

1.  Go to VS Code and open the file at path `ejected-app/src/App.test.tsx`. This is a test for the `App` component. We'll go over the contents of the test in just a moment.

2.  Open your terminal to `ejected-app` and run this command:

```
npm run test
```

As stated earlier, there are already several npm scripts to help manage the project and one of them is the script to run our tests, called `test`. Additionally, this `test` script is actually running our tests in **watch mode**, which simply means that the script stays active and autoruns each time we update or add new tests. If your tests don't run and you get this prompt, select option `a`:

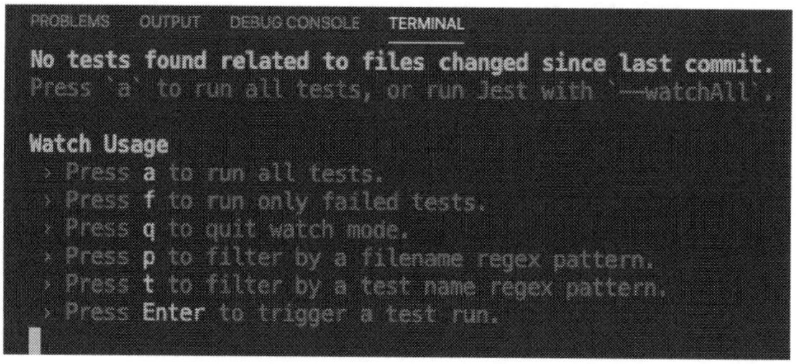

Figure 6.7 – Test run options

If your tests did run or you selected `a`, you should see the following result:

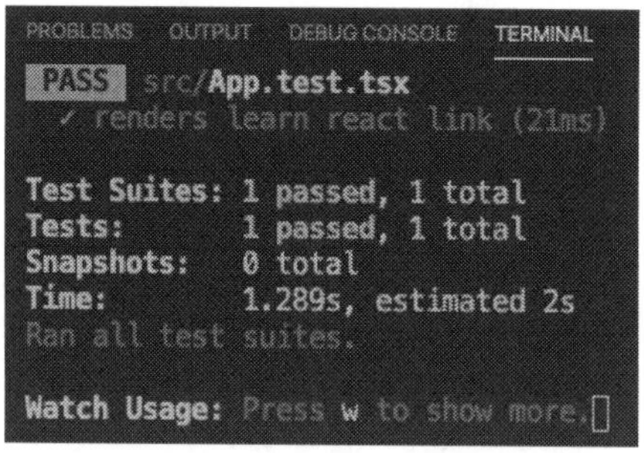

Figure 6.8 – Tests completed successfully

As you can see, our tests have automatically been found and run (although, currently, we only have one). And in this run, the one test is successful, meaning what was expected did occur. If any failed, the same UI would indicate how many tests failed and how many succeeded.

Now, let's take a look at the test in `App.test.tsx`:

```
import React from 'react';
import { render } from '@testing-library/react';
import App from './App';

test('renders learn react link', () => {
  const { getByText } = render(<App />);
  const linkElement = getByText(/learn react/i);
  expect(linkElement).toBeInTheDocument();
});
```

First, you will notice the filename has the text `test` in it. This is what tells Jest that this is a test file. Some teams like to place all their tests into a single folder. Some teams prefer to have the test right next to the actual file being tested, as in this case. There is no right answer. Do what works best for you and your team. In this book, we will put our tests right next to the file being tested. Let's take a look at the contents of our `test` file:

1.  Notice among the imports that we have a reference to `@testing-library/react`. As mentioned, this library will give us some extra tooling to make the testing of the component output easier.

2.  Now, notice the `test` function. This function acts as an encapsulated wrapper for our single test. This means that all the things relative to this one test live inside this function and cannot be accessed from outside of it. This ensures that our test is not impacted by other tests.

3.  The first parameter of this function is a description. Descriptions are totally arbitrary, and your team will have its own standard for how these descriptions should be written. The only thing we need to focus on is making the description brief but clear about what is being tested.

4.  The second parameter is a function that runs the actual test. In this case, the test is checking whether a certain specific text appears within the emitted HTML of our `App` component. Let's go over the code line by line.

5.  On *line 6*, we run `render`, passing it the `App` component. This `render` function executes our component and gets back certain properties and functions that allow us to test the emitted HTML. In this case, we decide only to receive the function `getByText`, which simply means to return an element that has certain text in it.

6.  In *line 7*, we get our HTML DOM element by calling `getByText` with the parameter `/learn react/i`, which is syntax for running a regular expression, but in this case, it's hardcoded for text.

7.  Finally, on *line 8*, an assertion is made called `expect`, which expects the element object called `linkElement` to be in the DOM using the `toBeInTheDocument` function. So, an easy way of understanding tests in general is to read their assertions like a sentence. For example, we can read this assertion like this, "I expect the linkElement to be in the document" (the document is, of course, the browser DOM). By reading it this way, it's pretty clear what is intended.

8.  Now, let's see what happens if we change the code a bit. Update `App.tsx` with the following (I'm only showing the `App` function for brevity):

```
function App() {
  return (
    <div className="App">
      <header className="App-header">
        <img src={logo} className="App-logo" alt="logo"
          />
        <p>
          Edit <code>src/App.tsx</code> and save to
            reload.
        </p>
        <a
          className="App-link"
          href="https://reactjs.org"
          target="_blank"
          rel="noopener noreferrer"
        >
          Learn
        </a>
      </header>
    </div>
  );
}
```

Notice I've left everything the same except I removed the text `React` in `Learn React`.

9. Once you save this file, you should immediately see an error like this:

```
PROBLEMS    OUTPUT    DEBUG CONSOLE    TERMINAL                          1: node          +  □  🗑  ∧  ×

FAIL  src/App.test.tsx
  × renders learn react link (25ms)

  ● renders learn react link

    Unable to find an element with the text: /learn react/i. This could be because the text is broken
    up by multiple elements. In this case, you can provide a function for your text matcher to make your m
    atcher more flexible.

      <body>
        <div>
          <div
            class="App"
          >
            <header
              class="App-header"
            >
              <img
                alt="logo"
                class="App-logo"
                src="logo.svg"
              />
              <p>
                Edit
                <code>
                  src/App.tsx
                </code>
                 and save to reload.
              </p>
              <a
                class="App-link"
                href="https://reactjs.org"
                rel="noopener noreferrer"
                target="_blank"
              >
                Learn
              </a>
            </header>
          </div>
        </div>
      </body>

       5 | test('renders learn react link', () => {
       6 |   const { getByText } = render(<App />);
    >  7 |   const linkElement = getByText(/learn react/i);
         |                       ^
       8 |   expect(linkElement).toBeInTheDocument();
       9 | });
      10 |

      at Object.getElementError (node_modules/@testing-library/dom/dist/config.js:34:12)
      at node_modules/@testing-library/dom/dist/query-helpers.js:71:38
      at getByText (node_modules/@testing-library/dom/dist/query-helpers.js:54:17)
      at Object.<anonymous> (src/App.test.tsx:7:23)

Test Suites: 1 failed, 1 total
Tests:       1 failed, 1 total
Snapshots:   0 total
Time:        0.862s, estimated 1s
Ran all test suites.

Watch Usage: Press w to show more.
```

Figure 6.9 – Error after changing App.tsx

Again, the test runner is running in watch mode so you should see the test results as soon as you save your change. As you can see, our test fails because the text `learn react` was not found and therefore the assertion `expect(linkElement).toBeInTheDocument()` is not true.

OK, so we've taken a look at a built-in test that `create-react-app` provided. Let's now create a new component so we can write our own tests from scratch. Do the following:

1. Let's leave our test running in watch mode, even though it's showing an error, and create a new terminal window by clicking the plus button at the upper-right side of the terminal window in VS Code. The button is the plus sign shown here:

Figure 6.10: Plus sign for a new terminal

2. Now, create a new file called `DisplayText.tsx` in the `src` folder and add this code:

```tsx
import React, { useState } from "react";

const DisplayText = () => {
  const [txt, setTxt] = useState("");
  const [msg, setMsg] = useState("");

  const onChangeTxt = (e: React.
    ChangeEvent<HTMLInputElement>)
  => {
      setTxt(e.target.value);
  }

  const onClickShowMsg = (e: React.
    MouseEvent<HTMLButtonElement, MouseEvent>) => {
      e.preventDefault();

      setMsg(`Welcome to React testing, ${txt}`);
  }
```

This component will simply display a new message after someone enters their name into the input and clicks the **Show Message** button. First, you can see we declare our new component called `DisplayText`.

3.  We then create some state necessary for the workings of our component and event handlers to deal with new text and the display of our message (we've already covered how to create a React component in *Chapter 5, React Development with Hooks*):

```
return (
    <form>
        <div>
            <label>Enter your name</label>
        </div>
        <div>
            <input data-testid="user-input"
                value={txt} onChange={onChangeTxt} />
        </div>
        <div>
            <button data-testid="input-submit"
                onClick={onClickShowMsg}>Show
                Message</button>
        </div>
        <div>
            <label data-testid="final-msg"
                >{msg}</label>
        </div>
    </form>
    )
}
export default DisplayText;
```

4.  Finally, we return our UI, which includes an input and a submit button. Note the `data-testid` attributes to allow elements to be easily found by our tests later. If you run this code and enter your name and click the button, you should see something like this:

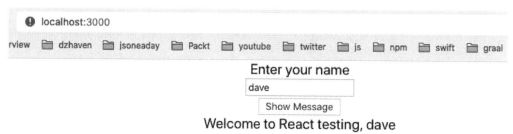

Figure 6.11 – New component for testing

As you can see, our display simply returns the entered text with a welcome message. However, even this simple example has several different things to test. For one, we would like to make sure that there is text entered into the input and that it is words and not numbers or symbols. We also want to make sure that when we click the button, the message is displayed and that it starts with the string `"Welcome to React testing"` and ends with the user's input text.

Now that we have our component, let's build our test for it:

1.  We need to be aware of a small issue in our `tsconfig.json` file. As I stated earlier, you can place your tests inside of a separate folder, usually called __test__, or you can place it side by side with your component file. We will be placing it side by side for convenience. If we do so, we will need to update our `tsconfig.json` file to include this `compilerOption`:

    ```
    "types": ["node", "jest"]
    ```

2.  Create the test file for this component by creating a new file called `DisplayText.test.tsx` and add this initial code into it:

```
import React from 'react';
import { render, fireEvent } from '@testing-library/react';
import DisplayText from './DisplayText';
import "@testing-library/jest-dom/extend-expect";


describe("Test DisplayText", () => {
    it("renders without crashing", () => {
        const { baseElement } = render(<DisplayText />);
        expect(baseElement).toBeInTheDocument();
    });

    it("receives input text", () => {
        const testuser = "testuser";
        const { getByTestId } = render(<DisplayText />);
        const input = getByTestId("user-input");
        fireEvent.change(input, { target: { value:
        testuser } });
        expect(input).toBeInTheDocument();
        expect(input).toHaveValue(testuser);
    })
});
```

From the top, you'll notice we have imported `render` from `@testing-library/react` and we've also imported the `@testing-library/jest-dom/extend-expect` extension, which allow us to do assertions. The extensions of the `expect` keyword give us additional functions that allow us to test in more ways. For example, we are using `toHaveValue` to get the value of `input`.

After the imports, you'll notice some new syntax. `describe` is, as the name implies, simply a way to create a grouping container with a helpful label. This container can have more than one test, but these tests should all be related to testing a specific component or feature. In this case, we are trying to test the `DisplayText` component so all the tests within `describe` will be testing only that.

So, our first test is started using the function called `it`. This function checks that our component, `DisplayText`, can be rendered out as HTML without crashing or erroring out. The `render` function attempts to do the rendering and the `expect` and `toBeInTheDocument` functions determine whether the rendering was a success by checking whether it is in the DOM. As an experiment, add this code, `console.log(baseElement.innerHTML)`, within the first test `it` function below the line starting with `const { baseElement }`. You should see this HTML string in the terminal:

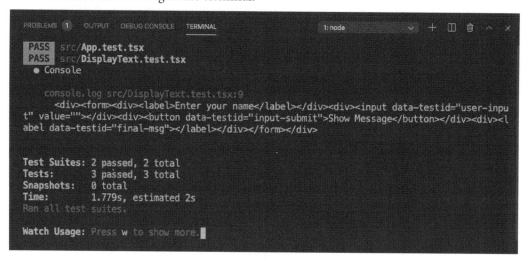

Figure 6.12 – Log: resultant test HTML

As you can see, there is a log of a `div` with a form in it and the rest of our component's HTML. Using this method, you will be able to check what is being rendered out and, if needed, how you can parse it.

Our next test, also starting with the `it` function, sees whether our input element is rendered correctly and gets the value we are typing into it. This may seem strange, but remember, in React, filling an input control is not straightforward and involves reacting to the `onChange` event. So, we pass our `data-testid` attribute to the `getByTestId` function to find the specific input element, as there could be more than one. Now, in order to insert the changed value, we use the `fireEvent.change` function to accept and send a string value. And then we test whether that value is indeed added to our input. Here's what it looks like:

```
it("receive input text", () => {
    const username = "testuser";


    const { getByTestId } = render(<DisplayText />);
    const input = getByTestId("user-input");
    fireEvent.change(input, { target: { value:
        username } });
    expect(input).toBeInTheDocument();
    expect(input).toHaveValue(username);
});
```

3.  Now, let's create one more test to show an end-to-end test of our component. Add the following code after our second `it` function:

```
it("shows welcome message", () => {
    const testuser = "testuser";
    const msg = `Welcome to React testing,
        ${testuser}`;
    const { getByTestId } = render(<DisplayText />);
    const input = getByTestId("user-input");
    const label = getByTestId("final-msg");
    fireEvent.change(input, { target: { value:
        testuser } });
    const btn = getByTestId("input-submit");
    fireEvent.click(btn);


    expect(label).toBeInTheDocument();
    expect(label.innerHTML).toBe(msg);
});
```

This test is similar to our second test in that it adds a value within our `input`, but then it goes on and gets our `button`, and then our `label`. It then creates a `click` event to simulate a button press that in regular code would cause our `label` to be populated with our welcome message. It then tests the contents of our `label`. Again, once you save this file, our tests should rerun and all of them should pass.

4.  Now, let's also look at something called snapshots. Obviously, a big part of React development is not just the behavior or actions available within our app, but the actual UI presented to our users. So, by doing snapshot testing, we are able to check that the desired UI, HTML elements, are indeed created by our components. Let's add this code to our tests after our "renders without crashing" test:

```
it("matches snapshot", () => {
    const { baseElement } = render(<DisplayText />);
    expect(baseElement).toMatchSnapshot();
});
```

As you can see, our `render` function is set to return the root most element of the `DisplayText` component by using the `baseElement` property. In addition, we can see that we have a new `expect` function called `toMatchSnapshot`. This function does a couple of things:

- The first time it runs, it creates a folder called `__snapshot__` at the root of our `src` folder.

- It then adds or updates a file that has the same name as our test file and ends with the extension .snap. So, in this case, our test file snapshot file would be `DisplayText.test.tsx.snap`.

The contents of this snapshot file are the emitted HTML elements of our component. So the snapshot you have should look something like this:

```
// Jest Snapshot v1, https://goo.gl/fbAQLP
exports[`Test DisplayText matches snapshot 1`] = `
<body>
  <div>
    <form>
      <div>
        <label>
          Enter your name
        </label>
      </div>
```

```
      <div>
        <input
          data-testid="user-input"
          value=""
        />
      </div>
      <div>
        <button
          data-testid="input-submit"
        >
          Show Message
        </button>
      </div>
      <div>
        <label
          data-testid="final-msg"
        />
      </div>
    </form>
  </div>
</body>
`;
```

As you can see, this is an exact duplicate of our desired HTML as emitted by our `DisplayText` component. Notice also the description given and the indication that it is snapshot 1. As you add more, the number will increment.

5.  OK, so now we have a snapshot and our first test run has succeeded. Let's see what happens if we change our `DisplayText` JSX. Update the `DisplayText.tsx` file, not your test file, like this (I'll just show the component definition for brevity's sake):

```
const DisplayText = () => {
  const [txt, setTxt] = useState("");
  const [msg, setMsg] = useState("");
  const onChangeTxt = (e: React.
    ChangeEvent<HTMLInputElement>)
    => {
      setTxt(e.target.value);
```

```
        }
    const onClickShowMsg = (e:
        React.MouseEvent<HTMLButtonElement, MouseEvent>) =>
        {
            e.preventDefault();

            setMsg(`Welcome to React testing, ${txt}`);
        }
```

The preceding code remains entirely the same, however, in the `return`, we add a dummy `div` tag as shown:

```
    return (
        <form>
            <div>
                <label>Enter your name</label>
            </div>
            <div>
                <input data-testid="user-input"
                value={txt}
                    onChange={onChangeTxt} />
            </div>
            <div>
                <button data-testid="input-submit"
                onClick={onClickShowMsg}>Show
                    Message</button>
            </div>
            <div>
                <label data-testid="final-msg" >{msg}
                    </label>
            </div>
            <div>
                this is just a test entry
            </div>
        </form>
    )
}
```

If we save this file and our test reruns, we should see the following:

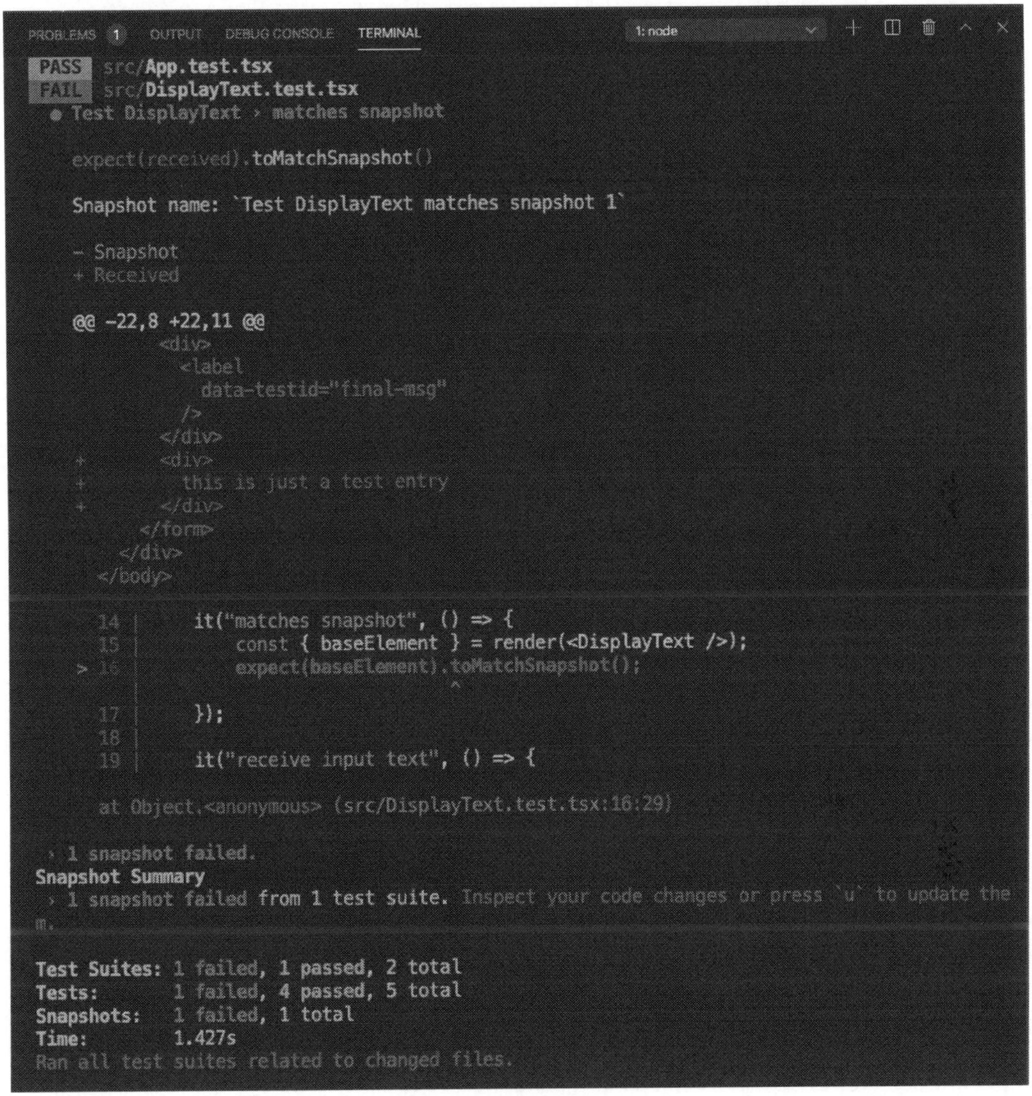

Figure 6.13 – Failed snapshot test

As you can see, our snapshot test failed since our UI now does not match our snapshot. So then, what if we meant to make this change to our `DisplayText` component UI? In this case, we can force a snapshot update by entering the u character under the **Watch Usage** list by first entering the w character. If this does not work for you, just stop and restart your test. This is what the **Watch Usage** list looks like:

```
Watch Usage
 > Press a to run all tests.
 > Press f to run only failed tests.
 > Press u to update failing snapshots.
 > Press i to update failing snapshots interactively.
 > Press q to quit watch mode.
 > Press p to filter by a filename regex pattern.
 > Press t to filter by a test name regex pattern.
 > Press Enter to trigger a test run.
```

Figure 6.14 – Watch Usage list

6.  And after selecting u, our snapshot file should update successfully and our snapshot test should complete. If you open your local snapshot file, you should see the same new `div` tag we added to our component earlier.

So now we've seen some simple tests to help us get started. Next, we'll get introduced to the topic of mocking.

# Mocking

Mocking is simply replacing specific functionality in our test with default values. An example of mocking could be to only pretend to make a network call but instead return a hardcoded value. The reason we want to do this is we want to only test a single unit or a small piece of our code. By mocking some portions of our code that are not specific to what we are testing, we are avoiding confusion and making certain our test works consistently. For example, if we were trying to test input in our code, we wouldn't want a network call failure to affect the result of that test, because a network call has nothing to do with the input element specifically. When we want to do end-to-end testing or integration testing, we can worry about the network call as well. But that is a different animal from unit testing (in some teams, integration testing is handled by the QA team separately) and we won't cover it here. Now, when it comes to React components, testing-library actually recommends against mocking, because this effectively makes our test less like actual code. Having said that, sometimes mocking can still be helpful to do, so I will show how to mock components as well.

# Mocking with jest.fn

Let's learn about mocking with Jest as it is also used with Node development. The first way to do mocking in Jest is to mock a specific function using fn. This function takes another function as a parameter that will do whatever you need to be done to set up your desired mock. But also, in addition to this ability to replace arbitrary existing code and values, creating a mock will give you access to a member called mock. This member provides metrics about your mock call. This is difficult to conceptualize so let's create an example:

1.  Let's update our DisplayText component to make a network call to a web API. We will use the **JsonPlaceholder** web API. This is a free service that provides you with a web API that returns JSON. Let's create a new property for DisplayText that is a function that returns a user's full name based upon their username. We need to first update the App function file like this:

```
function App() {
    const getUserFullname = async (username: string):
    Promise<string> => {
        const usersResponse = await
        fetch('https://jsonplaceholder.typicode.com/
        users');
        if (usersResponse.ok) {
            const users = await usersResponse.json();
            const userByName = users.find((usr: any) => {
                return usr.username.toLowerCase() === username;
            });
            return userByName.name;
        }
        return "";
    }
    return (
        <div className="App">
            <DisplayText getUserFullname={getUserFullname} />
        </div>
    );
}
```

So, here, we are creating the function called `getUserFullname` and then passing that as a property to our `DisplayText` component. As you can see, it is based on a network call to the web API of JsonPlaceholder. It calls into the `users` collection and then it filters the collection using the `find` array function. The result will get a user's full name from their username by calling `userByName.name`.

2.  Now, let's see the updated `DisplayText` component code:

```tsx
import React, { useState, FC } from "react";

interface DisplayTextProps {
    getUserFullname: (username: string) =>
    Promise<string>;
}

const DisplayText: FC<DisplayTextProps> =
({ getUserFullname }) => {
    const [txt, setTxt] = useState("");
    const [msg, setMsg] = useState("");

    const onChangeTxt = (e: React.
    ChangeEvent<HTMLInputElement>)
    => {
        setTxt(e.target.value);
    }

    const onClickShowMsg = async (e:
        React.MouseEvent<HTMLButtonElement, MouseEvent>) =>
        {
        e.preventDefault();

        setMsg(`Welcome to React testing, ${await
            getUserFullname(txt)}`);
    }
```

For the most part, this code remains the same, except of course we have defined a new interface called `DisplayTextProps` to house our `getUserFullname` function. This function is being passed in as a prop from our `App` component. And then we use that function within the `onClickShowMsg` event handler to show the welcome message with the user's full name:

```
    return (
        <form>
            <div>
                <label>Enter your name</label>
            </div>
            <div>
                <input data-testid="user-input"
                    value={txt}
                    onChange={onChangeTxt} />
            </div>
            <div>
                <button data-testid="input-submit"
                    onClick={onClickShowMsg}>Show Message</
                    button>
            </div>
            <div>
                <label data-testid="final-msg" >{msg}</
                    label>
            </div>
        </form>
    )
}
export default DisplayText;
```

The rest of the code is the same but is shown for completeness. So then, now if we run our app, we should see something like this:

Figure 6.15 – User's full name

As you can see, the full name of the user with the username **bret** is **Leanne Graham**.

Now let's write our test and mock out our network call using Jest:

1.  Open `DisplayText.test.tsx` and notice that all our tests are failing since none of them will have the new property `getUserFullname`. So, let's update our test and mock this function. Here are the new tests:

```
import React from 'react';
import { render, fireEvent, cleanup, wait } from
  "@testing-library/react";
import DisplayText from './DisplayText';
import "@testing-library/jest-dom/extend-expect";
```

Near the top, we see a new function import called `wait` from `@testing-library/react`. This is to handle asynchronous calls within our test items. For example, `getUserFullname` is an asynchronous call and so we need to `await` it. But if we do not `await` it, our test will fail because it will not have waited for the call to finish before moving to the next step:

```
afterEach(cleanup);

describe("Test DisplayText", () => {
    const userFullName = "John Tester";

    const getUserFullnameMock = (username: string):
      [Promise<string>, jest.Mock<Promise<string>,
        [string]>] => {
        const promise = new Promise<string>((res, rej) =>
      {
```

```
            res(userFullName);
    });
    const getUserFullname = jest.fn(
        async (username: string): Promise<string> => {
        return promise;
    });


    return [promise, getUserFullname];
}
```

The next thing you see is two new members, userFullName and getUserFullnameMock. Since we will be running our mock function in several tests, we are creating the getUserFullnameMock function so that we can reuse it to give us our mock function getUserFullname and a few other needed items.

But then the question may be why do they look so complicated? Let's go through the code and figure out what it's doing:

- After we set the userFullName, variable we create the getUserFullnameMock. function As you can see, the getUserFullnameMock function takes a username as a parameter, just like the real getUserFullname function, and returns a promise and a Mock object.

- Inside of getUserFullnameMock, the definition instantiates a promise object and it mocks our getUserFullname function by using jest.fn. We need a promise to simulate a network call and also to await on it later with the wait call from testing-library.

- As mentioned, jest.fn is used to instantiate a mock and have the mock do whatever it is that we may need. In this case, since the getUserFullname function we are mocking is making a network call, we need to have our jest.fn mock return a promise. And it does so by returning the promise we created on the line immediately above it.

- And then, finally, both the promise and the new mock function, getUserFullname, are returned.

- We are going to quite a bit of trouble here, but in this case, it is a good idea to eliminate the use of a slow and error-prone network call. Otherwise, if the network call fails, we may incorrectly believe our test and code have failed.

- Next, let's see how our mock is used within our tests:

```
it("renders without crashing", () => {
    const username = "testuser";
    const [promise, getUserFullname] =
        getUserFullnameMock(username);

    const { baseElement } = render(<DisplayText
        getUserFullname={getUserFullname} />);
    expect(baseElement).toBeInTheDocument();
});

it("matches snapshot", () => {
    const username = "testuser";
    const [promise, getUserFullname] =
        getUserFullnameMock(username);

    const { baseElement } = render(<DisplayText
        getUserFullname={getUserFullname} />);
    expect(baseElement).toMatchSnapshot();
});

it("receive input text", () => {
    const username = "testuser";
    const [promise, getUserFullname] =
        getUserFullnameMock(username);

    const { getByTestId } = render(<DisplayText
        getUserFullname={getUserFullname} />);
    const input = getByTestId("user-input");
    fireEvent.change(input, { target: { value:
        username } });
    expect(input).toBeInTheDocument();
    expect(input).toHaveValue(username);
});
```

The first few tests simply take the `getUserFullname` function and pass it as a property to `DisplayText`. They don't otherwise use it, but it's still needed since it's a required property of `DisplayText`.

2.  The last test is updated since it tests the welcome message. Update your last test like this:

```
it("shows welcome message", async () => {
    const username = "testuser";
    const [promise, getUserFullname] =
        getUserFullnameMock(username);

    const msg = `Welcome to React testing,
        ${userFullName}`;
    const { getByTestId } = render(<DisplayText
        getUserFullname={getUserFullname} />);
    const input = getByTestId("user-input");
    const label = getByTestId("final-msg");
    fireEvent.change(input, { target: { value:
        username } });
    const btn = getByTestId("input-submit");
    fireEvent.click(btn);

    expect(label).toBeInTheDocument();
    await wait(() => promise);
    expect(label.innerHTML).toBe(msg);
});
});
```

The last test tests the welcome message because the `getUserFullname` function provides the user's `fullname` and that is fed into the welcome message that's shown in our label. In order to test that, we do an assertion with `expect` and `toBe`. Additionally, notice the `await wait` call just above `toBe`. This call must run first because our `getUserFullname` function is an `async` function and needs therefore to be awaited in order to get its results.

So by using `jest.fn`, we can mock out a piece of code so that it can give us a consistent value. Again, this helps us create consistent, reproducible tests where we are testing only a specific unit of code.

# Component mocking

The second form of mocking is to replace whole components entirely and use them in place of real components when we want to test other code. In order to test this, follow the steps given here:

1. Let's make our `DisplayText` component show a list of user todos based on the inserted username. Update the component like this:

```
import React, { useState, FC } from "react";

interface DisplayTextProps {
    getUserFullname: (username: string) =>
        Promise<string>;
}

const DisplayText: FC<DisplayTextProps> = ({
getUserFullname })
  => {
    const [txt, setTxt] = useState("");
    const [msg, setMsg] = useState("");
    const [todos, setTodos] = useState<Array<JSX.
    Element>>();
```

Here, we've created some state to use later:

```
    const onChangeTxt = (e: React.
      ChangeEvent<HTMLInputElement>)
      => {
        setTxt(e.target.value);
    }
```

Here, we update our input with the value of the username given by the user:

```
    const onClickShowMsg = async (e:
      React.MouseEvent<HTMLButtonElement, MouseEvent>) =>
      {
        e.preventDefault();

        setMsg(`Welcome to React testing, ${await
          getUserFullname(txt)}`);
        setUsersTodos();
    }
```

Once the **Show Message** button is clicked, we update the message to be displayed as well as the list of todos to be shown.

2.  We are going to accept a prop to use as our message prefix:

```
const setUsersTodos = async () => {
    const usersResponse = await
        fetch('https://jsonplaceholder.typicode.com/
        users');
    if (usersResponse.ok) {
        const users = await usersResponse.json();
        const userByName = users.find((usr: any) => {
            return usr.username.toLowerCase() ===
                txt;
        });
        console.log("user by username", userByName);
```

Similarly to how we got the user's `fullname` by using their `username`, we get the user's list of todos by calling the JSONPlaceholder API. First, we find the user by calling into the users collection:

```
        const todosResponse = await
            fetch('https://jsonplaceholder.typicode.com/
            todos');
        if (todosResponse.ok) {
            const todos = await todosResponse.json();
            const usersTodos = todos.filter((todo:
                any) => {
                return todo.userId === userByName.id;
            });
            const todoList = usersTodos.map((todo:
                any) => {
                return <li key={todo.id}>
                    {todo.title}
                </li>
            });
            setTodos(todoList);
            console.log("user todos", usersTodos);
        }
    }
}
```

Then we call into the todos collection and match the todos to the previously found user.

3.  Finally, we return an unordered list of todos via the UI:

```
    return (
        <form>
            <div>
                <label>Enter your name</label>
            </div>
            <div>
                <input data-testid="user-input"
                    value={txt}
                    onChange={onChangeTxt} />
            </div>
            <div>
                <button data-testid="input-submit"
                    onClick={onClickShowMsg}>Show Message</
                    button>
            </div>
            <div>
                <label data-testid="final-msg" >{msg}</
                label>
            </div>
            <ul style={{marginTop: '1rem', listStyleType:
            'none'}}>
                {todos}
            </ul>
        </form>
    )
}
```

This is what you should see in your browser (note that on the web API, only the username bret has any todos). Note that the text that you see is *lorem ipsum*. It is just placeholder text. It is coming straight from the JSONPlaceholder API:

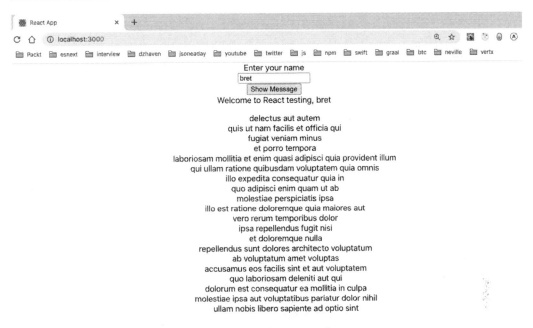

Figure 6.16 – List user todos

Here, we are displaying the user bret's list of todos.

Now, let's pretend we wanted to test our `DisplayText` component without testing this list of todos. How could we refactor this code so that our test wouldn't be so monolithic? Let's refactor our `DisplayText` component and pull out the todos capability as its own component:

1.  Update the `DisplayText` file like this:

```
import React, { useState, FC } from "react";
import UserTodos from "./UserTodos";


interface DisplayTextProps {
    getUserFullname: (username: string) =>
    Promise<string>;
}


const DisplayText: FC<DisplayTextProps> = ({
getUserFullname }) => {
    const [txt, setTxt] = useState("");
    const [msg, setMsg] = useState("");
    const [todoControl, setTodoControl] =
```

```
useState<ReturnType<typeof UserTodos>>();
```

```
const onChangeTxt = (e: React.
ChangeEvent<HTMLInputElement>)
   => {
     setTxt(e.target.value);
}
```

First, we create a state called `todoControl`. The type of this state is the type of our new `UserTodos` component, which we'll show later. We've gotten this type by using the utility type `ReturnType`. As you can see, it is a simple way of creating a type definition by using an object:

```
const onClickShowMsg = async (e:
   React.MouseEvent<HTMLButtonElement, MouseEvent>) =>
      {
      e.preventDefault();
      setTodoControl(null);
      setMsg(`Welcome to React testing, ${await
         getUserFullname(txt)}`);
      setTodoControl(<UserTodos username={txt} />);
}
```

Our `onClickShowMsg` event handler will call `setTodoControl` and pass our `UserTodos` component the `username`:

```
return (
   <form>
      <div>
         <label>Enter your name</label>
      </div>
      <div>
         <input data-testid="user-input"
         value={txt}
            onChange={onChangeTxt} />
      </div>
      <div>
         <button data-testid="input-submit"
         onClick={onClickShowMsg}>Show Message</
            button>
```

```
            </div>
            <div>
                <label data-testid="final-msg" >{msg}</
                label>
            </div>
            {todoControl}
        </form>
    )
}

export default DisplayText;
```

And finally, `todoControl` gets displayed with our UI.

2.  Now let's create our new `UserTodos` component. Create a file called `UserTodos.tsx` and add this code:

```
import React, { FC, useState, useEffect } from 'react';


interface UserTodosProps {
    username: string;
}
```

We are now taking the username as a prop from our parent:

```
const UserTodos: FC<UserTodosProps> = ({ username }) => {
    const [todos, setTodos] = useState<Array<JSX.
      Element>>();

    const setUsersTodos = async () => {
        const usersResponse = await
        fetch('https://jsonplaceholder.typicode.com/
          users');
        if(usersResponse) {
            const users = await usersResponse.json();
            const userByName = users.find((usr: any) => {
                return usr.username.toLowerCase() ===
                  username;
            });
            console.log("user by username", userByName);
```

First, we grab our users again from the users collection and filter to find our one user by matching the username:

```
const todosResponse = await
  fetch('https://jsonplaceholder.typicode.com/
  todos');
if (userByName && todosResponse) {
    const todos = await todosResponse.json();
    const usersTodos = todos.filter((todo:
    any) => {
        return todo.userId === userByName.id;
    });
    const todoList = usersTodos.map((todo:
    any) => {
        return <li key={todo.id}>
            {todo.title}
        </li>
    });
    setTodos(todoList);
    console.log("user todos", usersTodos);
    }
  }
}
```

Then we grab the matching todos of the found user. We then run the JavaScript map function to create a collection of li elements for each todo:

```
useEffect(() => {
    if (username) {
    setUsersTodos();
    }
}, [username]);
```

By using useEffect, we are indicating that any time our username prop changes, we want to update our list of todos:

```
return <ul style={{marginTop: '1rem', listStyleType:
    'none'}}>
        {todos}
    </ul>;
```

```
    }


export default UserTodos;
```

And finally, we output our todos as unordered list elements. If you run this code, you should see this once you click **Show Message**:

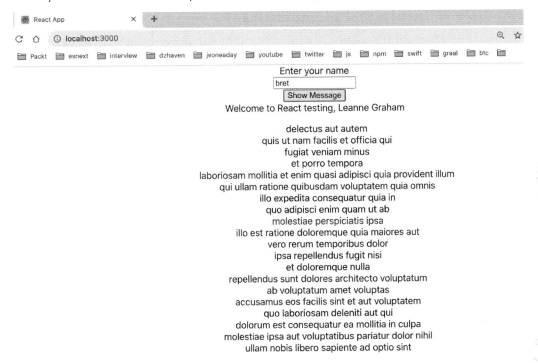

Figure 6.17 – Refactored todos

OK, so now we can add a new test that mocks out our `UserTodos` component and therefore allows `DisplayText` to be tested independently. Note also that there are two main ways of doing mocks with Jest. We can do an inline call to mock or we can use a mock file. For this example, we will use a mock file. Let's look at the steps:

1.  In the `src` folder, create a new folder, `__mocks__`. Inside that folder, create a file called `UserTodos.tsx` and add this code into it:

```
import React, { ReactElement } from 'react';


export default (): ReactElement => {
    return <></>;
};
```

This file will be the mocked version of the function component. As you can see, it returns nothing and has no real members. This means that unlike the real component, it will not make any network call or emit any HTML, which for testing is what we want.

2.  Let's now update `DisplayText.test.tsx` with the following code:

```
import React from 'react';
import { render, fireEvent, cleanup, wait } from '@
testing-library/react';
import DisplayText from './DisplayText';
import "@testing-library/jest-dom/extend-expect";


jest.mock("./UserTodos");


afterEach(cleanup);


describe("Test DisplayText", () => {
    const userFullName = "John Tester";


    const getUserFullnameMock = (username: string):
    [Promise<string>, jest.Mock<Promise<string>,
        [string]>] => {
        const promise = new Promise<string>((res, rej) =>
    {

            res(userFullName);
        });
        const getUserFullname = jest.fn(async (username:
            string):
        Promise<string> => {
            return promise;
        });


        return [promise, getUserFullname];
    }
```

First, we can see that we import our mock `UserTodos` component outside of any test. This is necessary as doing it inside a test will not work.

The rest of the tests are the same but they now internally use the mock of `UserTodos`. Therefore, the test runs faster as there's no network call. As a trial of your newfound testing skills, try creating your own test for the `UserTodos` component separately.

In this section, we learned about testing React applications using Jest and testing-library. Unit testing is a very important part of application development and you will be coding tests almost daily as a professional programmer. It can help both to write and refactor code.

In the next section, we'll continue adding to our developer skillset by discussing common tools used in the development of React applications.

# Learning common tools and practices for React development

There are many tools that can help in writing React applications. There are too many to list them exhaustively but we will review some of the most common here. These tools are vital for writing and debugging your code, so you should spend some time familiarizing yourself with them.

## VS Code

We've been using VS Code as our code editor for the entirety of this book. And for JavaScript development, VS Code is clearly the most popular editor currently in use. Here are a few facts you should know in order to make optimal use of VS Code:

- VS Code has a large ecosystem of extensions to help in coding. Many of them are dependent upon developer preferences, so you should do a quick search and take a look. However, here are some common extensions you should consider using:

  **Visual Studio IntelliCode**: Provides a language service for AI-driven code completion and syntax highlighting.

  **Apollo GraphQL**: Code completion and formatting helpers for GraphQL.

**React-related plugins**: There are many React-related plugins that can help by providing code snippets or Hooks into services like NPM. Here are just a few:

Figure 6.18 – React VS Code plugins

- VS Code has a built-in debugger that allows you to break (stop) on code and review variable values. I won't demonstrate it here as the standard for frontend development is to use the Chrome debugger, which also allows breaking on code, but I will demonstrate it once we start using Node.

- Configuration files: In VS Code, there are two ways of setting preferences for your project, a workspace and the `settings.json` file. There is an enormous number of ways VS Code can be configured with regard to fonts, extensions, windows, and so on. These configurations can be done globally, or they can be done per project. I've included a `.vscode/settings.json` file in the `ejected-app` project for demonstration purposes. Workspace files are basically the same as settings files, except they're intended for use with multiple projects in a single folder. Workspace files are named `<name>.code-workspace`.

# Prettier

When writing code, it is very important to use a consistent style to improve readability. For example, if you imagine a large team with many developers, if they each write code in their own style with various ways of doing indentation, variable naming, and so on, it would be chaos. Additionally, there are industry-standard ways of formatting JavaScript that can make it more readable and therefore more understandable. This is what tools like Prettier provide.

Prettier will automatically format your code into a consistent and readable format upon every save, no matter who is writing the code. Just remember, after installing Prettier, you need to set up `settings.json` or your workspace file to use it. Again, I have a sample `settings.json` file in our `ejected-app` project.

# Chrome Debugger

The Chrome browser provides built-in tools for web development. These include the ability to see all the HTML of a page, view console messages, break on JavaScript code, and view network calls made by the browser. Even without any plugins, it is quite extensive. For many frontend developers, Chrome is the main tool for debugging code.

Let's take a look at the debugger for `ejected-app` and learn some of the basics:

1. If your local instance of `ejected-app` is not running, start it again and open your Chrome browser to the default `localhost:3000` URL. Once there, open your Chrome debugger by either pressing the *F12* key or going to **Chrome Settings | More Tools | Developer Tools**. In the debugger, which will probably show at the bottom of your Chrome screen, you should see the **Elements** tab like this:

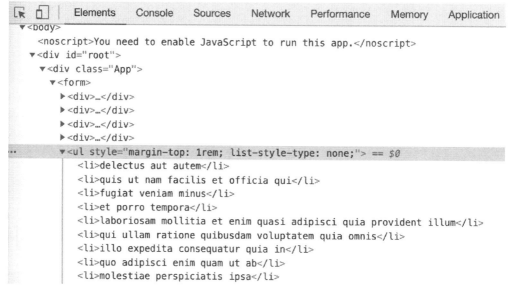

Figure 6.19: Chrome Debugger Elements tab

As you can see, we have our original `root div` tag where the rest of our app resides. And in this screenshot, we can see the state where we've made our call to the web API to get todos for the user `Bret`. So, then we can use the Chrome Debugger to find our HTML elements and check their attributes and play with CSS values to get our UI precisely how we would want it.

2. Next, go to the **Console** tab and you should see something like this:

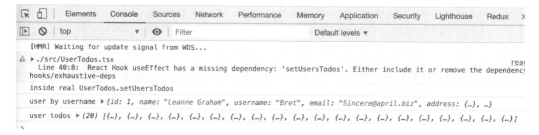

Figure 6.20: Chrome Debugger Console tab

So, here, we can check the values for variables and function return data, making sure they are what we want and are expecting.

3.  Using the Chrome Debugger, it is possible to break on running code. Open the **Sources** tab and find the `UserTodos.tsx` file, then add the breakpoint as shown:

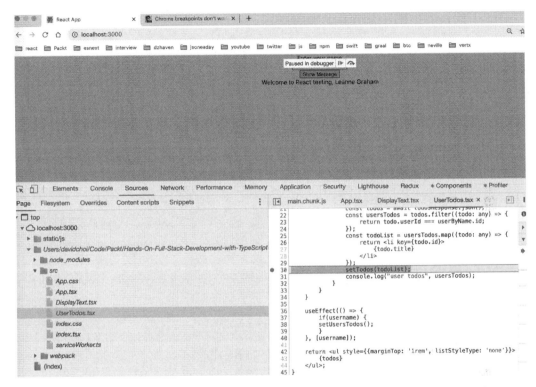

Figure 6.21 – Chrome Debugger Sources tab

As you can see, we are able to stop on our breakpoint, as indicated by the dot next to *line 30*. If you hover over certain variables, you will be able to see their current values, even when they contain objects such as other components. This is a really useful feature for debugging issues in code. This feature is enabled by something called source maps. Source maps are files that map or tie source code to minified runtime code. They get created and sent to the browser during development time and allow the ability to break on and view variable values during runtime.

4.  Now let's remove our breakpoint and move to the **Network** tab. This tab shows all the network connections made by our browser. This includes not only calls for network resources such as data but can include calls to get images or static files such as HTML files. If we open this tab and then make our call to get todos for the user Bret, we should see this:

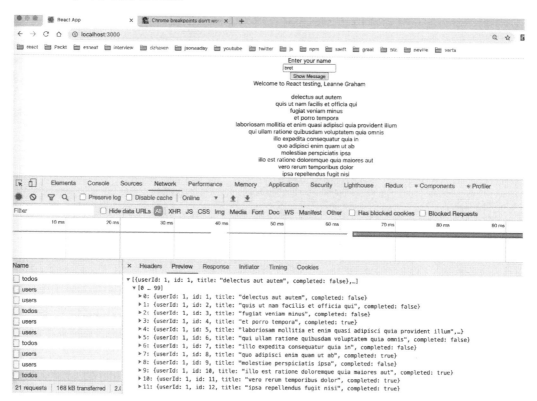

Figure 6.22 – Chrome Debugger Network tab

As you can see, we can view all the data that comes back from our call to the web API. This is a handy tool that allows us to compare the data coming from our network resource and compare it to what our code seems to be using. We will also use this tool later when we do GraphQL calls as well.

OK, so that was a quick overview of the Chrome Debugger, but Chrome also provides extensions that enable React-specific help. React Developer Tools provides information about our component hierarchy and attribute information about each component; for example, here's a sample in our app:

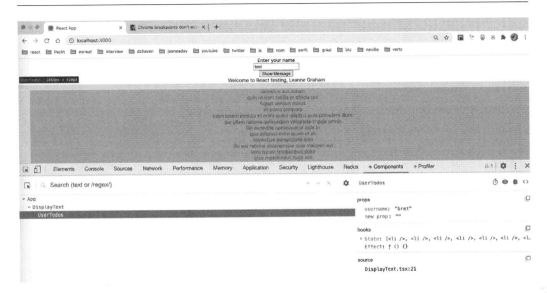

Figure 6.23 – React Developer Tools

As you can see, this tool reveals our component hierarchy and it shows the currently selected component's attributes. It also shows a highlight on the screen of the elements that make up our component, when we select the specific component within the hierarchy. It's a handy tool for viewing our elements from the standpoint of React component structure, as opposed to HTML structure. The Chrome ecosystem of extensions is vast and there are also extensions for Redux and Apollo GraphQL. We'll explore those in *Chapter 8, Learning Server-Side Development with Node.js and Express*, and *Chapter 9, What is GraphQL?*, respectively.

# Alternative IDEs

In this book, we use VS Code as our code editor. It works great and has become the most popular JavaScript and TypeScript editor. However, there is no reason why you have to use it. And there are alternatives you should be aware of. I will only list out a few of them here, just so you are aware of some options:

- **Atom**: Probably the most popular free editor after VS Code.
- **Sublime Text**: One of the faster and more responsive editors. Also has a free version.
- **Vim**: A Unix text editor, often used for editing code.
- **Webstorm**: A commercial editor from JetBrains.

Try some of these editors for yourself, as having a good code editor can definitely enhance your productivity.

This section reviewed some of the more commonly used tools in React development. Although these tools don't do the main work of writing code for our application, they are nevertheless enormously important for helping us to write code faster and of higher quality. They will also reduce our pain points while writing code, because finding bugs can often be as challenging as resolving them.

# Summary

In this chapter, we learned about the many tools professional frontend developers use to help write high-quality code. Whether it's the VS Code editor used to write the code, or the source code repository Git used to share it, all of the tools mentioned here are vitally important in doing the work of a frontend engineer.

By learning about these tools, you will become a much better programmer and your code quality will increase substantially. Additionally, your quality of life as a developer will improve because many of these tools can help track down issues more quickly and help you resolve them more easily than trying to tackle it entirely on your own.

In the next chapter, we will extend our knowledge of React by learning about Redux and React Router. Redux will help us manage global state and React Router will help us create client-side URLs. Both frameworks are very popular in the React community and provide many features that will help us create a more sophisticated, capable application.

# 7

# Learning Redux and React Router

In this chapter, we'll learn about Redux and React Router. Redux is still the most common method of managing global state shared across a React application. Using Redux global state, we can reduce a great deal of boilerplate code and streamline the application. React Router is also the most popular framework for managing client-side URL routing. Client-side URL routing allows a SPA application to behave in ways that are familiar to users expecting a classic-style web application that indicates where they are in the app. Both of these technologies are necessary for building SPA applications that look and feel like standard web apps.

In this chapter, we're going to cover the following main topics:

- Learning about Redux state
- Learning about React Router

## Technical requirements

You should have a basic understanding of web development using React. We will once again be using Node and Visual Studio Code.

The GitHub repository is at `https://github.com/PacktPublishing/Full-Stack-React-TypeScript-and-Node`. Use the code in the `Chap7` folder.

To set up this chapter's code folder, go to your `HandsOnTypescript` folder and create a new folder called `Chap7`.

# Learning about Redux state

Redux is still the most popular enterprise-level framework for creating and managing global state in a React application (although we can use Redux in any JavaScript app, not just React). Many newer frameworks have been created, and some of them have gained their own considerable following; however, Redux is still the most commonly used. You may find that Redux is difficult to understand at first. However, once we do learn it, we'll see its many benefits and why it is so often the go-to framework for large, complex React applications.

We learned about React state in *Chapter 4*, *Learning Single-Page Application Concepts and How React Enables Them*, and *Chapter 5*, *React Development with Hooks*. So, to reiterate, state, or a component's data, is the main driver of all UI changes in React. This is the reason why the React framework has the word "react" in its name, because it is reacting to these state changes (this is also known as being reactive). So, when creating and managing state, we generally want to associate local state with the component or the component's root parent most of the time.

Component-based state can be limiting. There are cases where state is not specific to a component or even to a component hierarchy. State can sometimes be necessary for several components or other non-component services that make up an application. In addition to this, state in React is passed down only one way, from the parent down to children as props. It should not be done upstream. And this further constrains how state can be used in React. Redux therefore provides a mechanism not only to share state globally but also to allow injection and updating of state from any component as needed.

Let's give an example to flesh this out a bit. In a typical enterprise-class application, we will always have authentication. And once a user is authenticated, we may receive certain data about the user – for example, the user's full name, user ID, email, and so on. It should not seem unreasonable to think that these data points may be used by a significant portion of the components within an application. It would be tedious and error-prone therefore to have each component call to get this data and then save it locally in their own state. Doing it this way would mean that there were multiple copies of the data and as it changed, some components may end up keeping older versions of the data.

This sort of conflict can be the source of bugs. Therefore, it would be helpful to be able to maintain this data on the client in only one place and share it with whatever component needed it. This way, if this data ever did get updated, we could be assured that all components, no matter what section of the app they are in, would get the latest valid data. This is what Redux can do for our application. We can consider it a **single source of truth**.

Redux is a data storage service that maintains all the globally shared data in our React application. Redux provides not only the store itself, but also the base functions needed to add, remove, and share this data. One difference with React state, however, is that Redux state is not necessarily going to trigger UI updates. It certainly can if we desire to do so, but there is no explicit necessity for doing so. So, we should keep that in mind.

Let's take a look at how to set up Redux:

1.  Create a new React project in the Chap7 folder like this:

    ```
    create-react-app redux-sample --template typescript
    ```

2.  Once our project is set up, open it and use your command line to cd into the redux-sample folder.

3.  We will now install Redux, which is actually several different dependencies. First, run this command:

    ```
    npm i redux react-redux @types/redux @types/react-redux
    ```

    This command gives us the main dependencies, including the TypeScript types.

OK, now that we've done some basic setup, we need to understand a few more things about Redux before we continue. Redux uses a pair of concepts called reducers and actions. Let's see what each of these does.

## Reducers and actions

In Redux, there is only a single store for all data. So, all our global data will live inside of a single Redux object. Now, the issue with this design is that, since this is global state, different app features will require different types of data and the entirety of the data is not always relevant to all parts of the application. So, the Redux creators came up with a scheme that uses reducers to filter and split up the single store into separated chunks. So, if component A only needs a specific piece of data, it does not have to deal with the entire store.

This design is a good way of separating data concerns. But the side effect of having such a design is that we need some way of updating the relevant portion of data without affecting any of the other pieces. This is what actions do. Actions are objects that provide the data for specific reducers only.

Now that we have a high-level view of what reducers and actions are, let's look at some examples in code:

1.  Create a new folder called `store` under `src`.

2.  Then, create a file called `AppState.ts`. This file will store our aggregated reducer object called `rootReducer` of type `AppState`, which represents the global state. Insert this code into the file:

    ```typescript
    import { combineReducers } from "redux";

    export const rootReducer = combineReducers({
    });

    export type AppState = ReturnType<typeof rootReducer>;
    ```

    `rootReducer` represents an aggregated object of all of our reducers. We don't have any reducers yet, but we will add the actual reducers once our setup is complete. `combineReducers` takes each of our reducers and combines them into a single object. At the bottom, we are creating a TypeScript type based upon our `rootReducer` by using the `ReturnType utility type`, and then exporting the new type called `AppState`.

    > **Note**
    >
    > A utility type is simply a helper class that the TypeScript team created to give specific functionality. There are many different utility types and a list can be found here: `https://www.typescriptlang.org/docs/handbook/utility-types.html`.

3.  Next, we create a file called `configureStore.ts`, which will contain our actual store object used by Redux and the app. This is what it should look like:

    ```typescript
    import { createStore } from "redux";
    import { rootReducer } from "./AppState";

    const configureStore = () => {
    ```

```
    return createStore(rootReducer, {});
};
export default configureStore;
```

As we can see, Redux's `createStore` method is used to build the actual store based upon our `AppState` object, `rootReducer`. `configureStore` is exported and used later to execute the creation of the store.

4.  Now, we must update our `index.tsx` file to call our `configureStore` method and initialize Redux for our app. Update `index.tsx` like this:

```
import React from 'react';
import ReactDOM from 'react-dom';
import './index.css';
import App from './App';
import { Provider } from "react-redux";
import configureStore from "./store/configureStore";
import * as serviceWorker from './serviceWorker';

ReactDOM.render(
  <React.StrictMode>
    <Provider store={configureStore()}>
    <App />
    </Provider>
  </React.StrictMode>,
  document.getElementById('root')
);
```

First, we import `Provider` from `react-redux`. `Provider` is a React component that acts as a parent component to all other components and *provides* our store data. In addition, `Provider`, as shown, is receiving the initialized store by accepting the return value of the `configureStore` function:

```
// If you want your app to work offline and load faster,
    // you can change
// unregister() to register() below. Note this comes with
    // some pitfalls.
// Learn more about service workers:
    // https://bit.ly/CRA-PWA
serviceWorker.unregister();
```

This commented code is coming from the `create-react-app` project. It is included here for completeness. OK, so now we have a base-level setup of Redux. So, our example will continue by creating a call to get a user object. We will use the JSONPlaceholder API we learned about in *Chapter 6, Setting Up Our Project Using create-react-app and Testing with Jest*. After a successful login, it shares the user information by putting it into Redux as a reducer. Let's do that now:

1. Create a new file, `UserReducer.ts`, inside of the `store` folder, like this:

```
export const USER_TYPE = "USER_TYPE";
```

The first thing we do is create a constant for the action type called `USER_TYPE`. This is optional but helps us avoid issues such as typos:

```
export interface User {
    id: string;
    username: string;
    email: string;
    city: string;
}
```

Then, we create a type representing our `User`:

```
export interface UserAction {
    type: string;
    payload: User | null;
}
```

Now, by convention, an action has two members: type and payload. So, we create a `UserAction` type with those members in it:

```
export const UserReducer = ( state: User | null = null,
action:
  UserAction): User | null => {
    switch(action.type) {
        case USER_TYPE:
            console.log("user reducer", action.payload);
            return action.payload;
        default:
            return state;
    }
};
```

And then, finally, we create our reducer called `UserReducer`. A reducer always takes the `state` and `action` parameters. Note, `state` is not the entire state, it is only the partial state relevant to some reducer. This reducer will know whether the passed-in `state` is its own based on the `action` type. Also notice that the original state is never mutated. This is extremely important. *Never* change the state directly. You should either return the state as is, which is done in `case default`, or return some other data. In this case, we return `action.payload`.

2. So now, we have to go back into our `AppState.ts` file and add this new reducer. The file should now look like this:

```
import { combineReducers } from "redux";
import { UserReducer } from "./UserReducer";


export const rootReducer = combineReducers({
  user: UserReducer
});


export type AppState = ReturnType<typeof rootReducer>;
```

Our Redux store has one new member called `user`, which is updated by `UserReducer`. If we had more reducers, we would simply give them a name and add them below `user` with their reducer, and the `combineReducers` Redux function would combine all of them into a single aggregate `rootReducer`.

3. Now, let's start using our new state. Update the `App.tsx` file like this:

```
import React, { useState } from 'react';
import ContextTester from './ContextTester';
import './App.css';


function App() {
  const [userid, setUserid] = useState(0);
  const onChangeUserId = (e: React.
    ChangeEvent<HTMLInputElement>)
  => {
    console.log("userid", e.target.value);
    setUserid(e.target.value ? Number(e.target.value) :
      0);
  }
```

```
      return (
        <div className="App">
          <label>user id</label>
          <input value={userid} onChange={onChangeUserId} />
        </div>
      );
    }


    export default App;
```

We will take `userid` as a parameter and then, based upon that ID, we will get the associated user from the JSON Placeholder API. Now, in order to do this, we need to use some Redux-specific Hooks so we can add our found user to the Redux store.

4.  Let's update the App component in `App.tsx` like this:

```
    function App() {
      const [userid, setUserid] = useState(0);
      const dispatch = useDispatch();
```

As you can see, we added a Redux Hook called `dispatch`. We get an instance of `dispatch` with the `useDispatch` Hook. `dispatch` is a Redux function that sends our action data to Redux. Redux then sends the action to each of our reducers for processing. Then the reducer that recognizes the action type accepts it as its state payload:

```
      const onChangeUserId = async (e:
        React.ChangeEvent<HTMLInputElement>) => {
        const useridFromInput = e.target.value ?
          Number(e.target.value) : 0;
        console.log("userid", useridFromInput);
        setUserid(useridFromInput);

        const usersResponse = await
          fetch('https://jsonplaceholder.typicode.com/
          users');
        if(usersResponse.ok) {
          const users = await usersResponse.json();
```

```
        console.log("users", users);
        const usr = users.find((userItem: any) => {
            return userItem && userItem.id ===
            useridFromInput;
        });
        console.log("usr", usr);
        dispatch({
            type: USER_TYPE,
            payload: {
                id: usr.id,
                username: usr.username,
                email: usr.email,
                city: usr.address.city
            }
        });
    }
```

Inside of the onChangeUserId handler, we make a call to the JSONPlaceholder API. Then we use the usersResponse response object to get the result from our network API. We then get our desired user by filtering with the user ID we got from our UI. Then we use dispatch to send our action to our reducer. Also notice onChangeUserId is now an async function:

```
    }
    return (
        <div className="App">
            <label>user id</label>
            <input value={userid} onChange={onChangeUserId} />
        </div>
    );
}
```

This UI will take userid as an input.

Now, let's create a child component that can display all of our user-related data:

1.  Create a new component called `UserDisplay.tsx` and add this code:

```tsx
import React from 'react';
import { AppState } from './store/AppState';
import { useSelector } from 'react-redux';
const UserDisplay = () => {
    const user = useSelector((state: AppState) =>
    state.user);

    if(user) {
        console.log("user", user);
        return (<React.Fragment>
            <div>
                <label>username:</label>
                 {user.username}
            </div>
            <div>
                <label>email:</label>
                 {user.email}
            </div>
            <div>
                <label>city:</label>
                 {user.city}
            </div>
        </React.Fragment>);
    } else {
        return null;
    }
}
export default UserDisplay
```

The `useSelector` Hook gets the specific `user` reducer. It takes a function as a parameter and this function takes the entire aggregated reducer state and only returns the `user` reducer. Also in this component, we are displaying the properties of our found user but taken from Redux and the `user` reducer. Notice also how we return `null` if no user is found.

2.  Now, let's add the `UserDisplay` component to our App component:

```
import React, { useState } from 'react';
import './App.css';
import { useDispatch } from 'react-redux';
import { USER_TYPE } from './store/UserReducer';
import UserDisplay from './UserDisplay';
```

Here, we import the new `UserDisplay` component:

```
function App() {
  const [userid, setUserid] = useState(0);
  const dispatch = useDispatch();
  const onChangeUserId = async (e:
    React.ChangeEvent<HTMLInputElement>) => {
    const useridFromInput = e.target.value ?
      Number(e.target.value) : 0;
    console.log("userid", useridFromInput);
    setUserid(useridFromInput);
    const usersResponse = await
      fetch('https://jsonplaceholder.typicode.com/
      users');
    if(usersResponse.ok) {
      const users = await usersResponse.json();
      const usr = users.find((userItem: any) => {
        return userItem && userItem.id ===
        useridFromInput;
      });
      dispatch({
        type: USER_TYPE,
        payload: {
          id: usr.id,
          username: usr.username,
          email: usr.email,
          city: usr.address.city
        }
      });
    }
  }
```

No real changes up to here:

```
    return (
        <React.Fragment>
            <div className="App">
                <label>user id</label>
                <input value={userid} onChange={onChangeUserId}
                />
            </div>
            <UserDisplay />
        </React.Fragment>
    );
}


export default App;
```

Now use `UserDisplay` in the returned JSX UI so that our user information is displayed.

3.  Now if you load the browser at `http://localhost:3000` and enter `1` in the input, you should see this:

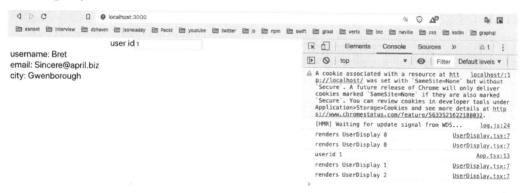

Figure 7.1 – User object from the Redux store

So, now that we've seen a sample of a simple Redux store use case, let's take it a step further and show what will happen when we have multiple reducers in the same store:

1.  Create a new file called `PostDisplay.tsx` and add the following code. This component will display posted comments from the JSON Placeholder API:

```
import React, { useRef } from 'react';
import { AppState } from './store/AppState';
```

```
import { useSelector } from 'react-redux';

const PostDisplay = React.memo(() => {
    const renderCount = useRef(0);
    console.log("renders PostDisplay", renderCount.
      current++);
    const post = useSelector((state: AppState) => state.
      post);
```

Again, like our previous example, here, we set up which state data we want using
`useSelector`:

```
    if(post) {
        return (<React.Fragment>
            <div>
                <label>title:</label>
                 {post.title}
            </div>
            <div>
                <label>body:</label>
                 {post.body}
            </div>
        </React.Fragment>);
    } else {
        return null;
    }
});

export default PostDisplay
```

As you can see, it looks very similar to `UserDisplay`, but it displays
`post`-related information such as `title` and body.

2.  Now, we update our Redux code to add our new reducer. First, add a new file inside
    of the `store` folder called `PostReducer.ts` and then add this code:

```
export const POST_TYPE = "POST_TYPE";

export interface Post {
    id: number;
```

```
        title: string;
        body: string;
    }


export interface PostAction {
    type: string;
    payload: Post | null;
}


export const PostReducer = ( state: Post | null = null,
    action: PostAction): Post | null => {
        switch(action.type) {
            case POST_TYPE:
                return action.payload;
            default:
                return state;
        }
};
```

Again, this is very similar to `UserReducer`, but focused on posts instead of users.

3.  Next, we want to update the `AppState.tsx` file and add our new reducer to it. Add this code:

```
import { combineReducers } from "redux";
import { UserReducer } from "./UserReducer";
import { PostReducer } from "./PostReducer";


export const rootReducer = combineReducers({
    user: UserReducer,
    post: PostReducer
});


export type AppState = ReturnType<typeof rootReducer>;
```

All we did is add our `PostReducer`.

4. OK, so now we'll update our `App` component and add code specifically for finding a specific post by ID from the JSON Placeholder API. Update `App` with this code:

```
function App() {
    const [userid, setUserid] = useState(0);
    const dispatch = useDispatch();
    const [postid, setPostId] = useState(0);
```

Notice we don't have a `dispatch` specific to any reducer. That's because dispatchers are just generic execution functions. The action will be routed to the appropriate reducer eventually.

`onChangeUserId` has not changed but is shown here for completeness:

```
const onChangeUserId = async (e:
React.ChangeEvent<HTMLInputElement>) => {
    const useridFromInput = e.target.value ?
    Number(e.target.value) : 0;
    console.log("userid", useridFromInput);
    setUserid(useridFromInput);

    const usersResponse = await
        fetch('https://jsonplaceholder.typicode.com/
        users');
    if(usersResponse.ok) {
        const users = await usersResponse.json();

        const usr = users.find((userItem: any) => {
            return userItem && userItem.id ===
            useridFromInput;
        });

        dispatch({
            type: USER_TYPE,
            payload: {
                id: usr.id,
                username: usr.username,
                email: usr.email,
                city: usr.address.city
```

```
            }
        });
    }
}
```

onChangePostId is a new event handler for handling post-related data
changes:

```
const onChangePostId = async (e:
    React.ChangeEvent<HTMLInputElement>) => {
    const postIdFromInput = e.target.value ?
        Number(e.target.value) : 0;
    setPostId(postIdFromInput);

    const postResponse = await
        fetch("https://jsonplaceholder.typicode.com/posts/"
            + postIdFromInput);
    if(postResponse.ok) {
        const post = await postResponse.json();
        console.log("post", post);
        dispatch({
            type: POST_TYPE,
            payload: {
                id: post.id,
                title: post.title,
                body: post.body
            }
        })
    }
}
```

OnChangePostId dispatches a relevant action via the dispatch function.

The UI has been slightly updated to handle the new PostDisplay component and separate it from the UserDisplay components:

```
return (
  <React.Fragment>
    <div style={{width: "300px"}}>
      <div className="App">
        <label>user id</label>
        <input value={userid} onChange={onChangeUserId}
        />
      </div>
      <UserDisplay />
    </div>
    <br/>
    <div style={{width: "300px"}}>
      <div className="App">
        <label>post id</label>
        <input value={postid} onChange={onChangePostId}
        />
      </div>
      <PostDisplay />
    </div>
  </React.Fragment>
);
}
```

If you run this code and update only `postid`, you should see an interesting thing:

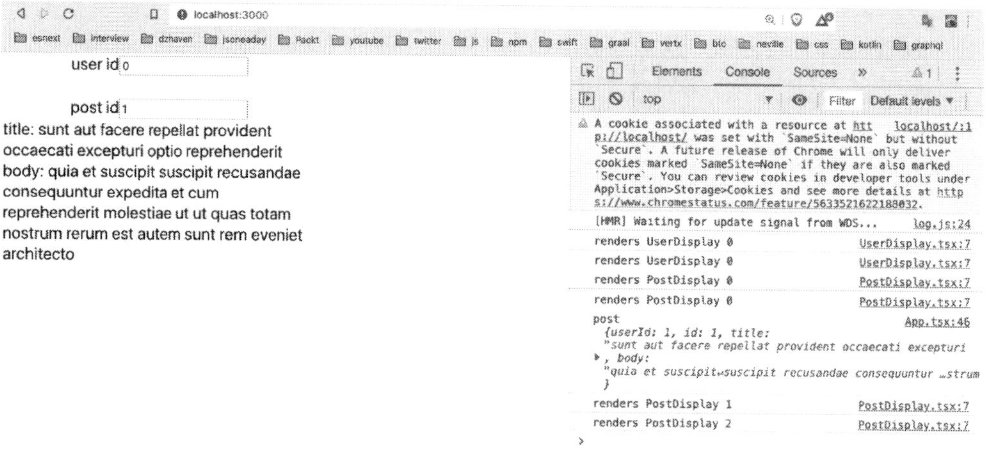

Figure 7.2 – PostDisplay result

Notice that in the console, when updating the `postid` input, there is no log for `UserDisplay`. This shows that the Redux store is not directly attached to the React render pipeline and only the components associated with a particular state change will re-render. This is different behavior from React Context and can be a benefit to performance by reducing unwanted renders (we'll talk about Context in the next section).

In this section, we learned about Redux, the most popular way of managing global state in React. In larger apps, we will use a global state manager frequently, as there is generally a lot of global data sharing happening. In our application, we will store information about our logged-in user and other data that will be shared across the app, so having this capability will be valuable.

# React Context

Context is a newer feature that came out a little before Hooks. Context is not a separate dependency but is built into React core. It allows similar functionality to Redux in that it allows state to be stored in a single source and then shared across components, without having to manually pass down props through the component hierarchy.

This capability is very efficient from a developer coding perspective because it eliminates the need to write a lot of boilerplate code to pass state down from a parent to its children. Here's a visualization of a possible set of hierarchies in a larger React app:

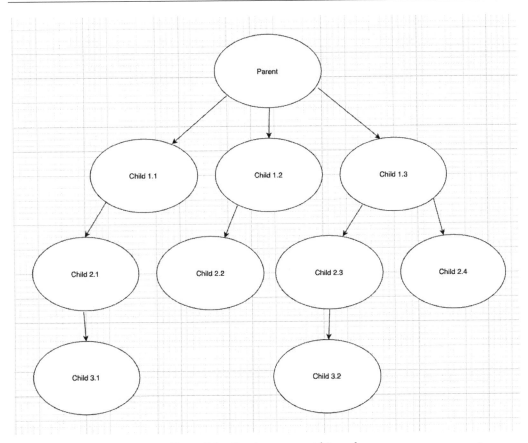

Figure 7.3 – React component hierarchy

In this example diagram, we have a single parent component and it has several children, which it is using in its own JSX. Those children also have their own children, and so on. So, if we were to configure the passing of props all the way down for every component hierarchy, it would be quite a bit of code, especially knowing that some hierarchies involve passing functions that may call back to some arbitrary parent. Having these sorts of prop relationships also causes additional cognitive load for developers, as they need to think about data relationships and how data is being moved among the components.

Both React Context and Redux are good ways of avoiding this state-passing boilerplate code, when appropriate. And for smaller projects, the simplicity of Context works well. However, for larger projects, I recommend against using Context.

React Context can have multiple parent providers, meaning it is possible to have more than one root context. For larger apps, this can be confusing and adds more boilerplate code. Additionally, the mixing of global state providers can be confusing. If a team decides to use both Context and Redux, when do we use each one? And if we use both now, we must maintain two styles for global state management.

In addition, Context, unlike Redux, has no concept of reducers. Therefore, all users of Context will receive the entire set of state data, which is not a good practice in terms of the separation of concerns. Over time, it can become confusing as to what subset of the data a particular component should deal with.

One additional side effect of having all state data available to all component users is that, even if a component does not actually access the specific state member, any Context changes will trigger a re-render. For example, let's say that the Context state looks like this { username, userage } and our component only uses username. Even if userage alone changes, it triggers a re-render in that component. This is true even when memo is used (we covered memo in *Chapter 5, React Development with Hooks*). Let's look at an example demonstrating this effect:

1.  Remove React.StrictMode and Provider from index.tsx to avoid confusion. We'll put this back later. Now, the index.tsx file should look like this:

    ```
    import React from 'react';
    import ReactDOM from 'react-dom';
    import './index.css';
    import App from './App';
    import { Provider } from "react-redux";
    import configureStore from "./store/configureStore";
    import * as serviceWorker from './serviceWorker';

    ReactDOM.render(
        <App />
        ,
        document.getElementById('root')
    );
    ```

Again, these comments are coming from `create-react-app` and are included here only for completeness:

```
// If you want your app to work offline and load faster,
 // you can change
// unregister() to register() below. Note this comes with
 // some pitfalls.
// Learn more about service workers:
 // https://bit.ly/CRA-PWA
serviceWorker.unregister();
```

You can also remove any unused imports to avoid triggering warning messages.

2.  Now, create these two child components, where each one will use a unique member of our Context state. First, create the `UserAgeComp.tsx` component with this code in it:

```
import React, { useContext } from 'react';
import { TestContext } from './ContextTester';

const UserAgeComp = () => {
    const { userage } = useContext(TestContext);

    return <div>
        {userage}
    </div>
};

export default UserAgeComp;
```

This code uses object destructuring to only use the `userage` member of `TestContext` by using the `useContext` Hook, which we will create later, and displays it only. Now, create the `UserNameComp.tsx` component with this code:

```
import React, { useContext, useRef } from 'react';
import { TestContext } from './ContextTester';


const UserNameComp = React.memo(() => {
    const renders = useRef(0);
    console.log("renders UserNameComp", renders.
        current++);


    const username   = "dave"; //useContext(TestContext);
    console.log("username UserNameComp", username);


    return <div>
        {username}
    </div>
});


export default UserNameComp;
```

You may be surprised that we are not using Context for `username` (note, I have it commented out), but before we can show the ramifications of using Context, I wanted to show this component working as expected first. So, this component has two main features. One is a `ref` that counts the number of times this component was rendered, and a variable called `username` that gets displayed. It will also log the renders count as well in order to show when a re-render is triggered.

3.   Now, we need to create a parent component that has Context in it. Create the `ContextTester.tsx` file and add this code into it:

```
import React, { createContext, useState } from 'react';
import UserNameComp from './UserNameComp';
import UserAgeComp from './UserAgeComp';
```

Here, we use `createContext` to create our `TestContext` object, which will hold our state:

```
export const TestContext = createContext<{ username:
   string, userage: number }>({ username: "",
   userage:0 });
const ContextTester = () => {
    const [userage, setUserage] = useState(20);
    const [localState, setLocalState] = useState(0);
    const onClickAge = () => {
        setUserage(
            userage + 1
        );
    }
    const onClickLocalState = () => {
        setLocalState(localState + 1);
    }


    return (<React.Fragment>
        <button onClick={onClickAge}>Update age</button>
        <TestContext.Provider value={{ username: "dave",
           userage }}>
            <UserAgeComp />
        </TestContext.Provider>
        <UserNameComp />
        <br/>
        <button onClick={onClickLocalState}>Update
           localstate</button>
         <label>{localState}</label>
    </React.Fragment>);
}
export default ContextTester;
```

This component will show two main things. One is the incremented value of localState, which is incremented by the onClickLocalState handler, and the other is the renders of the two child components, UserNameComp and UserAgeComp. Notice UserNameComp, for now, lives outside of the TestContext Context component, and therefore is not affected by TestContext changes. *This is very important to note.*

4. Now, if we click on Update age or Update localstate, you will see that the console.log statement in UserNameComp is never executed. That log statement was only executed one time when the page first loaded, which is what is supposed to happen since UserNameComp is using memo (memo only allows re-renders when props change). You should see only one set of logs in your **Console** tab (ignore the warnings, as we'll re-add our dependencies soon):

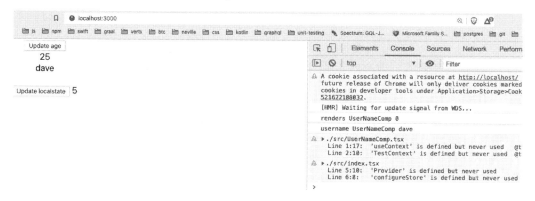

Figure 7.4 – Context render result

5. OK, so then now, let's force UserNameComp to use the username from our TestContext. So now, UserNameComp should look like this:

```
import React, { useContext, useRef } from 'react';
import { TestContext } from './ContextTester';

const UserNameComp = React.memo(() => {
    const renders = useRef(0);
    console.log("renders UserNameComp", renders.
        current++);

    const { username } = useContext(TestContext);
    console.log("username UserNameComp", username);
```

```
    return <div>
        {username}
    </div>
});

export default UserNameComp;
```

As you can see, now `UserNameComp` is using the `username` variable from the `TestContext` context. It never makes use of the `userage` variable and you will recall `username` has a hardcoded value so it never changes. So, theoretically, the `username` state of `UserNameComp` never changes and therefore should not cause a re-render. Now we need to place `UserNameComp` inside the `TestContext` tag as well. We are doing this because if a component needs to use a Context's state, it must be inside that Context's tag. Edit `ContextTester` like so:

```
const ContextTester = () => {
    const [userage, setUserage] = useState(20);
    const [localState, setLocalState] = useState(0);

    const onClickAge = () => {
        setUserage(
            userage + 1
        );
    }

    const onClickLocalState = () => {
        setLocalState(localState + 1);
    }

    return (<React.Fragment>
        <button onClick={onClickAge}>Update age</button>
        <TestContext.Provider value={{ username: "dave",
        userage
            }}>
            <UserAgeComp />
            <br/>
            <UserNameComp />
```

```
            </TestContext.Provider>


            <br/>
            <button onClick={onClickLocalState}>Update
              localstate</button>
             <label>{localState}</label>
        </React.Fragment>);
    }
```

Notice username is hardcoded to "dave" and never changes. And as you can see, UserNameComp was moved into TestContext.

6. Now, if we run this code and then click on the buttons several times, we should see something like this:

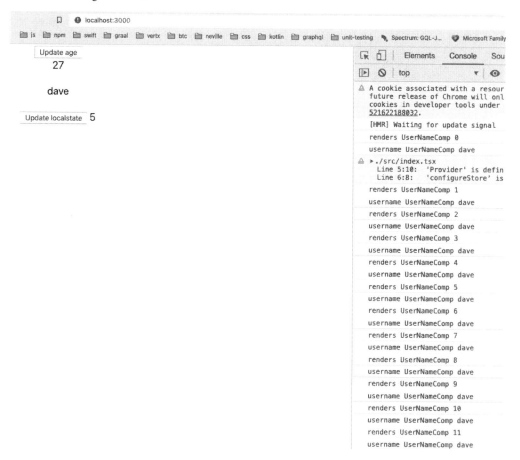

Figure 7.5 – Re-renders when using Context

As you can see, our `UserNameComp` component keeps getting re-rendered, even when we only change the `localState` variable. Why is this happening? `TestContext` is a component just like any other React component. And it does not use `memo`. So, when the parent component, `ContextTester`, gets re-rendered, it also gets re-rendered, which has a knock-on effect for any of its children. This is why `UserNameComp` keeps getting re-rendered although it never uses the `userage` variable.

So, as you can see, Context has some issues with its use, and it is my opinion that for large React applications, if you had to choose between the two, it would be better, albeit more complex, to use Redux.

In this section, we learned about Context basics. Context is relatively easy to learn and use. And for smaller projects, it works very well. However, due to its simple design, for more complex projects, a more sophisticated global state management system may be preferable.

# Learning about React Router

React Router is the most commonly used routing framework in React. It is relatively simple to learn and use. Routing, as we discovered in *Chapter 4, Learning Single-Page Application Concepts and How React Enables Them*, is ubiquitous in web development. It is a feature expected by users of web apps, so learning how to use it for our React app is a requirement.

Routes in React Router are simply React Router components that contain our own application components, and these components in turn represent our screens. In other words, a route in React Router is a logical representation of a virtual location (by virtual location, I mean a URL that is just a label and does not actually exist on any server). The "routers" in React Router act as parent components and our screen rendering components act as children. This is a bit difficult to understand by simply reading about it, so let's create an example:

1. Create a new React project under the `Chap7` folder in your terminal by calling this command:

```
create-react-app try-react-router --template typescript
```

2. Once it has completed creating our project, `cd` into the new `try-react-outer` folder, then let's add some packages:

```
npm i react-router-dom @types/react-router-dom
```

Note that React Router has several versions, so we will use the one for dom.

3.   Now, let's update our index.tsx file so that it includes the root React Router component in our app. Update index.tsx like this:

```
import React from "react";
import ReactDOM from "react-dom";
import "./index.css";
import App from "./App";
import * as serviceWorker from "./serviceWorker";
import { BrowserRouter } from "react-router-dom";

ReactDOM.render(
  <React.StrictMode>
    <BrowserRouter>
      <App />
    </BrowserRouter>
  </React.StrictMode>,
  document.getElementById("root")
);

// If you want your app to work offline and load faster,
// you can change
// unregister() to register() below. Note this comes with
// some pitfalls.
// Learn more about service workers:
// https://bit.ly/CRA-PWA
serviceWorker.unregister();
```

As you can see, we've added a new root component wrapping our App component, called BrowserRouter. BrowserRouter is a bit like Redux's Provider in the sense that it is a single parent component that provides various props to child components that are relevant to doing routing. We will go over these props soon, but for now, let's finish our setup of React Router.

4.  So now, since this tool is giving us routing, we must set up our individual routes. However, since routes ultimately are just containers for components that represent our screens, let's create two of those screens first. Create a file called `ScreenA.tsx` and add this code:

```
import React from "react";

const ScreenA = () => {
  return <div>ScreenA</div>;
};

export default ScreenA;
```

It's a simple component that displays **ScreenA** in the browser.

5.  Now, create a file called `ScreenB.tsx` and add this code:

```
import React from "react";

const ScreenB = () => {
  return <div>ScreenB</div>;
};

export default ScreenB;
```

Again, it is a simple component displaying **ScreenB** in the browser.

6.  Now, let's give our routes a try. Open `App.tsx` and add this code into it:

```
import React from "react";
import "./App.css";
import { Switch, Route } from "react-router-dom";
import ScreenA from "./ScreenA";
import ScreenB from "./ScreenB";

function App() {
  return (
    <Switch>
      <Route exact={true} path="/" component={ScreenA} />
      <Route path="/b" component={ScreenB} />
    </Switch>
```

```
    );
}
```

```
export default App;
```

So, what's happening here is that our app is rendering out a possible route based on several options. The `Switch` component indicates a parent that determines which route to choose by matching the browser URL to a path property of a `Route` instance. For example, if we start our app and go to the `"/"` route (the root of our application), we should see this:

Figure 7.6 – Routed to ScreenA

But if we were to go to route `"/b"`, we should see **ScreenB** instead, like this:

Figure 7.7 – Routed to ScreenB

So, as I stated at the beginning of the section, React Router routes are React components. This may seem weird as they have no visible UI. Nevertheless, they are parent components, except they render their children but have no UI of their own.

Now, we know that when our app first loads, it is the `index.tsx` file that runs before anything else. And this is also where the core React Router service lives. When this service encounters a URL, it looks through the set of routes defined in our `App.tsx` file and selects a matching route. Once the matching route is selected, that route's child component is rendered. So, for example, the route with `path="/b"` would render the `ScreenB` component.

Let's drill into the details of our routing code. If we look back at our routes, we should see that our first route has a property called exact. This tells React Router not to use regular expressions in determining a route match but instead to look for an exact match. Next, we see a property called path, which of course is supposed to be our URL path after the root domain. This path is by default a "contains" path, meaning that any URL that contains the same value as the path property will be accepted and the first matching route will be rendered, unless we included the exact property.

Now, you will also notice that we have a property called component, which of course refers to the child component that is to be rendered. And for simple scenarios, using this property works fine. But what if we need to pass some additional props to our component? React Router provides another property called render, which allows us to use what's called a **render property**.

A render property is a property that takes a function as its parameter. When the parent component does its rendering, it will call the render function internally. Let's look at an example:

1. Create a new component called ScreenC.tsx and add this code in it:

```tsx
import React, { FC } from "react";

interface ScreenCProps {
   message: string;
}

const ScreenC: FC<ScreenCProps> = ({ message }) => {
   return <div>{message}</div>;
};

export default ScreenC;
```

The ScreenC component is much like the other components. However, it also receives a prop called message and uses that as its display. Let's see how we pass this prop in via our render property of React Router.

2.  Now let's update our App component and add this new component as a route:

```
import React from "react";
import "./App.css";
import { Switch, Route } from "react-router-dom";
import ScreenA from "./ScreenA";
import ScreenB from "./ScreenB";
import ScreenC from "./ScreenC";

function App() {
  const renderScreenC = (props: any) => {
    console.log("ScreenC props", props);
    return <ScreenC {...props} message="This is Screen C"
      />;
  };

  return (
    <Switch>
      <Route exact={true} path="/" component={ScreenA} />
      <Route path="/b" component={ScreenB} />
      <Route path="/c" render={renderScreenC} />
    </Switch>
  );
}

export default App;
```

So, as you can see, we've created a function, renderScreenC, and it takes props as a parameter and then passes it to the ScreenC component and then returns that component. Along with passing props, we also have it passing the string "This is Screen C" into the message property. If we had tried to use the component property of Route, there would be no way to pass the message property and so we are using the render property instead.

3.  Next, we add a new `Route` that uses the `render` property and pass it the `renderScreenC` function. If we go to the `"/c"` path, we see basically the same thing as the other screens, but with our message, **This is Screen C**:

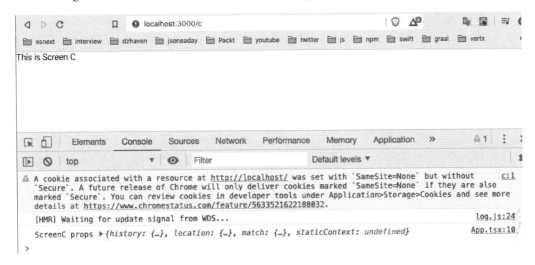

Figure 7.8 – Routed to ScreenC

But also, I've included a log of the props that are being passed into the component and we can see things such as `history`, `location`, and `match` members being included. You will recall our render function, `renderScreenC`, had a signature of `(props:any) => { ... }`. That `props` parameter is being passed in by our `Route` component from the React Router service. We'll take a look at these routing properties later.

So, now we know how to get better control of our screen component renders by using the `render` property, but a typical URL can also have parameters that pass data to the screen. Let's look at how to do this with React Router:

1.  Let's update our `Route` for `ScreenC` like this:

    ```
    <Route path="/c/:userid" render={renderScreenC} />
    ```

    The `userid` field is now a parameter on the URL.

2.  Now let's update our `ScreenC` component to accept Route props and handle our new `userid` parameter field:

    ```
    import React, { FC } from "react";

    interface ScreenCProps {
    ```

```
  message: string;
  history: any;
  match: any;
}


const ScreenC: FC<ScreenCProps> = (props) => {
  return (
    <div>
      <div>{"Your id is " + props.match.params.userid}
      </div>
      <div>{props.message}</div>
    </div>
  );
};


export default ScreenC;
```

We've stopped using object destructuring in order to get every `props` member without having to write them out. And now our component takes the `history` and `match` props members as its own props and it is also handling the `userid` field by using the `match.params.userid` property. Since the `history` object already contains `location` as a member, we did not add that member to our `ScreenCProps` interface. The screen should look like this:

Figure 7.9 – Routed to ScreenC with a parameter

As you can see, our `userid` parameter of value **1** is shown.

OK, so now we've used React Router more realistically, but there's another important characteristic to note about how React Router works. React Router acts basically like a stack of URLs. In other words, when a user visits the URLs of a site, they do so in a linear fashion. They go to A, then B, and maybe back to A, then C, and so on. And the result of this is that the browser history of a user can be saved as a stack, where you can go forward to a new URL or backward to a previously visited one. This characteristic of browser behavior is mostly maintained in React Router's `history` object.

So, again, let's update our code and take a look at some of the capabilities provided by the `history` object:

1. Update the `ScreenC` component like this:

```
import React, { FC, useEffect } from "react";

interface ScreenCProps {
  message: string;
  history: any;
  match: any;
}

const ScreenC: FC<ScreenCProps> = (props) => {
  useEffect(() => {
    setTimeout(() => {
      props.history.push("/");
    }, 3000);
  });

  return (
    <div>
      <div>{"Your id is " + props.match.params.userid}
        </div>
      <div>{props.message}</div>
    </div>
  );
};

export default ScreenC;
```

As you can see, we introduced `useEffect` and in this function, we are waiting 3 seconds with a timer and then by using the `history.push` function, we are redirecting our URL to `"/"`, which is rendered by the `ScreenA` component.

2.  Let's use another function inside of the `history` object. Update `ScreenC` again, like this:

```tsx
import React, { FC } from "react";

interface ScreenCProps {
  message: string;
  history: any;
  match: any;
}

const ScreenC: FC<ScreenCProps> = (props) => {
  const onClickGoback = () => {
    props.history.goBack();
  };

  return (
    <div>
      <div>{"Your id is " + props.match.params.userid}
      </div>
      <div>{props.message}</div>
      <div>
        <button onClick={onClickGoback}>Go back</button>
      </div>
    </div>
  );
};

export default ScreenC;
```

So, this time, we've created a button that will try and go back to the previous URL by using the `history.goBack` function. In order to test this code, we need to open the web page to URL `localhost:3000/b` first and then go to URL `localhost:3000/c/2`. Your screen should then look like this:

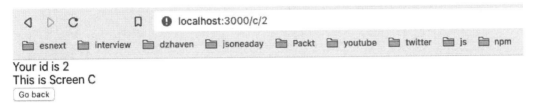

Figure 7.10 – Routed to ScreenC with a Go back button

3. You can see we have a button called **Go back**. If you click it, you will go back to the original `"/b"` route.

4. One more thing to review: React Router recently added the Hooks capability. So, we no longer have to pass down route properties using a child's props; we can just use Hooks. Here's what it looks like (i've kept the non-Hooks as comments for your convenience):

```
import React, { FC } from "react";
import { useHistory, useParams } from "react-router-dom";
```

Here, we have our new `useHistory` and `useParams` Hooks imports:

```
interface ScreenCProps {
    message: string;
    history: any;
    match: any;
}
const ScreenC: FC<ScreenCProps> = (props) => {
    // useEffect(() => {
    //   setTimeout(() => {
    //     props.history.push("/");
    //   }, 3000);
    // });
    const history = useHistory();
    const { userid } = useParams();
```

Here, we call our `useHistory` and `useParams` Hooks to get `history` and the `userid` URL parameter:

```
const onClickGoback = () => {
    // props.history.goBack();
    history.goBack();
};


return (
    <div>
        {/* <div>{"Your id is " + props.match.params.
           userid}</div>
        */}
        <div>{"Your id is " + userid}</div>
        <div>{props.message}</div>
        <div>
            <button onClick={onClickGoback}>Go back</button>
        </div>
    </div>
    );
};
export default ScreenC;
```

And here, we use the Hooks objects to display the same messages as before. It's quite easy and nice to use.

There are of course more capabilities of the `history` object and React Router overall, but this is a good introduction to those capabilities and we will use more of these features as we begin to build our app in the coming chapters.

Routing is a vital part of web development. Routes help users know where they are in the application and can provide a sense of context. Routing also helps us as developers structure the logical sections of our application and group relevant items together. React Router allows us to do all these things by providing many programmatic features that allow us to build sophisticated routing into our applications.

# Summary

This chapter covered some of the most important React-related frameworks. Redux is a sophisticated tool for managing global application state. React Router provides client-side URL management that looks and feels like classic-style web URLs.

Working with high-quality technologies such as Redux and React Router will help us to write better code. And this in turn will help us give our users the best experience.

We have reached the end of *Part 2*, which focused on client-side technologies. We will now begin learning about server-side technologies in *Part 3*.

# Section 3: Understanding Web Service Development Using Express and GraphQL

In this section, we will learn what a web service does and understand how Express and GraphQL can help us build high-performance services.

This section comprises of the following chapters:

# 8

# Learning Server-Side Development with Node.js and Express

In this chapter, we'll learn about Node and Express. We'll understand how Node can help us create performant web services. We'll also understand what the relationship between Node and Express is and how we can use them together to build our web API.

In this chapter, we're going to cover the following main topics:

- Understanding how Node works
- Learning Node's capabilities
- Understanding how Express improves Node development
- Learning Express's capabilities
- Creating a web API with Express

# Technical requirements

You should have a basic understanding of web development with JavaScript. We will once again be using Node and **Visual Studio Code** (**VSC**).

The GitHub repository is again at `https://github.com/PacktPublishing/Full-Stack-React-TypeScript-and-Node`. Use the code in the `Chap8` folder.

To set up this chapter's code folder, go to your local `HandsOnTypescript` folder and create a new folder called `Chap8`.

# Understanding how Node works

Node is one of the world's most popular JavaScript frameworks. It is used as the core technology for millions of websites. The reasons for this are many. It is relatively easy to code for. It is also very fast, and when used with things such as clustering and worker threads, it is very scalable. Also, since it uses JavaScript, it allows creating a full-stack application, front to back, using only a single language. All of these characteristics make Node a terrific choice if you are targeting the web. In this section, we will explore Node's architecture and how it achieves its strong performance.

To start, it is important to realize that Node is not a server-specific framework. It is actually a general-use runtime environment, and not just a web server. Node provides JavaScript with capabilities it normally does not have, such as the ability to access the filesystem and accept incoming network connections.

To explain how Node works, let's use the web browser as an analogy. The browser is also a runtime environment for our JavaScript code (as well as HTML and CSS). The browser works by having a core JavaScript engine that provides base-level JavaScript language features. This includes a language interpreter that reads our code for valid JavaScript and a virtual machine that runs our code across differing devices.

Above this core, the browser provides a secure memory container for apps to run on, the sandbox. But it also provides additional JavaScript capabilities generally known as the web API (not the server-side kind but at the browser level). The web API augments the base JavaScript engine, providing things such as **Document Object Model** (**DOM**) access so that JavaScript code can access the HTML document and manipulate it. It provides calls such as fetch that allow asynchronous network calls to other machines, as well as WebGL for graphics and many more. You can see a complete list here: `https://developer.mozilla.org/en-US/docs/Web/API`.

These features are provided as extras, above and beyond what JavaScript comes with "out of the box," which, if you think about it, does make sense since, at its core, JavaScript is just a language and therefore not specific to any particular platform, even the web.

Node follows a similar model to the browser as it also uses a core JavaScript engine (the V8 engine from Google Chrome) and provides a runtime container for our code to run in. However, since it is not a browser, it provides different additional capabilities that are not so focused on a graphical display.

So then, what is Node? Node is a general-use runtime environment that is focused on high performance and scalability. You can build many types of applications with Node, including computer management scripts and terminal programs. But Node's scaling capabilities make it well suited as a web server as well.

Node has many features that make it very capable as a programming runtime, but at its heart is **libuv**. Libuv is a Node service written in C that interfaces with the operating system kernel and provides asynchronous input/output facilities. In order to make timely access to these services, libuv uses something called an event loop, which we'll explain shortly, to process these tasks. On top of libuv, Node has an add-ons system, which is analogous to Chrome's extensions. It allows developers to extend Node using C++ and add high-performance features that do not exist by default. Also, in order to allow developers to keep using JavaScript to call into C++, a JavaScript-to-C++ binding system is available called Addons. Let's explore libuv and the event loop a bit more.

## Event loop

At the heart of Node are libuv and the event loop. This is the main feature of Node that makes it scale. Libuv's primary job is to provide access to asynchronous **input/output (I/O)** capabilities of the underlying operating system (Node supports Linux, macOS, and Windows). However, this is not always possible, so it also possesses a thread pool that can be used to make synchronous tasks effectively asynchronous by running them inside a thread. However, the core driver of Node scalability is asynchronous I/O, not threads. The ability to run timers, allow network connections, use operating system sockets, and access the filesystem comes from libuv.

So then, what is the event loop? The event loop is a task runner in libuv, similar to the Chrome event loop, that runs asynchronous callback tasks iteratively. At a high level, here's how it works.

When certain asynchronous tasks are triggered, they get executed by the event loop. The event loop does processing in phases or sets. As shown in the following diagram, it first runs **timers**, and if any timer callbacks are already queued, it executes them in sequence (if not, it comes back later, and if timers have completed, it queues their callbacks). Then, it handles any **pending callbacks** (callbacks set by the operating system – for example, TCP errors), and so on, down the line of phases. Note that tasks are asynchronous in nature if they are being executed by libuv, but the callbacks themselves may not be. Therefore, it is possible to block the event loop as it will not trigger the next callback in the queue until the present one returns. Here's a diagram showing roughly how this works:

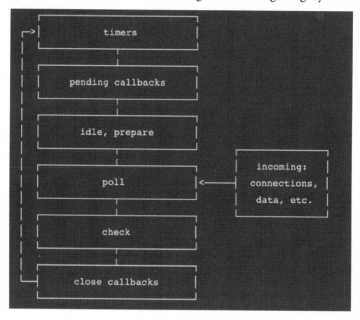

Figure 8.1 – Node event loop from the Node documentation

You can also consider phases as categories of asynchronous tasks and their callbacks.

All frameworks have their strengths and weaknesses. Node's main strength lies in asynchronous I/O-bound scalability. Therefore, Node is best used for highly concurrent workloads that require many simultaneous connections. In later versions of Node, starting at 10.5, the Node team did introduce worker threads to add multithreading capability for running CPU-bound tasks, which are tasks that are mostly about performing long-running computations. However, this is not Node's main strength. For computation-heavy workloads, there are probably better options. But since our priority with Node is to create a highly scalable API for our React frontend, Node works nicely for our needs.

In the next section, we'll start digging deeper into Node by writing code in Node without using any wrapper libraries, such as Express or Koa. This will not only give us a clearer understanding of how the Node core works, but it will also help us to better understand the differences between Node and Express.

# Learning Node's capabilities

In the previous section, we gave a high-level conceptual overview of what Node is and why it scales so well. In this section, we will begin making use of this scalability by writing code with Node. We'll install Node, set up a project, and start exploring the Node API.

## Installing Node

Before we can write code with Node, we need to install it. To follow along, in the previous chapters, you may have already done this, but let's refresh our memory of how to install it again as Node gets updated quite frequently:

1.  Go to `https://nodejs.org`. The following screenshot shows this page as of the time of writing this book:

Node.js® is a JavaScript runtime built on Chrome's V8 JavaScript engine.

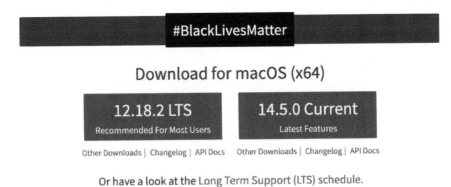

Figure 8.2 – Node website

For production use, you may want to go down the more conservative route and use the **Long-Term Support (LTS)** version, as shown, but since we want to learn about the latest version for this book, let's select the **Current** version.

> **Note**
>
> In general, later versions of Node will be slightly faster and have more security and bug fixes. However, it is possible that new issues have been introduced, so you should be careful when upgrading a production server.

By installing Node, we get the runtime as well as the latest npm package manager.

2. Once you click on your selected version, you will be asked to save an install package that matches your operating system. Save the package and then start it. You should then see a screen like the following:

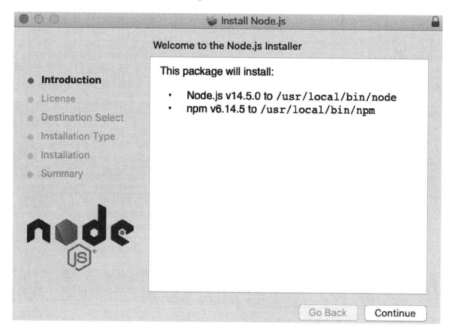

Figure 8.3 – Node setup

Complete the installation as guided by the setup window.

Great, now we have installed or updated our Node runtime and npm package manager. As mentioned previously, Node is not just a server framework but also a complete runtime environment that allows you to write a great variety of different applications. For example, Node has a command-line interface called REPL. If you open your command line or terminal and type node, you will see that it converts to accept JavaScript commands, like this:

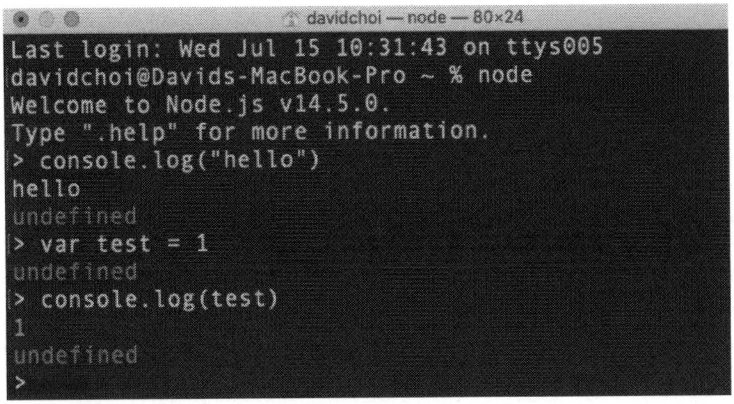

Figure 8.4 – Node REPL

We will not be using REPL in this book, but I included it here so that you are aware that it exists and may be of use for your future projects. You can learn more about REPL in the official documentation, `https://nodejs.org/api/repl.html#repl_design_ and_features`. Also, in case you're curious, `undefined` is returned because each command has not returned anything and in JavaScript, that is always `undefined`.

Okay, so now, let's create our first Node application and explore some more of Node's features:

1.  Open VSCode, and then open the terminal to the `Chap8` folder.

2.  Then, create a new folder called `try-node` in the `Chap8` folder.

3.  Now, create a file called `app.js`. Let's avoid TypeScript for now so that we can keep things simple.

4.  Add a simple console message to `app.js`, like so:

```
console.log("hello world");
```

Then, run it:

```
node app.js
```

You should see the following output:

Figure 8.5 – Run app.js

Not a particularly useful application, but nevertheless, as you can see, Node is running standard JavaScript code. Now, let's do something more useful. Let's access the filesystem using the following steps:

1.  In the same `app.js` file, delete the console message and enter the following code:

    ```
    const fs = require("fs");
    ```

    You may be confused by this code since it's not the current style of doing imports. But I wanted to include it here since a great deal of older Node code still uses this CommonJS-style syntax for importing dependencies. So, you should be aware of it.

2.  Next, write the following code to create a file and then read its contents:

    ```
    fs.writeFile("test.txt", "Hello World", () => {
      fs.readFile("test.txt", "utf8", (err, msg) => {
        console.log(msg);
      });
    });
    ```

    If you run this code, you will see the following output and a file called `test.txt` created in your `try-node` folder:

Figure 8.6 – app.js output

The syntax of `fs` is a bit cumbersome because it uses the older callback style. Node was created long before JavaScript received Promises and `async await`, and therefore some calls still use the callback style of asynchrony. However, there is a newer, Promise-enabled version of `fs` – which is, therefore, `async await`-capable – that can be used instead. Its syntax looks like this:

```
const fs = require("fs/promises");

(async function () {
  await fs.writeFile("test-promise.txt", "Hello
    Promises");
  const readTxt = await fs.readFile("test-promise.txt",
    "utf-8");
```

```
    console.log(readTxt);
})();
```

Notice we are using an IIFE to allow us to make a top-level await call.

If you are on an older version of Node, `fs/Promises` became stable after version 11, so you can use a tool called `promisify` to wrap callback-style calls to get them to work in an `async await` style.

Nevertheless, it is important that you are aware of the older callback-style calls since this is historically how Node code was written and there is probably a great deal of Node code that remains in this style today.

3.  We saw, at the top of our code, that we used `require` to do our `fs` import. Let's switch to the newer import syntax. We'll need to do two things: change the file extension from `.js` to `.mjs` and update the `require` statement like this:

```
import fs from "fs";
```

If you run `app.mjs` again, you will see that it still works. We could set the configuration flag inside of `package.json` "type" : "module" instead, but for this example app, we did not use npm. Additionally, if we set this flag globally, we can no longer use `require`. This can be an issue as some older npm dependencies still use `require` for importing.

> **Note**
> There is an older command-line flag called `--experimental-modules` that allows the use of `import`, but it is now deprecated and should be avoided for newer versions of Node.

# Creating a simple Node server

We learned that Node is based on some older JavaScript technologies, such as callbacks and CommonJS. Node was created before JavaScript Promises and the newer versions of JavaScript, such as ES6 and beyond. Nevertheless, Node still works well, continues to be updated, and later, when we add additional libraries, we'll be able to use `async await` and Promises in most cases.

Now, let's work on a more realistic Node server example. We'll create a new project with npm:

1.  On the root of Chap8, create a new folder called node-server.

2.  Cd into the node-server folder and initialize npm with the following command:

    ```
    npm init
    ```

3.  Let's call our package name node-server and accept defaults for the other package.json attributes.

4.  Create a new file on the root called server.mjs and add the following code:

    ```
    import http from "http";
    ```

    Don't worry, we'll start using TypeScript soon. Right now, let's keep things simple so that we can focus on learning Node.

5.  We have imported the http library from the Node core. We then use createServer in order to create a server object. Notice that our createServer function takes a function as an argument with two parameters. The parameters, req and res, are of the Request and Response type, respectively. A Request object will have all the members relevant to the request that was made by our users and the response allows us to modify our response before sending it back out.

    At the end of our createServer handler function, we are explicitly ending our calls by using res.end and returning text. If we did not send end, our response would never complete and nothing would appear on the browser:

    ```
    const server = http.createServer((req, res) => {
        console.log(req);
        res.end("hello world");
    });
    ```

6.  Finally, we use our new server object to wait and listen for new requests using the listen function with a port number and a callback function that prints that the server has started:

    ```
    const port = 8000;
    server.listen(port, () => {
        console.log(`Server started on port ${port}`);
    });
    ```

7. Run this code by executing our `server.mjs` script (make sure to use the correct extension of `.mjs`):

```
node server.mjs
```

Please remember, as we work, that there is no auto-reload function currently. So, upon code changes, we will have to do a stop and restart manually. We'll add this later as we continue adding more features to our projects.

8. If you open your browser to `http://localhost:8000`, you should see **hello world** printed in your browser and the following in your console:

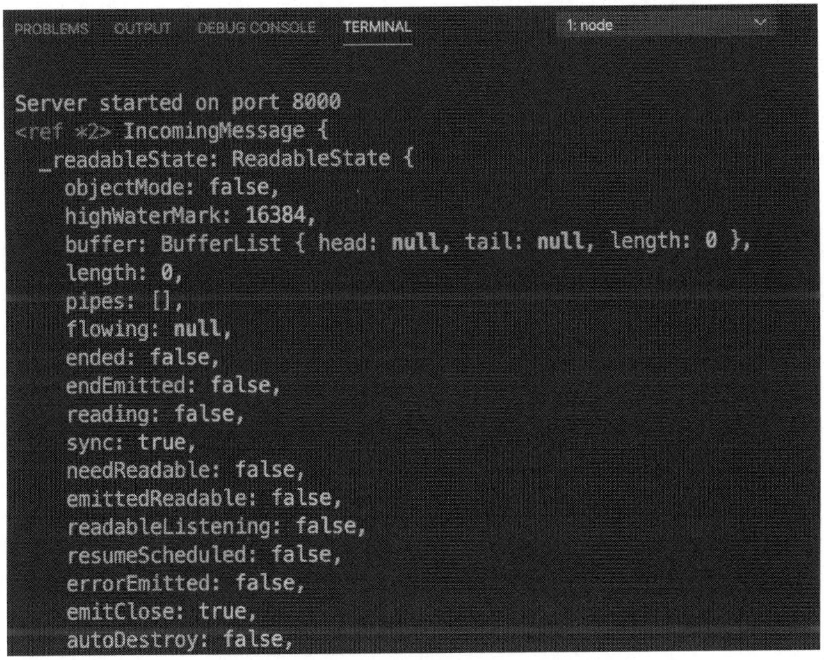

Figure 8.7 – First node server run

The terminal is showing the `req` object and its members. We'll of course go over `Request` and `Response` in more detail soon.

Another interesting thing is that no matter what URL we give, it always returns the same **hello world** text. This is because we have not implemented any route handling. Handling routes is another item we must learn in order to use Node properly.

You can keep refreshing your browser and the server will keep responding with **hello world**. As you can see, the server remains up no matter how many requests we send it, as opposed to returning and ending like a typical script program. This is because the event loop, the core of Node, is a kind of infinite loop that will keep waiting for new tasks and processing them dutifully.

Congratulations, you've now run your first Node server! Humble beginnings for sure, but nevertheless, you can now make real browser calls and our server will respond. So, you are well on your way.

## Request and Response

When a request from a browser gets to the server, all server frameworks will generally have two objects: `Request` and `Response`. These two objects represent the relevant data for the request that came from the browser and the response that will be returned to it. Let's take a look at these objects from the browser to see what they're made of. Reload your browser but this time with the Chrome dev tools open on the `Network` tab:

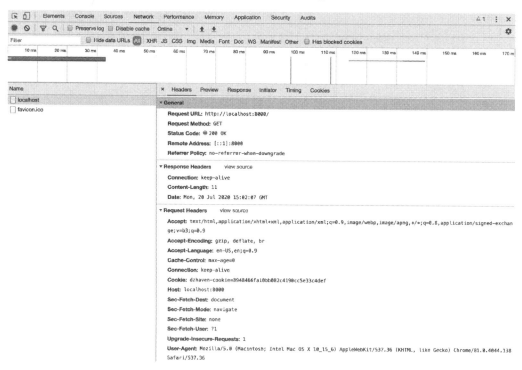

Figure 8.8 – Chrome dev tools Network tab

This view is only from the browser's perspective and in Node, there's a lot more information in these objects. However, we need to first understand what a web request is made of before we can try and create any real web server. So, let's list out some of the more important items and describe what they mean.

## Request URL

Obviously, this represents the complete URL path sent to the server. But the reason the server needs to know the complete path is that a lot of additional information can often be sent in the URL. For example, if our URL was `http://localhost:8000/home?userid=1`, there's actually a fair amount of information here. First, we tell our server that we're looking for either a web page or API data within the `home` subdirectory. This allows the server to tailor its returned response with only an HTML page or data specific to that URL. Additionally, we've passed a parameter called `userid` (parameters start after the question mark and multiple parameters can be separated by the & symbol), which can be used by the server to provide unique data in the request.

## Request method

A request method represents what's called an HTTP verb. A verb is simply a description that tells the server what action the client is intending to do. The default verb is GET, which means, as the name indicates, the browser would like to read some data. The other verbs are POST, which indicates creation or insertion, PUT, which indicates updating, and then DELETE, indicating deletion. In *Chapter 9, What Is GraphQL?*, we'll see that GraphQL only uses the POST method, but this isn't actually an error as the verbs are not hard rules but more like guidelines. One additional thing to note is that when using GET, any parameters needed will be provided in the URL, as the request URL bullet item example showed. However, for POST, the parameters are provided in the body of the request. We'll go over these differences more in the *Learning Express capabilities* section.

## Status code

All web requests will return these codes to indicate the result of the request. For example, a status of 200 indicates success. I won't list all of them here, but we should know some of the most common ones, as it can sometimes help in debugging:

| Error Code | Description |
| --- | --- |
| 201 Created | Indicates successful creation of something. |
| 400 Bad Request | Indicates the request, as sent by browser, has an issue or error in it. |
| 401 Unauthorized | Indicates a permission failure of the specified URL. |
| 403 Forbidden | Generally, indicates the URL is not available to public. |
| 404 Not Found | The given URL was not found. |
| 500 Internal Server Error | An exception or other error occurred on the server during processing. |
| 502 Bad Gateway | Strange status label, but indicates that the requesting server was a proxy for another server, but that upstream server returned an invalid response. |
| 503 Service Unavailable | Usually indicates a temporary situation that makes the server unable to respond to requests. |

Figure 8.9 – Error codes

## Headers

Headers provide additional information that acts as descriptions or metadata. As shown, there are multiple types of headers: general, request, response, and entity. Again, I won't go over all of them, but there are a few we should be familiar with. Here are the request headers:

| Request Header | Description |
| --- | --- |
| User-Agent | The browser and OS that is sending the request. |
| Referrer | The URL a user was on before linking to the current URL. |
| Cookie | Cookies are small text files that contain information about a user and their session specific to the current website. The server can add whatever they like into a cookie but usually there is some sort of session identifier and possibly a user identifying token. |
| Content-Type | The media type of the body of the request. For example, for POST and PUT it would be "application/json", which indicates that json string is in the body. |

Figure 8.10 – Request headers

And here are the response headers:

| Response Header | Description |
| --- | --- |
| Access-Control-Allow-Origin | Used with CORS to allow a different URL when making requests. An asterisk, *, allows any URL. |
| Allow | Indicates which HTTP verbs are allowed. |

Figure 8.11 – Response headers

This is, of course, dry information. However, knowing what's involved in making these requests and responses helps us better understand how the web works and therefore write better web apps. Let's look more deeply now at routing.

# Routing

Routing is in some sense a lot like passing parameters to a server. When the server sees a specific route, it will know that the response needs to be a certain way. The response could be returning some specific data or writing data to a database, but having routes helps us manage how our server should behave for each request.

Let's do some route handling in Node:

1.  Update the `server` object in the `server.mjs` file in the `node-server` project, like this:

```
const server = http.createServer((req, res) => {
    if (req.url === "/") {
        res.end("hello world");
    } else if (req.url === "/a") {
        res.end("welcome to route a");
    } else if (req.url === "/b") {
        res.end("welcome to route b");
    } else {
        res.end("good bye");
    }
});
```

As you can see, we take the `req.url` field and compare it to several URLs. For each one that matches, we end our response with some unique text.

2. Run the server again and try each route. For example, if your route is `http://localhost:8000/a`, then you should see this:

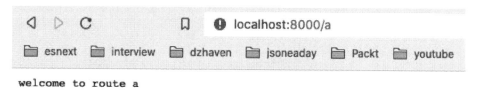

welcome to route a

Figure 8.12 – Route /a

3. Okay, now let's see what happens if we receive a POST request. Update your `createServer` function like this:

```
const server = http.createServer((req, res) => {
  if (req.url === "/") {
    res.end("hello world");
  } else if (req.url === "/a") {
    res.end("welcome to route a");
  } else if (req.url === "/b") {
    res.end("welcome to route b");
  } else if (req.url === "/c" && req.method === "POST") {
    let body = [];
    req.on("data", (chunk) => {
      body.push(chunk);
    });
    req.on("end", () => {
      const params = Buffer.concat(body);
      console.log("body", params.toString());
      res.end(`You submitted these parameters:
        ${params.toString()}`);
    });
  } else {
    res.end("good bye");
  }
});
```

As you can see, we added another if else statement with the /c route and the POST method type. You may be surprised to see that in order to get the posted data from our call, we need to handle the data event and then the end event so that we can return the call.

Let me explain what this is about. Node is very low level, meaning it does not hide its intricate details to make things easier, in order to be more performant. So, when a request is made and some information is being sent to the server, this data will be sent as a stream. This simply means the data is not sent in one shot, but in pieces. Node does not hide this fact from the developer and uses an event system to receive the data in chunks, since it's not clear upfront how much data is coming in. Then, once this data is finished being received, that's when the end event triggers.

In this sample, the data event is used to aggregate our data into an array. Then, the end event is used to put that array into a memory buffer, from which it can then be processed as a whole. In our case, it's just JSON, so we convert to a string.

4. To test this, let's submit a POST request using curl. curl is just a command-line tool that allows us to make web server requests without using a browser. It's great for testing. Execute the following code in your terminal (if you're on Windows, you may need to install curl first; on macOS, it should already be there):

```
curl --header "Content-Type: application/json" --request
POST --data '{"userid":"1","message":"hello"}' "http://
localhost:8000/c"
```

You should get the following back:

```
davidchoi@Davids-MacBook-Pro ~ % curl --header "Content-Type: application/json" --
request POST --data '{"userid":"1","message":"hello"}' "http://localhost:8000/c"
You submitted these parameters: {"userid":"1","message":"hello"}
```

Figure 8.13 – Result of curl POST

Clearly, all of this works but is not ideal from a development productivity perspective. We would not want 30 of these if else statements in a single createServer function. It's difficult to read and maintain. We'll see how Express helps us avoid these types of issues by providing extra wrappers on top of Node to make development faster and more reliable. We'll see this in the *Understanding how Express improves Node development* section. Let's learn about some tools to help our Node coding first.

# Debugging

As we saw with React, a debugger is a very important tool to help in troubleshooting code. In the case of Node, we cannot use a browser tool, of course, but VSCode does have a built-in debugger that will allow us to break on code and view values. Let's take a look at that as we'll also use it with Express:

1.  Click on the debugger icon in VSCode and you'll see the following screen. In the current version, as of the time of writing, it looks like this:

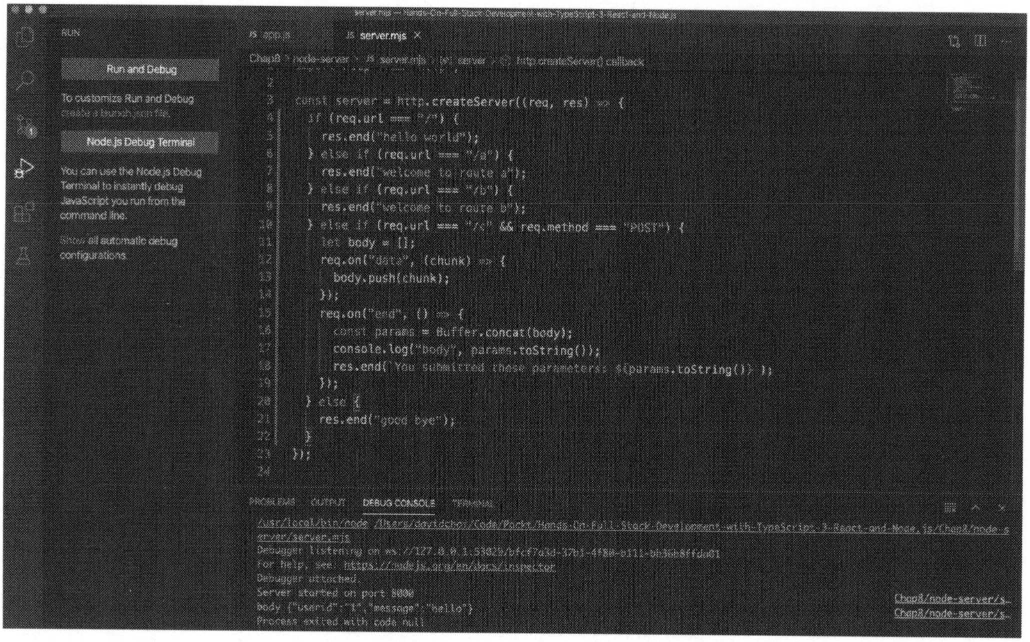

Figure 8.14 – The VSCode debugger menu

The first button runs the debugger and the second shows the debugger version of the terminal. When running the debugger, you generally want to be looking at the debugger console as it can show errors that happen at runtime.

2.  When running the VSCode debugger, you want to click on the **Run and Debug** button. Then, you will see the dropdown shown in the following screenshot. Select **Node.js** and that will start your Node session as a debug session. Notice the continue, pause, restart, and stop buttons at the upper right. Note also that running in debug mode using VSCode is a completely different run of Node from the running of Node using the `npm start` command:

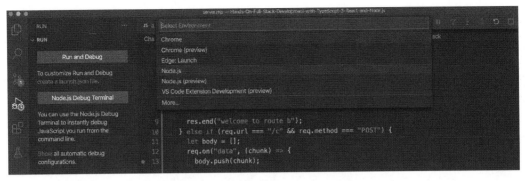

Figure 8.15 – Node.js debugger selection

3.  Once you start your debugger, if you have set a breakpoint by clicking next to any
    line number, you will be able to have the code pause there. Then, you can view
    values that are relevant to that scope:

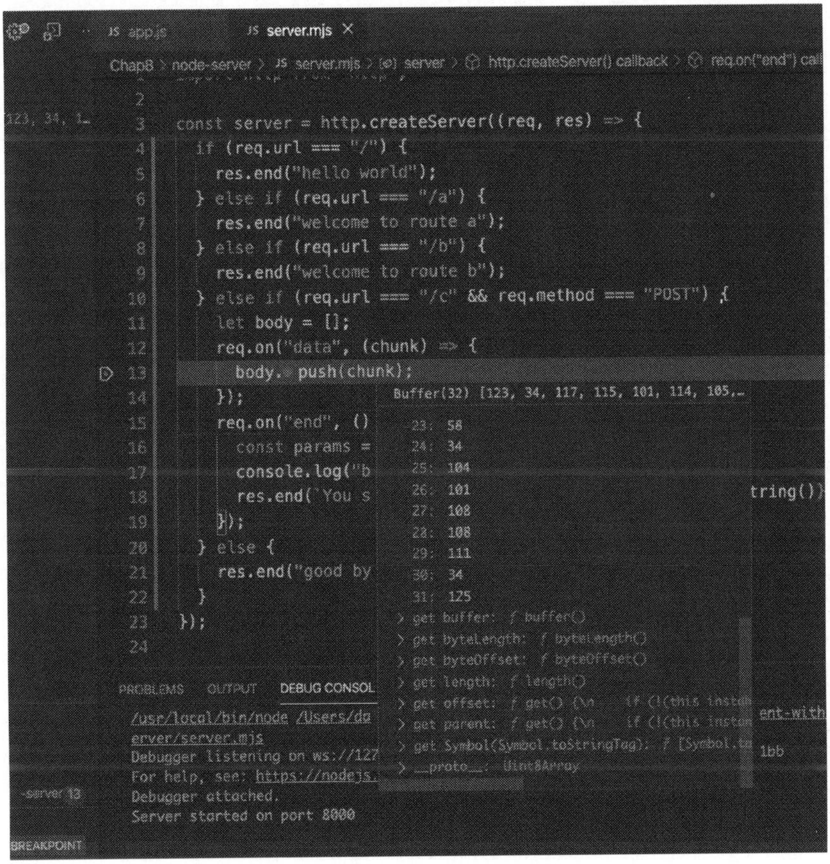

Figure 8.16 – Break on line view

As you can see, we have set a breakpoint on line 13 within the `data` event and are able to view the current chunk. Hit the continue button or click *F5* to continue running the program.

4.  Hovering over values while on a breakpoint is useful but not the only way to help debug our app. We can also use the debugger screens to help us understand what our values are at the moment we have stopped at a breakpoint. Take a look at the following screenshot:

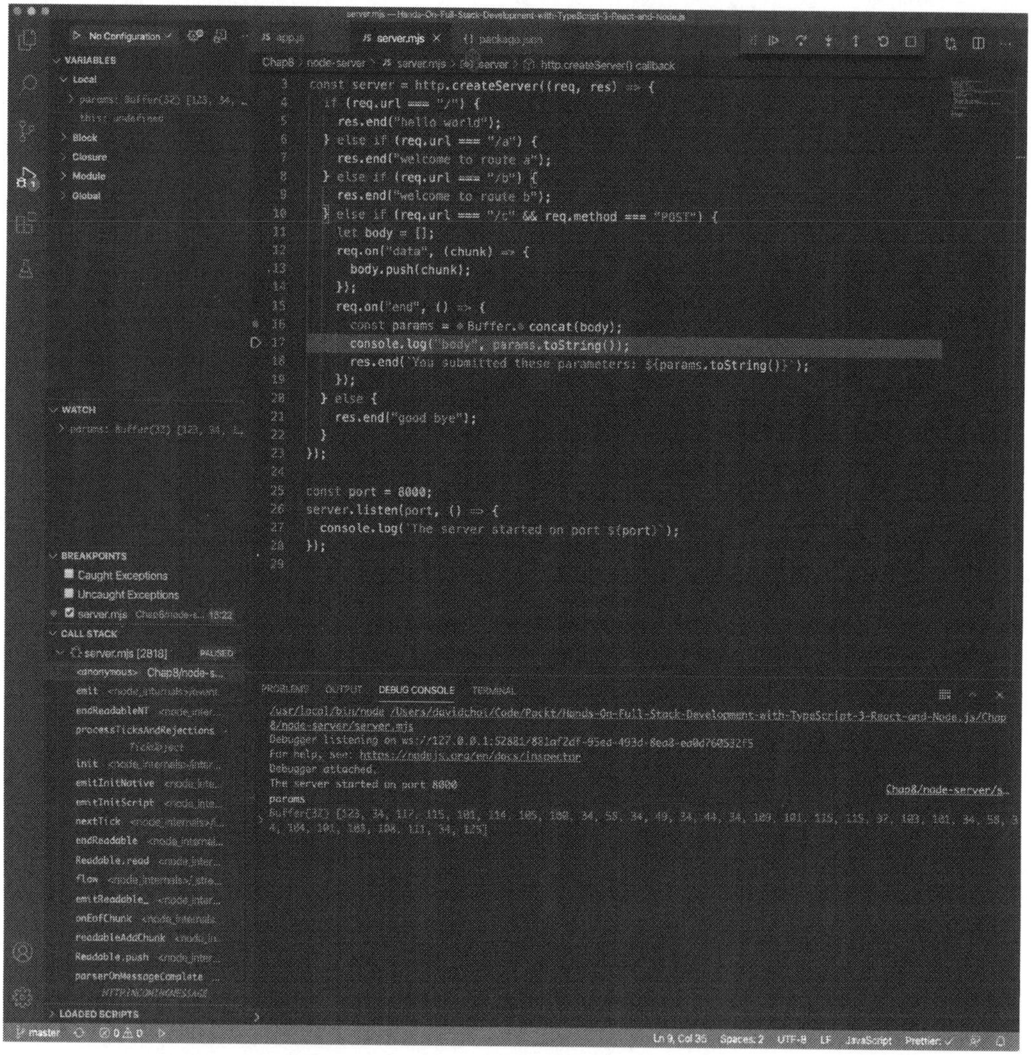

Figure 8.17 – Debug windows full view

Look at our breakpoint, toward the middle of the screenshot. We can see that we have broken inside of the end event handler scope. Let's look at some of the features listed:

- Starting with the upper-left menu, called **VARIABLES**, we can see the **Local** section and two variables that exist in our currently stopped-on code scope: params and this. Again, we are looking at the **Local** scope, which right now is the event handler for the end event, and that's why we only have those two variables.

- Near the middle left, on the **WATCH** menu, we see a single variable called params, which I added. There is a plus sign in this section that allows us to add variables that we are interested in and when they come into scope, the current value will show there.

- Then, toward the bottom left, we see **CALL STACK**. The call stack is the list of calls that our program is running. The list will show in reverse order, with the last command on top. Often, many of these calls will be code from either Node or some other framework we did not write ourselves.

- Then, at the bottom right, we have our **DEBUG CONSOLE** tab, which displays any logs or errors while the app is running. Notice that at the bottom of this tab, we can also type in code to see results. For example, I typed the params variable and its buffer was displayed.

- Finally, at the upper right, we see the debug continuation buttons. The first button on the left is the continue button, which continues running our app from the last breakpoint. Next is the step over button, which will go to the immediate next line and stop there. Next is the step into button, which will take you inside the definition of a function or class as it runs. Then, there's the step out button, which will bring you out and back into the parent caller. The last, square button stops our app completely.

That was a quick introduction to the VSCode debugger. We will be using more of it as we get into Express, and then later with GraphQL.

Now, as you've seen, having to manually restart the Node service every time we make any changes is a bit of a pain and slows down development. So, let's use a tool called nodemon, which will automatically restart our Node server whenever we save script changes:

1. Install nodemon globally by running the following command:

```
npm i nodemon -g
```

This installs `nodemon` to our entire system. Installing it globally allows all apps to run `nodemon` without needing to keep installing it. Note that on macOS and Linux, you may need to prefix this command with `sudo`, which will elevate your rights so that you can install it globally.

2. Now, we want to start it upon app start. Update the `package.json` file by finding the `"scripts"` section and adding a sub-field called `"start"`, and then add the following command to it:

```
nodemon server.mjs
```

Your `package.json` `"scripts"` section should look like this now:

```
"scripts": {
    "test": "echo \"Error: no test specified\" && exit 1",
    "start": "nodemon server.mjs"
},
```

Figure 8.18 – package.json "scripts" section

3. Now, run the new script using the following command:

```
npm start
```

Note that normally, when running the npm command, you need to run `npm run <file name>`. However, for `start` scripts, we can skip the `run` sub-command.

You should see the app start up as usual.

4. Now that the app is running, let's try changing and then saving the `server.mjs` file. Change the string inside the `listen` function to be `` `The server started on port ${port}` ``. Once you save this change, you should see Node restart and the new text showing on the terminal.

5. The settings within `package.json` do not affect our VSCode debugger. So, to set auto-restart, we'll need to set that up as well. Go to your debugger menu again and click the **create a launch.json file** button, as shown here:

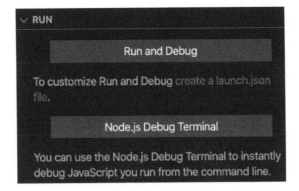

Figure 8.19 – Creating a new launch.json file

If you click this button, you will then see the `launch.json` file in the `.vscode` folder in the root of the GitHub repository (not the root of the project). It should contain the following configurations (note that this one file can contain multiple configurations):

```
{
    // Use IntelliSense to learn about possible attributes.
    // Hover to view descriptions of existing attributes.
    // For more information, visit:
    // https://go.microsoft.com/fwlink/?linkid=830387
    "version": "0.2.0",
    "configurations": [
        {
            "type": "node",
            "request": "launch",
            "name": "Launch node-server Program",
            "skipFiles": ["<node_internals>/**"],
            "program": "${workspaceFolder}/Chap8/node-
                server/server.mjs",
            "runtimeExecutable": "nodemon",
            "restart": true,
            "console": "integratedTerminal"
        }
    ]
}
```

You can see that the `configurations` field is an array, which means you can keep adding configurations to this one file. But for our configuration, notice that `type` is `node`, of course. We've also updated `name` to `"Launch node-server Program"`. But also, notice that we switched `runtimeExecutable` to be `nodemon` instead of `node`, and `console` is now the integrated terminal. In order to use `nodemon` with the debugger, we must switch to the **TERMINAL** tab and *not* the debugger console.

6.  Now that we have at least one `launch.json` configuration, our debug menu will show the following view:

Figure 8.20 – Debugger from launch.json

If your dropdown does not show **Launch node-server Program**, select it and then press the play button. Then, you should see the debugger launch again, only this time it will auto-restart.

7.  Now, try and make a small change and the debugger should auto-restart. I removed the `T` from the `listen` function log message:

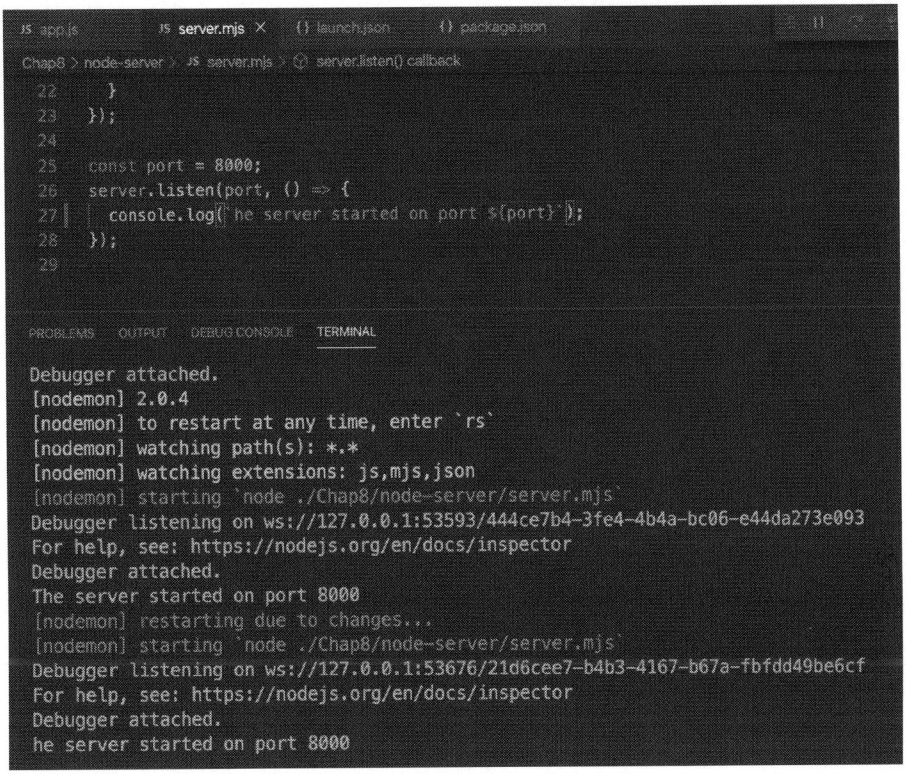

Figure 8.21 – Debugger auto-restarted

8.    Sweet, now we can easily break on and debug our Node code!

That was a fast introduction to some tools that will help with our development and debugging.

In this section, we learned about using Node directly to code our server. We also learned about debugging and tooling to improve our development flow. Coding with Node directly can be time-consuming and unintuitive. In the next sections, we will learn about Express and how it helps make our Node development experience better.

# Understanding how Express improves Node development

As we have seen, coding with Node directly has an awkward and cumbersome sort of feel. Having an easier-to-use API would make us more productive. This is what the Express framework attempts to do. In this section, we will learn what Express is and how it can help us write code more easily for our Node apps.

Express is not a standalone JavaScript server framework. It is a layer of code that sits on top of Node, and therefore uses Node, to make developing JavaScript servers with Node both easier and more capable. Just like Node, has its own core capabilities and then some additional features via dependency packages. Express also has its core abilities as well as a rich ecosystem of middleware that provides extra capabilities.

So then, what is Express? According to the website, Express is just an application that is a series of middleware calls. Let's explain this by first looking at a diagram:

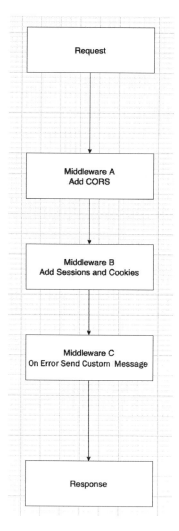

Figure 8.22 – Express request response flow

Whenever a new server request comes in, it travels along a sequential path for processing. Normally, you would just have a request, and then once the request is understood and processed, you would then get some response. When using Express, however, you can have multiple intermediate functions that inject themselves into the process and do some unique work.

So, in the example shown in *Figure 8.22*, we see that first there is middleware that adds CORS ability, which is a way to allow requests from different URL domains than the one that the server resides on. Then, we have middleware that handles sessions and cookies. Sessions are just unique data that gets collected about the user's current usage of the website – for example, their login ID. Then, finally, we see an on-error handler that will determine some unique message that will be shown depending on the error that has occurred. Of course, you could add more middleware as needed. The key point here is that Express enables this injection of extra capabilities that Node normally does not have in a fairly straightforward way.

On top of this middleware ability, Express adds additional features to the `Request` and `Response` objects that further enhance the developer's productivity. We'll take a look at those features and further explore Express in the next section.

# Learning Express's capabilities

Express is basically a middleware runner for Node. But, like most things in life, a simple explanation seldom provides the information necessary to make proper use of it. So, in this section, we will explore Express and learn about its capabilities with examples.

Let's install Express onto our `node-server` project. Type the following command into your terminal:

```
npm I express -S
```

This should give you an updated `package.json` file that has a new dependencies section:

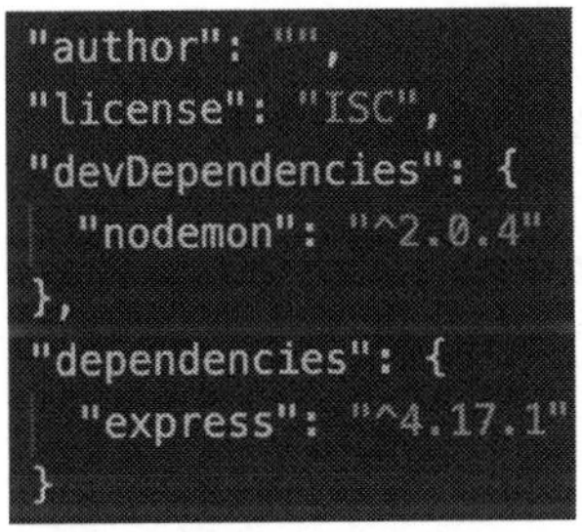

```
"author": "",
"license": "ISC",
"devDependencies": {
    "nodemon": "^2.0.4"
},
"dependencies": {
    "express": "^4.17.1"
}
```

Figure 8.23 – Updated package.json

Now, before we start writing code, we need to understand a few things. Again, as mentioned, Express is a wrapper around Node. This means that Express already uses Node internally. So, when we write code with Express, we will not be directly calling Node. Let's see what this looks like:

1. Create a new server file called `expressapp.mjs` and add the following code to it:

```
import express from "express";

const app = express();

app.listen({ port: 8000 }, () => {
  console.log("Express Node server has loaded!");
});
```

As you can see, we create an instance of `express` and then we call a function called `listen` on it. Internally, the `express.listen` function calls Node's `createServer` and `listen` functions. If you run this file, you will see the following log message:

```
davidchoi@Davids-MacBook-Pro node-server % nodemon expressapp.mjs
[nodemon] 2.0.4
[nodemon] to restart at any time, enter `rs`
[nodemon] watching path(s): *.*
[nodemon] watching extensions: js,mjs,json
[nodemon] starting `node expressapp.mjs`
Express Node server has loaded!
```

Figure 8.24 – The expressapp.mjs file running

So, now we have a running Express server. However, it does not do anything until we add some middleware. Middleware for Express runs under several main umbrellas or sections. There is middleware that runs for the entire application, there is middleware that runs only during routing, and there is middleware that runs on errors. There is also middleware that is core to Express that it uses internally. And, of course, instead of implementing our own code to do the work of middleware, we can also use npm packages that provide third-party middleware. We already saw some of these in the previous section, *Understanding how Express improves Node development*, in *Figure 8.22*.

2. Let's start by adding our own middleware. Update `expressapp.mjs` with the following code:

```
import express from "express";

const app = express();

app.use((req, res, next) => {
    console.log("First middleware.");
    next();
});
app.use((req, res, next) => {
    res.send("Hello world. I am custom middleware.");
});

app.listen({ port: 8000 }, () => {
    console.log("Express Node server has loaded!");
});
```

So, for this first example, we have decided to use the app-level middleware by using the `use` function on the `app` object. This means that any requests for the entire application, regardless of route, will have to process these two middleware.

Let's go through them. First, note that all middleware is processed in the order that they are declared in code. Second, unless ending a call at the end of a middleware, we must call the `next` function to go to the next middleware, or else the processing will stop.

The first middleware is just logging some text, but the second middleware will write to the browser screen by using the Express `send` function. The `send` function is a lot like the `end` function in Node, as it ends processing, but it also sends back a content-type header of the `text/html` type. If we were using Node, we would have to send headers explicitly ourselves.

3.  Now, let's add middleware for routes. Note that technically, you can pass routes – for example, the /routea route – to the use function. However, it is better to use the router object and contain our routes under one container. In Express, a router is also middleware. Let's see an example:

```
import express from "express";

const router = express.Router();
```

First, we have created our new router object from the express.Router type:

```
const app = express();

app.use((req, res, next) => {
  console.log("First middleware.");
  next();
});
app.use((req, res, next) => {
  res.send("Hello world. I am custom middleware.");
});
app.use(router);
```

So, we have the same set of middleware as before added to the app object, which makes it run globally across all routes. But then, we have also added the router object to our app as middleware. The router middleware, however, runs only for the specific routes that are defined:

```
router.get("/a", (req, res, next) => {
  res.send("Hello this is route a");
});
router.post("/c", (req, res, next) => {
  res.send("Hello this is route c");
});
```

So again, we added two middleware to our router object: one for the /a route, which uses the get method function and the other for the /c route, which uses the post method function. Again, these functions represent the HTTP verbs that are possible. The listen function call is identical to before:

```
app.listen({ port: 8000 }, () => {
  console.log("Express Node server has loaded!");
});
```

Now, a peculiar thing will happen if we run this code by going to the following URL: `http://localhost:8000/a`. Instead of seeing the **Hello this is route a** text, we will instead see the **Hello world. I am custom middleware.** text. Can you guess why? It is because middleware order matters and since our second app-level middleware is calling `res.send`, all calls will end there and not go to the next middleware.

Remove the second `app.use` call that sends the `Hello world...` message and try going to `http://localhost:8000/a`. You should see the following message now:

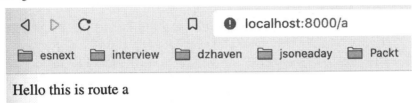

Figure 8.25 – Middleware for route /a

Great, that worked, but now try using your browser to go to `http://localhost:8000/c`. Does that work? No, it does not, and you get the **Cannot GET /c** message. As you might have guessed, browser calls are defaulted to GET calls but our `/c` route is a POST-only route. If you bring up your terminal and run the last POST `curl` command that we used in the *Learning Node's capabilities* section, you'll see this:

```
davidchoi@Davids-MacBook-Pro ~ % curl --header "Content-Type: application/json"
equest POST --data '{"userid":"1","message":"hello"}' "http://localhost:8000/c"
Hello this is route c
davidchoi@Davids-MacBook-Pro ~ %
```

Figure 8.26 – Route /c

As you can see, we receive the appropriate text message.

4. Now, let's add third-party middleware. In the *Learning Node's capabilities* section, we saw how to parse POST data and how arduous that can be using Node. For our example, let's use the body parser middleware to make doing this easier. Update the code like this:

```
import express from "express";
import bodyParser from "body-parser";
```

We first import the body parser middleware. Then, we add the body parser at the top so that all of our handlers can be automatically converted from a JSON string to a parsed object when needed:

```
const router = express.Router();
const app = express();

app.use(bodyParser.json());
```

Then, we update our /c route handler so that its text message shows the value passed in the message field:

```
app.use((req, res, next) => {
  console.log("First middleware.");
  next();
});

app.use(router);
router.get("/a", (req, res, next) => {
  res.send("Hello this is route a");
});
router.post("/c", (req, res, next) => {
  res.send(`Hello this is route c. Message is
    ${req.body.message}`);
});
```

As you can see, most of this work is quite a bit easier than using Node events such as data and end.

5.  Now, finally, let's do an on error middleware. Simply add the following code to just below the bodyParser.json() middleware call:

```
import express from "express";
import bodyParser from "body-parser";

const router = express.Router();
const app = express();

app.use(bodyParser.json());

app.use((req, res, next) => {
```

```
    console.log("First middleware.");
    throw new Error("A failure occurred!");
});
```

Then, we throw an error from our first custom middleware:

```
app.use(router);
router.get("/a", (req, res, next) => {
    res.send("Hello this is route a");
});
router.post("/c", (req, res, next) => {
    res.send(`Hello this is route c. Message is ${req.body.
        message}`);
});


app.use((err, req, res, next) => {
    res.status(500).send(err.message);
});
```

Now, we've added our error handler as the last middleware in our code. This middleware will catch all errors that were not previously handled and send the same status and message:

```
app.listen({ port: 8000 }, () => {
    console.log("Express Node server has loaded!");
});
```

6.  Go to http://localhost:8000/a and you should see the following message:

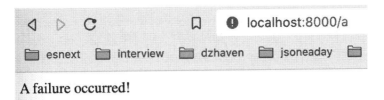

Figure 8.27 – Error message

Since our top-level middleware is throwing an exception, all routes will throw this exception and therefore will be caught by our error handler middleware.

This was an overview of the Express framework and its features. As you can see, it can make developing with Node quite a bit simpler and clearer. In the next section, we will take a look at using Express and Node to build a web API that returns JSON, which is the default data schema of the web.

# Creating a web API with Express

In this section, we will learn about the web API. Currently, it is one of the most popular ways of providing data across the web. In our final application, we will not be using the web API since it is our intention to use GraphQL. However, it is good to have some understanding of web API design since on the internet, it is very commonly used and under the covers, GraphQL also works similarly.

What is a web API? **API** stands for **application programming interface**. This means that it's a way for one programming system to interact with another. Therefore, a web API is an API that uses web technologies to provide programming services to other systems. A web API sends and receives data as a string, as opposed to binary data, and usually in JSON format.

All web APIs will have an endpoint that is represented by a URI, basically the same thing as a URL. This path must be static and not changing. If a change is desired, then it is expected that the API vendor will do a version update, leaving the old URI intact and creating a new URI delineated by a version upgrade. For example, if a URI started as /api/v1/users, then the next iteration would be /api/v2/users.

Let's create a simple web API for demonstration purposes:

1. Let's update our expressapp.mjs file with the following new routes:

```
import express from "express";
import bodyParser from "body-parser";

const router = express.Router();
const app = express();

app.use(bodyParser.json());

app.use((req, res, next) => {
  console.log("First middleware.");
  next();
});
```

Everything up to here was the same, except notice we removed the exception that was thrown:

```
app.use(router);
router.get("/api/v1/users", (req, res, next) => {
  const users = [
    {
      id: 1,
      username: "tom",
    },
    {
      id: 2,
      username: "jon",
    },
    {
      id: 3,
      username: "linda",
    },
  ];
  console.log(req.query.userid);
  const user = users.find((usr) => usr.id == req.query.
    userid);
  res.send(`User ${user?.username}`);
});
```

This first middleware is showing the /api/v1/users path. This type of pathing is fairly standard for web APIs. It indicates the version and a related container of data to query – in this case, users. For example purposes, we are using a hardcoded array of users and finding only one with a matching ID. Since id is a number and anything coming from req.query is a string, we are using == as opposed to ===. If you load the browser to the URI, you should see this:

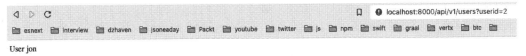

User jon

Figure 8.28 – User GET request

As you can see, our second user, jon, is returned.

2.  Next, for this middleware, we are doing something almost identical for groups. Notice how the pathing is consistent between both resource paths. This is an important feature for a web API. Again, we take a single item from an array, but in this case, we are using a POST method, so the parameter is gotten from the body:

```
router.post("/api/v1/groups", (req, res, next) => {
  const groups = [
    {
      id: 1,
      groupname: "Admins",
    },
    {
      id: 2,
      groupname: "Users",
    },
    {
      id: 3,
      groupname: "Employees",
    },
  ];
  const group = groups.find((grp) => grp.id == req.body.
   groupid);
  res.send(`Group ${group.groupname}`);
});
```

If you run the terminal command to this URI, you should see the following:

```
davidchoi@Davids-MacBook-Pro ~ % curl --header "Content-Type: application/json" --re
quest POST --data '{"groupid":"1"}' "http://localhost:8000/api/v1/groups"
Group Admins
davidchoi@Davids-MacBook-Pro ~ %
```

Figure 8.29 – Group POST request

As shown, our first group, `Admins`, is returned. The rest of the code is identical:

```
app.use((err, req, res, next) => {
    res.status(500).send(err.message);
});


app.listen({ port: 8000 }, () => {
    console.log("Express Node server has loaded!");
});
```

> **Important Note**
> Since the web API is specific to web technologies, it supports calls with all the HTTP methods: GET, POST, PATCH, PUT, and DELETE.

This was a quick introduction to building a web API using Express and Node. We now have had a broad overview of Node and its most important framework, Express.

# Summary

In this chapter, we learned about Node and Express. Node is the core server-side technology that drives a huge percentage of servers on the web, and Express is the most popular and often used Node-based framework for building web applications. We now have a complete picture of how frontend and backend technologies work to create websites.

In the next chapter, we'll learn about GraphQL, an extremely popular and relatively new standard for creating web-based API services. Once we've covered this, we will have all the knowledge we need to start building our project.

# 9
# What is GraphQL?

In this chapter, we'll learn about GraphQL, one of the hottest web technologies currently being used. Many large companies have adopted GraphQL for their APIs, including companies such as Facebook, Twitter, New York Times, and GitHub. We'll learn what makes GraphQL so popular, how it works internally, and how we can take advantage of its features.

In this chapter, we're going to cover the following main topics:

- Understanding GraphQL
- Understanding GraphQL schemas
- Understanding typedefs and resolvers
- Understanding queries, mutations, and subscriptions

## Technical requirements

You should have a basic understanding of web development using Node. We will once again be using Node and Visual Studio Code.

The GitHub repository is at `https://github.com/PacktPublishing/Full-Stack-React-TypeScript-and-Node`. Use the code in the `Chap9` folder.

To set up the `Chap9` code folder, go to your `HandsOnTypescript` folder and create a new folder called `Chap9`.

# Understanding GraphQL

In this section, we will explore what GraphQL is, why it was created, and what problems it attempts to solve. It is important to understand the underlying reasons for GraphQL's existence as it will help us design better web APIs.

So, what is GraphQL? Let's list some of its main characteristics:

- **GraphQL is a data schema standard developed by Facebook.**

  GraphQL provides a standard language for defining data, data types, and related data queries. You can think of GraphQL as roughly analogous to an interface that provides a contract. There's no code there, but you can still see what types and queries are available.

- **GraphQL works across platforms, frameworks, and languages.**

  When we create an API using GraphQL, the same GraphQL language will be used to describe our data, its types, and queries no matter what programming language or operating system we use. Having a consistent and reliable representation of data across a wide variety of systems and platforms is, of course, a good thing for clients and systems. But it's also beneficial to programmers, since we can continue to use our normal programming language and frameworks of choice.

- **GraphQL returns control for what is queried to the caller.**

  In a standard web service, it is the server that controls what fields of the data will be returned. However, in a GraphQL API, it is the client that determines which fields they would like to receive. This gives clients better control and reduces bandwidth usage and cost.

Broadly speaking, there are two main uses of a GraphQL endpoint. One is as a gateway to consolidate other data services, and the other is as the main web API service that directly receives data from a datastore and provides it to clients. Here's a diagram of GraphQL being used as a gateway for other data:

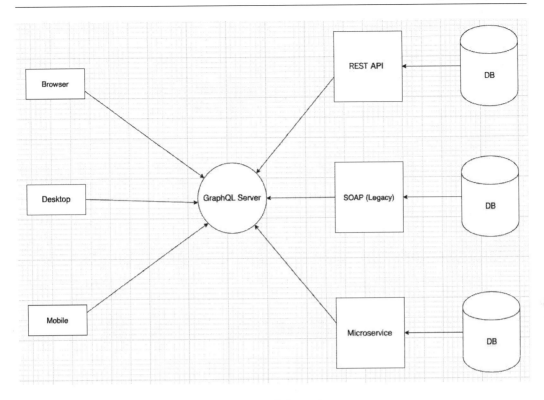

Figure 9.1 – GraphQL as a gateway

As you can see, GraphQL is acting as the single source of truth for all clients. It works well in this capacity due to its standards-based language that is supported across a wide variety of systems.

For our own application, we will use it as our entire web API, but it is possible to mix it in with existing web services so that GraphQL handles only a part of the service calls being made. This means you do not need to rewrite your entire application. You can introduce GraphQL slowly and deliberately where it makes sense to do so, without disrupting your current application services.

In this section, we took a look at GraphQL at a conceptual level. GraphQL has its own data language, meaning it can be used regardless of server framework, application programming language, or operating system. This flexibility allows GraphQL to be a powerful means of sharing data throughout an organization or even across the web. In the next section, we will explore the GraphQL schema language and see how it works. It will help us structure our data models and understand how to set up our GraphQL server.

# Understanding GraphQL schemas

As stated, GraphQL is a language used to provide structure and type information to our entity data. Regardless of which vendor's implementation of GraphQL is used on the server, our client can expect the same data structures to be returned. This ability to abstract away the implementation details of servers to clients is one of the strengths of GraphQL.

Let's create a simple GraphQL schema and see what it looks like:

1. In the `Chap9` folder, create a new folder called `graphql-schema`.

2. Open your terminal in that folder and then run this command, accepting the defaults:

```
npm init
```

3. Now install these packages:

```
npm i express apollo-server-express @types/express
```

4. Initialize TypeScript with this command:

```
tsc -init
```

Notice, after this command completes, that the default `tsconfig.json` setting is strict.

5. Create a new TypeScript file called `typeDefs.ts` and add this to it:

```
import { gql } from "apollo-server-express";
```

This import gets the `gql` object, which allows syntax formatting and highlighting of the GraphQL schema language:

```
const typeDefs = gql`
  type User {
    id: ID!
    username: String!
    email: String
  }

  type Todo {
    id: ID!
    title: String!
```

```
    description: String
  }

  type Query {
    getUser(id: ID): User
    getTodos: [Todo!]
  }
`;
```

The language is fairly simple and looks a lot like TypeScript. Starting from the top, first we have a `User` entity, as indicated by the `type` keyword. `type` is a GraphQL keyword that indicates that an object of a certain structure is being declared. As you can see, the `User` type has multiple fields. The `id` field is of type `ID!`. The `ID` type is a built-in type that indicates a unique value, basically a GUID of some kind. The exclamation mark indicates that the field cannot be `null`, whereas no exclamation mark would indicate that it can be `null`. Next, we see the `username` field and its type of `String!`, which of course means it is a non-nullable string type. Then, we have the `description` field, but it has a `String` type without an exclamation mark, so it is nullable.

The `Todos` type has similar fields, but notice the `Query` type. This shows that even queries are types in GraphQL. So, if you look at the two queries, `getUser` and `getTodos`, you can see why we created the `User` and `Todos` types, as they become the return values for our two `Query` methods. Also notice that the `getTodos` function returns an array of non-nullable `Todos`, which is indicated by the brackets. Finally, we export our type definitions using the `typeDefs` variable:

```
export default typeDefs;
```

Type definitions are used by Apollo GraphQL to describe the schema types in a schema file. Before your server can start providing any GraphQL data, it must first have a complete schema file that lists *all* of your application's types, their fields, and queries that will be served in its API.

Another thing to note is that GraphQL has several default scalar types that are built into the language. These are `Int`, `Float`, `String`, `Boolean`, and `ID`. As you noticed in the schema file, we did not have to create a type notation for these types.

In this section, we reviewed what a simple GraphQL schema file looks like. We will be using this syntax as we build out our API. In the next section, we will dive deeper into the GraphQL language and also learn what resolvers are.

# Understanding Typedefs and Resolvers

In this section we will further explore GraphQL schemas, but we will also implement resolvers, which are the functions that do the actual work. This section will also introduce us to Apollo GraphQL and how to create a GraphQL server instance.

What are resolvers? Resolvers are the functions that get or edit the data from our datastore. This data is then matched with the GraphQL type definition.

In order to see what the role of resolvers is in more depth, we need to continue building out our previous project. Let's look at the steps:

1.  Install the dependency UUID. This tool will allow us to create a unique ID for our ID types:

    ```
    npm i uuid @types/uuid
    ```

2.  Create a new file called server.ts, which will start our server, with this code:

    ```
    import express from "express";
    import { ApolloServer, makeExecutableSchema } from
    "apollo-server-express";
    import typeDefs from "./typeDefs";
    import resolvers from "./resolvers";
    ```

    Here we import dependencies needed to set up our server. We already created the typeDefs file and we will soon create the resolvers file.

3.  Now we create our Express server app object:

    ```
    const app = express();
    ```

4.  makeExecutableSchema builds a programmatic schema from the combination of our typeDefs file and our resolvers file:

    ```
    const schema = makeExecutableSchema({ typeDefs, resolvers
    });
    ```

5.  Finally, we create an instance of our GraphQL server:

    ```
    const apolloServer = new ApolloServer({
      schema,
      context: ({ req, res }: any) => ({ req, res }),
    });
    apolloServer.applyMiddleware({ app, cors: false });
    ```

`context` is made up of the request and response objects of Express. Then, we add our middleware, which for GraphQL is our Express server object called `app`. The `cors` option indicates to disable GraphQL from acting as our CORS server. We'll discuss CORS in later chapters as we build out our app.

In this code, we are now starting up our Express server by listening on port `8000`:

```
app.listen({ port: 8000 }, () => {
    console.log("GraphQL server ready.");
});
```

The `listen` handler just logs a message to announce it has started.

Now let's create our resolvers:

1.  Create the `resolvers.ts` file and add this code to it:

```
import { IResolvers } from "apollo-server-express";
import { v4 } from "uuid";
import { GqlContext } from "./GqlContext";

interface User {
    id: string;
    username: string;
    description?: string;
}

interface Todo {
    id: string;
    title: string;
    description?: string;
}
```

2.  Since we are using TypeScript, we want to use types to represent our returned objects, and that's what `User` and `Todo` represent. These types will be matched by GraphQL to the GraphQL types of the same name we had created in our `typeDefs.ts` file:

```
const resolvers: IResolvers = {
    Query: {
        getUser: async (
```

```
        obj: any,
        args: {
            id: string;
        },
        ctx: GqlContext,
        info: any
    ): Promise<User> => {
        return {
            id: v4(),
            username: "dave",
        };
    },
```

Here is our first resolver function, matching the getUser query. Notice that the parameter is more than just the id parameter. This is coming from the Apollo GraphQL server and adds additional information for our call. (Note that to save time, I am hardcoding a User object.) Also, we will create the GqlContext type later, but basically, it is a container that holds our request and response objects that we learned about in *Chapter 8, Learning Server-Side Development with Node.js and Express.*

3.  Similarly to getUser, our getTodos resolver receives similar parameters and also returns a hardcoded set of Todo:

```
    getTodos: async (
        parent: any,
        args: null,
        ctx: GqlContext,
        info: any
    ): Promise<Array<Todo>> => {
        return [
            {
                id: v4(),
                title: "First todo",
                description: "First todo description",
            },
            {
                id: v4(),
```

```
        title: "Second todo",
        description: "Second todo description",
      },
      {
        id: v4(),
        title: "Third todo",
      },
    ];
  },
```

4. Then we export the `resolvers` object:

```
  },
};

export default resolvers;
```

As you can see, our actual data getters are just normal TypeScript code. If we had used Java or C# or any other language, the resolvers would simply be **Create Read Update Delete** (**CRUD**) operations in those languages as well. The GraphQL server, then, is just translating the data entity models into the types in our type definition schema file.

5. Now let's create our `GqlContext` type. Create a file called `GqlContext.ts` and add this code:

```
import { Request, Response } from "express";

export interface GqlContext {
  req: Request;
  res: Response;
}
```

This is just a simple shell interface that allows us to provide type safety to our context in our GraphQL resolver calls. As you can see, this type contains the Express `Request` and `Response` objects.

6. So, now we need to compile our code to JavaScript since we are using TypeScript. Run this command:

```
Tsc
```

This will have created js versions of all the ts files.

7. Now we can run our new code; enter this:

```
nodemon server.js
```

8. If you go to the URL http://localhost:8000/graphql, you should see the GraphQL Playground screen. This is a query testing page provided by Apollo GraphQL that allows us to manually test our queries. It looks like this:

Figure 9.2 – The GraphQL dev client

Notice that I have already run one of the queries, which looks like JSON and is on the left, and the result is shown, which is also JSON and on the right. If you look at our query on the left, I am explicitly asking for only the id field, which is why only the id field is returned. Notice that the standard result format is data > <function name> > <fields>. Try running the getTodos query as a test.

9. Another thing to note is the **DOCS** tab, which shows all the available queries, mutations, and subscriptions (we will go over these in the next section). It looks like this:

Figure 9.3 – The DOCS tab

10. Finally, the **SCHEMA** tab shows the schema type information of all our entities and queries:

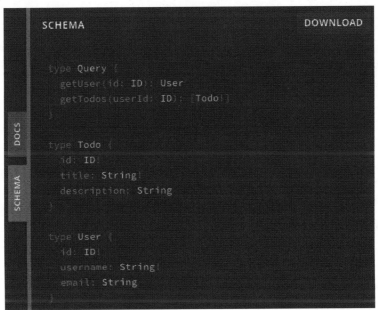

Figure 9.4 – The SCHEMA tab

As you can see, it looks identical to our `typeDefs.ts` file.

In this section, we took a look at resolvers by running a small GraphQL server. Resolvers are the other half that makes GraphQL actually function. We also saw how relatively easy it is to get a small GraphQL server running by using the Apollo GraphQL library.

In the next section, we will delve more deeply into queries by looking at mutations and subscriptions.

# Understanding queries, mutations, and subscriptions

When creating a GraphQL API, we want to do more than just get data: we may also want to write to a datastore or be notified when some data changes. In this section, we'll see how to do both actions in GraphQL.

Let's take a look at how to write data using mutations first:

1.  We will create a mutation called addTodo, but in order to make the mutation more realistic, we will need a temporary datastore. So, we will create an in-memory datastore for testing purposes. Create the db.ts file and add this code to it:

```
import { v4 } from "uuid";

export const todos = [
  {
    id: v4(),
    title: "First todo",
    description: "First todo description",
  },
  {
    id: v4(),
    title: "Second todo",
    description: "Second todo description",
  },
  {
    id: v4(),
    title: "Third todo",
  },
];
```

We have just added `Todos` from our previous list into an array that we are exporting.

2.  Now we need to update our `typeDefs.ts` file to include our new mutation. Update it like this:

```
import { gql } from "apollo-server-express";

const typeDefs = gql`
  type User {
    id: ID!
    username: String!
    email: String
  }

  type Todo {
    id: ID!
    title: String!
    description: String
  }

  type Query {
    getUser(id: ID): User
    getTodos: [Todo!]
  }

  type Mutation {
    addTodo(title: String!, description: String): Todo
  }
`;

export default typeDefs;
```

As you can see, other queries remain the same, but we added a new type called `Mutation`, which is where any queries that change data will reside. We also added our new mutation called `addTodo`.

3.  Now we want to add our `addTodo` resolver. Add this code to your `resolvers.ts` file:

```
Mutation: {
    addTodo: async (
      parent: any,
      args: {
        title: string;
        description: string;
      },
      ctx: GqlContext,
      info: any
    ): Promise<Todo> => {
      todos.push({
        id: v4(),
        title: args.title,
        description: args.description
      });
      return todos[todos.length - 1];
    },
  },
```

As you can see, we have a new container object called `Mutation`, and inside of it is our `addTodo` mutation. It has similar parameters to the queries, but this mutation will add a new `Todo` to the `todos` array. If we run this code in the playground, we see this:

Figure 9.5 – The GraphQL playground for the addTodo mutation

When our query is of type Query, we can leave out the query prefix. However, since this is a mutation, we must include it. As you can see, we only get back `id` and `title`, because that is all we asked for.

Now let's take a look at subscriptions, which are a way of being notified when certain data changes. Let's get notified when our `addTodo` adds a new `Todo` object:

1. We need to add an object of type `PubSub` from the `apollo-server-express` library into the GraphQL server `context`. This object is what allows us to both subscribe (ask to be notified when changes occur) and publish (send a notification when changes occur). Update the `server.ts` file as follows:

```
import express from "express";
import { createServer } from "http";
import {
  ApolloServer,
  makeExecutableSchema,
  PubSub,
} from "apollo-server-express";
import typeDefs from "./typeDefs";
import resolvers from "./resolvers";
```

First, we get an import of the `PubSub` type. Notice we also get `createServer`; we'll use that later.

2. Here is our `pubsub` object, based on the `PubSub` type:

```
const app = express();
const pubsub = new PubSub();
```

3. Now we add the `pubsub` object to the GraphQL server's `context` so that it can be used from our resolvers:

```
const schema = makeExecutableSchema({ typeDefs, resolvers
});
const apolloServer = new ApolloServer({
  schema,
  context: ({ req, res }: any) => ({ req, res, pubsub }),
});
```

4. Create an `httpServer` instance from Node directly and then use the `installSubscription Handlers` function on it. Then, when we call `listen`, we are now calling `listen` on the `httpServer` object and *not* the app object:

```
apolloServer.applyMiddleware({ app, cors: false });
const httpServer = createServer(app);
apolloServer.installSubscriptionHandlers(httpServer);

httpServer.listen({ port: 8000 }, () => {
  console.log("GraphQL server ready." +
    apolloServer.graphqlPath);
  console.log("GraphQL subs server ready." +
    apolloServer.subscriptionsPath);
});
```

5. Now let's update our `typeDefs.ts` file to add our new mutation. Just add this type:

```
type Subscription {
    newTodo: Todo!
}
```

6. Now we can update our `resolvers.ts` file with our new subscription resolver:

```
import { IResolvers } from "apollo-server-express";
import { v4 } from "uuid";
import { GqlContext } from "./GqlContext";
import { todos } from "./db";

interface User {
  id: string;
  username: string;
  email?: string;
}

interface Todo {
  id: string;
  title: string;
```

```
    description?: string;
}
```

```
const NEW_TODO = "NEW TODO";
```

Here we've created a new NEW_TODO constant to act as the name of our new subscription. Subscriptions require a unique label, sort of like a unique key, so that they can be correctly subscribed to and published:

```
const resolvers: IResolvers = {
  Query: {
    getUser: async (
      parent: any,
      args: {
        id: string;
      },
      ctx: GqlContext,
      info: any
    ): Promise<User> => {
      return {
        id: v4(),
        username: "dave",
      };
    },
```

As you can see, nothing in our query changes, but it's included here for completeness:

```
    getTodos: async (
      parent: any,
      args: null,
      ctx: GqlContext,
      info: any
    ): Promise<Array<Todo>> => {
      return [
        {
          id: v4(),
          title: "First todo",
          description: "First todo description",
```

```
        },
        {
            id: v4(),
            title: "Second todo",
            description: "Second todo description",
        },
        {
            id: v4(),
            title: "Third todo",
        },
    ];
    },
},
```

Again, our query remains the same:

```
Mutation: {
    addTodo: async (
        parent: any,
        args: {
            title: string;
            description: string;
        },
        { pubsub }: GqlContext,
```

Notice that in place of the ctx object, we have deconstructed it to just use the pubsub object, as it's the only one we need:

```
        info: any
    ): Promise<Todo> => {
        const newTodo = {
            id: v4(),
            title: args.title,
            description: args.description,
        };
        todos.push(newTodo);
        pubsub.publish(NEW_TODO, { newTodo });
```

Here we have `publish`, which is a function to notify us when we have added a new Todo. Notice the `newTodo` object is being included in the `publish` call, so it can be provided to the subscriber later:

```
        return todos[todos.length - 1];
      },
    },
  Subscription: {
    newTodo: {
      subscribe: (parent, args: null, { pubsub }:
      GqlContext) =>
        pubsub.asyncIterator(NEW_TODO),
```

Here we subscribe to new `Todo` adds. Notice that our subscription `newTodo` is not a function. It's an object with a member called `subscribe`:

```
      },
    },
  };

export default resolvers;
```

The rest is the same as before.

7.  Let's try testing this. First, make sure you have compiled your code with `tsc`, started your server, and refreshed the playground. Then, open a new tab in the playground, enter this subscription, and click the play button:

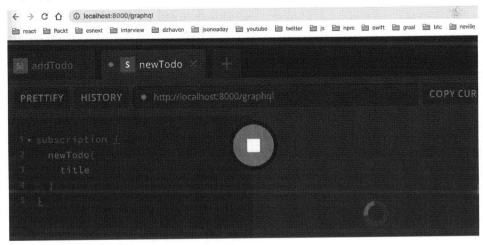

Figure 9.6 – The newTodo subscription

When you click the play button, nothing happens, because a new `Todo` has not been added yet. So, let's go back to our `addTodo` tab and add a new `Todo`. Once you've done that, come back to the `newTodo` tab and you should see this:

Figure 9.7 – The newTodo subscription result

As you can see, that works, and we get the newly added `Todo`.

In this section, we learned about GraphQL queries, mutations, and subscriptions. We will be using these to build out our application API. Because GraphQL is an industry standard, all GraphQL client frameworks can work with any vendor's GraphQL server framework. Furthermore, clients using a GraphQL API can expect consistent behavior and the same query language regardless of server or vendor. This is the power of GraphQL.

## Summary

In this chapter, we explored the power and capabilities of GraphQL, one of the hottest new technologies for creating web APIs. GraphQL is an extremely capable technology, but also, because it is an industry standard, we can always expect consistent behavior across servers, frameworks, and languages.

In the next chapter, we will start bringing together the technologies we've learned about thus far and create an Express server using TypeScript, GraphQL, and helper libraries.

# 10

# Setting Up an Express Project with TypeScript and GraphQL Dependencies

One of the biggest hurdles for learning modern JavaScript programming is the enormous number of packages and dependencies available. It can be overwhelming and daunting trying to select the right set of packages for your project. In this chapter, we'll learn how to set up a well-configured TypeScript, Express, and GraphQL project. We'll see what dependencies are popular and how we can benefit by using them for our project.

In this chapter, we're going to cover the following main topics:

- Creating a TypeScript-based Express project
- Adding GraphQL and dependencies to a project
- Reviewing ancillary packages

# Technical requirements

You should have a basic understanding of web development using Node, Express, and GraphQL. We will once again be using Node and Visual Studio Code.

The GitHub repository is available at `https://github.com/PacktPublishing/Full-Stack-React-TypeScript-and-Node`. Use the code in the `Chap10` folder.

To set up the `Chap10` code folder, go to your `HandsOnTypescript` folder and create a new folder called `Chap10`.

# Creating a TypeScript-based Express project

In this section, we'll build a starting project that we will use to base our server on. We'll manually review and select each dependency and understand what role each will play in our application. When we're done, we will have a strong base for building out our server app.

There are many pre-made project templates that can be used to build Node projects. A common one for TypeScript users is the TypeScript-Node-Starter project from Microsoft. It has a good variety of useful dependencies. Unfortunately, it's geared toward MongoDB users, but our app will use Postgres.

Another project template, from the team that makes Express, is `express-generator`. It is a CLI that takes parameters and sets up a base project. However, this template generator is geared toward servers that do server-side HTML using template engines such as `pug` and `ejs`. This would be unnecessary for us since we are creating an API for an SPA application. In addition, it has no GraphQL packages to help us create our API.

Therefore, in order to eliminate extraneous packages and as a learning exercise, let's build out our project manually. This will allow us to see every piece that is needed to build out our app and understand what each one does. Follow the steps given here:

1. Create a new folder in the `Chap10` folder and call it `node-server`.

2. In your terminal, run the following command:

```
npm init
```

3. Next, we install TypeScript and initialize it:

```
npm i typescript
tsc -init
```

4. Update the `tsconfig.json` file like this:

```
{
  "compilerOptions": {
    "target": "es6",
    "module": "commonjs",
    "lib": ["ES6", "ES2017", "ES2018", "ES2019",
      "ES2020"],
    "sourceMap": true,
    "outDir": "./dist",
    "rootDir": "src",
    "moduleResolution": "node",
    "removeComments": true,
    "noImplicitAny": true,
    "strictNullChecks": true,
    "strictFunctionTypes": true,
    "noImplicitThis": true,
    "noUnusedLocals": true,
    "noUnusedParameters": false,
    "noImplicitReturns": true,
    "noFallthroughCasesInSwitch": true,
    "allowSyntheticDefaultImports": true,
    "esModuleInterop": true,
    "emitDecoratorMetadata": true,
    "experimentalDecorators": true
```

```
    },
    "exclude": ["node_modules"],
    "include": ["./src/**/*.tsx", "./src/**/*.ts"]
}
```

We've already learned about the `tsconfig.json` file in *Chapter 2, Exploring TypeScript*, but let's review what we see here:

- We can target ES6 since we are running on our own server and can control the V8 version by using an appropriate version of Node.

- We are using `commonjs` as the `module` system to avoid issues with mixing `require` and `import` for modules.

- We want to use the latest JavaScript versions, so `lib` is set to allow them.

- The `outDir` field represents the folder that transpiled `js` files will be saved into.

- `rootDir` represents the code source directory.

- We are allowing `emitDecoratorMetadata` and `experimentalDecorator` as TypeORM; the dependency for the repository layer that accesses our database will need to use them.

- The `exclude` and `include` folders, as implied, represent folders we would like to either hide or make available to the TypeScript compiler.

5.  Now let's add some of our base dependencies:

```
npm i express -S
npm i @types/express jest @types/jest ts-jest nodemon
ts-node-dev faker @types/faker -D
```

Let's go over some of these packages:

- We installed both `Express` and its TypeScript types.

- We installed `jest` and its types for testing.

- The `ts-jest` package allows us to write our tests in TypeScript.

- I am showing `nodemon` for completeness, but we will be running the globally installed version that we installed in *Chapter 8, Learning Server-Side Development with Node and Express*.

- faker is a fake data generator for testing and mocking.

- ts-node-dev will help our Node server to restart when any TypeScript code is changed.

Now that we have our base dependencies installed, let's start up our plain Express server to make sure everything is working:

1.  We'll need to create a server setup script to initialize our server as we've done before in *Chapter 8, Learning Server-Side Development with Node and Express.* Create a folder called src and then create another file called index.ts inside of it. Then, add this code:

```
import express from "express";
import { createServer } from "http";

const app = express();

const server = createServer(app);

server.listen({ port: 8000 }, () => {
  console.log("Our server is running!");
});
```

Basically, this is what we've done before: creating an express instance and then using it to create our server.

2.  Now, we'll need to create a "start" script inside of package.json. Open that file and find the "scripts" section. Then, under the existing "test" entry, add this code:

```
"scripts": {
    "test": "echo \"Error: no test specified\" &&
        exit 1",
    "start": "ts-node-dev --respawn src/index.ts"
},
```

The command uses ts-node-dev to monitor when TypeScript changes occur and then "respawn". This means it will automatically restart Node as needed.

3.  Now if you type this command, your server should run:

```
npm start
```

You should see something like this once it is running:

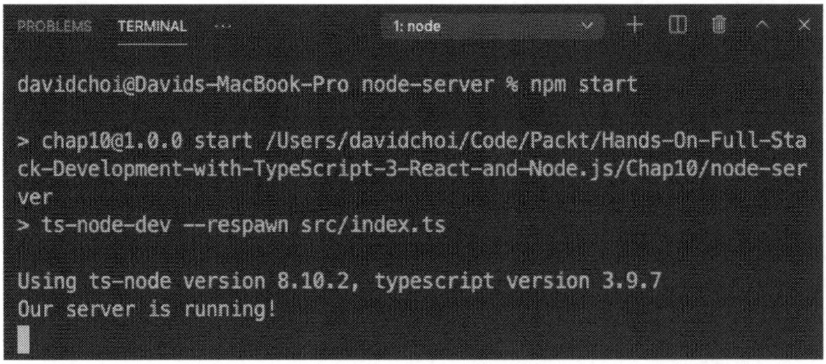

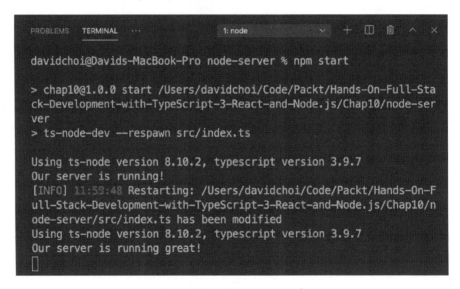

Figure 10.1 – First server run

As you can see, our server started with our command and the emitted console log message.

4.  If you update the index.ts file by changing the log message, you'll see that the server is auto-restarted, as this screenshot shows:

Figure 10.2 – Server restarted

The server restarts and then our new message, Our server is running great!, is shown.

In this section, we started learning about important dependencies for our server. We will be using all of these packages as well as other packages to build our GraphQL API. In the next section, we'll add our GraphQL dependencies.

# Adding GraphQL and dependencies to a project

We've already taken a look at GraphQL in *Chapter 9, What is GraphQL?*. In this chapter, let's review these packages as well as introduce some new related packages that we will be using.

Let's list some of the GraphQL-related packages we will be using for our app:

- `graphql`

  This package is the reference implementation for JavaScript of GraphQL. It is created by the GraphQL foundation and we will be using it to do some of our GraphQL query testing.

- `graphql-middleware`

  This is a package that allows us to inject our code either before or after a resolver runs. Some possible actions include, but are not limited to, authentication checks and logging.

- `graphql-tools`

  This package provides some helpers for testing and mocking our GraphQL queries when needed.

- `apollo-server-express`

  This is the main library we will use to create our Express GraphQL server, which we already used in *Chapter 9, What is GraphQL?*.

These are the main packages we will use for our GraphQL implementation. Next, we will create a GraphQL server and also build some tests for it. In later chapters, we'll merge the various packages we use here into a single project. Let's look at the steps:

1. Create another folder inside our `Chap10` folder called `gql-server`. Then, `cd` into it from the terminal and run these commands:

   ```
   npm init
   ```

2. Accept all defaults and then run this command:

   ```
   npm i express graphql graphql-tools graphql-middleware
   apollo-server-express uuid -S
   ```

3. Once that completes, run this:

```
npm i @types/express typescript @types/faker @types/jest
faker jest nodemon ts-jest ts-node-dev @types/uuid -D
```

4. Now initialize TypeScript with this command:

```
tsc -init
```

5. Once this is complete, copy the contents of the tsconfig.json file from our node-server project into the tsconfig.json file in this new gql-server project folder.

6. Now, in our package.json file, add a start entry to our scripts section like this:

```
"scripts": {
  "test": "echo \"Error: no test specified\" && exit 1",
  "start": "ts-node-dev --respawn src/server.ts"
},
```

Figure 10.3 – The start script

7. Now let's create a new src folder in the root of our gql-server folder. Then copy these files from the Chap9/graphql-schema project and paste them into the src folder: db.ts, GqlContext.ts, resolvers.ts, server.ts, and typeDefs.ts.

8. Let's test that our app will run by starting it up with this command:

```
npm start
```

Now let's add some middleware and see how it runs:

1. Create a new file called Logger.ts in the src folder and add this code to it:

```
export const log = async (
  resolver: any,
  parent: any,
  args: any,
  context: any,
  info: any
) => {
  If(!parent) {
    console.log("Start logging");
```

```
    }

    const result = await resolver(parent, args, context,
      info);


    console.log("Finished call to resolver");


    return result;
  };
```

In this code, we are intercepting any resolver calls and logging them before the
`resolver` function runs. Notice that we check that the `parent` object is `null`,
which indicates that the `resolver` call has not yet run. Let's also add logging to
our `getTodos` resolver. Open `resolvers.ts` and add this line at the start of the
`getTodos` function body, just before the `return` statement:

```
console.log("running getTodos");
```

2. Now we need to update our `server.ts` file so that it makes use of this logger.
   Update `server.ts` like this:

```
import express from "express";
import { createServer } from "http";
import {
  ApolloServer,
  makeExecutableSchema,
  PubSub,
} from "apollo-server-express";
import typeDefs from "./typeDefs";
import resolvers from "./resolvers";
import { applyMiddleware } from "graphql-middleware";
import { log } from "./Logger";
```

Here we have imported the `applyMiddleware` function and the `log` middleware
we created earlier. Note that this `applyMiddleware` function is coming
from the `graphql-middleware` package and is distinct from the Apollo
`applyMiddleware` function, which merely associates the Express instance with
our Apollo server:

```
const app = express();


const pubsub = new PubSub();
```

```
const schema = makeExecutableSchema({ typeDefs, resolvers
   });
const schemaWithMiddleware = applyMiddleware(schema,
   log);
const apolloServer = new ApolloServer({
   schema: schemaWithMiddleware,
   context: ({ req, res }: any) => ({ req, res, pubsub }),
   });
```

Here we have taken our schema that was created by `makeExecutableSchema` and used the `applyMiddleware` function to create a schema that has a middleware association. Then, we apply this schema, `schemaWithMiddleware`, to our Apollo server. The rest of the code is unchanged, so I won't include it here.

3.  Start your server if you have not done so already and open your browser to the GraphQL server URL. If you run the call to `getTodos`, you will see the `todos` data come back as shown:

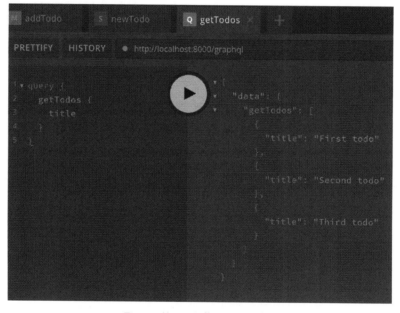

Figure 10.4 – Calling getTodos

Additionally, you should see in the Visual Studio Code terminal the `console.log` messages we set up earlier:

```
davidchoi@Davids-MacBook-Pro gql-server % npm start

> gql-server@1.0.0 start /Users/davidchoi/Code/Packt/Hands-On-Full-Stack-Developm
ent-with-TypeScript-3-React-and-Node.js/Chap10/gql-server
> ts-node-dev --respawn src/server.ts

Using ts-node version 8.10.2, typescript version 3.9.7
GraphQL server ready./graphql
GraphQL subs server ready./graphql
Start logging
running getTodos
```

Figure 10.5 – The getTodos result

Our middleware runs and does its log. Then, the actual resolver runs and returns the data.

So, we've now seen GraphQL middleware that allows us to intercept calls and inject our own code into the GraphQL process. Let's now try to create some tests with GraphQL:

1.  We need to create a GraphQL query runner for testing purposes. Create a new file called `testGraphQLQuery.ts` and add this code to it:

    ```
    import { graphql, GraphQLSchema } from "graphql";
    ```

    We import `graphql` and `GraphQLSchema` so that we can make manual queries and type schema files.

2.  Import `Maybe` as it is a GraphQL type indicating whether parameters may or may not be used:

    ```
    import { Maybe } from "graphql/jsutils/Maybe";
    ```

3.  Create our `Options` interface, which will later act as the `testGraphQLQuery` function's parameters type to run our query:

    ```
    interface Options {
        schema: GraphQLSchema;
        source: string;
        variableValues?: Maybe<{ [key: string]: any }>;
    }
    ```

The code [key: string] represents object property names – for example, myObj["some name"]. The testGraphQLQuery function is called with the required parameters and will return the relevant data:

```
export const testGraphQLQuery = async ({
  schema,
  source,
  variableValues
}: Options) => {
  return graphql({
    schema,
    source,
    variableValues,
  });
};
```

4.  Now let's write our test. Create a getUser.test.ts file and add this code to it:

```
import typeDefs from "./typeDefs";
import resolvers from "./resolvers";
import { makeExecutableSchema } from "graphql-tools";
import faker from "faker";
import { testGraphQLQuery } from "./testGraphQLQuery";
import { addMockFunctionsToSchema } from "apollo-server-express";
```

The imports are pretty self-explanatory, but the faker import is used to help us create fake entries for the field values of our test objects.

5.  We set up our test using describe and then we create our query for getUser with the fields that we want:

```
describe("Testing getting a user", () => {
  const GetUser = `
    query GetUser($id: ID!) {
      getUser(id: $id) {
        id
        username
        email
      }
```

```
        }
    `;
```

6. Now in our test, we first create our `schema` from the merger of `typeDefs` and `resolvers` and then we set up our fake data fields for our mocked `User` object:

```
it("gets the desired user", async () => {
    const schema = makeExecutableSchema({ typeDefs,
      resolvers });
    const userId = faker.random.alphaNumeric(20);
    const username = faker.internet.userName();
    const email = faker.internet.email();
    const mocks = {
      User: () => ({
        id: userId,
        username,
        email,
      }),
    };
```

As shown in *Chapter 6, Setting Up Our Project Using create-react-app and Testing with Jest*, mocking allows us to focus on the unit of code we want to test without having to worry about other items.

7. Using `addMockFunctionsToSchema`, we add our mocked `User` object to the schema so that it will be returned when relevant queries are made:

```
console.log("id", userId);
console.log("username", username);
console.log("email", email);

addMockFunctionsToSchema({ schema, mocks });
```

8. Finally, we run the `testGraphQLQuery` function to get back our mocked data:

```
const queryResponse = await testGraphQLQuery({
    schema,
    source: GetUser,
    variableValues: { id: faker.random.alphaNumeric(20)
      },
});
```

```
const result = queryResponse.data ? queryResponse.
    data.getUser : null;
console.log("result", result);
expect(result).toEqual({
    id: userId,
    username,
    email,
});
});
});
```

If the returned object has the same fields, it shows that the logic of querying the
getUser query is working, since the call has gone through the entire code path to
get our User object.

9.  Before we run our test, we need to add a configuration to the package.json file
    for jest. Add this to the end of the configuration:

```
"jest": {
    "transform": {
        ".(ts|tsx)": "<rootDir>/node_modules/ts-
            jest/preprocessor.js"
    },
    "testRegex": "(/__tests__/.*|\\.(test|spec))
        \\.(ts|tsx|js)$",
    "moduleFileExtensions": [
        "ts",
        "tsx",
        "js"
    ]
}
```

This configuration makes certain that all files with spec or test in the name
are tested (this is the testRegex section), and that any TypeScript files are first
transpiled to JavaScript before running (this is the transform section).

10. If you run the jest command on your terminal, you should see this result; make
    sure you are on the gql-server path:

```
davidchoi@Davids-MacBook-Pro gql-server % jest
ts-jest[main] (WARN) Replace any occurrences of "ts-jest/dist/preprocessor.js" or
  "<rootDir>/node_modules/ts-jest/preprocessor.js" in the 'transform' section of
your Jest config with just "ts-jest".
 PASS  src/getUser.test.ts
  Testing getting a user
    ✓ gets the desired user (26 ms)

  console.log
    id oz3zqctmuf57ohres88m

      at src/getUser.test.ts:31:13

  console.log
    username Adonis34

      at src/getUser.test.ts:32:13

  console.log
    email Gavin_Crist@yahoo.com

      at src/getUser.test.ts:33:13

  console.log
    result [Object: null prototype] {
      id: 'oz3zqctmuf57ohres88m',
      username: 'Adonis34',
      email: 'Gavin_Crist@yahoo.com'
    }

      at src/getUser.test.ts:43:13

Test Suites: 1 passed, 1 total
Tests:       1 passed, 1 total
Snapshots:   0 total
Time:        4.293 s
Ran all test suites.
```

Figure 10.6 – The GraphQL query test result

As you can see, the test passes. I've added several `log` statements in order to show that the fields of the mocked `User` are the same. You should avoid this in your tests as it is difficult to read.

> **Note**
>
> In your `package.json` file's scripts section, you can replace the "test"
> entry with "test" : "jest". This way, it will be more consistent with other NPM
> scripts. As with any NPM script, you would run it with the `npm run test`
> command.

In this section, we learned about some of the NPM packages available for GraphQL. These packages can help us build and test our servers, making them more reliable. In the next section, we'll look at some other packages that will help us build our servers.

# Reviewing ancillary packages

In this section, we'll review some of the ancillary dependencies of our project. Our server, at its heart, is Node, Express, and GraphQL, of course. But there are also many other activities our server will need to perform in order to be complete and fully functional.

Let's list some packages we will be using throughout our application that should allow us to write less code and focus more on our core business logic:

- `bcryptjs`

  Every server will have some need to encrypt data for security purposes. An obvious example would be our users' passwords. Bcrypt is an industry-standard encryption algorithm that exists on numerous platforms, including C++ and Java. `bcryptjs` is a JavaScript implementation of the algorithm and will help us secure our application.

- `cors`

  The web is full of security hazards and hackers attempting to break servers. Because of this, the standard behavior of any web server is to only allow client requests coming from the same domain as the server. For complex server setups, such as microservices and proxies, this would not be feasible. So, **Cross-Origin Resource Sharing (CORS)** was created to allow requests from other domains. The `cors` package provides tools for executing CORS on our server.

- `date-fns`

  The JavaScript Date object is notoriously cumbersome to deal with directly and `date-fns` provides lots of useful methods for parsing, formatting, and displaying dates and times.

- `dotenv`

  Every large application needs to store configuration information in a central place, both to manage and secure sensitive data and settings. Using `dotenv` will allow us to maintain our sensitive information settings without revealing it to end users.

- `nodemailer`

  `nodemailer` allows us to send emails from within our Node server. We can send emails, for example, to allow users to reset their password or notify them of activity on the site.

- `request`

  This package will allow us to make HTTP requests from within our Node server. This can be useful, for example, when we need to grab data from another API, whether it be third-party or internal.

- `querystring`

  `querystring` will allow us to easily create URL querystring parameters from objects and parse the body of POST requests into fields. This package can be used together with the `request` package.

- `randomstring`

  `randomstring` can be used to generate random temporary passwords.

There are many more packages we will be using as we build out our application – for example, packages that allow us to connect to our Postgres database and to our Redis storage. However, I will introduce those packages in the relevant sections as it will be clearer what those packages do at that time.

In this section, we learned about some of the miscellaneous packages we will be using in our project. Although these tools are not the main focus of our application, they are nonetheless extremely valuable. If we were to write these dependencies ourselves, we would have to become experts in various fields such as encryption and date time management, which would be a huge waste of time for us since it is not central to our goals.

## Summary

In this chapter, we learned about additional NPM package dependencies that we will use to build out our application. These tools are well used by the community and therefore well tested and reliable. Using packages from the Node ecosystem is one of the most valuable benefits of Node. It saves us from having to write, test, and maintain this extra code ourselves.

In the next chapter, we will review what we will be building in detail. We'll see what the various components of our application will be, and we'll start coding the React side of our application.

# 11
# What We Will Learn – Online Forum Application

No matter how many books we study, we as developers cannot truly learn how to program with a certain technology stack without building a realistic application that uses it. In this chapter, we'll learn about the application that we intend to build. We'll see how we will apply some of the topics we've covered. We'll see what features our application will have and some of the rationale for including those features. This author also has a fair amount of experience of building forum-style applications, such as my latest app, DzHaven. So, you can rest assured that what you'll learn is production-grade code that's actually being used in real-world applications.

In this chapter, we're going to cover the following main topics:

- Analyzing what we will build – The forum application
- Analyzing forum authentication
- Analyzing thread management
- Analyzing the thread points system

# Analyzing what we will build – The forum application

As noted, we are building a forum application. It will be somewhat similar in style to other forum applications, such as StackOverflow and Bitcointalk.org. A user will be able to post a topic or ask a question and receive responses from other users in the application's community.

**Why build a single forum application?**

We could have demonstrated JavaScript development by building several smaller simpler applications. The problem with demonstrating full-stack programming with simple apps is that they do not show all the capabilities of a modern JavaScript application. In other words, it could leave holes in your knowledge of how to implement certain features, such as authentication or database access.

We could, of course, build a graphically intense photo or video application, but the issue with these apps is the enormous focus needed on graphical design and aesthetics. Also, working on editing photos or video is nice, but those skills don't translate well to general full-stack programming. There's nothing wrong with apps like these, but in a book such as this, the main goal is obviously to learn how to code a full-stack app, and not necessarily become a graphics specialist.

So, a forum application will give us a good depth of understanding of the myriad frameworks necessary in a large full-stack application. It will also show the kind of features we need to implement in an app that will serve many users in a publicly accessible website. At a high level, we will be implementing the following technology features:

- **Security**

  Broadly speaking, web security entails two main parts. Authentication is the server's ability to verify that a user is who they say they are, and authorization is the ability to control user access to features of the application.

- **Sessions and cookies**

  Server-side sessions allow a server to maintain data about a user's current activity on the site. We will use sessions and cookies to identify users and provide an easier experience while they are using the site.

- **Object Relational Mapper**

  An **Object Relational Mapper** (**ORM**) is technology that allows code, in our case TypeScript, to be used to interact with a database instead of SQL.

- **Database access and repository layer**

  Database access is complex, so we will use a design pattern called Repository to separate our database access code from the rest of our application code.

These days, an application needs to be mobile-enabled by default. We need to make sure users on mobile phones are able to access and engage with our application community. Therefore, we'll build our application using responsive methods so that our app will work on both desktops and mobile devices. Responsive web design simply means that our application's screen will change to best fit the device screen size and dimensions. We will use modern CSS and JavaScript techniques to do this.

In this section, we reviewed what type of application we will be building and the reasons for our selection. In the next section, we'll look at forum authentication and some of its features.

# Analyzing forum authentication

In any large multi-user application, we need to use a system to recognize and authorize users. Our forum application is no different.

Users will be able to post forum topics and answer forum questions. They therefore need to be able to distinguish their own activity from that of other users. So, we will build a login system to allow users to authenticate and perform activities on the site with their own unique account. We will therefore build the following features:

- **Login and logout**

  This feature will include not only the **GraphQL** resolvers to allow logging in and logging out, but also the screens to allow the user to enter their ID and password. We will also be using several technologies to provide a unique session state for the user's activities at any given time.

- **Registration system**

  A registration system will include both screens and resolvers that allow a user to create a unique account in order to distinguish their activities on the site.

- **Password reset**

  The ability for users to change their password when required, but in a secure way.

- **Profile screen**

  A screen and features that show a user's account information. This information will include their email and user ID. In addition to that, it provides the ability for the user to view all of their prior posts, including both topic posts and responses.

- **Categories**

  Groupings based on categories should be created to allow users to view only the posts in categories that they are interested in and reduce noise.

- **Notification emails**

  A system for contacting users via email and notifying them of additional requirements or news about the site. For example, this could include a verification email that checks that the email they registered with is valid and accessible by the same user.

In this section, we went over the list of features we will be building to allow users to authenticate and uniquely identify themselves and their activities on the site. In the next section, we'll review how we will implement **threads**, the main means of communication within our application.

# Analyzing thread management

Every post on the site can be considered the beginning of a thread; that is to say, the initial thread posting kicks off a discussion on a topic and creates a chain of responses. So, our application needs to be able to allow a user to start the discussion by adding the initial thread post. This post would then be viewable to all users and they can respond to it. Each thread item, including the initial post, will be uniquely identified to the user that made the post. So, in order to create this functionality, we will need the following features:

- **Topic thread posting and editing**

  This feature will, of course, include the ability to be viewed by anyone, as well as adding and editing topic posts by an author. Users will also be able to see all their posts from their **UserProfile** screen.

- **Responding to a thread topic**

  This feature will include the ability for the topic-starting user and other users to respond to a topic post with their own comments. It has the ability to view a topic post and all responses related to that topic on one screen.

  In order to keep the application's complexity down to a minimum, users will not be allowed to respond to specific responses, but only respond to the main topic. They will, however, be able to quote other posts in their response.

In this section, we reviewed the features for the main capabilities of the application. Creating and responding to new threads will be the core feature of the application, although we will add other related features in order to enhance its capabilities. In the next section, we will review what we will build for the thread points system.

# Analyzing the thread points system

Users should be able to tag comments that they like and upvote them. Showing which postings are popular also helps users be more engaged in the communication. In this section, we'll review how we'll enable users to indicate their approval of posts.

To enable this capability, we will include the following features in our app:

- **Points system**

  A points system will be created to allow users to upvote or downvote thread postings and responses.

- **Display view count**

  Show the number of times a thread post was viewed by users.

- **Display response count**

  Show the number of responses a post has to let users know what topics are popular or trending.

In this section, we reviewed how the system is important to enable users to indicate how they feel about certain posts and view the popularity of topics. The points system will enhance user engagement and activity.

# Summary

In this chapter, we looked at the application we will be building, the list of features it will have, and some of the reasons for going with this type of application. Since we are building a full-stack application, the code we are about to build will be quite complex and challenging. You may even be surprised by the ultimate size and scope of this app. However, once we are done, we will have built a modern, sophisticated, and complete end-to-end application.

In the next chapter, we will start coding the React client-side portion of our application. We won't be able to entirely finish it since we've not started our backend. However, we will build a very large portion of it, and you will be able to see many of the screens.

# 12

# Building the React Client for Our Online Forum Application

We've come a long way. In this chapter, we'll start coding our application, starting with the React client. We will take everything we learned about in the previous chapters and build our React app using the new Hooks API. We will also use Responsive techniques to build a mobile client that will adapt its views to handle both mobile and desktop devices.

## Technical requirements

You should now have a good understanding of web development using React, Node, Express, and GraphQL. You should also be familiar with CSS. We will once again be using Node and Visual Studio Code to write our code.

The GitHub repository for this book can be found at https://github.com/PacktPublishing/Full-Stack-React-TypeScript-and-Node. Use the code in the Chap12 folder.

To set up the Chapter 12 code folder, go to your HandsOnTypescript folder and create a new folder called Chap12.

# Creating the initial version of our React application

In this section, we will be building out our React client. We won't be able to complete the client entirely since it will need our backend features, such as our GraphQL API, the ability to authenticate, post threads, and so on. However, we'll begin creating our main screens and set up Redux and React Router.

There will be a very large amount of code in this section. Please take frequent breaks and pace yourself. The code will evolve and get iterated and refactored numerous times during our build. Sometimes, it will be for better code reuse. Sometimes, it will be to improve our design and its readability. So, if you get stuck, please refer to the source code. This will be the most challenging section of this book so far.

> **Note**
> We will not be showing every line of code as that would be redundant. Please download and open the source code in your editor to follow along.

In this section, we will be covering the following topics:

- React project setup and dependency configuration

- Styling and layout

- Core component and feature creation

> **Tip**
> Having everything compile and work from the beginning is actually not of any benefit to your learning. Do not focus on getting stuff to simply compile and run the first time you do this. Instead, try experimenting and making changes. In other words, break the code so that it does not compile and then fix it. This is the only way to ensure you understand what you're doing.

Let's start by creating our base project by using `create-react-app`. Then, we will add Redux and React Router:

1.  Go to the `Chap12` folder from your Terminal and run the following command:

```
create-react-app super-forum-client --template typescript
```

2. Next, cd into the new `super-forum-client` folder and run the `start` command to make sure it's working:

```
npm start
```

3. Now, let's install Redux and React Router:

```
npm i redux react-redux @types/redux @types/react-redux
react-router-dom @types/react-router-dom
```

> **Note**
>
> If you ever have issues with NPM packages where the app does not start properly, try deleting the `package-lock.json` file and the `node_modules` folder. Then, do a clean install using `npm install`.

So, now, we have our core packages installed. Before we start coding, we need to discuss how we will lay out our application. In our case, we want our application to work on both mobile devices and desktops. This way, we can have a single application that runs on phones, desktops, and laptops.

There are multiple ways of approaching this goal. We can use a library such as **Bootstrap** or a UI framework such as **Ionic** to help us build out a UI and layout. These frameworks are great and work well, but they also hide some of the details about how layout and styling work on the web. You can also lose some control when using frameworks and end up with a site that looks similar to other sites that use the same framework.

# CSS Grid

For our application, we will use Responsive Web Design. Responsive Web Design is simply the intent that our web application adapts to different devices and screen dimensions. There are many ways, when using web technologies, that we can do this. One of them is CSS Grid. With this system, we can structure our application screen to make optimal use of desktop space, while at the same time automatically reconfigure it for mobile devices. Due to this, we will be using CSS Grid, as well as other web technologies, to create our layout.

CSS Grid gives us most of the capabilities that programs such as Bootstrap could accomplish. However, CSS Grid is part of the CSS web standard, instead of being part of a third-party library. So, we know that our layout will always work with the web and will never suddenly become unsupported.

So, what is CSS Grid? CSS Grid is a layout method built into standard CSS that allows us to create flexible layouts using rows and columns. It was created to replace the use of tables for layouts. CSS Grid is very capable and there are numerous ways of doing the same thing. To keep things simple, I will show you one specific way to do this, though you can explore more options later if you think you'll find that useful. Let's get started using CSS Grid:

1. First, go back to our project, open App.tsx, and remove the contents of the App object. Do the following:

```
import React from "react";
import "./App.css";
function App() {
  return (
    <div className="App">
      <nav className="navigation">Nav</nav>
      <div className="sidebar">Sidebar</div>
      <div className="leftmenu">Left Menu</div>
      <main className="content">Main</main>
      <div className="rightmenu">Right Menu</div>
    </div>
  );
}
export default App;
```

As you can see, we've gotten rid of most of the contents and replaced it with layout placeholders. Of course, we will make components out of these elements eventually, but for now, we'll focus on getting our Grid layout working.

2. Now, let's replace the contents of the App.css file, like this:

```
:root {
  --min-screen-height: 1000px;
}
```

First, there's a `:root` pseudoclass, which we will use as a container for the CSS Variables for our app theme. To make styling and theming more consistent and easier, we will use variables instead of hardcoding values. As we build out our app, you will see more and more variables being added here:

```css
.App {
    margin: 0 auto;
```

The following margin settings centers our layout:

```css
    max-width: 1200px;
    display: grid;
    grid-template-columns: 0.7fr 0.9fr 1.5fr 0.9fr;
    grid-template-rows: 2.75rem 3fr;
    grid-template-areas:
        "nav nav nav nav"
        "sidebar leftmenu content rightmenu";
    gap: 0.75rem 0.4rem;
}
```

Here's a rundown of the Grid-related attributes:

- `display`: Here, we declare that our element will be of the `grid` type.

- `grid-template-columns`: This attribute tells our app the width of our columns in a relative way. In our setup, it indicates we have four columns. The `fr` value indicates that some portion of the available width should be given to the column. So, for example, in our case, we have four columns, so if each column had exactly equal amounts of the available width, each column's value would be `1fr`. But in our case, each column will be using a different amount of width smaller or greater than the equal distribution, which is why we have the varying values. Possible values can be specific, such as `100px` or `2rem`, percentages, such as example `20%`, or implicit, such as `.25fr`.

- `grid-template-rows`: Indicates the number and size of rows. Possible values are the same as columns.

- `grid-template-areas`: Every Grid can have labeled sections called areas. As this example shows, you simply add the labels for each area in Grid form to the columns and rows that you want them to be in. So, in our case, `"nav nav nav nav"` represents the first of our two rows with four columns, while `"sidebar leftmenu content rightmenu"` represents our second row and each of its columns.

- gap: This is a way of adding padding in-between columns and rows. The first entry indicates the row, while the second indicates the column.

3.  Now that we've explained the basic features of CSS Grid, let's look at the styling for the related sections of the Grid. The remaining styles are for the Grid content areas:

```
.navigation {
  grid-area: nav;
}
.sidebar {
  min-height: var(--min-screen-height);
  grid-area: sidebar;
  background-color: aliceblue;
}
.leftmenu {
  grid-area: leftmenu;
  background-color: skyblue;
}
.content {
  min-height: var(--min-screen-height);
  grid-area: content;
  background-color: blanchedalmond;
}
.rightmenu {
  grid-area: rightmenu;
  background-color: coral;
}
```

As you can see, they have a grid-area attribute, which indicates which area of the Grid the element belongs to. The nav area will be for navigation. sidebar will show a menu of user-specific settings and will only appear for desktops and laptops; it will be hidden for mobile devices. leftmenu will be used to store our Thread categories list. content will house our main list of Threads, filtered by category. Finally, rightmenu will show a list of popular or otherwise relevant Threads.

> **Note**
>
> I am using these awkward background-color settings temporarily, only to distinguish between each area clearly. Eventually, we will remove them.

Now, we have a basic layout for our app that works for desktop and laptop devices. But how can we make this auto reconfigure itself for smaller screens, such as phones and tablets? There is a CSS technology called **Media Queries** that could be of help in situations like this. However, for our needs, it alone is insufficient.

We are building our app dynamically, using React driven by state changes. This means that certain screen components should not be drawn if they are not needed or cannot be displayed on smaller devices. So, although we could use Media Queries to hide elements when smaller screens are detected, it would be an inefficient use of resources to have React render something that is never going to be seen or directly used by the user.

Instead, let's see what we can do in code using event handling and React Hooks to take care of this issue:

1. The first thing we want to do is convert our elements into React components. Let's create a new folder inside the src folder called components.

2. Then, inside that folder, create a container component for each of the elements that were inside the root div of our App component. Your src folder and the App.tsx file should now look like this:

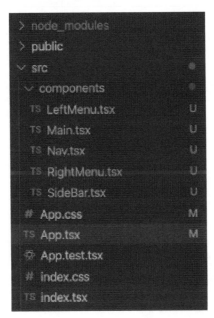

Figure 12.1 – Refactored App.tsx file

Due to brevity, I won't review every single file we need to create here since it is highly repetitive code, but here's a sample of the updated `Main` component (the source code will, of course, contain the complete application code for all components):

```
import React from "react";
const Main = () => {
  return <main className="content">Main</main>;
};
export default Main;
```

As you can see, we just moved our code from `App.tsx` into the component's `Main.tsx` file. This means you'll need to create the remaining components; that is, `Nav`, `SideBar`, `LeftMenu`, and `RightMenu`. Here's a screenshot of the React Developer Tools screen showing our component hierarchy so far. React Developer Tools was discussed in *Chapter 6, Setting Up Our Project Using create-react-app and Testing with Jest*:

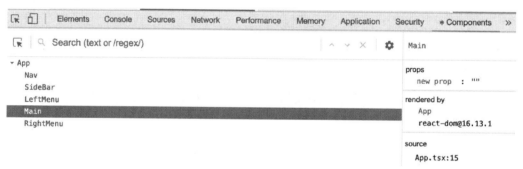

Figure 12.2 – Component hierarchy view

Notice that we have the **Nav**, **SideBar**, **LeftMenu**, **Main**, and **RightMenu** components here. Each component represents the areas of our app on the root of our website. Note that we will have more screens than this as we build out our app.

We had to do this componentization anyway because we are building a React application. But how does this help us with our desire to make our web app responsive so that it auto-configures to different device screens? By separating out each area of the Grid into its own component, we can allow each component to use a React Hook that looks for screen size information. Due to this, if the component is not appropriate for a certain screen size, it will not render or render differently.

In order to make this responsive system work, we'll need two main features. First, we'll need some additional CSS styles that use Media Queries to lay out our Grid differently when smaller devices are detected. Additionally, we'll need to have our components become aware when certain screen sizes are being used and either not render the component or render it differently. Let's see what that code looks like.

First, let's create our media queries for mobile devices. Open your `App.css` file and add the following Media Query to the bottom of our file:

```
@media screen and (orientation: portrait) and (max-width:
768px) {
  .App {
    grid-template-columns: 1fr;
    grid-template-areas:
      "nav"
      "content";
  }
}
```

Here, we are overriding the original `App` class definition whenever the device's `orientation` is in `portrait` mode and the resolution is `768px` or less. If you run the app using Chrome Developer Tools in mobile mode as an iPhone X, you should see this:

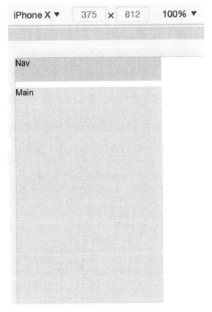

Figure 12.3 – Chrome Developer Tools view of our app in mobile mode

The app has a white right-hand side because we are still rendering the elements that existed in the original desktop mode. We'll fix this soon. Now, let's create our **Hook**, which helps handle device size-based rendering:

1.  Create a folder inside the `src` folder called `hooks`. Then, add a file called `useWindowDimensions.ts`. Notice that it is not a component since it has a `ts` extension. Copy the source code from this book's GitHub repository and let's go through it.

    First, we create an interface called `WindowDimension` so that we can type in what is returned by our Hook, which in this case is the browser's `window` object dimensions.

    Then, on *line 8*, we name our `useWindowDimensions` Hook. Then, on the next line, we create a state object called `dimension` and give it a value of `0` for `height` and `0` for `width`.

2.  Next, we create our handler function, `handleResize`, which will use the state update method, `setDimension`, to set our dimension values. The `window` object of our browser provides the dimension values.

3.  Finally, starting no *line 21*, we use the `useEffect` Hook to handle the window's `resize` event. Note that an empty array, `[]`, means that this will run only once on first load. Also, note that when we add an event handler, we must also return an event remover (this prevents memory leaks and redundant event handlers from being added).

4.  Now, we need to update our `SideBar`, `LeftMenu`, and `RightMenu` components so that they will use our `useWindowDimensions` Hook and know not to render when a device has a width of less than or equal to `768` (the same as our media query). The code to use with the Hook is identical across each of these components, so I will only show the `SideBar` component here. Please update the other components yourself in a similar manner:

```
import React from "react";
import { useWindowDimensions } from "../hooks/
useWindowDimensions";
const SideBar = () => {
  const { width } = useWindowDimensions();
  if (width <= 768) {
    return null;
  }
```

```
    return <div className="sidebar">Sidebar</div>;
};
export default SideBar;
```

As you can see, we use the `useWindowDimensions` Hook to get the `width` dimension. We then check if it is `768` or lower and if it is, we return `null`; otherwise, we return the normal JSX. The other components will have the same code for the `useWindowDimensions` Hook.

If you run the app, you will see that the white gap is now gone and that these components are not rendered in the HTML. Note that to save time, we will only support desktop and mobile portrait mode for iPhone X. Supporting every possible device configuration is beyond the scope of this book. Here is a good link on the topic of supporting multiple device screens from Google: `https://developers.google.com/web/fundamentals/codelabs/ your-first-multi-screen-site`.

Before we continue, let's flesh out our client base configurations, such as Redux and React Router.

5. Update your `index.tsx` file so that it includes Redux and React Router. We covered Redux and React Router in *Chapter 7, Learning Redux and React Router*. As always, the source code is available if you get stuck.

6. Now, let's create a folder inside the `src` folder called `store` and add our Redux files there. Create the `AppState.ts` and `configureStore.ts` files and enter the code as shown in the source files. We are not ready for `UserProfileReducer` yet, so you can leave it out for now. We won't be using Redux middleware since I showed this in *Chapter 7, Learning Redux and React Router*.

Now, before we continue and start creating components, let's add a newer React feature to our app that will help us add more polish.

# Error Boundaries

Error Boundaries is a lot like exception handling for React Components. In a large app, it is not always possible to prevent all errors that may occur. So, by using Error Boundaries with our components, we can "catch" unanticipated errors and provide a better user experience to our users. When errors occur, we'll display an error screen that we pre-create rather than some ominous looking technical error message. Let's get started:

1.   First, let's create our Error Boundary file. Inside of the `components` folder, create a file called `ErrorBoundary.tsx` and add the source code from this book's GitHub repository to it. Note that Error Boundaries still uses the older class style because we need the `getDerivedStateFromError` and `componentDidCatch` life cycle event handlers to catch errors. The React team does plan to add a Hooks equivalent eventually.

     At the top of the file, notice that we also have a matching CSS style file. It's trivial, so I won't show it here, but you can find it in the source code.

     First, we will create a type for our Error Boundary's props called `ErrorBoundaryProps`.

     Next, we must create another type for our Error Boundary's local state called `ErrorBoundaryState`. At the beginning of the `ErrorBoundary` class definition, we will see some boilerplate with the constructor for setting up the state. Immediately following this, we will use the `getDerivedStateFromError` function to tell React to show the error UI if `hasError` is true.

     On *line 31*, it is in our `componentDidCatch` function that our component realizes an error of some kind occurred and sets our `hasError` state variable to true. We can also run our own code here to log errors and notify support if needed.

     Finally, if `hasError` is true, we render our message so that users do not have to see strange technical messages that can be confusing. You can, of course, write your own custom message.

     > **Warning**
     >
     > Error Boundaries do not catch errors that are occurring inside event handlers, asynchronous code, or server-side rendered React, as well as errors thrown by Error Boundaries themselves. You must deal with those yourself generally using `try catch`.

2.  Now, let's test our Error Boundary by throwing an error inside one of our components. Update the `Main.tsx` file's `Main` function, like this:

```
const Main = () => {
  const test = true;
  if (test) throw new Error("Main fail");
  else {
    return <main className="content">Main</main>;
  }
};
```

As you can see, we deliberately throw an `Error`.

3.  Try running the app now. You should see the type of screen we were trying to avoid. Why is this happening? This is happening because we are currently in development mode and React deliberately shows all errors in this mode. If we were in production mode, by running `npm run build`, we would see the Error Boundary message.

However, we can still view our Error Boundary screen while in development mode if we click on the **x** button on the Chrome browser's upper right-hand corner. If you do this, you should see the following message:

**Something has gone wrong. Please reload your screen.**

Figure 12.4 – Error Boundary message

As you can see, our normal error message now appears. And again, feel free to style this message as you see fit. To save time, we will leave it as-is.

# Data Service layer

In our application, we will be making calls to either a GraphQL API or a Web API, or fetching network calls. However, none of these backend services are ready yet. For now, we'll create a file that will contain fake network calls to simulate a real backend. Once our real backend arrives, we will remove this feature:

1. First, create a folder called `services` inside `src` and then create the `DataService.ts` file inside it. Since this is code we will soon discard, I won't show it here, but you can grab the code from the source files. Note that some references to Model types will be in this service, so you'll need to add those and we'll cover them as this chapter progresses.

2. Now that we have a way of getting data, let's update our `LeftMenu` component so that it uses it. But first, we need to create our `Category` type since we are using TypeScript. Create a new folder called `model` inside `src`. Then, create the `Category.ts` file and add the source code to it.

3. Now, update the `LeftMenu.tsx` file. First, we will update the imports by adding the model type called `Category` and then the `LeftMenu.css` file. We'll be using these later in our code.

4. Then, on *line 9*, create our state object called `categories` that contains our list of categories. Before we can load `Category` data, we need some default text, `Left Menu`.

5. Then, on *line 13*, we have `useEffect`, where we make a call to our `getCategories` function and get our `Categories`. Then, we use the ES6 `map` function to convert our objects into JSX.

6. Finally, in the returned JSX, we use the `Categories` state object in our UI.

If you reload your browser, you will see a 2-second delay due to the timers in our fake `DataService`, and then the list of categories, like this:

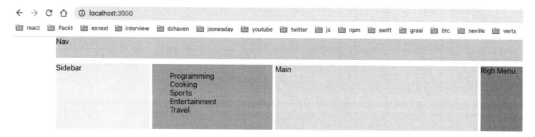

Figure 12.5 – Loaded categories

Again, we'll remove `DataService` once our real server calls are ready.

# Navigation menu

Now that we have a base configuration and layout, we can start creating our SideBar menu. The interesting thing about our SideBar menu items is that they will be used on both the SideBar and as a drop-down modal for mobile devices. This way, we can write less code by having only a single component for both display types.

Now, in order to create the SideBar with a correct set of links, we need to know if the user is logged in. If they are not logged in, we will show them login and register menus. If they are logged in, we will show them logout and UserProfile menus. The UserProfile menu screen will show the user's settings, as well as a list of posts that they have made. Since the login state of our user will be shared across the application, let's put this data into our Redux store:

1. We will use the existence of a `UserProfile` object instance, or lack thereof, as an indication that a user is logged in. First, let's add a new reducer to our currently empty reducers set. Create a new folder inside `store` called `user`. Now, create a file called `Reducer.ts` and add the required source code.

2. Then, create an action type called `UserProfileSetType` so that our `UserProfileReducer` can be distinguished from other reducers.

3. Next, we must create a payload type called `UserProfilePayload`. This is the data that will be in our actions when they are dispatched later.

4. Then, we must create the `UserProfileAction` interface, which is of the `action` type. This is used to distinguish an action for UserProfiles from some other action type.

5. Finally, we have our actual reducer, `UserProfileReducer`, which performs filtering based on our desired `UserProfileSetType`. Again, Redux was covered in *Chapter 7, Learning Redux and React Router*.

6. In order to help us style our components, we'll need to use icons to provide a better visual presentation. Let's install Font Awesome as it is a free and provides an attractive kit of styles and icons that are very popular for web development. Run the following command:

```
npm i @fortawesome/fontawesome-svg-core @fortawesome/
free-solid-svg-icons @fortawesome/react-fontawesome
```

7.  Now that we've added our icons, let's create a new folder inside `src/components` called `sidebar` and move our existing `SideBar.tsx` file into it. Now, create a new file called `SideBarMenus.tsx` and add the following code to it. Make sure you've added the necessary imports:

```
const SideBarMenus = () => {
    const user = useSelector((state: AppState) => state.
        user);
const dispatch = useDispatch();
```

We use the `useSelector` and `useDispatch` Hooks to access Redux's capabilities:

```
useEffect(() => {
    dispatch({
        type: UserProfileSetType,
        payload: {
            id: 1,
            userName: "testUser",
        },
    });
}, [dispatch]);
```

Then, we use a `useEffect` Hook to call, dispatch, and update our `UserProfile` object. Notice that it is now hardcoded, but we will use a GraphQL call later when our backend is ready:

```
    return (
    <React.Fragment>
        <ul>
            <FontAwesomeIcon icon={faUser} />
                <span className="menu-name">{user?.userName}
                </span>
        </ul>
    </React.Fragment>
    );
};
```

Next, we must add a FontAwesome font for the UserProfile and then show the current username. This menu item will eventually be clickable so that our user's profile screen appears:

```
export default SideBarMenus;
```

As we build out our screens to log in, log out, register, and so on, we will add these menu items to this JSX.

I personally find bullet points distracting, so let's remove all the bullets from all the app's unordered lists by adding the following style to the index.css file:

```
ul {
    list-style-type: none
}
```

8.  Now, we need to update SideBar.tsx so that it uses SideBarMenus.tsx. Update SideBar like this. First, add the appropriate imports, such as SideBarMenus, first:

```
const SideBar = () => {
  const { width } = useWindowDimensions();
  if (width <= 768) {
    return null;
  }
  return (
    <div className="sidebar">
      <SideBarMenus />
    </div>
  );
};
```

Now, we can update the JSX to include it.

Note that we will eventually write some code so that the UserProfile icon and userName will only appear when our user is actually logged in. We will also click enable it so that clicking on it opens our user's UserProfile screen. However, we cannot do this without our backend. For now, we will have it as a placeholder.

9.  Let's continue and reuse our `SideBarMenus` component for mobile display. Update the `Nav.tsx` file inside the `components` folder. Add the appropriate imports:

```
const Nav = () => {
  const { width } = useWindowDimensions();

  const getMobileMenu = () => {
    if (width <= 768) {
      return (
        <FontAwesomeIcon icon={faBars} size="lg"
          className="nav-mobile-menu" />
      );
    }
    return null;
  };
```

Again, we have used our `useWindowDimensions` Hook to determine if we are on a mobile device. However, this time, we have created a function called `getMobileMenu` to handle the logic of deciding what JSX to return. If we are not running a mobile device, it returns nothing; otherwise, it returns the `FontAwesome` icon for the hamburger menu:

```
  return (
    <nav className="navigation">
      {getMobileMenu()}
      <strong>SuperForum</strong>
    </nav>
  );
};
export default Nav;
```

The screen, when viewed on a mobile device, should look like this:

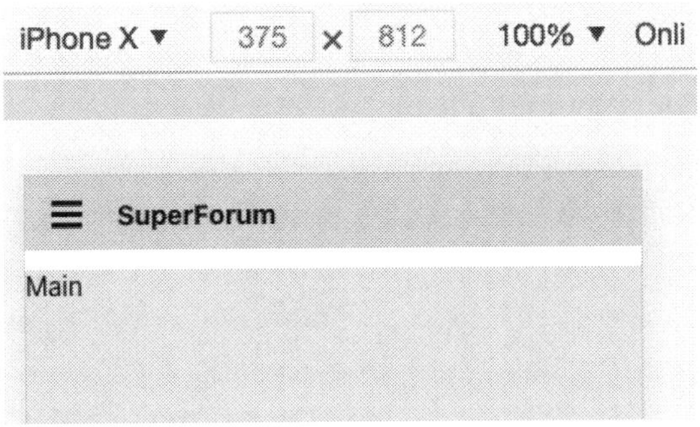

Figure 12.6 – Nav menu in mobile mode

10. As we build out our app, we need to be able to display modals. So, before we continue, we need to install `react-modal`. This package will allow us to make some components modal popups. This makes them more flexible in terms of when we can display them. Install `react-modal` like this:

```
npm i react-modal
npm i @types/react-modal -D
```

11. In order to use this modal and have it be responsive and adapt to different device screens, we need to update our styles. In our `App.css` file, you will see a class called `modal-menu` that has been applied to all our modals.

    This is the default style for modals that our non-mobile devices will get. The main thing to note here is that the modal starts its `left` position at 50% of the screen. Then, we use `transform` to pull it back halfway (50% of itself). This should center our modal so that it's in the middle of the screen. Notice that `z-index` is set high to ensure this modal always appears on top.

    For mobile devices, we use our `App.css` file's existing Media Query to hold an updated `modal-menu`. Basically, we are overriding the same attributes that were in the desktop styles with styles for the mobile Media Query. In this case, we are using `left`, `right`, and `top` to stretch out the modal to the ends of the available screen. This is why our transform is now 0, since it's not needed.

12. Moving on, we will add our click handler to the hamburger icon and then show our `SideBarMenus` component when the icon is clicked. So, we'll need to update our `Nav.tsx` file again so that it includes our modal, which displays `SideBarMenus`. Let's update `Nav.tsx`. Add the appropriate imports first. Then, add the code from the source.

13. If we start by looking on *line 10*, we will see we have a new local state called showMenu. We'll use this to control whether we show or hide our modal menu.

14. The onClickToggle handler is used in FontAwesomeIcon, inside the getMobileMenu function, to toggle the showMenu local state, which shows or hides the modal.

15. In a ReactModal, when any request to close comes into the component, we need to set the state controlling display so that it can be explicitly set to false; otherwise, the modal will not go away. This is what onRequestClose does. The shouldCloseOnOverlayClick property allows us to close the modal, even when we click anywhere outside it. This is a commonly expected behavior by users, so it's good to have.

16. Finally, the JSX has been updated so that we can add our ReactModal, which includes our SideBarMenus component.

    As you can see, the modal is called ReactModal and that among its properties, there's the prop called isOpen. This determines whether the modal is shown or not.

17. If you run the code and then click on the hamburger icon, you will see this:

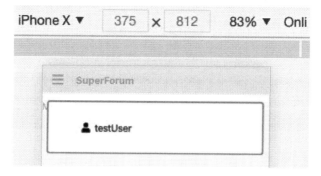

Figure 12.7 – ReactModel with SideBarMenus

Again, we will be building out this menu as we add more features.

## Authentication components

Now that we have our SideBar set up, let's start building our authentication components. We'll start by building our register, login, and logout screens:

1. Let's create the registration modal first. In order to do this, we'll need to add a link for registration inside our `SideBarMenus` component. Open the `SideBarMenus.tsx` file and update it like this:

```
As always add appropriate imports first.
```

The first few lines of code remain the same, so I haven't shown them here. Here is the updated JSX:

```jsx
    return (
      <React.Fragment>
        <ul>
          <li>
            <FontAwesomeIcon icon={faUser} />
            <span className="menu-name">{user?.userName}
            </span>
          </li>
          <li>
            <FontAwesomeIcon icon={faRegistered} />
            <span className="menu-name">register</span>
          </li>
        </ul>
      </React.Fragment>
    );
  };
```

We've added an additional `li` to the returned JSX and included the new icon and label for the register.

2.  Now, before we create our Registration component, let's create a helper service that validates our passwords for us. We want to make sure users enter sufficiently long and complex passwords, so we need a **validator**. Create a new folder inside `src` called `common` and then another folder called `validators`. In the `validators` folder, create a file called `PasswordValidator.ts` and add the following code to it. The code is pretty simple, so I won't show all of it here, but do notice the password strength and the Regular Expression. A Regular Expression is just a programmatic way of searching for patterns in a string:

```
const strongPassword = new RegExp(
    "^(?=.*[a-z])(?=.*[A-Z])(?=.*[0-9])(?=.*[!@#$%^&*])
    (?=.{8,})"
);
if (!strongPassword.test(password)) {
    passwordTestResult.message =
        "Password must contain at least 1 special
        character, 1 cap letter, and 1 number";
    passwordTestResult.isValid = false;
}
```

Here, we've used a Regular Expression to check for proper complexity by ensuring that we have both letters, numbers, and symbols in our password. Parantheses represent a set of related expressions. So, first, we have lowercase letters, then uppercase letters, then numbers, then symbols, and finally an expected length:

```
return passwordTestResult;
};
```

This code isn't particularly complicated, but since we are going to need this across several components, such as registration and on the server, having it in a separate file is better for code reuse.

> **Note**
>
> In SPA web development, validations are generally done twice – once on the client and again on the server. Doing this twice may seem redundant, but it's necessary for added security. Once we start building out our server code, we'll learn how to share dependencies like this across projects.

3.  Since we're creating multiple authentication-related components, let's create a folder inside `components` called `auth` and then place our authentication-related files there. Once you've created the `auth` folder, add a file called `Registration.tsx` in there. Add the following code to the file. If you look at the source code, you will be able to see the necessary imports. Make sure your `App.css` file is updated as well. Note that eventually, we'll move some of this code into a shared location, but for now, we'll use it directly in our `Registration` component:

```
const userReducer = (state: any, action: any) => {
  switch (action.type) {
    case "userName":
      return { ...state, userName: action.payload };
    case "password":
      return { ...state, password: action.payload };
    case "passwordConfirm":
      return { ...state, passwordConfirm: action.payload
        };
    case "email":
      return { ...state, email: action.payload };
    case "resultMsg":
      return { ...state, resultMsg: action.payload };
    default:
      return { ...state, resultMsg: "A failure has
        occurred." };
  }
};
```

Here, we are creating our reducer, which has many related fields:

```
export interface RegistrationProps {
  isOpen: boolean;
  onClickToggle: (
    e: React.MouseEvent<Element, MouseEvent> | React.
    KeyboardEvent<Element>
  ) => void;
}
```

Since this is a modal component, we are allowing our parent components to control how this component is viewed by passing props. The `isOpen` prop controls how the modal is displayed, while the `onClickToggle` function controls hiding and showing the modal:

```
const Registration: FC<RegistrationProps> = ({ isOpen,
onClickToggle }) => {
  const [isRegisterDisabled, setRegisterDisabled] =
    useState(true);
  const [
      { userName, password, email, passwordConfirm,
resultMsg },
      dispatch,
    ] = useReducer(userReducer, {
      userName: "davec",
      password: "",
      email: "admin@dzhaven.com",
      passwordConfirm: "",
      resultMsg: "",
    });
```

Here, we have the `isRegisterDisabled` local state value, which disables the register button if the given values are not correct, and, of course, our local reducer, `userReducer`:

```
const allowRegister = (msg: string, setDisabled:
    boolean) => {
    setRegisterDisabled(setDisabled);
    dispatch({ payload: msg, type: "resultMsg" });
  };
```

`allowRegister` is just a helper function for setting the register button to disabled and showing a message if needed.

4. Next, we have a series of `onChange` event handlers for each field, such as the `userName` field. They each do validation as needed, as well as update the typed-in text:

```
const onChangeUserName = (e: React.
ChangeEvent<HTMLInputElement>) => {
    dispatch({ payload: e.target.value, type: "userName"
  });
```

```
    if (!e.target.value) allowRegister("Username cannot
    be empty", true);
    else allowRegister("", false);
};
```

The onChangeUserName function is used to set a userName and validate whether registration is allowed to continue:

```
const onChangeEmail = (e: React.
ChangeEvent<HTMLInputElement>) => {
  dispatch({ payload: e.target.value, type: "email" });
  if (!e.target.value) allowRegister("Email cannot be
  empty", true);
  else allowRegister("", false);
};
```

The onChangeEmail function is used to set the email and validate whether registration is allowed to continue:

```
const onChangePassword = (e: React.
ChangeEvent<HTMLInputElement>) => {
  dispatch({ payload: e.target.value, type: "password" });
  const passwordCheck: PasswordTestResult =
  isPasswordValid(e.target.value);
  if (!passwordCheck.isValid) {
  allowRegister(passwordCheck.message, true);
  return;
  }
  passwordsSame(passwordConfirm, e.target.value);
};
```

The onChangePassword function is used to set the password and validate whether registration is allowed to continue:

```
const onChangePasswordConfirm = (e: React.
ChangeEvent<HTMLInputElement>) => {
    dispatch({ payload: e.target.value, type:
    "passwordConfirm" });
    passwordsSame(password, e.target.value);
};
```

The onChangedPasswordConfirm function is used to set passwordConfirm and validate whether registration is allowed to continue:

```
const passwordsSame = (passwordVal: string,
passwordConfirmVal: string) => {
  if (passwordVal !== passwordConfirmVal) {
    allowRegister("Passwords do not match", true);
    return false;
  } else {
    allowRegister("", false);
    return true;
  }
};
```

Finally, since this is a registration component, we use passwordsSame to check whether the password and the confirmation password are equal.

5.  Next, we have onClickRegister and onClickCancel. The onClickRegister button click handler will submit the attempted registration. Currently, since we have no backend, it does no actual submission, but we'll fill it in once we have the server up. On the other hand, the onClickCancel handler exits the Registration component:

```
const onClickRegister = (
  e: React.MouseEvent<HTMLButtonElement, MouseEvent>
) => {
  e.preventDefault();
  onClickToggle(e);
};
const onClickCancel = (
  e: React.MouseEvent<HTMLButtonElement, MouseEvent>
) => {
  onClickToggle(e);
};
```

Note that the e.preventDefault function simply prevents the standard behavior, which is different depending on the context. In the case of forms, our onClickRegister handler is associated with a button inside a form tag, so the default behavior is to submit and cause a page refresh. A page refresh is **not** what we want in a SPA, so we restrict it by using preventDefault.

6. Now that the event handlers have been set up we return the JSX that is tied to those handlers. First, we start with the `ReactModal` wrapper component:

```
return (
    <ReactModal
        className="modal-menu"
        isOpen={isOpen}
        onRequestClose={onClickToggle}
        shouldCloseOnOverlayClick={true}
    >
    <form>
        <div className="reg-inputs">
            <div>
                <label>username</label>
                <input type="text" value={userName}
                onChange={onChangeUserName} />
            </div>
```

Again, our modal is controlled externally by a parent component via the `isOpen` and `onClickToggle` props.

```
<div>
    <label>email</label>
    <input type="text" value={email}
    onChange={onChangeEmail} />
</div>
```

Here, we have our email field.

```
            <div>
            <label>password</label>
            <input
              type="password"
              placeholder="Password"
              value={password}
              onChange={onChangePassword}
            />
            </div>
```

This is our password field.

```
<div>
    <label>password confirmation</label>
    <input
        type="password"
        placeholder="Password Confirmation"
        value={passwordConfirm}
        onChange={onChangePasswordConfirm}
    />
    </div>
</div>
```

This is our password confirmation field.

```
<div className="reg-buttons">
    <div className="reg-btn-left">
        <button
            style={{ marginLeft: ".5em" }}
            className="action-btn"
            disabled={isRegisterDisabled}
            onClick={onClickRegister}
        >
        Register
        </button>
```

Here, we have our button to register.

```
        <button
            style={{ marginLeft: ".5em" }}
            className="cancel-btn"
            onClick={onClickCancel}
        >
        Close
        </button>
```

Here is our button to cancel.

```
    </div>
        <span className="reg-btn-right">
            <strong>{resultMsg}</strong></strong>
```

```
          </span>
        </div>
      </form>
    </ReactModal>
  );
};

export default Registration;
```

Finally, note that we have a message section that's using the `resultMsg` reducer field. This will show errors if something has gone wrong.

7.  Now, if you run the app in desktop mode, you should see something this:

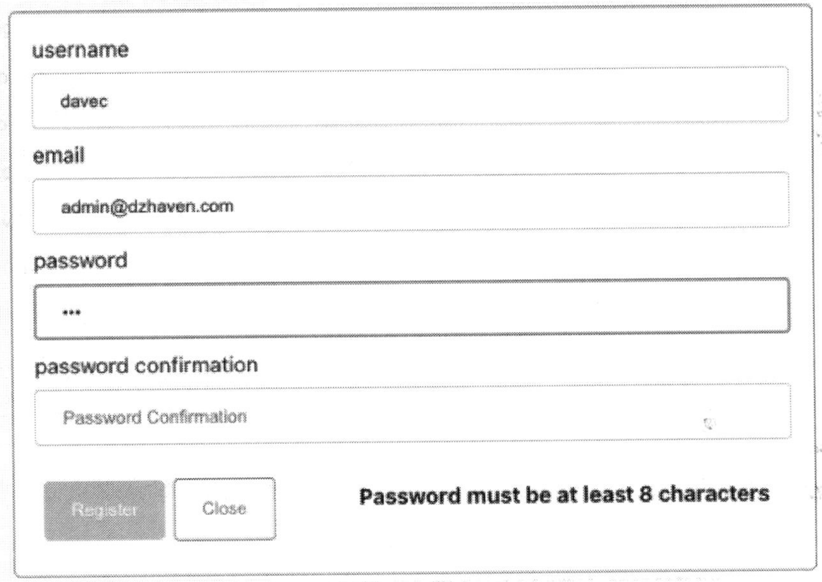

Figure 12.8 – Desktop registration modal view

If you run your Chrome debugger and switch to mobile mode, you will see the following screen after clicking on your hamburger icon and then the register label:

Figure 12.9 – Mobile registration modal view

As you can see, we were able to effectively get two screens with only a single component by using CSS responsive capabilities.

8.  Now, let's move on to the login modal. If we take a look at the existing `Registration` component, we will see that it contains some code that we could also use in our `Login` component. We really should refactor the code so that it can be reused. For example, `Registration`, `Login`, and `Logout` will all use `ReactModal` and therefore receive props to control the modal's display. So, let's see what we can do to reuse our existing code. First, let's extract the `RegistrationProps` interface from the `Registration.tsx` file and place it in its own file. Create a folder called `types` inside `components`. Then, create a file called `ModalProps.ts` and add the `RegistrationProps` interface. Rename it `ModalProps`.

As you can see, it's the same as `RegistrationProps` except for the name change. Now, open the `Registration.tsx` file, remove `RegistrationProps`, and import `ModalProps`. Then, replace `RegistrationProps` with `ModalProps`. Check that everything still runs.

9.  We refactored `ModalProps` so that it can be reused across components. Now, let's pull out `UserReducer` since `Login` uses some of its fields. Create a new folder called `common` inside the existing `auth` folder and create the `UserReducer.ts` file. Place the following code inside it:

```
const userReducer = (state: any, action: any) => {
  switch (action.type) {
    case "userName":
      return { ...state, userName: action.payload };
    case "password":
      return { ...state, password: action.payload };
    case "passwordConfirm":
      return { ...state, passwordConfirm: action.payload
      };
    case "email":
      return { ...state, email: action.payload };
    case "resultMsg":
      return { ...state, resultMsg: action.payload };
    case "isSubmitDisabled":
      return { ...state, isSubmitDisabled: action.payload
  };
    default:
      return { ...state, resultMsg: "A failure has
        occurred." };
  }
};
export default userReducer;
```

Notice that we added a new field called `isSubmitDisabled`. This field will replace the existing `isRegisterDisabled` so that it can be used to disable buttons across any authentication screens.

Now, remove `userReducer` from the `Registration.tsx` file and import it from the new `UserReducer.ts` file. Also, replace `isRegisterDisabled` with `isSubmitDisabled` and include `isSubmitDisabled` in your `destructured` object, as well as the state initializer of the `useReducer` Hook call.

10. Now, let's do one more refactor. The `allowRegister` function in `Registration` disables a button and updates the status message. This can also clearly be reused. Let's create a new file called `Helpers.ts` inside the common folder and add the following code inside it:

```
import { Dispatch } from "react";

export const allowSubmit = (
    dispatch: Dispatch<any>,
    msg: string,
    setDisabled: boolean
) => {
    dispatch({ type: "isSubmitDisabled", payload:
setDisabled });
    dispatch({ payload: msg, type: "resultMsg" });
};
```

As you can see, we changed the function name to `allowSubmit` and we are now taking `dispatch` as a parameter. Now, remove `allowRegister` from `Registration` and import the new `allowSubmit` function and update the `allowRegister` calls to `allowSubmit` calls. Check the code of your `Registration.tsx` file against the source code.

We'll leave the two `onClick` calls as-is, even though `Login` will also have similar calls, as we'll probably have to do some component-specific things for these calls later once our backend is ready.

You should now be able to run this code.

11. Now, we can use the newly extracted code in our new `Login` component. In the `auth` folder, create a new file called `Login.tsx` and add the relevant code from the source code. I'll highlight a few items here:

```
const [
    { userName, password, resultMsg, isSubmitDisabled },
    dispatch,
```

```
  ] = useReducer(userReducer, {
    userName: "",
    password: "",
    resultMsg: "",
    isSubmitDisabled: true,
  });
```

Since our `Login` component has different needs than our `Registration` component, we are only using a subset of the fields from our `userReducer` by using object destructuring.

In the JSX, notice that we've updated some of the CSS classes in order to align the buttons better. These new classes are in the `App.css` file.

12. Finally, we need to add a link for logging in. Update the `SideBarMenu.tsx` file, as shown in the source code.

Since `Logout` is very similar, I've added the component but will not cover it here. We'll add code to control which menu links are shown depending on user login status later as the backend gets more fleshed out. We'll also add additional validation. However, we have a lot more work to do before that, so let's continue.

# Routing and screens

Now, let's continue by creating the routes that our application will need. Up to this point, we have had only a single URL for our app. The root URL is `http://localhost:3000`. We now want to divide our application so that it has distinct routes for specific sections of our application. We'll start by taking our existing code, modifying it, and making that into our first root React Route. Let's get started:

1. First, let's move our Grid area-related components into distinct folders. First, create a folder called `areas` inside the `components` folder. Then, move the `Nav.tsx`, `Nav.css`, `RightMenu.tsx`, `Main.tsx`, `LeftMenu.tsx`, and `LeftMenu.css` files, as well as the entire `sidebar` folder, into the new `areas` folder. Your file path imports will need to be updated, including the `App.tsx` file. Take a look at the source code to learn how to do that.

2. Once you've done that, create a new folder inside `areas` called `main` and move the `Main.tsx` file inside it. Make sure to update your paths. We'll be adding all our main area-related components into this folder.

3.  The first new component we'll create in this folder is a `MainHeader` component. As the name implies, it will be used as a header for the main section. It will show what category of thread items we are currently looking at. Create the `MainHeader.tsx` file inside the `main` folder and add the code from the source into it.

    This control's only purpose is to display the current `Category` name.

Again, note that we have some new CSS classes in the `MainHeader.css` and `App.css` files.

## Home screen

Before we continue, let's perform some basic setup for our new route. Here, we'll create our new screen component, `Home`, and update any related files, such as `App.tsx`:

1.  When we first created our `App.tsx` file, we did so as if our application will have only one screen. Obviously, this is not true. Now that we have fleshed out our layout, let's begin adding our distinct screens and routes. Open the `App.tsx` file and update it like this.

    Here, we have added a new import called `Home` that represents the main page route. We will build this later:

    ```
    import Home from "./components/routes/Home";function
    App() {
    const renderHome = (props: any) => <Home {...props} />;
    ```

    We are defining a function here to send to our route's `render` property. This function allows all the route's props, as well as any custom props we would like to send, to be included in the initialization of our `Home` component:

    ```
    return (
        <Switch>
            <Route exact={true} path="/" render={renderHome} />
            <Route
                path="/categorythreads/:categoryId"
                render={renderHome}
            />
        </Switch>
    );
    }
    ```

So, the previous code that showed our Grid areas will now be in the Home component, which again, we will build shortly.

As shown in *Chapter 7, Learning Redux and React Router*, our Switch component allows React Router to change the rendering of route screens based on the URL provided. For now, we will have two routes pointing to the same Home screen, but we will add more later. The root path will show Threads for a default category, while the categorythreads route will show Threads for a specific category.

2.  Before we create our new Home component, let's refactor our CSS a bit and make it more reusable. First, update the App.css file by adding the following class above the App class:

```css
.screen-root-container {
    margin: 0 auto;
    max-width: 1200px;
    margin-bottom: 2em;
    border: var(--border);
    border-radius: 0.3em;
}
```

This will now become the root class for any components that represent route screens in our app.

3.  Next, create a new file called Home.css inside the components/routes folder. Now, cut this entire set of CSS styles from App.css:

```css
.App { // note this class is rename into home-container
    // later
    margin: 0 auto;
    max-width: 1200px;
    display: grid;
    grid-template-columns: 0.7fr 0.9fr 1.5fr 0.9fr;
    grid-template-rows: 2.75rem 3fr;
    grid-template-areas:
        "nav nav nav nav"
        "sidebar leftmenu content rightmenu";
    gap: 0.75rem 0.4rem;
}
```

The next set of CSS classes are the Grid areas:

```css
.navigation {
  grid-area: nav;
}
.sidebar {
  min-height: var(--min-screen-height);
  grid-area: sidebar;
  background-color: aliceblue;
}
.leftmenu {
  grid-area: leftmenu;
  background-color: skyblue;
}
.content {
  min-height: var(--min-screen-height);
  grid-area: content;
  background-color: blanchedalmond;
  padding: 0.5em 0.75em 0.5em 0.75em;
}
.rightmenu {
  grid-area: rightmenu;
  background-color: coral;
}
```

Now, copy this code into our new Home.css file. Once they've been copied over, change the name of the App class to home-container. We're changing the name so that the class' purpose is clearer. Now, let's create our new Home screen component and learn how to use these CSS classes.

4.  Create a folder inside the components folder called routes and add a new file called Home.tsx inside it. The code is short and simple, so you can just copy it from the source. It's mostly the old code from the previous version of App.tsx.

We've updated our root CSS App class so that it's now screen-root-container home-container. Using two classes in one class attribute simply means to first apply the first class style and then apply the next, which will override any settings from the prior. Also, we will now be able to use screen-root-container in the other screens.

We've successfully moved our original `App.tsx` code into the `Home.tsx` file. Notice that we also placed our `Nav` component inside a `div` tag. We're doing this so that we can reuse the `Nav` component later in other screens. You should now remove the `className="navigation"` attribute from your `Nav.tsx` component file.

5.  Now that we have updated our `Home` screen, we need to update our `Main` component so that it lists the threads within the given category. In order to do this, we actually need to do quite a few updates. First, we need to create two new models called `Thread` and `ThreadItem`. `Thread` is the initial post, while `ThreadItem` is a response. Let's start with our models.

    First, create `Thread.ts` in the `models` folder, as shown in the source code.

    There's not much to explain here as it's fairly obvious. However, note that `points` indicates the total number of likes.

    Next, let's do `ThreadItem.ts`. Create the required file and add the source code to it. It's pretty similar to `Thread`.

6.  Now, we will create the thread card file component. This component will represent a single Thread record and will show things such as its title, body, and points. Create a file called `ThreadCard.tsx` inside the `components/areas/main` folder. Then, add the code to it:

```
import React, { FC } from "react";
import "./ThreadCard.css";
import Thread from "../../../models/Thread";
import { Link, useHistory } from "react-router-dom";
import { faEye, faHeart, faReplyAll } from "@fortawesome/
free-solid-svg-icons";
import { FontAwesomeIcon } from "@fortawesome/react-
fontawesome";
import { useWindowDimensions } from "../../../hooks/
useWindowDimensions";
```

First, we have various imports, including the `Link` object and the `useHistory` Hook from React Router:

```
interface ThreadCardProps {
    thread: Thread;
}
```

Notice we are accepting the `Thread` object as our parameter. We will use this object and its members as we render our `ThreadCard` UI:

```
const ThreadCard: FC<ThreadCardProps> = ({ thread }) => {
  const history = useHistory();
  const { width } = useWindowDimensions();

  const onClickShowThread = (e: React.
  MouseEvent<HTMLDivElement>) => {
    history.push("/thread/" + thread.id);
  };
```

Here, we are using the React Router `useHistory` Hook to get the `history` object. When someone clicks on our Thread, we use the `history` object to redirect the app to a new URL by `pushing` the new URL on top of the `history` object. We will build our thread route and component later:

```
const getPoints = (thread: Thread) => {
  if (width <= 768) {
    return (
      <label
        style={{
          marginRight: ".75em",
          marginTop: ".25em",
        }}
      >
        {thread.points || 0}
        <FontAwesomeIcon
          icon={faHeart}
          className="points-icon"
          style={{
            marginLeft: ".2em",
          }}
        />
      </label>
    );
  }
  return null;
};
```

The getPoints function creates the UI for displaying "likes" on our post. However, since our UI is responsive, it does not appear in desktop mode when we check the screen's width property:

```
const getResponses = (thread: Thread) => {
    if (width <= 768) {
        return (
            <label
                style={{
                    marginRight: ".5em",
                }}
            >
                {thread && thread.threadItems && thread.
                 threadItems.length}
```

This function shows the response count, as indicated by the thread.threadItems.length property:

```
            <FontAwesomeIcon
                icon={faReplyAll}
                className="points-icon"
                style={{
                    marginLeft: ".25em",
                    marginTop: "-.25em",
                }}
            />
            </label>
        );
    }
    return null;
};
```

The getResponses function shows how many ThreadItems responses there are for this Thread. However, since our UI is responsive, it does not appear in desktop mode when we check the screen's width property:

```
const getPointsNonMobile = () => {
    if (width > 768) {
        return (
            <div className="threadcard-points">
```

```
            <div className="threadcard-points-item">
            {thread.points || 0}
            <br />
            <FontAwesomeIcon icon={faHeart}
              className="points-icon" />
          </div>
          <div
            className="threadcard-points-item"
            style={{ marginBottom: ".75em" }}
          >
            {thread && thread.threadItems && thread.
            threadItems.length}
```

This function is getting the likes count, as indicated by the `thread.threadItems.length` property:

```
            <br />
            <FontAwesomeIcon icon={faReplyAll}
              className="points-icon" />
          </div>
        </div>
      );
    }
    return null;
  };
```

The `getPointsNonMobile` function returns the points column on the right of `ThreadCard`, but only renders it if the device is a desktop or laptop with a screen width bigger than 768 pixels.

Remember that every React component that may be used multiple times on the same screen must have a unique `key` value. So, later, when we use this component, you will see that each instance has been given a unique `key` value. The following JSX is returning the `Category` name as a `Link` so that when it's clicked, the user will be sent to the screen showing the Threads for that `Category`:

```
  return (
    <section className="panel threadcard-container">
      <div className="threadcard-txt-container">
        <div className="content-header">
          <Link
```

```
        to={`/categorythreads/${thread.category.id}`}
        className="link-txt"
    >
        <strong>{thread.category.name}</strong>
    </Link>
```

Link is a React Router component that renders a URL anchor (HTTP link). Notice that categorythreads is the second route we created earlier and that it takes categoryId as a parameter:

```
        <span className="username-header" style={{
            marginLeft: ".5em" }}>
            {thread.userName}
        </span>
    </div>
    <div className="question">
        <div
            onClick={onClickShowThread}
            data-thread-id={thread.id}
            style={{ marginBottom: ".4em" }}
        >
            <strong>{thread.title}</strong>
        </div>
        <div
            className="threadcard-body"
            onClick={onClickShowThread}
            data-thread-id={thread.id}
        >
            <div>{thread.body}</div>
        </div>
```

As you can see, we use the thread prop extensively while rendering our UI.

Here, we are using the getPoints and getResponses functions to render a subset of our UI so that it shows points and responses:

```
        <div className="threadcard-footer">
            <span
                style={{
                    marginRight: ".5em",
```

```
                }}
            >
                <label>
                    {thread.views}
                    <FontAwesomeIcon icon={faEye}
                        className="icon-lg" />
                </label>
            </span>
            <span>
                {getPoints(thread)}
                {getResponses(thread)}
            </span>              </div>
        </div>
    </div>
```

Here, we are using `getPointsNonMobile` to show our response count and likes:

```
            {getPointsNonMobile()}    </section>
    );
};

export default ThreadCard;
```

Notice that we have referenced many CSS classes in this component, all of which can be found in the `ThreadCard.css` and `App.css` files in the source code. I won't go over every single CSS class here, but if you look at the `ThreadCard.css` file, you'll notice that there is a reference to something called `flex`. Flexbox is another method of creating a layout in CSS similar to Grids. However, Flexbox is intended to be used for single-row or single-column layouts; for example:

```
.threadcard-txt-container {
    display: flex;
    flex-direction: column;
    width: 92%;
    margin: 0.75em 1em 0.75em 1.2em;
    border-right: solid 1px var(--border-color);
}
```

In this CSS, the display method is indicated as `flex` and `flex-direction` is column. This means that the layout of all the elements inside `threadcard-txt-container` will be in a single stacked column. So, even if we had elements such as labels or buttons, which are normally set in a horizontal line, if they live inside a column-based flex container, they will be laid out vertically. If we had used the row attribute, then the layout would be horizontal.

7. Now that we've created our Thread container, `ThreadCard`, let's update our `Main.tsx` file so that we can use it. Add the code from the source.

   if you look on *line 8*, you will see the `useParams` function being used. Previously, we created two routes for React Router in the `App.tsx` file. One of the routes, `categorythreads`, accepted a URL parameter. By using the `useParams` Hook, we can get route parameters – in this case, `categoryId` – so that we can use them.

   Then, on *line 9*, we have the `category` state. Once we've retrieved our category from the list of threads, we will update this state.

   On *line 10*, we have a state object, which is a list of our `ThreadCards`, called `threadCards`.

   Then, in `useEffect`, we are updating our list of `ThreadCards` if we get a new `categoryId`. When we get a valid `categoryId`, we use our `DataService` to query for a list of threads that are specific to that category and then build out a list of `ThreadCards`. We also take the first thread to get the name of the category, since they all have the same category.

   Finally, we return our UI.

> **Note**
>
> Sometimes, you will see warnings about missing dependencies on the array of the `useEffect` Hook. These are what I consider opinionated warnings and with experience, you will be able to judge which of them can be safely ignored. For example, in `useEffect` for `Main.tsx`, I am deliberately ignoring this warning about the `category` state object, because including the object in the array would trigger an unnecessary double run of `useEffect` (because `useEffect` runs whenever something in its array list has changed) and possibly a double render.

8.  Now, let's try running in desktop mode. Go to `http://localhost:3000/categorythreads/1`. You should see the following:

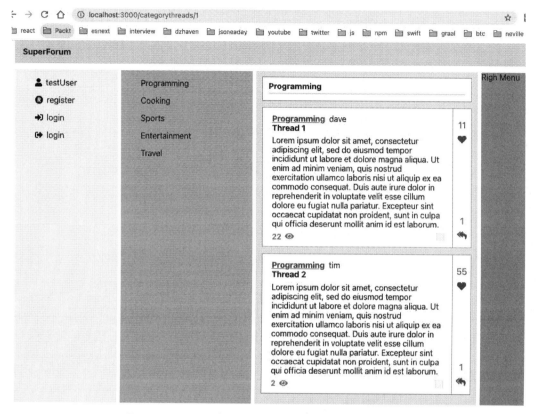

Figure 12.10 – Desktop view of the categorythreads URL

Here's what it looks like on mobile:

Figure 12.11 – Mobile view of the categorythreads URL

As you can see, in mobile mode, we don't have the right column of points. Instead, those points are in the bottom of the main text section. The icons show that, for the first post, two people have seen it. 55 people liked it, and one person responded.

Wow – that was a lot of code we just went through! However, we're not done yet! Let's continue by building our `RightMenu` component.

On our `RightMenu`, we want to show a list of the top three categories with the most thread postings. In each category, we'll show the topmost viewed threads. Let's get started:

1. First, create a folder for `RightMenu` inside the `areas` folder called `rightMenu`.

2. Now, create a new file inside that folder called `TopCategory.tsx`. This component will represent a single top category and its threads.

3. Create a new model that will represent the data coming from the server. Let's call it `CategoryThread`. Create a file called `CategoryThread.ts` inside the `models` folder and enter the source code.

4.  Now, we need to update our existing `RightMenu` component and create a new component that will display our `CategoryThread` items. To group and organize our `CategoryThread` items, we need to use a tool called Lodash to help us.

    Lodash is a dependency that provides an enormous library of JavaScript helper functions. It would be impossible to go through all its capabilities here. However, Lodash is particularly useful for managing arrays and collections. You will see it's pretty straightforward to use, but if you would like more details, here's a link to their documentation: `https://lodash.com/docs/`. Install Lodash like this:

    ```
    npm I lodash @types/lodash
    ```

    > **Note**
    >
    > Never import the entire Lodash library by using `import _ from "lodash"`. You will add an enormous amount of code to your project by doing so. Only import the specific call using `import groupBy from "lodash/groupBy"`.

    Now, we can update our `RightMenu.tsx` file as shown in the source code.

    First, notice that in addition to Lodash, we also imported a new `RightMenu.css` file, along with some minor styling. We also imported the `TopCategory` component, which we'll build after.

    Next, we have a new state object called `topCategories` that we will use to store our array of top categories.

    Then, in `useEffect`, we have our top categories from the `getTopCategories` function. Then, we group the results by category and create our array of `TopCategory` elements. The `TopCategory` component elements will display our data. Notice that the `TopCategory` component receives each group of top categories through the `topCategories` prop.

    The component then returns the `topCategories` elements.

5.  Now, we need to build our `TopCategory` component. Create the file called `TopCategory.tsx` in the same folder as `RightMenu` and add the relevant source code to it.

    At the top, notice that we have a complementary CSS file called `TopCategory.css`.

Next, we have a new interface called `TopCategoryProps` for receiving props. On *line 10*, the threads state object will store our JSX element when it's ready.

Then, on *line 12*, we have `useEffect`, which we will use to build our UI elements based on the passed in prop; that is, `topCategories`.

The returned JSX has a `strong` header, which is the name of the first category element that was found, since the array of top categories is always from one category. Then, we included our list of threads.

6.  Since this `RightMenu` does not render for mobile devices, let's see what it looks like on desktop:

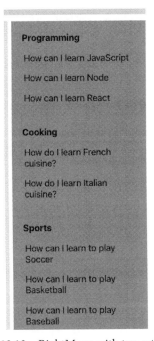

Figure 12.12 – RightMenu with top categories

OK – we're getting there! We've completed most of what we need for our main screen, but now, we need our application to show an individual **Thread posting**.

# Thread posts screen

This screen will be multi-use. Using this screen, we will be able to create a new posting or display an existing one. We will also show Thread responses on the same screen. Let's get started:

1.  First, we need to create our new route component. We'll call it `Thread.tsx` and place it inside a new folder called `thread`, which should be placed inside the `routes` folder. However, our `Thread` component will be complex, so we should split it into modular pieces known as child components. In this case, doing this will not give us code reuse benefits. However, it will make the code easier to read and refactor since it will be distributed in chunks instead of a single very large monolith. Let's create a new component file called `ThreadHeader.tsx` and add the source code to it.

    First, notice the new function we are importing, `getTimePastIfLessThanDay`. This function will look at a passed-in date and format it appropriately for ease of readability.

    This component will take the fields in as parameters and not have a state of its own. `ThreadHeader` is acting as a display-only component. It shows the thread's `title`, `userName`, and `lastModifiedOn` time.

2.  Now, create the `Thread.tsx` file and add the source code to it.

    Notice that we are importing a new `Thread.css` file and our new `ThreadHeader` component. Also, notice that since our component is also called `Thread`, as is our model, I am importing our model as `ThreadModel`. This type of issue can occur somewhat frequently in large projects, so you should be aware that you can import in this manner.

    Next, we must create our local `thread` state object, which is of the `ThreadModel` type. Then, we must use the `useParams` Hook once again to get the route parameter's `id`, which is the ID of the thread for this route.

    In `useEffect`, if the `id` route parameter exists and it is greater than `0`, we attempt to get our `thread`. Later, once our backend is ready, we'll write some code so that new threads can be inserted.

    Finally, we return our UI, which includes `ThreadHeader`. Notice that the `lastModifiedOn` field is non-nullable, so we are using a ternary check for a null `thread` and returning the current date if it is null.

3. Now, we need to create a new route for our `Thread` screen component. Open `App.tsx` again and update the code, like this:

```
function App() {
    const renderHome = (props: any) => <Home {...props} />;
    const renderThread = (props: any) => <Thread {...props} />;
```

Here, we've added the `renderThread` function for our `Thread` component:

```
    return (
        <Switch>
            <Route exact={true} path="/" render={renderHome} />
            <Route
                path="/categorythreads/:categoryId"
                render={renderHome}
            />
            <Route
                path="/thread/:id"
                render={renderThread}
            />
        </Switch>
    );
}
```

Notice that our route for `Thread` is `"/thread/:id"`, which means that after the thread path, it expects a parameter. Internally, React Router will label it `id`.

4. Now, we'll add the next section of our Thread screen. On this screen, we will be displaying the Thread's category via a drop-down menu. However, since the standard dropdown in HTML, called a `select` element, is ugly and does not integrate well with React, we'll use an NPM package called `react-dropdown` to help us get a more attractive and React integrated control.

Install `react-dropdown` like this:

```
npm I react-dropdown
```

Now, create a file called `ThreadCategory.tsx` in the `thread` folder and add the source code to it.

Once you've set up the imports, create the `ThreadCategoryProps` interface, which will represent our prop type.

Next, we start creating our `ThreadCategory` component and set up a constant variable, `catOptions`, that contains the items that will appear as selectable options in our dropdown. Again, we are only temporarily hardcoding values until our backend is ready.

Finally, we are returning the JSX with an initialized `DropDown` control.

5.  Now, let's create our `Title` component. We'll call it `ThreadTitle`. Create a file called `ThreadTitle.tsx` inside the `thread` folder and add the source code to it.

    This is just a simple renderer, so I won't explain it here. However, notice that, at the moment, our `onChangeTitle` handler is blank. Again, once our backend is ready, we will distinguish between read and write states and implement the `onChangeTitle` function.

6.  Now, let's update our `Thread.tsx` file and take a look at what we have so far. Update `Thread.tsx` like this. Note that as we've been adding these Thread-related components, we've been updating the `Thread.css` file, so keep your CSS file updated as well.

    The state and `useEffect` code is basically the same, so I won't show it here:

```
    return (
        <div className="screen-root-container">
            <div className="thread-nav-container">
                <Nav />
            </div>
            <div className="thread-content-container">
                <ThreadHeader
                    userName={thread?.userName}
                    lastModifiedOn={thread ? thread.lastModifiedOn
: new Date()}
                    title={thread?.title}
                />
                <ThreadCategory categoryName={thread?.category?.
name} />
                <ThreadTitle title={thread?.title} />
            </div>
        </div>
```

```
    );
  };
```

Here, we have added our new components to our returned JSX. As you can see, our code is a lot shorter and easier to read than if we had the individual elements and event handlers all in the `Thread.tsx` file.

If you run the app via `http://localhost:3000/thread/1`, you should see this:

Figure 12.13 – Thread screen

Note that the gap on the right is where we will add likes and response count information for the Thread.

Now, we're not reviewing every single CSS file here because we want to focus on the code, but since this is a major screen and route destination, let's review the CSS to see how we laid this out. This is what we have thus far. Update your `Thread.css` file so that we can take a look together.

As we did previously with the Home screen, we placed our nav control inside its own div container called `thread-nav-container`.

This `thread-content-container` class is where the actual Thread content is being laid out. As you can see, the layout is a Grid with two columns and an undefined indeterminate number of rows.

The rest of the content is being added to the first column using the `grid-column` attribute. We will add the second column to hold our Thread's points (likes) later.

7. Now, we need to add a section for the body of our Thread posting. The body entry is a bit more complicated because we will need to add a Rich Text entry formatter. This control will allow users to format their text and do more sophisticated editing.

To create our body, let's install an NPM package called Slate.js. This will be our Rich Text editor and formatter. We'll also need to install several dependencies, including something called Emotion. Emotion is a library that allows us to use CSS directly inside JavaScript:

```
npm i slate slate-react slate-history emotion is-hotkey @
types/is-hotkey @types/slate @types/slate-react
```

Using Slate.js and implementing Rich Text editing is quite complex. It could easily fill a book of its own. Due to this, we'll try and keep things somewhat simple, but as you'll soon see, there's no easy way to implement Rich Text editing. Let's create a folder called `editor` inside our `components` folder and create a new file called `RichTextControls.tsx`. This file contains the controls that we will be using in our editor. The source code I am using is from the Slate.js project at `https://github.com/ianstormtaylor/slate/blob/master/site/components.tsx`. This code is fairly large, so I'll show and explain the relevant code as we use each control.

8.  Next, we need to create the `RichEditor.tsx` file in the same `editor` folder and add this code to it.

    At the top of our imports section, we can see the usual React-related imports, but also two Slate.js imports. These are there to help us create our editor UI. I'll explain these in more detail later.

    The `isHotKey` import is a tool that helps us build keyboard shortcuts for our editor.

    The `withHistory` import allows the editor to save the edits that have occurred, in their correct order, so that they can be undone if needed.

    `Button` and `Toolbar` are controls that can be used to build our editor UI. We'll create the `RichTextControls` file in a moment.

    Now, we can import our icons and CSS stylesheet.

    The `HOTKEYS` variable is a dictionary that contains the various shortcut keys to formatting pairings. [keyName: string] on the left represents the dictionary key; the right-hand side shows the value.

On *line 26*, we have the `initialValue` variable. Our editor uses objects for its value, not strings. So, the `initialValue` variable represents the starting value object of the editor. The type is a `Node` array that comes from the Slate.js editor. In Slate.js, text is represented as hierarchical trees of nodes. This is to make sure that the structure of the text is kept intact, but also to allow formatting information to live alongside the text. You can think of it as text and metadata together.

The `LIST_TYPES` array is used to distinguish between whether an entry is a paragraph or a list of text.

On *line 38*, we start creating our `RichEditor` component. As we mentioned previously, in Slate.js, the value or content of the text inside the editor is not plain text. It is a JSON object and its root type is `Node`. So, our main text value, called `value`, is a state object of the Node array type.

Next, we have the `renderElement` function, which is used internally to render larger text pieces. An `Element` is a multi-line set of text. We'll build the `Element` component in a bit.

Then, we have the `renderLeaf` function, which is used to render smaller bits of text. A `Leaf` is a small snippet of text. We will create this component a bit later.

Note that we covered Hooks, such as `useCallback` and `useMemo`, in *Chapter 5, React Development with Hooks*.

We then have the editor variable. The editor is the React component that accepts and displays text, as opposed to the `Slate`, `Toolbar`, and `Editable` components, which act as wrappers around the editor and inject or modify text formatting for it.

The `useEffect` function is used to grab the `existingBody` prop and make it the local state value, assuming `existingBody` was passed in. Again, an `existingBody` is passed in only during view mode, not create mode.

The `onChangeEditorValue` event handler sets the local `value` state when it is changed in the UI. Again, notice how the value type is not text, but a `Node` array.

Starting on *line 59*, we start our JSX definition. We initialize our Slate wrapper component with our `editor` instance, local `value` state, and the `onChange` event.

Next, `Toolbar`, which is from the `RichTextControls.tsx` file, represents a layout container and contains our buttons for formatting. They look like this. I will explain `MarkButton` and `BlockButton` later:

Figure 12.14 – Slate.js Toolbar buttons

The Editable control contains the main formatters, shortcut keys, and base settings for our editor.

Notice that I've moved out most of the functions outside the main component for readability.

On *line 92*, we have our `MarkButton` control. `MarkButton` is a function that generates the button UI and also associates the actual formatter that triggers when that specific button is clicked. Generally, marks are used for words or characters, as opposed to blocks, which are usually multi-line statements. `Button` is from our `RichTextControls.tsx` file. It represents a styled button on our Toolbar.

Next, we have the `isMarkActive` function. The `isMarkActive` function determines if a formatter has been applied already.

Next, the `toggleMark` function will toggle the formatting based on whether it has been applied or not. It associates the editor with the format.

`BlockButton` sets the formatting for a block of text and creates its button. Usually, a block contains multiple `Nodes`.

The `isBlockActive` function determines if formatting was applied.

`ToggleBlock` toggles the applied formatting.

Next, the `Element` component determines which type of HTML to use. `Elements` are used quite frequently in Slate.js.

We use `Leafs` to determine smaller HTML to return. `Leafs` are frequently used in Slate.js.

We now have a reusable Rich Text editor. We will certainly use this component in our Thread display. Now, since it is its own component, we can reuse this code wherever we like.

9.  Now, we need to add our new `RichEditor` to our `ThreadBody.tsx` file. It is a small component, so just add the code from the source.

10. Finally, we need to reference our `ThreadBody` from our `Thread` component, like this. Make sure you have all the necessary imports. Then, in the JSX, just below `ThreadTitle`, add the following code:

```
<ThreadBody body={thread?.body} />
```

Again, notice how easy it is to read and understand this JSX now that we have put it into components.

Now, let's take a look at what this looks like:

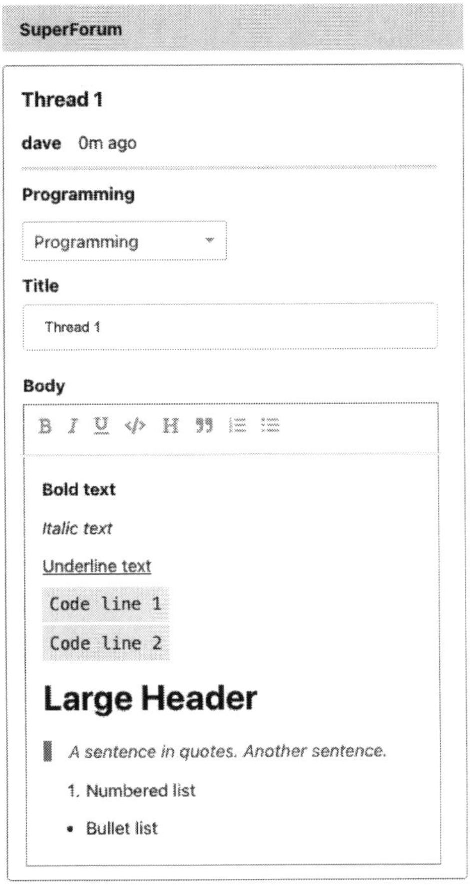

Figure 12.15 – Thread entry screen and its editor

Our Rich Text editor provides the following options: bold, italic, underline, show as code, make header, wrap in quotes, number list, and bullet list. As you can see, all our formatters work.

When using Slate.js, you might be wondering why the bullets appear, even though we added the CSS to remove `ul` styling to our `index.css` file earlier. In order to get proper styling in our editor, I updated that style like this:

```
ul:not([data-slate-node="element"]) {
    list-style-type: none;
}
```

This is a CSS selector that says "do not apply this style if the element has a custom attribute on it called `data-slate-node`". This is what Slate.js uses to distinguish its own elements from other standard HTML.

Wow, that was a lot of code! However, we're not done yet. We still have to create our points column on the right, add our response capability, and allow `ThreadItems` to be added. Let's leave the points column for a little later and work on our response system next:

1.  The first thing we want to do is some refactoring. In our `ThreadHeader` component, we displayed `userName` and `lastModifiedOn` to let users know who created the post and when. We can use this display for our responses as well. So, let's pull out this bit of code and put into a separate component so that we can reuse it. Create a file called `UserNameAndTime.tsx` in the `routes/` `thread` folder and add the source code to it. Since we're basically copying over the `ThreadHeader` code, I won't review it here.

2.  Now, we can use this by updating our `ThreadHeader` component code. Update it by replacing the JSX under the h3 tags for `title` with the following code. Don't forget to add the import statement:

```
    <UserNameAndTime userName={userName}
lastModifiedOn={lastModifiedOn} />
```

Great! Now, we can start building our `ThreadItems` component. But this time, we'll do things a little differently. In the case of Thread responses, it is possible that we might have more than one response. So, this scenario is somewhat analogous to a machine in a widget factory. There is only one machine but potentially many widgets that need to be created. This sort of situation in programming design would usually entail using something called a factory pattern.

So, what we're going to make is actually two components. One component will act as the factory "building" Thread responses. The other component will define what a response actually looks like. So, together these two components can churn out any number of responses. Note that we're not using the formal design pattern for the factory, just a rough conceptual model. Let's get started:

1.  First, we need to create our `ThreadResponse` component, which will define what our `ThreadItem` UI and behavior look like. Create a `ThreadResponse.tsx` file inside `routes/thread` and add the relevant source code.

    First, notice we are importing and reusing the `RichEditor` and `UserNameAndTime` components we created earlier. Can you imagine how much work it would take to have to recreate them again if we had not componentized them? Thank goodness we put them into their own components!

    Next, we have our `ThreadResponseProps` interface. Notice that all our props are optional. This is in preparation for when we refactor this component and make it capable of creating new response entries.

    Finally, we have the returned JSX. This is a pretty simple UI – we just display our `UserNameAndTime` and `RichEditor`.

2.  Now, let's create our `ThreadResponse` factory. Create a file called `ThreadResponseBuilder.tsx` in the same folder and add the relevant source code to it.

    First, we have the `ThreadResponsesBuilderProps` interface. This component will receive a `props` that contains a list of `ThreadItems`. We'll have to update our `Thread` parent component so that it passes the list down.

    Starting on *line 12*, since our builder is churning out multiple responses, our only state, `responseElements`, is a JSX element that's used to contain them.

    Next, we use `useEffect` to create our list of response elements. Each `ThreadResponse` instance has a unique key, which prevents rendering issues. Whenever our `threadItems` props change, we will create a `ul` of `ThreadResponses`.

    Finally, we return our JSX, which is a list of `TheadResponse` elements.

3.  We're almost done. Let's update our `Thread.tsx` file so that it now uses our `ThreadResponsesBuilder` component. Note that the styling has been updated in the `App.css` and `Thread.css` files.

In the JSX just below `ThreadBody`, add the highlighted tags shown in the following code:

```
    return (
        <div className="screen-root-container">
            <div className="thread-nav-container">
                <Nav />
            </div>
            <div className="thread-content-container">
                <ThreadHeader
                    userName={thread?.userName}
                    lastModifiedOn={thread ? thread.lastModifiedOn
: new Date()}
                    title={thread?.title}
                />
                <ThreadCategory categoryName={thread?.category?.
name} />
                <ThreadTitle title={thread?.title} />
                <ThreadBody body={thread?.body} />
                <hr className="thread-section-divider" />
                <ThreadResponsesBuilder threadItems={responses}
/>
            </div>
        </div>
    );
};
```

Notice that we also added a new line, hr, to separate out the Thread post from any responses.

Our screen should now look like this:

Figure 12.16 – A Thread and its responses

We now have an almost complete `Thread` posting and viewing UI. But again, we're not done yet. We still have to build our points viewer and enable `Thread` and `ThreadItem` posting. We'll build the points viewing component here, but let's leave the posting capability for later chapters, when we have our backend ready to tie it together. Also, when our backend is ready, it will become clearer as to why we did certain things the way we did them here.

For our `categorythreads` route, you saw that we had a vertical bar showing our likes and response count. If you take a look at how we created that section, you'll see we put that code into a function called `getPointsNonMobile`. We could extract this feature into its own React component. Obviously, this will allow us to use it in both our `ThreadCard` component and our `Thread` component, as well as anywhere else we may need it later. Let's get started:

1. Create a new file called `ThreadPointsBar.tsx` and place it inside the root of the `components` folder. We'll take the `getPointsNonMobile` function from the `ThreadCard` component and add it inside this new component.

   On *line 6*, we use `ThreadPointsBarProps` as our props type. You may be wondering why I didn't just pass the entire Thread object in. Adding only the member data that's needed allows us to keep better separation of concerns. If we passed the entire Thread, not only would we be telling our `ThreadPointsBar` about what model types we are dealing with, but we would be giving it information it does not actually use or need.

   Next, the returned JSX is basically the same as the original function as it does the same thing. Now, try updating the `ThreadCard` component so that the `getPointsNonMobile` function gets removed. In its place, we will add our new `ThreadPointsBar` component. Note that our `ThreadCard.css` file was updated slightly, so you should refresh it. The screen should look identical to our original screen since we only moved things around.

2. Now, let's add our new `ThreadPointsBar` component to our `Thread` route component. The JSX changes are small but significant, so let's go over them here and then look at our updated `Thread.css` file:

```
return (
    <div className="screen-root-container">
        <div className="thread-nav-container">
            <Nav />
        </div>
        <div className="thread-content-container">
            <div className="thread-content-post-container">
```

Here, we've moved the order of some of our elements around. Now, the main Thread post-related elements are under this `div` in the `thread-content-post-container` class:

```
            <ThreadHeader
                userName={thread?.userName}
                lastModifiedOn={thread ? thread.
    lastModifiedOn : new Date()}
                title={thread?.title}
            />
            <ThreadCategory categoryName={thread?.
    category?.name} />
            <ThreadTitle title={thread?.title} />
            <ThreadBody body={thread?.body} />
        </div>
        <div className="thread-content-points-container">
```

Here, we have a brand new `div` with a `thread-content-points-container` class that contains our new `ThreadPointsBar` component:

```
            <ThreadPointsBar
                points={thread?.points || 0}
                responseCount={
                    thread && thread.threadItems && thread.
    threadItems.length
                }
            />
        </div>
    </div>
    <div className="thread-content-response-container">
        <hr className="thread-section-divider" />
        <ThreadResponsesBuilder threadItems={thread?.
    threadItems} />
    </div>
```

We've also moved our responses down into their own parent, `thread-content-response-container`:

```
        </div>
    );
};
```

Let's look at our refreshed CSS `Thread.css` file to see what's going on.

Near the top of the file, I've explicitly given a definition for `grid-template-rows`. The Grid now has two rows: one for posts and one for responses. Posts take up one part of available space, but responses can take up as much space as needed, which is what `auto` means, since it could have 0 or more responses.

We now have this new class, `thread-content-points-container`. We need this to change the layout of our `ThreadPointsBar`, which is now different from the main screen. Notice that it puts itself into the second column start index and first Grid row. The `> div` element on the second definition means to give the `div` elements inside `ThreadPointsBar` and `threadcard-points` a specific height of all available.

Now, our main Thread post items, such as `ThreadTitle` and `ThreadBody`, live inside this `thread-content-post-container`.

Our responses – mainly `ThreadResponsesBuilder` – live inside this `thread-content-response-container`. Notice that `grid-row` is set to 2.

After the `thread-content-response-container` class, you'll notice that all the section-related classes no longer need references to any Grid column or Grid since they all live inside `thread-content-post-container`.

3.  Now, we want to give our points totals for our responses. However, because we could end up having many responses, it might not look that great to have 20 or 30 little vertical points bars for each response. So, to make things look cleaner, let's just put these points on the same line as our `userName` and `createdOn` dates. Luckily for us, we've already created most of the code to show these points in our `ThreadCard` component with the `getPoints` function. So, let's convert that into a component too.

    Create a new file called `ThreadPointsInline.tsx` and add the relevant source code to it. We've basically just copied and pasted our `getPoints` code into here, so there's not much to explain. However, notice that we reused the `ThreadPointsBarProps` interface from the `ThreadPointsBar` component. So, we need to make this type exportable.

I'll assume you know how to update the `ThreadCard.tsx` file since we did this earlier with `ThreadPointsBar`. Now, let's update the `ThreadResponse.tsx` file so that it uses our new `ThreadPointsInline` component. Try and do this on your own; only look at the code if you get stuck. So, here's what we have now:

Figure 12.17 – Displaying thread points

As you can see, both our points systems can be seen. Now, there's one final small trick we need to implement to get this screen showing up properly on mobile devices.

4.  Open the `Thread.css` file and make sure it contains the same Media Query as the source code.

Now, open the `Thread` component's code so that we can go through it.

On *line 32*, you will see that our Thread post-related items all live inside `thread-content-container`. The CSS class, via the Media Query, has been set so that it only has a **single** column on mobile devices. This setting will make sure that when we remove our `ThreadPointsBar` component from that area, we don't end up with an empty space, because we had two columns previously.

Next, we can see that our `ThreadPointsBar` actually lives inside `thread-content-points-container`. In the Media Query, we are making that element invisible. This is still efficient because, as you may recall, internally, `ThreadPointsBar` is using our `useWindowDimensions` Hook to determine if it should render itself or not. It will not do this for mobile devices.

Awesome! Let's take a look our screen now on mobile:

Figure 12.18 – Mobile view of the Thread screen

Terrific! Now, we have one code base and two screens.

For the final item in this chapter, we will build out our UserProfile screen. We want to do a few things with this screen:

- Allow users to reset their passwords.
- Show all user-generated Thread posts.
- Show all user-generated responses (ThreadItems).

Let's get started:

1. The very first thing we have to do is actually make a change to the SideBarMenus component. We need to move out the useEffect call in order to send our user to Redux, and then to the Login component. We're doing this so that when the user successfully logs in, the new user object will be sent to Redux. By now, you should be comfortable with making this kind of change. So, go ahead and remove this code from SideBarMenu and add it to Login.

   > **Tip**
   >
   > Make sure that when you put the code into Login, you change the name of dispatch to something else, as there is already a dispatch in the Login component.

2. This new screen will include a password reset feature, but you may recall we already have a lot of code for doing password confirmations in our Register component. Let's try to extract that code into its own component so that we can reuse it in both the Register component and our new UserProfile component.

   Create a file called PasswordComparison.tsx inside the components/ auth/common folder. Add the relevant source code to it.

   This is a fairly straightforward copy and paste, but there's a couple of things to note. Notice that this component does not use userReducer, instead taking props for its values. In particular, notice that one of them is the dispatch function. **This is what allows this component to share its password values with its parent**, because the dispatch call belongs to the parent. Everything else is basically a copy and paste.

   Try removing this code yourself from the original Register component. Ensure that you remove all the unnecessary imports.

3.  Now, let's create a new `userProfile` folder inside the `routes` folder so that we can create our new `UserProfile.tsx` file and add the relevant source code to it.

    Starting on *line 14*, we use our `userReducer` since we need some of its properties, such as `userName`. We also get the Redux user reducer and set some local state for the user's Threads and `ThreadItems`.

    On *line 28*, the `useEffect` function is using the `getUserThreads` function of `DataService`, which gets the user's Threads. We don't need another call to get `ThreadItems` because Threads contains related `ThreadItems`. However, I did update the `ThreadItem` class so that it includes its parent `ThreadId`. Take a look at those files for that code.

    Next, starting on *line 38*, we map each Thread in the query results to an `li`. We also add all `ThreadItems` to a single array so that we can use them later.

    Then, starting on *line 53*, we've taken our `ThreadItems` and mapped them to a set of `li` as well.

    On *line 77*, we use the `PasswordComparison` component that we created earlier.

    On *line 82*, notice we have our button using `isSubmitDisabled`. Can you guess how this disabling is working, even though `UserProfile` does not contain any code to change it? That's right – `PasswordComparison` is doing it internally using our UserProfile's `dispatch` function.

    Finally, we have our Threads and `ThreadItems` rendered off our local state objects.

4.  For the final change, let's update our `App.tsx` file so that it includes our new route for `UserProfile`. Note that we also need to temporarily add the `userName` Redux call until the same call, inside `Login.tsx`, is completely working (we'll finish the call in `Login.tsx` once our backend is ready). This is because when we load our `UserProfile`, there is no guarantee that the user has already loaded their `Login` screen. However, we know that if they've loaded any screen in the app, they must have loaded the `App.tsx` component. Update `App.tsx` from the source code.

    So, first, we have a `useEffect` with a hardcoded `userName` being sent to the Redux store. Again, this is only temporary until our backend is ready.

    On *line 26*, `renderUserProfile` is the function that returns our `UserProfile` component. That function is then used on *line 33* as the destination for the new route; that is, `"/userprofile/:id"`.

There's one more tiny change we need to make. In our `SideBarMenus` component, let's update our `userName` label so that it's a link to our new `UserProfile` screen. You can find this JSX in the `SideBarMenus.tsx` file:

```
<span className="menu-name">{user?.userName}</span>
```

Then, replace it with this:

```
<span className="menu-name">
            <Link to={`/userprofile/${user?.id}`}>{user?.userName}</Link>
        </span>
```

Now, if you run the app, you will see the following:

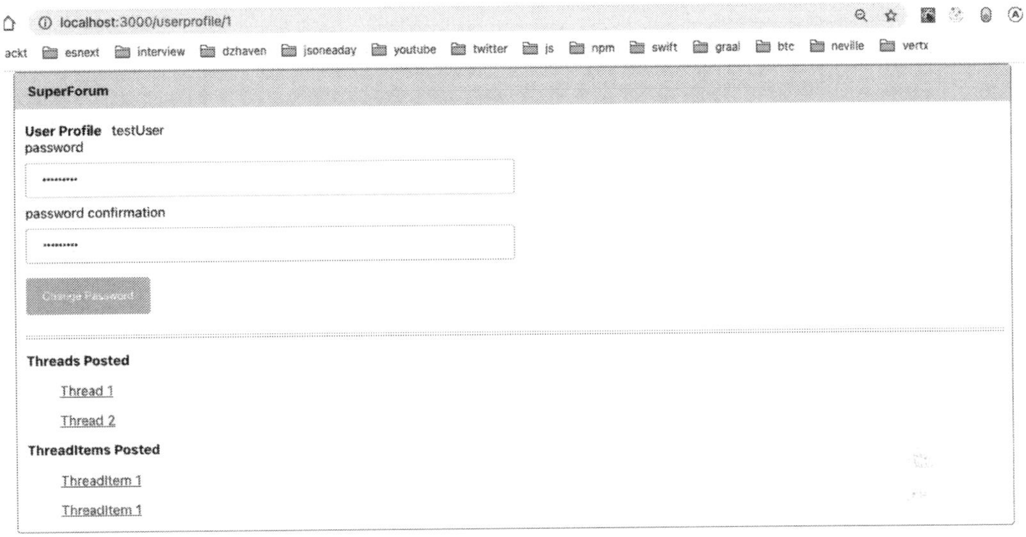

Figure 12.19 – UserProfile screen

If you click on any of the Thread links, you'll see that they take us to the thread route.

That was amazing! We've gone through so much React code in this chapter. We learned about the layout, folder structure, component creation, code reuse, code refactoring, styling, and more. Code refactoring in particular can be very time-consuming and even stressful. However, the reality is that most of the time, we will not be writing new code but refactoring existing code. So, this was a good way to build our skills.

In the next few chapters, we will be building out our backend and tying it together with our client side. You should now feel very confident – you've made a huge effort in getting through this complex chapter.

# Summary

In this chapter, we began our journey of building our full stack application by creating our React client. We used Hooks to create our components, implemented component hierarchies, and designed layouts using CSS Grid. We then refactored a ton of code, and we tried to reuse as much code as possible. Even though we're not done yet, we've built out a large important piece of our final application.

In the next chapter, we will learn about the session state on our backend server, what the session state is, how to use it, and the most popular tool for creating and managing session data: Redis.

# 13
# Set Up a Session State Using Express and Redis

In this chapter, we'll learn about creating session state using Express and the Redis data store. Redis is one of the most popular in-memory data stores. It is used by companies such as Twitter, GitHub, Stack Overflow, Instagram, and Airbnb. We'll use Express and Redis to create our session state, which will be the basis for our application's authentication capabilities.

In this chapter, we're going to cover the following main topics:

- Understanding session state
- Understanding Redis
- Building session state with Express and Redis

# Technical requirements

You should have a good understanding of web development using Node.js. We will once again be using Node and Visual Studio Code.

The GitHub repository is at `https://github.com/PacktPublishing/Full-Stack-React-TypeScript-and-Node`. Use the code in the `Chap13` folder.

To set up the Chapter 13 code folder, go to your `HandsOnTypescript` folder and create a new folder called `Chap13`.

# Understanding session state

In this section, we'll learn what session state is and why it's necessary. We'll revisit some of the concepts of how the web works and understand why we need session state.

The web is actually not one thing. It is a collection of many technologies. The core of the web is the HTTP protocol. This is the communication protocol that allows the web to work over the internet. A protocol is simply an agreed-upon set of rules for communication. This sounds somewhat straightforward, and for some things, it can be. However, for our application, it's a little more complicated.

The HTTP protocol is a connectionless protocol. This means that HTTP connections are made only at the time a request is made and then released. So, a connection is not maintained, even if a user is actively using a website for hours. This makes HTTP more scalable. However, this also means certain features that larger websites need are more difficult to create when using this protocol.

Let's take a look at a real-world example. Let's pretend we are Amazon and we have millions of users on our site trying to buy items. Now because people are trying to buy things, we need to be able to uniquely identify these users. For example, if we were both using Amazon at the same time and you were trying to add items into your cart, we would need to make sure that none of your items ended up in my cart and vice versa. This seems like it should be easy to do. However, with a connectionless protocol like HTTP, it's hard.

In HTTP, every request creates a new connection and each new request knows nothing about any prior requests. That is, it holds no state data. So, to go back to our Amazon example, this means that if a user makes a request to add an item to a cart, there is no built-in facility to distinguish this user's request from any other request. Of course, we could intervene with our own capabilities, and certainly, that's what we'll be discussing in this chapter. But the point is that there is nothing out of the box that we can just use.

To be clear, there are numerous ways of dealing with this particular issue. Perhaps we could give each user a unique ID and they could pass it on each call. Or maybe we could save session information onto the database, for example, to hold purchase items in a cart. And certainly, there are many more options than this depending on what specifically is the requirement. However, these simple ideas would need to be fleshed out and detailed. Then we would need to spend time testing them. So, realistically, wherever we can, we want to avoid rolling our own capabilities and, instead, we should select industry-standard solutions. If we use these, we know they have been tested for robustness and security and will use best practices.

The method we will use for distinguishing users will put the emphasis on server-side technology by using Express sessions and Redis as our data store. We will not use JWT as it is a client-side technology and is more susceptible to security vulnerabilities than a server-side solution.

> **Important note**
> Every solution has its pros and cons. Certainly, any server can be hacked. And having security solutions on a server does not guarantee anything. However, when it comes to your server, you can secure and control its settings to at least try and maximize its security. On a user's machine, you have no control at all.

In this section, we learned about what session state is and why it's necessary. We learned about some of the missing features of the HTTP protocol and how we can provide ourselves with those capabilities. In the next section, we will continue by learning about Redis, the data store that we will use to maintain our session data.

# Understanding Redis

In this section, we will learn about Redis and install it. We will also give a simple introduction to Redis and how it works.

Redis is an in-memory data store. It is extremely fast and scalable. You can use Redis to store strings, lists, sets of data, and more. Thousands of companies use Redis and it is free and open source. In general, Redis is most often used as an in-memory database or cache.

For our use case, we will use Redis to act as the data store for our Express sessions. Redis is supported on Linux and Mac. It is not officially supported on Windows. You can get unofficial support by using a Docker image on Windows, but that is beyond the scope of this book. However, you can usually get free Linux VM's on cloud providers for a trial period. So if you're on Windows, you could try one of those services.

> **Note**
>
> Redis.conf has a setting called bind which sets the local IP address, the Redis server will use as well as which external IP addresses will be allowed to access it. Leaving this setting commented will allow any IP address to access the server. This is ok for development purposes. However, once you go into production you should set this to a specific value and only allow the IP addresses you desire to have access to the server IP.

Let's begin by installing Redis. Currently, I am using a Mac:

1. Go to the Redis website at https://redis.io/download and select **Download** under the stable version. Here's a sample screenshot of the current 6.0.7 version:

> **Note**
>
> Please download a 6.0.x version as higher or lower versions may have breaking changes.

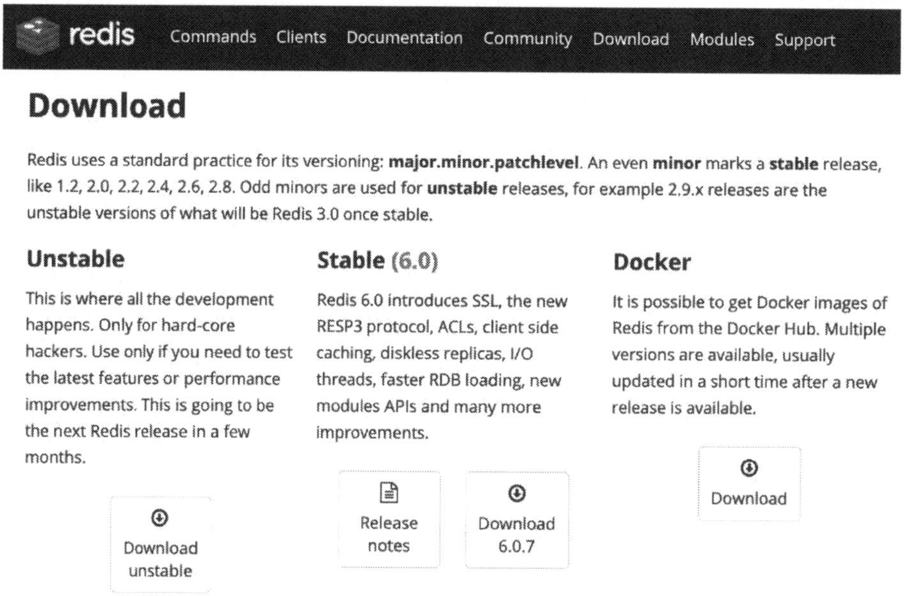

redis    Commands    Clients    Documentation    Community    Download    Modules    Support

## Download

Redis uses a standard practice for its versioning: **major.minor.patchlevel**. An even **minor** marks a **stable** release, like 1.2, 2.0, 2.2, 2.4, 2.6, 2.8. Odd minors are used for **unstable** releases, for example 2.9.x releases are the unstable versions of what will be Redis 3.0 once stable.

**Unstable**

This is where all the development happens. Only for hard-core hackers. Use only if you need to test the latest features or performance improvements. This is going to be the next Redis release in a few months.

⊕
Download unstable

**Stable (6.0)**

Redis 6.0 introduces SSL, the new RESP3 protocol, ACLs, client side caching, diskless replicas, I/O threads, faster RDB loading, new modules APIs and many more improvements.

📄              ⊕
Release      Download
notes         6.0.7

**Docker**

It is possible to get Docker images of Redis from the Docker Hub. Multiple versions are available, usually updated in a short time after a new release is available.

⊕
Download

Figure 13.1 – Redis download

2. Once you have downloaded and successfully unzipped or unpacked the file into a folder, use your terminal and go to that folder. For example, this is what my terminal looks like after I have unpacked the tar file:

```
davidchoi@Davids-MacBook-Pro ~ % cd Downloads
davidchoi@Davids-MacBook-Pro Downloads % cd redis-6.0.7
davidchoi@Davids-MacBook-Pro redis-6.0.7 % ls
00-RELEASENOTES        README.md             runtest-sentinel
BUGS                   TLS.md                sentinel.conf
CONTRIBUTING           deps                  src
COPYING                redis.conf            tests
INSTALL                runtest               utils
MANIFESTO              runtest-cluster
Makefile               runtest-moduleapi
```

Figure 13.2 – Redis stable unpacked

3.  Now we must make our source files into a runnable application. Simply type make into the terminal and let it run. It will take some time to finish. The beginnings of the make command run will look like this:

```
davidchoi@Davids-MacBook-Pro redis-6.0.7 % make
cd src && /Library/Developer/CommandLineTools/usr/bin/make all
/bin/sh: pkg-config: command not found
    CC Makefile.dep
/bin/sh: pkg-config: command not found
rm -rf redis-server redis-sentinel redis-cli redis-benchmark redis-check-rdb redis-
check-aof *.o *.gcda *.gcno *.gcov redis.info lcov-html Makefile.dep dict-benchmark
rm -f adlist.d quicklist.d ae.d anet.d dict.d server.d sds.d zmalloc.d lzf_c.d lzf_
d.d pqsort.d zipmap.d sha1.d ziplist.d release.d networking.d util.d object.d db.d
replication.d rdb.d t_string.d t_list.d t_set.d t_zset.d t_hash.d config.d aof.d pu
bsub.d multi.d debug.d sort.d intset.d syncio.d cluster.d crc16.d endianconv.d slow
log.d scripting.d bio.d rio.d rand.d memtest.d crcspeed.d crc64.d bitops.d sentinel
.d notify.d setproctitle.d blocked.d hyperloglog.d latency.d sparkline.d redis-chec
k-rdb.d redis-check-aof.d geo.d lazyfree.d module.d evict.d expire.d geohash.d geoh
ash_helper.d childinfo.d defrag.d siphash.d rax.d t_stream.d listpack.d localtime.d
 lolwut.d lolwut5.d lolwut6.d acl.d gopher.d tracking.d connection.d tls.d sha256.d
 timeout.d setpuaffinity.d anet.d adlist.d dict.d redis-cli.d zmalloc.d release.d
ae.d crcspeed.d crc64.d siphash.d crc16.d ae.d anet.d redis-benchmark.d adlist.d di
ct.d zmalloc.d siphash.d
(cd ../deps && /Library/Developer/CommandLineTools/usr/bin/make distclean)
(cd hiredis && /Library/Developer/CommandLineTools/usr/bin/make clean) > /dev/null
|| true
(cd linenoise && /Library/Developer/CommandLineTools/usr/bin/make clean) > /dev/nul
l || true
(cd lua && /Library/Developer/CommandLineTools/usr/bin/make clean) > /dev/null || t
rue
(cd jemalloc && [ -f Makefile ] && /Library/Developer/CommandLineTools/usr/bin/make
 distclean) > /dev/null || true
(rm -f .make-*)
(rm -f .make-*)
echo STD=-std=c11 -pedantic -DREDIS_STATIC='' >> .make-settings
echo WARN=-Wall -W -Wno-missing-field-initializers >> .make-settings
echo OPT=-O2 >> .make-settings
```

Figure 13.3 – Running the make command

4.  Now that we've built our server, feel free to move it wherever you would like. I moved it into my `Applications` folder. You'll need to run this command after changing directories into the `Redis` folder:

    ```
    src/redis-server
    ```

    Here's a screenshot of my local Redis server running:

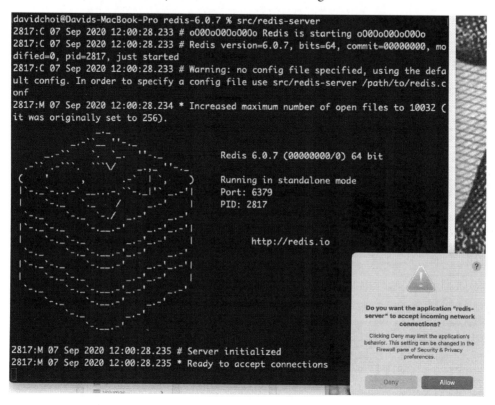

Figure 13.4 – Running Redis

---

**Warning**

On Mac, you may get a warning asking if you want to give Redis permission to accept incoming network requests. You should allow this.

---

5. Let's quickly test that Redis is working. Open a new terminal window while Redis is running, and from your Redis `src` folder, type this command:

```
redis-cli
```

Here's a test that I did:

```
Last login: Mon Sep  7 11:43:39 on ttys001
davidchoi@Davids-MacBook-Pro ~ % /Applications/redis-6.0.7/src/redis-cli
127.0.0.1:6379> ping
PONG
127.0.0.1:6379> set test 1
OK
127.0.0.1:6379> get test
"1"
```

Figure 13.5 – Test Redis

In *Figure 13.5*, we first `ping` to check that Redis is running. Then we use the `set` command to create a new value with the key `test` and value `1`. Then we `get` that value successfully.

6. Now that we know our server is installed properly, we need to do some minor configuration. Shutdown the server first with this command:

```
src/redis-cli shutdown
```

Once shut down, go to the `Chapter13` source code folder and copy the contents of the `redis/redis.conf` file. Then, in the terminal, run the following command:

```
sudo mkdir /etc/redis
```

If asked for a `sudo` password, enter your password. This is the default folder for most Redis configuration locations. Next, run this command:

```
sudo nano /etc/redis/redis.conf
```

Nano is a text editor for the terminal. Now paste the contents of the source code, `redis.conf`, file into this newly created file on `/etc/redis/redis.conf`.

If you view this file and search for the keyword `requirepass`, pressing *Ctrl + W* or viewing from VSCode, you will see the password we are going to use for testing purposes only. Please do not use this password in production.

For any other settings, we should be fine with the defaults.

7.  OK, now let's restart our Redis server, but this time pointing to our new `redis.conf` file. Type this command:

```
src/redis-server /etc/redis/redis.conf
```

Notice this time the log message says `Configuration loaded`.

Note that if you want to test the server again, this time you need to authenticate since we configured a password:

```
src/redis-cli
```

```
auth <password>
```

This is what it looks like:

```
davidchoi@Davids-MacBook-Pro redis-6.0.7 % src/redis-cli
127.0.0.1:6379> auth test-password-do-not-use-123
OK
127.0.0.1:6379> ping
PONG
```

Figure 13.6 – Test restart and auth of Redis

In this section, we discussed what Redis is and did a basic installation of the Redis service. In the next section, we will be starting our backend server code by creating a bare-bones Node and Express server and setting up Redis-based session state.

# Building session state with Express and Redis

In this section, we will start building out our backend. We'll create our Express project and set up Redis-based session state.

Now that we understand what Redis is and how to install it. Let's go over how Express and Redis will work together in our server. As we discussed in *Chapter 8, Learning Server-Side Development with Node.js and Express*, Express is basically a wrapper around Node. And this wrapper provides additional capabilities for Node by using middleware. Session state is also an Express middleware.

In our application, Express will provide a session object with relevant capabilities, such as creating cookies on the user browser and various functions to help set up and maintain the session. Redis will be the data store for our session data. Since Redis is ultra-fast at storing and retrieving data, it is a good use case of Redis.

Let's now create our project using Express and Redis:

1.  First, we need to create our project folder, super-forum-server. Once created, we need to initialize it as an NPM project by running this (make sure your terminal is already in the super-forum-server folder first):

    ```
    npm init -y
    ```

    Once it's complete, just update the name field inside of package.json to say super-forum-server. Feel free to also update the author field to your name as well.

2.  Now let's install our dependencies:

    ```
    npm i express express-session connect-redis ioredis
    dotenv
    ```
    ```
    npm i typescript @types/express @types/express-session @
    types/connect-redis @types/ioredis ts-node-dev -D
    ```

    As you can see, we installed our express package, but we also installed express-session. This package is what enables sessions in Express. We also installed connect-redis, which is what connects our Express session to a Redis data store. In addition to connect-redis, we need the ioredis package because it is the client that gives us access to the Redis server itself. I'll explain this further once we start coding. The dotenv package will allow us to use a config file, .env, to hold things like server passwords and other configurations.

    Then, in the second install command, we can see our development-related packages, which are mostly TypeScript definition packages like @types/express. However, notice in the end, we also install ts-node-dev. We use this package to help us start our server through the main index.ts file. The ts-node-dev package will trigger tsc, the TypeScript compiler, and get the final server up and running.

    > **Warning**
    > Never include your dotenv config file, .env, in your Git repository. It has sensitive information. You should have an offline process to maintain this file and share it with your developers.

3.  Let's now update our package.json file to use the ts-node-dev helper. This package is super useful because it also auto-restarts our server whenever we change any of our scripts. Add this line to the scripts section of package.json:

```
"start": "ts-node-dev --respawn src/index.ts"
```

Notice there are two dashes before respawn. The index.ts file will be our root file that starts our server.

4.  Now we should set up TypeScript in our project. We've seen the TypeScript config file, tsconfig.json, many times before so I won't list it here (you can of course find it in our source files). But do notice that we have target as ES6 and the production files are saved to the ./dist folder.

5.  Create the src folder on the root of the project.

6.  Now let's create our .env file and its entries. Copy these settings into your own file, but use your own unique secret values:

| Setting | Function |
|---|---|
| REDIS_PASSWORD | The password we set up for Redis in our redis.conf file from earlier. You must use the same password that you used. |
| REDIS_PORT | The port that Redis is using. The default is 6379. |
| REDIS_HOST | The IP address of your Redis server. Since we have installed our Redis service locally, we can use localhost. |
| COOKIE_NAME | The name of the cookie that will be associated with our Redis session. |
| SESSION_SECRET | Every session has a unique secret that allows access to that session in Express. You should create your own unique value. |
| SERVER_PORT | The port that the server will run on. You can add whichever port you like, but nothing else can be running on that same port. |

7.  Now let's create the index.ts file. Let's create a bare-bones file first, just to make sure our server will run. Enter this into the file:

```
import express from "express";
```

Here, we have imported Express.

```
console.log(process.env.NODE_ENV);
```

Here, we are showing which environment we are on – production or development. If you have not set your local environment already, use this command on your terminal to set it.

For Mac, use this command:

```
export NODE_ENV=development
```

For Windows, use this command:

```
SET NODE_ENV=development
```

On your production server, you may also need to run this command but set it to production:

```
require("dotenv").config();
```

Here, we import our dotenv package and set up default configurations. This is what allows our .env file to be used in our project.

```
const app = express();
```

Here, we instantiate our app object with express. So, we'll add all our middleware onto the app object. Since almost everything in Express is middleware, session state is also middleware.

```
app.listen({ port: process.env.SERVER_PORT }, () => {
  console.log(`Server ready on port ${process.env.
    SERVER_PORT}`);
});
```

And here, we have initialized our server and when it is running, it will show the log message shown. Run the following command:

```
npm start
```

You should see the following log message on your terminal:

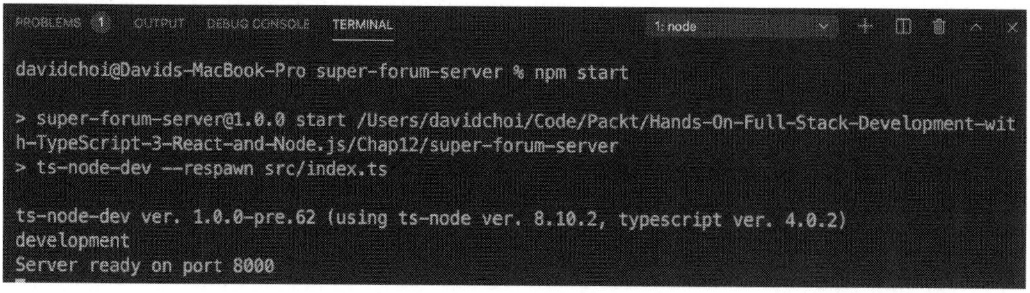

| PROBLEMS  1 | OUTPUT | DEBUG CONSOLE | **TERMINAL** | | 1: node | ⌄ | + | ⬚ | 🗑 | ^ | × |

```
davidchoi@Davids-MacBook-Pro super-forum-server % npm start

> super-forum-server@1.0.0 start /Users/davidchoi/Code/Packt/Hands-On-Full-Stack-Development-wit
h-TypeScript-3-React-and-Node.js/Chap12/super-forum-server
> ts-node-dev --respawn src/index.ts

ts-node-dev ver. 1.0.0-pre.62 (using ts-node ver. 8.10.2, typescript ver. 4.0.2)
development
Server ready on port 8000
```

Figure 13.7 First run of the Express server

8. Now that we know our base server is running properly, let's add our Express session state and Redis:

```
import express from "express";
import session from "express-session";
import connectRedis from "connect-redis";
import Redis from "ioredis";
```

To start, you can see we import `expression-session` and our Redis related packages.

```
console.log(process.env.NODE_ENV);
require("dotenv").config();


const app = express();
const router = express.Router();
```

Here, we've initialized our `router` object.

```
const redis = new Redis({
    port: Number(process.env.REDIS_PORT),
    host: process.env.REDIS_HOST,
    password: process.env.REDIS_PASSWORD,
});
```

The `redis` object is the client to our Redis server. As you can see, we've hidden the values to our configuration information behind our `.env` file. You can imagine how unsafe it would be if we could see the passwords and other security information hardcoded into our code.

```
const RedisStore = connectRedis(session);
const redisStore = new RedisStore({
  client: redis,
});
```

Now we've created our `RedisStore` class and the `redisStore` object, which we will make the data store for our Express session.

```
app.use(
  session({
    store: redisStore,
    name: process.env.COOKIE_NAME,
    sameSite: "Strict",
    secret: process.env.SESSION_SECRET,
    resave: false,
    saveUninitialized: false,
    cookie: {
      path: "/",
      httpOnly: true,
      secure: false,
      maxAge: 1000 * 60 * 60 * 24,
    },
  } as any)
);
```

The session object gets some options. One option, `store`, is where we are adding our `redisStore` object. The `sameSite` value indicates that cookies from other domains are not allowed, which enhances security. The `secret` field is again a kind of password or unique ID for our specific session. The `cookie` field sets up our cookie that gets saved onto user browsers. The `httpOnly` field means the cookie is not available from JavaScript. This makes the cookie much more secure and can prevent XSS attacks. The `secure` field is `false` because we are not using HTTPS.

```
app.use(router);
router.get("/", (req, res, next) => {
  if (!req.session!.userid) {
    req.session!.userid = req.query.userid;
    console.log("Userid is set");
    req.session!.loadedCount = 0;
  } else {
    req.session!.loadedCount = Number(req.session!.
      loadedCount) + 1;
  }
```

We've set up our `router` object and our one route, which is GET. Basically, what we're doing is taking `userid` from the URL query string and then setting our user's unique `session.userid` field with it. We also count how many times the call was made to show that the session is being kept alive between calls.

```
  res.send(
    `userid: ${req.session!.userid}, loadedCount:
      ${req.session!.loadedCount}`
  );
```

Here, we're responding by sending the session information as a string return.

```
});

app.listen({ port: process.env.SERVER_PORT }, () => {
  console.log(`Server ready on port ${process.env.SERVER_
    PORT}`);
});
```

And finally, we have our `express` server listen on port 5000, which is what our `SERVER_PORT` is set to. As shown in the following image, the cookie gets created on the first load:

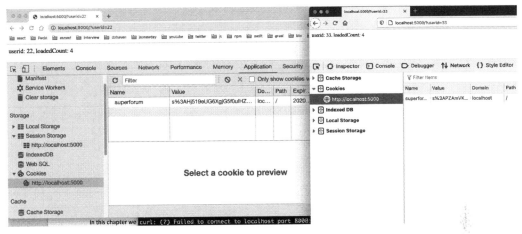

Figure 13.8 – Two browsers showing distinct session state

Note that we use two browsers to show that unique sessions are created. If we used one browser, the sessions would not be unique as the same cookie would be used.

In this section, we used our knowledge of Express and Redis and implemented a base project for our SuperForum application. We saw the role both Express and Redis play in creating the session. And we saw how to use the session to create a unique data container for each user that comes onto our site.

## Summary

In this chapter, we learned about sessions and the Redis data store service. We also learned how to integrate Redis with Express so we can create unique sessions for our users. This will be critical for building our authentication services in later chapters.

In the next chapter, we will set up our Postgres server and create our database schema. We will also learn about TypeOrm, which will allow us to integrate and use Postgres from our application. And finally, we will also build out our authentication service and tie it to our session state.

# 14

# Setting Up Postgres and a Repository Layer with TypeORM

In this chapter, we'll learn about setting up a repository layer using Postgres as our database and TypeORM as our library for accessing the database. We'll build our database schema and, with the help of TypeORM, we'll be able to perform **CRUD (Create, Read, Update, Delete)** operations for our application. This is a crucial chapter as the core activity of our backend will be to retrieve and update data.

In this chapter, we're going to cover the following main topics:

- Setting up our Postgres database
- Understanding object relational mappers by using TypeORM
- Building our repository layer using Postgres and TypeORM

# Technical requirements

This book will not be teaching you about relational databases. So, you should have a basic understanding of SQL, including simple querying and table structures, as well as web development using Node. We will once again be using Node and Visual Studio Code to write our code.

The GitHub repository is available at `https://github.com/PacktPublishing/Full-Stack-React-TypeScript-and-Node`. Use the code in the `Chap14` folder.

To set up the Chapter 14 code folder, go to your `HandsOnTypescript` folder and create a new folder called `Chap14`.

# Setting up our Postgres database

In this section, we will install and set up a Postgres database. Relational databases are still very relevant, and these days NoSQL databases are all the rage. However, according to StackOverflow, Postgres continues to be one of the world's most popular databases. Additionally, its performance is world class, beating MongoDB by a significant margin (`https://www.enterprisedb.com/news/new-benchmarks-show-postgres-dominating-mongodb-varied-workloads`). So, Postgres is what we will be using as our database technology.

Let's install our Postgres database. We will use the installer provided by EDB. EDB is a third-party company that provides tools and services for supporting Postgres:

1.  Go to the URL `https://www.enterprisedb.com/downloads/postgres-postgresql-downloads` and select the download for your platform. I will be using version 12.4 for Mac, which is the latest Mac version as of the time of writing.

2.  Accept all the defaults on the installer, including the list of components to be installed, as shown here:

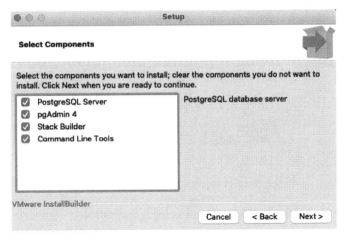

Figure 14.1 – Postgres Setup screen

3.   Once your install finishes, start up the pgAdmin application. This application is the administrator application for Postgres. You should see a screen like this:

Figure 14.2 – First view of pgAdmin

As you can see, it is a web browser application. I have some other servers on my installation, but your install should not have any if this is your first pgAdmin install.

4.   Now, let's create a new server group called HandsOnFullStackGroup so we can keep our work separate from others. A server group is just a container to house multiple server instances, and each server can have multiple databases inside them. Note that a server **does not** indicate a single physical machine.

5.  First, select the option for **Server Group** by right-clicking over the **Servers** item, as shown here:

Figure 14.3 – pgAdmin adding a server group

6.  Next, create a server by right-clicking on the new **HandsOnFullStackGroup** and selecting **Server**. Then, enter the name `SuperForumServers` on the first screen, as follows:

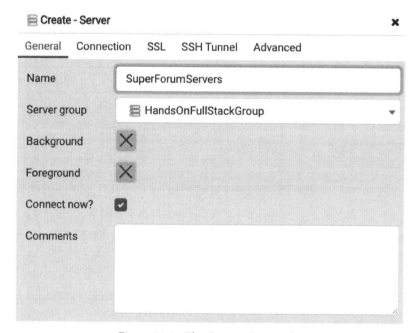

Figure 14.4 – The Create - Server tab

7.  Now, select the second tab, **Connection**, and enter `localhost` as the **Host name/ address**. Then enter the password for `postgres`. The Postgres account is the root administrator account, so you need to remember this password. Here's a screenshot of this tab:

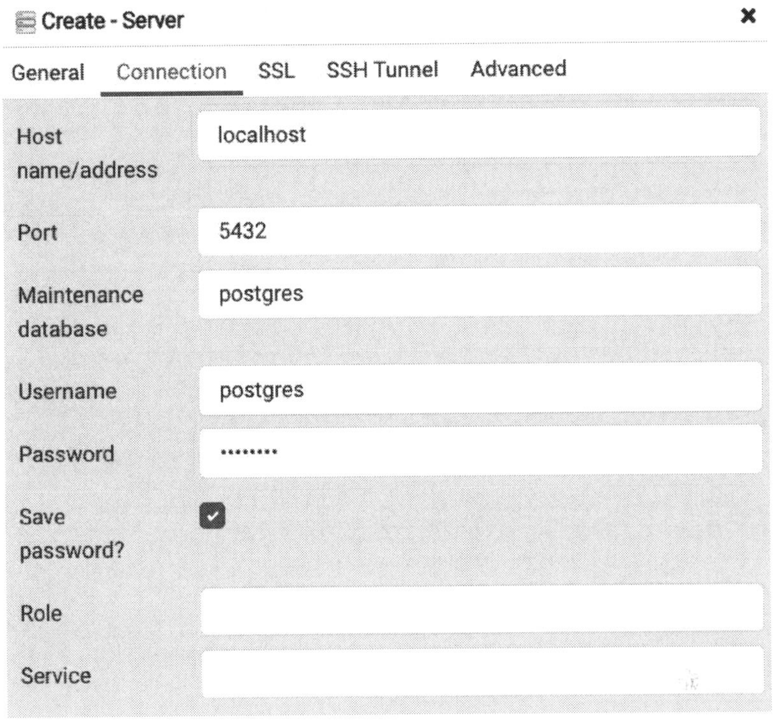

| Create - Server | ✕ |
|---|---|
| General    Connection    SSL    SSH Tunnel    Advanced | |
| Host name/address | localhost |
| Port | 5432 |
| Maintenance database | postgres |
| Username | postgres |
| Password | ········ |
| Save password? | ☑ |
| Role | |
| Service | |

Figure 14.5 – The Connection tab

8.  Select **Save** and your server will be created. You should see the following view:

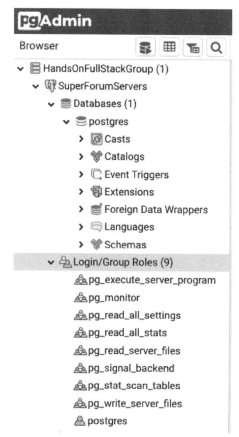

Figure 14.6 – View of the new HandsOnFullStackGroup and SuperForumServers

Notice that there is already a database called **postgres** there. This database is empty, but can be used to store global data.

Now, let's create the database for our application. However, before we can do that, we need to create a new account specifically to use in relation to our new database. Using the default administrator account, postgres, would not be a good idea as, if it were to be hacked, it would give the attacker access to our entire server:

1.  In pgAdmin, right-click on **Login/Group Roles** and select **Create | Login/Group Role**. Then, in the **General** tab, for a name, use superforumsvc. Then, in the **Definition** tab, set your own password. Next, go to the **Privileges** tab and **make sure** to enable login. The rest you can keep as the default settings.

2.  Next, right-click on the **Databases** item in the view and select **Create | Database**. Then, in the **General** tab, use the name SuperForum and select **superforumsvc** as **Owner**:

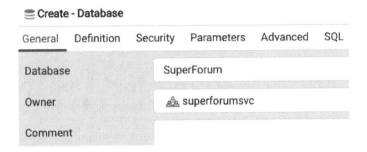

Figure 14.7 – Creating the SuperForum database

3.  Then, click **Save**. Your view should now show this:

Figure 14.8 – New database and user

Terrific! We now have a database. If we were not using an ORM, we would have to go through the tedious process of manually creating our tables and fields. But, as you'll see, TypeORM saves us from this grunt work, as well as providing us with great language features to query our database.

In the next section, we'll dig into TypeORM. We'll learn about how it works and how it helps us, at many levels, to interact with our database.

# Understanding object relational mappers by using TypeORM

In this section, we'll learn what **Object Relational Mapper** (**ORM**) technology is. We'll also learn about TypeORM, one of the most popular ORM frameworks for JavaScript. ORM can make working with databases a lot easier and reduce some cognitive load for the developer.

As a programmer, you know that different programming languages have types that are incompatible. For example, JavaScript, despite the name, cannot use or even access Java types directly. In order for either language to use the types from the other, we would need to do some sort of translation. In part, this is the reason for having services such as the Web API. The Web API provides all data to callers as a string format, like JSON. This allows any caller to use the data since it can be read by any language.

Database to coding language conversion has similar type incompatibilities. So, normally after making a query that returns data, we would have to take each field's value from the database and manually write code to convert it to a specific type in the coding language. However, if we use an ORM, most of this work goes away.

An ORM is designed so that it *knows* how to map database fields into code fields and handles that translation work for us. Additionally, most ORMs have some sort of capability to autocreate tables and fields on the database based on entity structures created in code. You can think of entities as types on the coding language side that represent similar objects to tables on the database side. For example, if we have an entity called User in our JavaScript, it would be expected that we would have a table called Users on the database to match it (it's plural because a table holds more than one user).

This feature alone can save an enormous amount of time and effort for developers, but on top of this, a good ORM will also have features to help build queries, insert parameters safely (reducing the chance of SQL injection attacks), and also handle transactions. Transactions are atomic database operations that must complete in their entirety or all the actions involved are undone.

> **Note**
>
> A SQL injection attack is an attempt by a malicious person to insert SQL code that is different from the one originally intended by the developers. It can result in issues such as data loss and application failure.

For our application, we will be using TypeORM. TypeORM is a popular and highly rated ORM for TypeScript, with over 20,000 likes on GitHub. It provides all of the features mentioned and is easy to get started with, although becoming an advanced user does take considerable effort. It supports multiple databases, including Microsoft SQL, MySQL, and Oracle.

It will save us a great deal of time with its rich feature set, and because many JavaScript projects use TypeORM, there is a large community of developers that can help if you run into issues when using it.

In this section, we learned about ORM technology. We learned what it is and why it's important and valuable to use. In the next section, we will be using TypeORM to build our own project. Let's get started.

# Building our repository layer using Postgres and TypeORM

In this section, we'll learn about the importance of using a repository layer. Having a separate layer for a large and important part of our application can help make code refactoring easier. It is also helpful in terms of understanding how the app works since major sections are logically separated out.

In *Chapter 1*, *Understanding TypeScript*, we learned about **Object-Oriented Programming** (**OOP**). One of the major mechanisms for implementing OOP design is the use of abstraction. By creating our database access code in its own separate layer, we are using abstraction. As you may recall, one of the benefits of abstraction is that it hides the implementation of the code internally and exposes an interface to outside callers. Additionally, because all code related to accessing the database is in one place, we don't have to hunt around to find our database query code. We know which layer of our application this code lives in. Keeping code logically separate is known as the separation of concerns.

So, let's get started with building our repository layer:

1. First, we need to copy our server code that we created in *Chapter 13, Setting Up Session State Using Express and Redis*. Go to the `Chapter13` folder in the source code and copy the `super-forum-server` folder into the `Chapter14` folder.

   > **Note**
   >
   > You will need to delete the `node_modules` folder and the `package-lock.json` file and then re-run the installation with the command.

   ```
   npm install
   ```

2. Next, we need to install TypeORM and its related dependencies. Run the following command:

   ```
   npm i typeorm pg bcryptjs cors class-validator
   npm i @types/pg @types/cors @types/bcryptjs -D
   ```

   With this command, we have installed `typeorm`. `pg` is the client to communicate with Postgres. `bcryptjs` is an encryption library that we will use to encrypt our passwords before inserting into the database. `cors` is needed to allow us to receive client-side requests from a different domain, other than our server's domain. In modern apps, it's possible the client-side code is not being served from the same server as the server-side code. This is especially true when we are creating an API such as GraphQL, which may be used by multiple clients. You'll also see this when we start integrating our client's React app with the server, as they will run on different ports.

   `class-validator` is a dependency for assigning decorators for validation. We'll discuss this in more detail later with the help of examples.

3. Now, before we can start creating our Entities database, we need to create a configuration file so that our TypeORM code can access our Postgres database. This means that we also have to update our `.env` file with our database configurations. Open the `.env` file and add these variables. Our server was installed locally, so PG_ HOST has the value `localhost`:

   ```
   PG_HOST=localhost
   ```

   The port the server uses for communication is as follows:

   ```
   PG_PORT=5432
   ```

Our database account name is as follows:

```
PG_ACCOUNT=superforumsvc
```

Use the password you created for your own database:

```
PG_PASSWORD=<your-password>
```

Our database name is as follows:

```
PG_DATABASE=SuperForum
```

As mentioned before, TypeORM will create our tables and fields for us and maintain them as they change. `PG_SYNCHRONIZE` enables that feature:

```
PG_SYNCHRONIZE=true
```

Of course, once you go live in production, you must disable this feature so as to prevent unwanted database changes.

The location of our Entity files, including subdirectories, is as follows:

```
PG_ENTITIES="src/repo/**/*.*"
```

The root directory for our entities is as follows:

```
PG_ENTITIES_DIR="src/repo"
```

`PG_LOGGING` determines whether to enable logging on the server:

```
PG_LOGGING=false
```

Logs should be enabled in production in order to trace issues. However, logs can create huge files, so we won't enable it for our development.

4. Now we can create our TypeORM configuration file. In the root of our project, `Chap13/super-forum-server`, create the file `ormconfig.js` and add this code to it:

```
require("dotenv").config();
```

First, we get our `.env` configurations by requiring them:

```
module.exports = [
    {
        type: "postgres",
```

Which database type will we connect to? Since TypeORM supports multiple databases, we need to indicate this.

The rest of the values use the configurations from our `.env` file, so they are self-explanatory:

```
        host: process.env.PG_HOST,
        port: process.env.PG_PORT,
        username: process.env.PG_ACCOUNT,
        password: process.env.PG_PASSWORD,
        database: process.env.PG_DATABASE,
        synchronize: process.env.PG_SYNCHRONIZE,
        logging: process.env.PG_LOGGING,
        entities: [process.env.PG_ENTITIES],
        cli: {
            entitiesDir: process.env.PG_ENTITIES_DIR
        },
    }
];
```

Now, we're ready to start creating our entities.

5.  Now that we've installed our dependencies and set up the configuration to the database, let's create our first entity, the User. Change the directory to the Chap14/super-forum-server folder and then create, inside the src folder, a folder called repo. We'll place all of our repository code there. Then, create a file inside repo called User.ts with the following code in it:

```
import { Entity, PrimaryGeneratedColumn, Column } from
"typeorm";
```

These TypeORM imports will allow us to create our User entity class. Entity, PrimaryGeneratedColumn, and Column are what are known as decorators. Decorators are attributes placed just before a relevant line of code that provide additional configuration information about a field or object. You can think of them as a shortcut. Instead of writing some long lines of code, you can simply add a tag that sets configurations. We'll see examples in this code:

```
import { Length } from "class-validator";
```

This is a validator for length.

Next comes our first use of decorators. The `Entity` decorator tells TypeORM that the class that is about to be defined is an entity with the name `Users`. In other words, in our code we will have objects called `User` that map directly to tables in our database called `Users`:

```
@Entity({ name: "Users" })
```

In databases, every table must have a unique identifying field. This is what `PrimaryGeneratedColumn` indicates. The field name will be `id`. Notice that the `""` in `id` is not capitalized. We'll fix this issue later:

```
export class User {
    @PrimaryGeneratedColumn({ name: "id", type: "bigint" })
    id: string;
```

Next, we have our first use of the `Column` decorator:

```
@Column("varchar", {
    name: "Email",
    length: 120,
    unique: true,
    nullable: false,
})
email: string;
```

As you can see, it is used to define the database field `Email`, which will be called `email` in our TypeScript code. So again, decorators are being used to map our code objects to database entities. Now, let's go through the `Column` decorator more closely. First, it defines that our column is of the `varchar` database type. Again, database types are different from code types, as shown here. Next, we see the `name` field, which is set to `Email`. This will be the exact name of this field in the `Users` table. Then we have `length`, which indicates the maximum allowed character count of this field. The `unique` attribute tells Postgres to enforce the fact that each `User` entry must have a unique email. And finally, we have `nullable` set to `false`, which means this field must have a value in the database:

```
@Column("varchar", {
    name: "UserName",
    length: 60,
    unique: true,
    nullable: false,
})
```

```
    userName: string;
    @Column("varchar", { name: "Password", length: 100,
        nullable: false })
    @Length(8, 100)
```

Here, we used the `Length` decorator to make sure that the field entered has a minimum and maximum character length:

```
    password: string;
```

The two fields, `userName` and `password`, have `varchar` as columns, with similar settings to `email`:

```
    @Column("boolean", { name: "Confirmed", default: false,
        nullable: false })
    confirmed: boolean;
```

Now, here we see a `confirmed` field that is of the `boolean` type. The `confirmed` field will show whether the newly registered user account has been email verified yet. Note, it's pretty self-explanatory, but the default setting indicates that at the moment the record is inserted into the database, unless explicitly set, it will be set to `false`:

```
    @Column("boolean", { name: "IsDisabled", default:
        false, nullable: false })
    isDisabled: boolean;
}
```

And finally, here's the `isDisabled` field, which will allow us to disable an account for management purposes.

6.  Great! Now we can see whether TypeORM will create our new `Users` table on our behalf. The last thing we need to do is connect to the Postgres database from our code. Update `index.ts` like this:

```
import express from "express";
import session from "express-session";
import connectRedis from "connect-redis";
import Redis from "ioredis";
import { createConnection } from "typeorm";
require("dotenv").config();
```

We have imported the `createConnection` function from TypeORM:

```
const main = async () => {
  const app = express();
  const router = express.Router();


  await createConnection();
```

Here, we've called `createConnection`. But notice that our code is now wrapped in a function called `main` that is `async`. The reason we needed this is that `createConnection` is an `async` call and requires an `await` prefix. So, we had to wrap it in an `async` function, which is what the `main` function does.

The remaining code is the same, as follows:

```
const redis = new Redis({
  port: Number(process.env.REDIS_PORT),
  host: process.env.REDIS_HOST,
  password: process.env.REDIS_PASSWORD,
});
const RedisStore = connectRedis(session);
const redisStore = new RedisStore({
  client: redis,
});
app.use(
  session({
    store: redisStore,
    name: process.env.COOKIE_NAME,
    sameSite: "Strict",
    secret: process.env.SESSION_SECRET,
    resave: false,
    saveUninitialized: false,
    cookie: {
      path: "/",
      httpOnly: true,
      secure: false,
      maxAge: 1000 * 60 * 60 * 24,
    },
```

```
  } as any)
);
```

Again, the code is the same:

```
app.use(router);
router.get("/", (req, res, next) => {
  if (!req.session!.userId) {
    req.session!.userId = req.query.userid;
    console.log("Userid is set");
    req.session!.loadedCount = 0;
  } else {
    req.session!.loadedCount = Number(req.session!.
    loadedCount) + 1;
  }
  res.send(
    `userId: ${req.session!.userId}, loadedCount:
      ${req.session!.loadedCount}`
  );
});
app.listen({ port: process.env.SERVER_PORT }, () => {
  console.log(`Server ready on port
    ${process.env.SERVER_PORT}`);
});
};
main();
```

And finally, we've called our `main` function to execute it.

7.  Now, let's run our application by running the following command:

```
npm start
```

Nothing has changed on the terminal. However, if you open pgAdmin and go to the **Tables** view, you'll see our new Users table with all of its columns created for us:

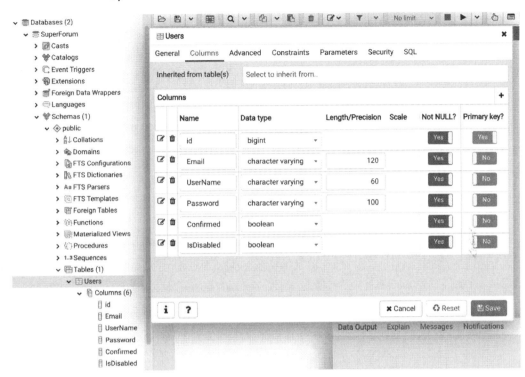

Figure 14.9 – New Users table

This is such a huge time saver! Could you imagine if we had to create each of our tables manually ourselves? With all of their fields and constraints? This would take hours.

Notice that our columns have the same settings as from our decorators. For example, our email has a variety of characters, with a length of 120, and is not nullable.

8.  However, we have a small issue. Our `id` column is not using capitalization even though our other columns are. Let's fix that. Open the `User.ts` file again and simply change the name setting of the `PrimaryGeneratedColumn` decorator to be `Id` instead of `id` (only in the decorator; leave the `id` field name in our JavaScript). If your server is not running, start it again. But after it restarts, refresh the **Tables** view by right-clicking on it and selecting **Refresh**. You should see that our `id` column has been updated to `Id`. This is a terrific feature of TypeORM, as manually changing column names or constraints can sometimes be painful.

9.  Great! Now we just need to create our other entities: `Thread` and `ThreadItem`. Again, `Thread` is the initial starting post in our forum and `ThreadItems` are the responses. First, stop your server so that it doesn't create our database items before we're ready. Now, since this is mostly repetitive, I'll just show the code here without comment.

    The imports for both these files will be identical and as shown here:

    ```
    import { Entity, PrimaryGeneratedColumn, Column } from
    "typeorm";
    import { Length } from "class-validator";
    ```

    The `Thread` entity looks like this for now (we'll be adding more fields once we build our table relationships):

    ```
    @Entity({ name: "Threads" })
    export class Thread {
      @PrimaryGeneratedColumn({ name: "Id", type: "bigint" })
      id: string;

      @Column("int", { name: "Views", default: 0, nullable:
        false })
      views: number;

      @Column("boolean", { name: "IsDisabled", default:
        false, nullable: false })
      isDisabled: boolean;

      @Column("varchar", { name: "Title", length: 150,
        nullable: false })
      @Length(5, 150)
      title: string;
    ```

```
@Column("varchar", { name: "Body", length: 2500,
  nullable: true
})
@Length(10, 2500)
body: string;
}
```

`ThreadItem` looks like this:

```
@Entity({ name: "ThreadItems" })
export class ThreadItem {
  @PrimaryGeneratedColumn({ name: "Id", type: "bigint" })
  id: string;

  @Column("int", { name: "Views", default: 0, nullable:
    false })
  views: number;

  @Column("boolean", { name: "IsDisabled", default:
    false, nullable: false })
  isDisabled: boolean;

  @Column("varchar", { name: "Body", length: 2500,
    nullable: true
  })
  @Length(10, 2500)
  body: string;
}
```

10. As you can see, both entities are pretty straightforward. Now, restart your server and you should see the two new tables: **Threads** and **ThreadItems**:

Figure 14.10 – Threads and ThreadItems

We still have many fields to add, such as the points column. But first, let's build out some relationships between tables. For example, every table should have an association with a specific user. Let's begin by adding these relationships:

1. First, stop your server. Then, in your User.ts file, add this to the bottom of your class. I'll assume you know how to add any required imports by now and won't mention them further:

```
@OneToMany(() => Thread, (thread) => thread.user)
    threads: Thread[];
```

The OneToMany decorator shows that for each individual User, there are potentially multiple Threads associated.

2.  Now, add this to the bottom of your Thread.ts file's Thread class:

```
@ManyToOne (
    () => User,
    (user:User) => user.threads
)
user: User;
```

The ManyToOne decorator shows that every Thread, of multiple threads, has only one User associated with it. Although teaching SQL is beyond the scope of this book, put simply, these relationships act as constraints on the database, meaning we are prevented from inserting data that does not make sense; for example, having multiple Users *owning* a single Thread.

3.  Now, let's establish the relationship of our Thread to ThreadItems. Add this code to the Thread class:

```
@OneToMany (
    () => ThreadItem,
    threadItems => threadItems.thread
)
threadItems: ThreadItem[];
```

Again, this shows that one Thread can have multiple ThreadItems associated with it. Now, let's update our ThreadItem:

```
@ManyToOne(() => User, (user) => user.threads)
user: User;
```

A ThreadItem, like a Thread, can only have one User associated with it as the owner:

```
@ManyToOne(() => Thread, (thread) => thread.
  threadItems)
thread: Thread;
```

4. Each `ThreadItem` can only have one parent `Thread`. Now, if you restart the server, you should see these new relationships:

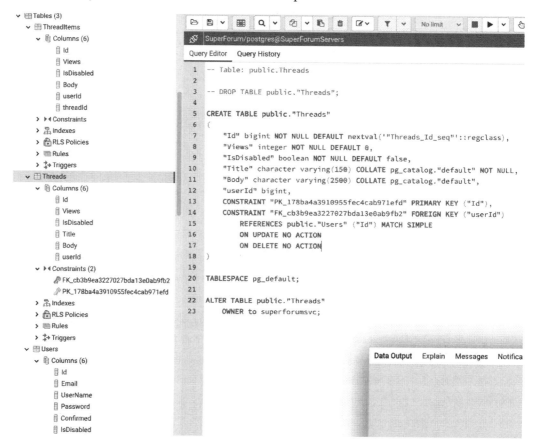

Figure 14.11 – Relationships

You will see in the `Threads` and `ThreadItems` tables that new columns have been added. For example, in `ThreadItems`, `userId` and `threadId` were added to indicate their respective relationships. However, in the `Users` table, nothing was added. This is because the `Users` table has a `OneToMany` relationship with the `Threads` table. Therefore, this relationship is indicated by the constraint shown in the image for the `CREATE TABLE public."Threads"` script. As you can see, there is a constraint for the `userId` column. So, by indicating that each thread has a single `User` associated with it, it implicitly indicates that each `User` can have one or more `Threads` that it owns.

Now, let's set up our points system. In the case of points, that is, likes or dislikes, we need to allow users to be able to vote either up or down only once. However, there's no way to indicate that in terms of a single table. So, we'll create two new tables, `ThreadPoints` and `ThreadItemPoints`, which will have associations with relevant `Users`, `Threads`, and `ThreadItems`.

1. First, shut down your server and then create the `ThreadPoint.ts` file. Then, add this code to it:

```
@Entity({ name: "ThreadPoints" })
export class ThreadPoint {
    @PrimaryGeneratedColumn({ name: "Id", type: "bigint" })
    // for typeorm
    id: string;

    @Column("boolean", { name: "IsDecrement", default:
      false, nullable: false })
    isDecrement: boolean;

    @ManyToOne(() => User, (user) => user.threadPoints)
    user: User;

    @ManyToOne(() => Thread, (thread) => thread.
      threadPoints)
    thread: Thread;
}
```

So, what we're doing here in this code is saying that this point is for a specific `User` and `Thread`. We are also indicating that if the `isDecrement` field is `true`, then this constitutes a dislike. This means that points have three possible states: no points at all, a like, or a dislike. We'll write some code in our repository queries later to handle these three states.

2. Now, add this code to the `User.ts` class:

```
@OneToMany(() => ThreadPoint, (threadPoint) =>
threadPoint.user)
    threadPoints: ThreadPoint[];
```

Again, this code completes the associations in code.

3.  Next, add the following to the `Thread.ts` class:

```
@OneToMany(() => ThreadPoint, (threadPoint) =>
  threadPoint.thread)
  threadPoints: ThreadPoint[];
```

This also completes the association with `ThreadPoint`.

4.  Now, we need to do the same thing for `ThreadItemPoints`. Create `ThreadItemPoint.ts` and add the following code:

```
@Entity({ name: "ThreadItemPoints" })
export class ThreadItemPoint {
  @PrimaryGeneratedColumn({ name: "Id", type: "bigint" })
    // for typeorm
  id: string;

  @Column("boolean", { name: "IsDecrement", default:
  false,
    nullable: false })
  isDecrement: boolean;

  @ManyToOne(() => User, (user) => user.threadPoints)
  user: User;

  @ManyToOne(() => ThreadItem, (threadItem) =>
    threadItem.threadItemPoints)
  threadItem: ThreadItem;
}
```

This is a pretty similar setup to `ThreadPoint`.

5.  Now we update our `User` class by adding the following:

```
@OneToMany(() => ThreadItemPoint, (threadItemPoint) =>
  threadItemPoint.user)
  threadItemPoints: ThreadItemPoint[];
```

And we update our `ThreadItem` class by adding this:

```
@OneToMany(
    () => ThreadItemPoint,
    (threadItemPoint) => threadItemPoint.threadItem
)
threadItemPoints: ThreadItemPoint[];
```

And this completes the associations needed in relation to `ThreadItemPoint`.

We're not done yet though. You may recall from *Chapter 11, What We Will Learn – Online Forum Application*, that our threads will have categories, so we need to create that entity and its relationship as well:

1.  First, create the `ThreadCategory.ts` file and add this code to it:

```
@Entity({ name: "ThreadCategories" })
export class ThreadCategory {
    @PrimaryGeneratedColumn({ name: "Id", type: "bigint" })
    // for typeorm
    id: string;
    @Column("varchar", {
        name: "Name",
        length: 100,
        unique: true,
        nullable: false,
    })
    name: string;
    @Column("varchar", {
        name: "Description",
        length: 150,
        nullable: true,
    })
    description: string;
    @OneToMany(() => Thread, (thread) => thread.category)
    threads: Thread[];
}
```

`ThreadCategory` has a pretty similar setup to the other entities.

2.  Now, add this to the `Thread.ts` class:

```
@ManyToOne(() => ThreadCategory, (threadCategory) =>
  threadCategory.threads)
category: ThreadCategory;
```

This, of course, creates the relationship between `Thread` and `ThreadCategory`.

3.  Now, run the server and it should create the tables and associations.

Now we've created the entities that we need and also their associations. But whenever we add data to a database, we want to log when it was created or changed. However, implementing this will create identical fields across all entities, and we don't want to write the same code over and over again.

Well, since TypeScript allows us to use inheritance in classes, let's create a base type that has these fields that we need and then have each entity simply inherit from this base class. Additionally, TypeORM requires that our entities inherit from its own base class in order to be able to connect to its API. So, then let's add the TypeORM base class in our own base class as well:

1.  Create a file called `Auditable.ts` and add this code:

```
import { Column, BaseEntity } from "typeorm";


export class Auditable extends BaseEntity {
  @Column("varchar", {
    name: "CreatedBy",
    length: 60,
    default: () => `getpgusername()`,
    nullable: false,
  })
  createdBy: string;
```

`Getpgusername` is the service account `superforumsvc` and that's what this field will default to, unless explicitly set:

```
  @Column("timestamp with time zone", {
    name: "CreatedOn",
    default: () => `now()`,
    nullable: false,
  })
  createdOn: Date;
```

This field will default to the current time and date, now(), unless explicitly set.

As you can see, the fields are pretty self-explanatory as to what they do. However, notice that our base class, Auditable, also extends the TypeORM base class called BaseEntity. This BaseEntity inheritance is what allows our entities to access the Postgres database through TypeORM:

```
@Column("varchar", {
    name: "LastModifiedBy",
    length: 60,
    default: () => `getpgusername()`,
    nullable: false,
})
lastModifiedBy: string;

@Column("timestamp with time zone", {
    name: "LastModifiedOn",
    default: () => `now()`,
    nullable: false,
})
lastModifiedOn: Date;
}
```

2.  OK, so that's the new Auditable base class covered. Now we want to make our entities inherit it. This is simple. For example, in the User class, just add the extends keyword and add the Auditable class like this:

```
export class User extends Auditable {
```

Repeat this process for every entity and then restart your server (remember to add your import statements as needed). Once you refresh your view, you should see the new fields like this:

Figure 14.12 – User updated for Auditable

Awesome! Now we can create our repository library that will actually call into our database. Since we created our Session State in the last chapter, *Chapter 13*, *Setting Up Session State Using Express and Redis*, let's create our authentication-related calls first:

1.  Before we create our main code, we need to do something first. You may recall from *Chapter 11, What We Will Learn – Online Forum Application*, we used a function called `isPasswordValid` to check that the user's password was sufficiently long and complex. We will need to reuse that code on our server because, as I mentioned then, validation in general should be done on both the client and server. So, let's temporarily copy the `PasswordValidator.ts` file and the `common/validators` folder structure into our server project, and later I'll show a method for sharing code across multiple projects.

2.  Let's also create a validator for email addresses. Create an `EmailValidator.ts` file in the same `common/validators` directory and add this code:

```
export const isEmailValid = (email: string) => {
    if (!email) return "Email cannot be empty";
```

Here, I've checked for an empty address.

```
    if (!email.includes("@")) {
        return "Please enter valid email address.";
```

And here, I've checked for the @ symbol.

```
    }
    if (/\s+/g.test(email)) {
        return "Email cannot have whitespaces";
```

And finally, here I've checked for white space.

```
    }
    return "";
};
```

If no issue is found, an empty string is returned.

3.  Create the `UserRepo.ts` file and add this code:

```
import { User } from "./User";
import bcrypt from "bcryptjs";
import { isPasswordValid } from "../common/validators/
PasswordValidator";
import { isEmailValid } from "../common/validators/
EmailValidator";
```

First, we have our imports, including our validators.

```
const saltRounds = 10;
```

`saltRounds` is for password encryption, as you'll soon see.

```
export class UserResult {
    constructor(public messages?: Array<string>, public
    user?:
    User) {}
}
```

We will use the `UserResult` type to indicate whether an error occurred during authentication. As you can see, it is basically a wrapper around the `User` object. We're using this object as the return type of our functions. We're doing this because when making network calls or other complex calls, it's not unusual for something to go wrong. Therefore, having the ability to include error or status messages with our objects is beneficial. Note how both members, `messages` and `user`, are optional. This will come in handy once we start using this type.

```
export const register = async (
    email: string,
    userName: string,
    password: string
): Promise<UserResult> => {
```

This is the start of our `register` function.

```
const result = isPasswordValid(password);
if (!result.isValid) {
    return {
        messages: [
            "Passwords must have min length 8, 1 upper
                character, 1 number, and 1 symbol",
        ],
    };
}

const trimmedEmail = email.trim().toLowerCase();
const emailErrorMsg = isEmailValid(trimmedEmail);
if (emailErrorMsg) {
    return {
        messages: [emailErrorMsg],
    };
}
```

Here, we've run our two validators, isPasswordValid and isEmailValid. Notice how we've used an object literal as our return object and not included the user member. Again, TypeScript only cares about the shape of our objects matching the shape of the type. So, in this case, since our UserResult member, user, is optional, we can create a UserResult object that does not include it. TypeScript is really flexible.

```
const salt = await bcrypt.genSalt(saltRounds);
const hashedPassword = await bcrypt.hash(password,
   salt);
```

Here, we've encrypted our password using the saltRounds constant and bcryptjs.

```
const userEntity = await User.create({
   email: trimmedEmail,
   userName,
   password: hashedPassword,
}).save();
```

And then, if we pass our validations, we create our User entity and then immediately save it. These two methods are both from TypeORM, and note that when making changes to the Entities database, you **must** always run the save function or else it will not complete on the server.

```
userEntity.password = ""; // blank out for security
return {
   user: userEntity
};
};
```

Then, we return the new entity and again, since our call has no errors, we only return the user object without any messages.

4.  Let's try this new function, `register`, with a real network call. Update the `index.ts` file like this:

```typescript
import express from "express";
import session from "express-session";
import connectRedis from "connect-redis";
import Redis from "ioredis";
import { createConnection } from "typeorm";
import { register } from "./repo/UserRepo";
import bodyParser from "body-parser";
```

Notice that we now import `bodyParser`.

```typescript
require("dotenv").config();

const main = async () => {
  const app = express();
  const router = express.Router();

  await createConnection();
  const redis = new Redis({
    port: Number(process.env.REDIS_PORT),
    host: process.env.REDIS_HOST,
    password: process.env.REDIS_PASSWORD,
  });
  const RedisStore = connectRedis(session);
  const redisStore = new RedisStore({
    client: redis,
  });

  app.use(bodyParser.json());
```

Here, we have set up our `bodyParser`, so we can read `json` parameters from posts.

```typescript
  app.use(
    session({
      store: redisStore,
      name: process.env.COOKIE_NAME,
      sameSite: "Strict",
```

```
      secret: process.env.SESSION_SECRET,
      resave: false,
      saveUninitialized: false,
      cookie: {
        path: "/",
        httpOnly: true,
        secure: false,
        maxAge: 1000 * 60 * 60 * 24,
      },
    } as any)
  );
```

All this code remains the same:

```
  app.use(router);
  router.post("/register", async (req, res, next) => {
    try {
      console.log("params", req.body);
      const userResult = await register(
        req.body.email,
        req.body.userName,
        req.body.password
      );
      if (userResult && userResult.user) {
        res.send(`new user created, userId: ${userResult.
          user.id}`);
      } else if (userResult && userResult.messages) {
        res.send(userResult.messages[0]);
      } else {
        next();
      }
    } catch (ex) {
      res.send(ex.message);
    }
  });
```

As you can see, we removed the previous `get` route and replaced it with `post` on the register URL. This call now runs our `UserRepo register` function and, if it is successful, it sends a message back with the new user's ID. If it's not successful, it sends back the error message from the repo call. In this case, we just use the first message, as we'll be removing these routes and replacing them with GraphQL in *Chapter 15, Adding GraphQL Schema – Part I*:

> **Warning**
>
> We are sending back errors for learning purposes only. You do not want to send error messages emanating from exceptions to users in production. It is confusing and, in some cases, can open your site up to attack.

```
app.listen({ port: process.env.SERVER_PORT }, () => {
    console.log(`Server ready on port
    ${process.env.SERVER_PORT}`);
  });
};
main();
```

Now we'll start testing. However, we need to switch to using Postman instead of curl. Postman is a free application that will allow us to make GET and POST calls to our server while accepting session cookies. It's very easy to use:

1.  First, go to `https://www.postman.com/downloads` and download and install Postman for your system.

2.  Following installation, the first thing you should do is run a GET call on the root of the site using Postman. I've created a simple route for the root, in `index.ts`, that will initialize the session and its cookie. Run the GET call on our site like this:

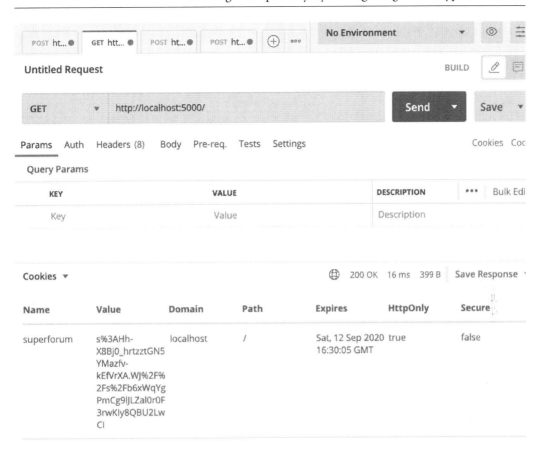

Figure 14.13 – Running Postman on the root of the site

This is how you can run this same GET call:

1. Below the top tab labelled **GET**, you should see a dropdown to the left. Select **GET** and add the local URL. There are no parameters, so just click **Send**.

2. Then, toward the bottom-left, you will see another dropdown. Select **Cookies** and you should see our cookie called **superforum**.

Now you have the cookie required to maintain the Session State. So, we can now continue our testing, starting with the `register` function:

1.  Open a new tab, select **POST**, and then add the URL `http://localhost:5000/register`.

2.  Click on the **Headers** tab and insert **Content-Type**, as shown here:

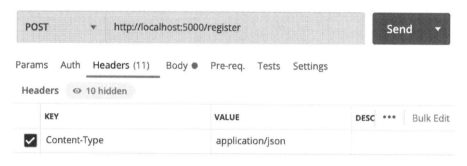

Figure 14.14 – Content-Type

3.  Now, select the **Body** tab right next to **Headers** and enter the **JSON** shown in *Figure 14.15*. Running this should show the same error result:

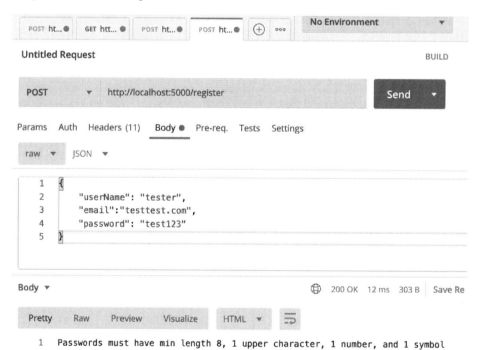

Figure 14.15 – Register fail

As you can see, we are passing the `email`, although it's invalid, the `userName`, and a `password`, which is also invalid.

But still, this failure is good, as we have confirmed our validation is working.

4.  Let's fix the password and try again. Update the password to `Test123!@#` and run it again like this:

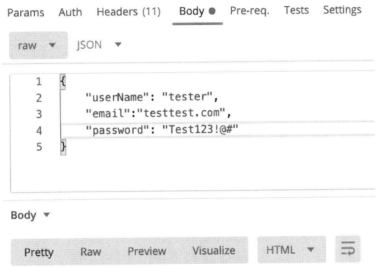

Figure 14.16 – Trying to register again

Now you should see the message **Please enter valid email address**. Again, this is what we want, as clearly the email given is not valid.

5.  Let's try one more time. Update the email to test@test.com and run this:

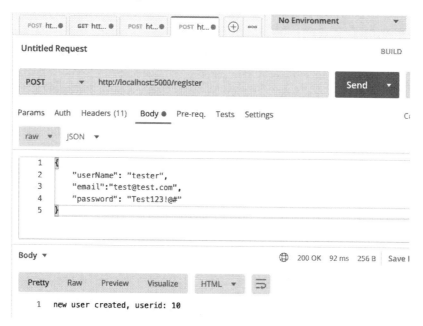

Figure 14.17 – Successful registration

The output message, **new user created, userId: 10**, shows that our user was indeed created and saved.

> **Note**
>
> I am showing an ID of 10 as I was doing some testing in preparing this book. ID fields will normally start at 1. If you don't see this result again, make sure you ran Postman on the root of our website while using a GET call.

6.  Sweet! That worked! Now, let's look at our Users table to check that the user was indeed added:

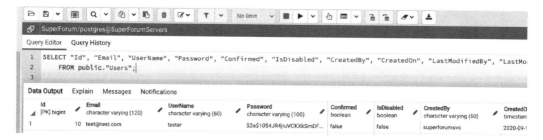

Figure 14.18 – A new user added to the Users table

You can run the query shown by right-clicking on the Users table in pgAdmin and selecting Scripts > SELECT Script. You can run the script by clicking on the play button at the top. But, as you can see, our user was inserted into the database.

7.  Now, let's update UserRepo with our login function. Add the following code to the end of UserRepo:

```
export const login = async (
  userName: string,
  password: string
): Promise<UserResult> => {
  const user = await User.findOne({
    where: { userName },
  });
  if (!user) {
    return {
      messages: [userNotFound(userName)],
    };
  }
  if (!user.confirmed) {
    return {
      messages: ["User has not confirmed their
        registration email yet."],
    };
  }
  const passwordMatch = await bcrypt.compare(password,
    user?.password);
  if (!passwordMatch) {
    return {
      messages: ["Password is invalid."],
    };
  }
  return {
    user: user,
  };
};
```

Not much to show here. We try and find a user with the given `userName`. If not found, a message is sent back that the `user` is not found, using a function called `userNotFound`. I'm using a function because we will reuse this message later. It's a simple function, so I won't cover it here (it's in the source code). If the user is found, then we first see whether the account was confirmed. If not, we provide an error regarding it. Next, we check their password by using `bcryptjs`, since we used that tool to encrypt it during registration. If it does not match, we also provide an error regarding that. If all goes well and the `user` exists, we return the `user`.

8.  Let's try running this as well. Update `index.ts` by adding this new route just below the register route:

```
router.post("/login", async (req, res, next) => {
    try {
        console.log("params", req.body);
        const userResult = await login(req.body.userName,
          req.body.password);
        if (userResult && userResult.user) {
            req.session!.userId = userResult.user?.id;
            res.send(`user logged in, userId:
              ${req.session!.userId}`);
        } else if (userResult && userResult.messages) {
            res.send(userResult.messages[0]);
        } else {
            next();
        }
    } catch (ex) {
        res.send(ex.message);
    }
});
```

This is quite similar to our `register` route. However, here we save the user's `id` to the Session State and then send back a message using that session.

9.  Let's run this route and see what happens. Again, open a new tab in Postman and run the settings as shown here. **Remember** to add the **Content-Type** header in the **Headers** tab:

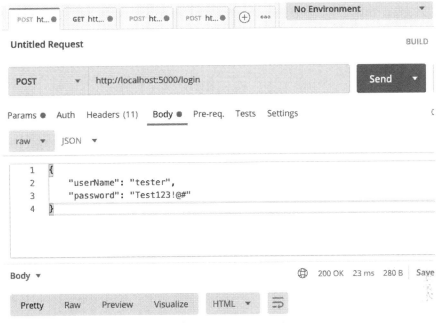

Figure 14.19 – Login route

Again, this is good to see as our validations are working.

10. Go to your pgAdmin and open the same screen you used to run the SELECT query to see our first inserted user. Then, run this SQL to update our user's confirmed column to be true:

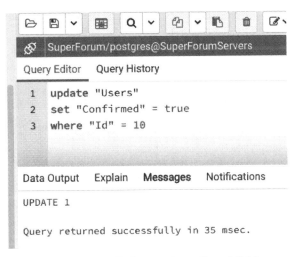

Figure 14.20 – Update user's confirmed field

Once you run your query, you should see the same message, as shown in *Figure 14.20*.

11. Now, let's run Postman to try and log in again:

Figure 14.21 – Logging in the user

Now, our users can log in and, based on the returned message, we can now see that our Session State is being used. I've created the `logout` function and route in the source code. I won't show it here since it's simple.

> **Note**
>
> If you're attempt to save to the session fails, make sure that your Redis service is running.

Awesome! We've come a long way. We now have working session-based authentication, but we're not done yet. We need to create ways of inserting `Threads` and `ThreadItems`, as well as retrieving them. Let's start with `Threads`:

1. Before we create our new `ThreadRepo` repository, let's build a small helper. In `UserRepo`, we had a type called `UserResult` that had an array of messages and a user as members. You'll notice that any repo of `Threads`, `ThreadItems`, and `Categories` will need a similar construction. It should have an array of messages and entities, although the entity returned will be an array of items and not just one.

This seems like a good place to use TypeScript Generics, so that we can share a single result type across all these entities. Let's create a new general-purpose result object type called `QueryResult`. We learned about TypeScript Generics in *Chapter 2, Exploring TypeScript*.

Create a file called `QueryArrayResult.ts` and add this code to it:

```
export class QueryArrayResult<T> {
    constructor(public messages?: Array<string>, public
        entities?: Array<T>) {}
}
```

As you can see, it's very similar to the original `UserResult`. However, this type uses a generic of type `T` to indicate any of our entities.

> **Warning**
>
> The pg dependency also has a type called `QueryArrayResult`. When importing our dependency, please make sure you import our file, and not pg.

2.  Now, let's use this new `QueryArrayResult` type in our `ThreadRepo`. Create a new file, `ThreadRepo.ts`, inside the `repo` folder and add the following code:

```
export const createThread = async (
    userId: string,
    categoryId: string,
    title: string,
    body: string
): Promise<QueryArrayResult<Thread>> => {
```

The parameters shown are needed because every `Thread` must be associated with a user and a category. Do note, however, that `userId` is coming from our session.

```
    const titleMsg = isThreadTitleValid(title);
    if (titleMsg) {
      return {
        messages: [titleMsg],
      };
    }
    const bodyMsg = isThreadBodyValid(body);
    if (bodyMsg) {
      return {
```

```
    messages: [bodyMsg],
  };
}
```

Here we validate our `title` and `message`.

```
// users must be logged in to post
const user = await User.findOne({
  id: userId,
});
if (!user) {
  return {
    messages: ["User not logged in."],
  };
}
```

Here, we take our session provided `userId` and try and find a matching `user`. We need this `user` object later to create our new `Thread`.

```
const category = await ThreadCategory.findOne({
  id: categoryId,
});
if (!category) {
  return {
    messages: ["category not found."],
  };
}
```

Here we get a `category` object, because again we need to pass it during the creation of our new `Thread`.

```
const thread = await Thread.create({
  title,
  body,
  user,
  category,
}).save();
if (!thread) {
  return {
    messages: ["Failed to create thread."],
```

```
    };
  }
```

As you can see, we pass `title`, `body`, `user`, and `category` in order to create our new `Thread`.

```
  return {
    messages: ["Thread created successfully."],
  };
};
```

We are only returning messages as we don't need to return the actual object. Also, returning an object that is not required is inefficient in terms of API payload size.

3. Before we can continue, we need to add some `ThreadCategories` to our database so that we can actually use the `createThread` function. Go to the source code and find the `utils/InsertThreadCategories.txt` file. Copy and paste these `insert` statements into a query screen of `pgAdmin` and run it. This will create the listed `ThreadCategories`.

4. Next, we need to add our route for creating `Threads`. Add the following code to `index.ts`:

```
router.post("/createthread", async (req, res, next) => {
  try {
    console.log("userId", req.session);
    console.log("body", req.body);
    const msg = await createThread(
      req.session!.userId, // notice this is from
        session!
      req.body.categoryId,
      req.body.title,
      req.body.body
    );
```

In this super simple call, we pass parameters to the `createThread` function. Again, our `userId` comes from our session, since a user should be logged in in order to be allowed to post, and then we simply return the result message.

```
    res.send(msg);
  } catch (ex) {
    console.log(ex);
```

```
        res.send(ex.message);
    }
});
```

5.  Let's try running this route. First, however, run the logout route in Postman. You'll find it on the `http://localhost:5000/logout` URL. I'm sure you can set up Postman yourself now. Once that is done, let's try and run the `createthread` route and hopefully, it should fail validation:

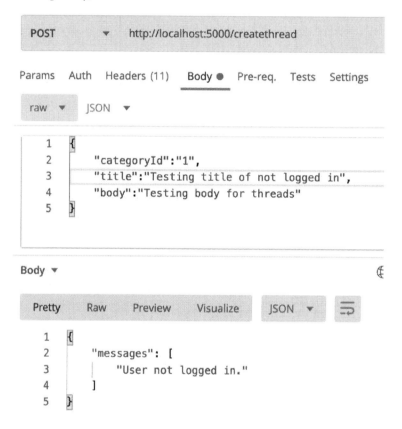

Figure 14.22 – Test createthread route

Yes, it failed validation as expected.

6.  Now, let's log in again so that our session gets created. Go ahead and do that with Postman again, and then run the `createthread` route again. This time, it should work with the message, **Thread created successfully**.

7.  OK. Now we need two more functions, one to get a single `Thread` by its ID, and another to get all the threads for `ThreadCategory`. Add this code to `ThreadRepo`:

```
export const getThreadById = async (
   id: string
): Promise<QueryOneResult<Thread>> => {
   const thread = await Thread.findOne({ id });
   if (!thread) {
     return {
       messages: ["Thread not found."],
     };
   }

   return {
     entity: thread,
   };
};
```

This `getThreadById` function is pretty simple. It just looks for a single thread based on an ID.

```
export const getThreadsByCategoryId = async (
  categoryId: string
): Promise<QueryArrayResult<Thread>> => {
  const threads = await Thread.
  createQueryBuilder("thread")
    .where(`thread."categoryId" = :categoryId`, {
      categoryId })
    .leftJoinAndSelect("thread.category", "category")
    .orderBy("thread.createdOn", "DESC")
    .getMany();
```

This `getThreadsByCategoryId` function is much more interesting. `Thread.createQueryBuilder` is a special function in TypeORM that allows us to build more sophisticated queries. The function's `thread` parameter is an alias used to represent the Threads table in our query. So, if you look at the rest of the query, such as the `where` clause, you can see that we use `thread` as a prefix for fields or relationships. The `leftJoinAndSelect` function means that we want to do a SQL left join, but also we want to return the related entity, in this case,

ThreadCategory, with the result set. OrderBy is pretty self-explanatory, and getMany just means to return all items.

```
    if (!threads) {
      return {
        messages: ["Threads of category not found."],
      };
    }
    console.log(threads);
    return {
      entities: threads,
    };
  };
```

8. The rest of the code is pretty straightforward. Let's test getThreadsByCategoryId as a route. Add this to the index.ts file:

```
router.post("/threadbycategory", async (req, res, next)
=> {
    try {
      const threadResult = await
      getThreadsByCategoryId(req.body.categoryId);
```

Here, we have made our call to getThreadsByCategoryId using the categoryId parameter.

```
      if (threadResult && threadResult.entities) {
        let items = "";
        threadResult.entities.forEach((th) => {
          items += th.title + ", ";
        });
        res.send(items);
      } else if (threadResult && threadResult.messages) {
        res.send(threadResult.messages[0]);
      }
```

In this `if else` code, we either have all titles displayed or the error displayed.

```
      } catch (ex) {
        console.log(ex);
        res.send(ex.message);
      }
    });
```

9. The rest of the code is as before. Run this in your Postman client and you should see this. Again, your ID numbers may vary:

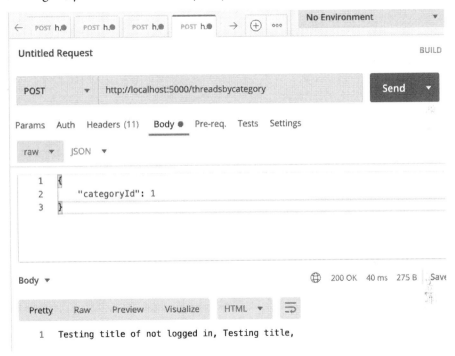

Figure 14.23 – Test threadsbycategory route

I'll leave the testing of `getThreadById` up to you, as it's pretty easy. Again, the source code is in our project repository.

The code for `ThreadItems` is almost identical and is in our source code. So, I won't review it here. Now, we do need a few more functions for getting things such as `ThreadCategories` to populate our React app's `LeftMenu`. We also need to retrieve points for our `Threads` and `ThreadItems`. And we also need relevant `Thread` data for our `UserProfile` screen. However, those calls will repeat a lot of the concepts we learned in this section, and we'll have to create routes that we'll ultimately end up deleting once we start our GraphQL server code. Therefore, let's leave those for *Chapter 15*, *Adding GraphQL Schema – Part I*, where we can also start integrating the backend GraphQL code with our React frontend.

In this section, we learned how to build a repository layer and make queries into Postgres using TypeORM. We'll be reusing our query skills once we start integrating GraphQL in the next chapter, so this is important knowledge that we'll continue to use.

## Summary

In this chapter, we learned how to set up a Postgres database and how to query it using an ORM, TypeORM. We also learned how to keep our code cleanly separated by using a repository layer.

In the next chapter, we'll learn how to enable GraphQL on our server. We'll also finish our database queries and integrate our backend into our React frontend.

# 15
# Adding GraphQL Schema Part I

In this chapter, we'll continue building out our application by integrating GraphQL. We'll do this on both the client and the server. We'll also finish building out our backend Express server and integrating that backend with our React client.

In this chapter, we're going to cover the following main topics:

- Creating GraphQL server-side typedefs and resolvers
- Integrating authentication with GraphQL resolvers
- Creating React client-side Hooks for querying Apollo GraphQL

## Technical requirements

You should have a basic understanding of GraphQL and a good understanding of React, Node.js, Postgres, and Redis. We will once again be using Node and **Visual Studio Code (VSCode)** to write our code.

The GitHub repository is at `https://github.com/PacktPublishing/Full-Stack-React-TypeScript-and-Node`. Use the code in folder `Chap15`.

To set up the Chapter 15 code folder, do this:

1. Go to your HandsOnTypescript folder and create a new folder called Chap15.

2. Now go to the Chap14 folder and copy the super-forum-server folder into the Chap15 folder. Make certain all files have been copied.

3. Within the super-forum-server folder delete the node_modules folder and the package-lock.json file. Make sure you're in the super-forum-server folder and run this command:

```
npm install
```

4. Now make sure your Postgres server and Redis server are running, as shown in *Chapter 13, Setting Up a Session State Using Express and Redis*, and *Chapter 14, Setting Up Postgres and Repository Layer with TypeORM*. Then, test your server by running this command:

```
npm start
```

5. Now let's copy our client app. Go to the Chap13 folder and copy super-forum-client to the root of Chap15. Make sure all files are copied over.

6. Delete the node_modules folder and the package-lock.json file. Now make sure you're in the super-forum-client folder and run this command:

```
npm install
```

7. Test that it works by running this:

```
npm start
```

# Creating GraphQL server-side typedefs and resolvers

In this section, we'll add our GraphQL service to our Express server. We'll also start transforming our routes into GraphQL queries, which we created in *Chapter 14, Setting Up Postgres and Repository Layer with TypeORM*. We'll also flesh out the rest of the calls that we need, as GraphQL queries.

Let's start by first integrating GraphQL into our Express application (we covered GraphQL in *Chapter 9*, *What is GraphQL?*, and *Chapter 10*, *Setting Up an Express Project with TypeScript and GraphQL Dependencies*):

> **Note**
>
> There will be a very large amount of code in this chapter and not all of it can be shown in text. Please refer to the chapter source code, which is the GitHub repository code, frequently. Note also the chapter source code is the final running project and will contain only the final working code.

1. Let's begin by installing GraphQL. Run this command:

```
npm i apollo-server-express graphql graphql-middleware
graphql-tools
```

2. Next, let's create our initial type definitions, typeDefs. Create a folder called gql inside of the src folder. Then create the file typeDefs.ts inside of it. Now add this code:

```
import { gql } from "apollo-server-express";

const typeDefs = gql`
  scalar Date
```

We define a new custom scalar type, Date, not available by default in GraphQL for dates and times:

```
  type EntityResult {
    messages: [String!]
  }
```

This EntityResult type will be used when errors or messages are returned instead of entities from our resolvers:

```
  type User {
    id: ID!
    email: String!
    userName: String!
    password: String!
    confirmed: Boolean!
    isDisabled: Boolean!
    threads: [Thread!]
```

```
        createdBy: String!
        createdOn: Date!
        lastModifiedBy: String!
        lastModifiedOn: Date!
    }
```

We created our `User` type here. Notice the relations to `Thread` and `ThreadItem`. We've also used our `Date` type:

```
    type Thread {
        id: ID!
        views: Int!
        isDisabled: Boolean!
        title: String!
        body: String!
        user: User!
        threadItems: [ThreadItem!]
        category: ThreadCategory
        createdBy: String!
        createdOn: Date!
        lastModifiedBy: String!
        lastModifiedOn: Date!
    }
```

We created our `Thread` type and its relations:

```
    union ThreadResult = Thread | EntityResult
```

Now that we are implementing our real application, it's time to use some more sophisticated features of GraphQL. The `union` type is the same concept as in TypeScript. It will allow us to return any type from a list of possible GraphQL types. For example, in this example, this type may represent *either* a Thread or an EntityResult, but not both at the same time. I'll show the usage of this type soon and it will become clearer how it works.

```
    type ThreadItem {
        id: ID!
        views: Int!
        isDisabled: Boolean!
        body: String!
        user: User!
```

```
    thread: Thread!
    createdBy: String!
    createdOn: Date!
    lastModifiedBy: String!
    lastModifiedOn: Date!
  }
```

We created our `ThreadItem` type.

```
type ThreadCategory {
    id: ID!
    name: String!
    description: String
    threads: [Thread!]!
    createdBy: String!
    createdOn: Date!
    lastModifiedBy: String!
    lastModifiedOn: Date!
}
```

The `ThreadCategory` type also refers to the `Threads` that it contains.

```
type Query {
    getThreadById(id: ID!): ThreadResult
}
`;
```

Here, we have our `Query` with the `getThreadById` function. Notice it returns our union `ThreadResult`. We'll flesh this out more later.

```
export default typeDefs;
```

3. Now let's create a simple resolvers file to get started with our GraphQL installation. Create a file called `resolvers.ts` in the `gql` folder and add this code:

```
import { IResolvers } from "apollo-server-express";
interface EntityResult {
  messages: Array<string>;
}
```

We'll be using `EntityResult` as our return type for errors and status messages. Also, add our type mapping to the same type in the `typeDefs` file:

```
const resolvers: IResolvers = {
  ThreadResult: {
    __resolveType(obj: any, context: GqlContext, info:
      any) {
      if (obj.messages) {
        return "EntityResult";
      }
      return "Thread";
    },
  },
```

Here's another new feature of GraphQL we are using. `ThreadResult` is the `union` that represents the two types, `Thread` and `EntityResult`, in GraphQL. This resolver notices when a `ThreadResult` is about to be returned and figures out which type it is internally. The method you use is entirely up to you to determine the type sent back, but here we have used a simple check for the `EntityResult` type's `message` field by checking `obj.message`:

```
  Query: {
    getThreadById: async (
      obj: any,
      args: { id: string },
      ctx: GqlContext,
      info: any
    ): Promise<Thread | EntityResult> => {
      let thread: QueryOneResult<Thread>;
      try {
        thread = await getThreadById(args.id);
        if (thread.entity) {
          return thread.entity;
        }
        return {
          message: thread.messages ? thread.messages[0] :
            "test",
        };
      } catch (ex) {
```

```
        throw ex;
      }
    },
  },
};

export default resolvers;
```

We learned about GraphQL queries in *Chapter 9, What is GraphQL?*, so I won't go over it too deeply here. Just note that in this call, I accept the result type from the call to getThreadById, QueryOneResult, and after some processing, I return the actual entity itself or EntityResult. Again, since our typeDefs file has our query as returning a ThreadResult, it will go to the ThreadResult query and figure out which type to return. This is a pattern that we'll repeat for most of our repository calls. Repositories were covered in *Chapter 14, Setting Up Postgres and Repository Layer with TypeORM*.

> **Note**
>
> For this sample application, we are just rethrowing the errors that may occur. But in your production app, you should handle the error as appropriate to your app, which, in general, means to at least log the issue so it can be looked at later.

We will populate this code with more queries and mutations later, but for now, let's focus on completing our base setup.

4. Copy and paste the GqlContext.ts file from the Chap10/gql-server/src folder into the gql folder. As shown in *Chapter 9, What is GraphQL?*, this is where our Request and Response objects live inside of a GraphQL call.

5. Now let's open our index.ts file and add GraphQL into it. Update it by adding this code just before the call to listen and make sure to add the necessary imports, which you should be able to do yourself now:

```
const schema = makeExecutableSchema({ typeDefs, resolvers
});
const apolloServer = new ApolloServer({
    schema,
    context: ({ req, res }: any) => ({ req, res }),
});
apolloServer.applyMiddleware({ app });
```

This is basically similar code to *Chapter 9, What is GraphQL?*, where we instantiate our `ApolloServer` and bring it our `typeDefs`, `resolvers`, and Express `app` instance.

6. Let's test this to make sure it's working. Open the URL `http://localhost:5000/graphql`. This is the GraphQL playground we reviewed in *Chapter 9, What is GraphQL?*. Run it as shown:

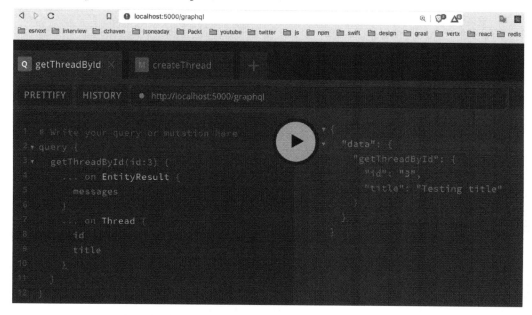

Figure 15.1 – First query into GraphQL

So, as you can see, our call now works. The only difference from some of our prior calls into GraphQL is that since our call could return two different types, we use the `... on <some type>` syntax to decide which entity and fields we want upon return (this feature is called inline fragments). Also, again, please remember your local ID numbers will not necessarily be the same as mine, so you need to send IDs that definitely exist in your database.

7. OK, let's do another. This time, we'll pick one that does not return an entity – the `createThread` function. First, add this mutation to the end of your `typeDefs` file:

```
type Mutation {
    createThread(
        userId: ID!
        categoryId: ID!
```

```
        title: String!
        body: String!
    ): EntityResult
}
```

Notice we are not returning a `ThreadResult`. Our `createThread` function only returns a string message. So that's all we need.

8.  Now let's update the `resolvers` file. Add this function as a mutation. Again, you'll need to import anything that is needed yourself:

```
Mutation: {
    createThread: async (
        obj: any,
        args: { userId: string; categoryId: string; title:
            string; body: string },
        ctx: GqlContext,
        info: any
    ): Promise<EntityResult> => {
```

Again, the same parameters list as always, but this time we return only the `EntityResult` as there is no need to return the entire entity:

```
        let result: QueryOneResult<Thread>;
        try {
            result = await createThread(
                args.userId,
                args.categoryId,
                args.title,
                args.body
            );
```

Here, we made our call to the repository's `createThread` and got back our result.

```
            return {
                messages: result.messages
                    ? result.messages
                    : ["An error has occurred"],
            };
```

And now we're returning the list of possible messages to indicate the status of the result.

```
} catch (ex) {
    throw ex;
```

Again, in production, you should not simply rethrow but log or otherwise deal with an error. We rethrow here in order to simplify and focus on the concepts at hand, without getting sidetracked.

```
        }
    },
},
```

9.  So, now if we run our code, we should see this:

Figure 15.2 – createThread function

10. OK, so let's do one more call for Threads. In the `ThreadRepo` is the call `getThreadsByCategoryId`, which returns an array of Threads. This is a problem because the GraphQL `union` operator does not support arrays. So we'll need to create another new entity in the `typeDefs` file to represent an array of Threads and then we can create our union. Update the `typeDefs` file by adding this under the ThreadResult union:

```
type ThreadArray {
    threads: [Thread!]
}
union ThreadArrayResult = ThreadArray | EntityResult
```

So we created an entity that returns an array of Threads first. Then we created our union that either returns that entity type or the `EntityResult`.

Now add this after the getThreadById query:

```
getThreadsByCategoryId(categoryId: ID!):
ThreadArrayResult!
```

11. Now we can build our resolver. Update the resolvers Query section by adding this:

```
getThreadsByCategoryId: async (
    obj: any,
    args: { categoryId: string },
    ctx: GqlContext,
    info: any
): Promise<{ threads: Array<Thread> } | EntityResult>
=> {
    let threads: QueryArrayResult<Thread>;
    try {
        threads = await getThreadsByCategoryId(args.
          categoryId);
        if (threads.entities) {
            return {
                threads: threads.entities,
            };
        }
}
```

Here, we return our array of threads.

```
        return {
            messages: threads.messages
                ? threads.messages
                : ["An error has occurred"],
        };
```

And here we return our messages if there are no threads.

```
    } catch (ex) {
        throw ex;
    }
},
```

12. We're missing just one more item. When we first started using `union`, we had to create a query for the `EntityResult` type. So, we need to do the same thing for our new `ThreadArrayResult` type. Enter this code just after the `EntityResult` definition inside the `resolvers` file:

```
ThreadArrayResult: {
    __resolveType(obj: any, context: GqlContext, info:
    any) {
        if (obj.messages) {
            return "EntityResult";
        }
        return "ThreadArray";
    },
},
```

It's the same situation as before. If `obj` has a `messages` property, we return the type `EntityResult`; if not, then we return the `ThreadArray` type.

13. If we run this Query, we should see something like this (note my results are filled with duplicate testing data):

Figure 15.3 – The getThreadsByCategoryId function

Notice we added an additional field called `__typename`. This field will tell us which type is coming back, which as shown is `ThreadArray`.

OK, so now we have a working GraphQL server with queries for Threads. Try and integrate the non-authentication related calls from *Chapter 14, Setting Up Postgres and Repository Layer with TypeORM*, yourself. If you get stuck, you can refer to the source code. But it's important you try and do this *without* looking as that's how you know for sure you understand the material.

# ThreadPoint System

Now that we've integrated our existing resolver calls, let's create some of the calls that we still need. We created a points system for our Threads and ThreadItems. Let's now implement a way to increment and decrement points. If it's been a while, take a look at the ThreadPoint and ThreadItemPoint entities before continuing. You'll notice a new field called `points`, which I'll explain once we start writing our code:

1.  First, create a file called `ThreadPointRepo.ts` inside of the repo folder and add this code into it (again, I assume you know how to add the necessary imports):

    ```
    export const updateThreadPoint = async (
      userId: string,
      threadId: string,
      increment: boolean
    ): Promise<string> => {
    ```

    Notice the parameters have an `increment` boolean. This determines whether we are trying to add or remove a point.

    ```
    // todo: first check user is authenticated
    ```

    Once we create our authentication calls, we'll revisit this comment and fill it in with code. Note that adding a `todo` comment is a good way of keeping track of the items remaining to be completed. It also notifies team members of this fact.

    ```
    let message = "Failed to increment thread point";
    const thread = await Thread.findOne({
      where: { id: threadId },
      relations: ["user"],
    });
    if (thread!.user!.id === userId) {
      message = "Error: users cannot increment their own
        thread";
      return message;
    }
    ```

So, we start by getting the `Thread` for the given `threadId`. Notice we also check that the given `User` is not the same `User` who owns the thread. If you have only one `User` in your database, you'll need to add another `User`, so that the owner of the `Thread` is not the same one trying to increment its point. You can add a user by using a SQL insert query or reusing our register route from *Chapter 14, Setting Up Postgres and Repository Layer with TypeORM*.

```
const user = await User.findOne({ where: { id: userId }
});
```

Here, we've gotten the matching `User` a bit before we actually need to use them. We'll see in a bit why we're doing something that may seem inefficient.

```
const existingPoint = await ThreadPoint.findOne({
  where: {
    thread: { id: threadId },
    user: { id: userId },
  },
  relations: ["thread"],
});
```

Here, we are seeing if an existing point entity already exists. We will use this object to make decisions on how to add or remove points later:

```
await getManager().transaction(async
(transactionEntityManager) => {
```

As you can see, we have a bit of new TypeORM code. The `getManager().transaction` call is creating a SQL transaction. A transaction is a way of doing multiple SQL operations as a single atomic operation. In other words, either every single one will complete successfully or all will fail. So then everything running inside of this scope is part of the transaction.

Additionally, we noticed previously that we had created a `User` entity in advance of using it. This is because it is a best practice to avoid making selection queries inside of a transaction. This is not a hard rule. But in general, having selection queries inside of transactions makes things slower.

```
if (existingPoint) {
  if (increment) {
    if (existingPoint.isDecrement) {
      await ThreadPoint.remove(existingPoint);
      thread!.points = Number(thread!.points) + 1;
```

```
            thread!.lastModifiedOn = new Date();
            thread!.save();
        }
    } else {
        if (!existingPoint.isDecrement) {
            await ThreadPoint.remove(existingPoint);
            thread!.points = Number(thread!.points) - 1;
            thread!.lastModifiedOn = new Date();
            thread!.save();
        }
    }
```

In this section, we checked if a ThreadPoint already exists by checking for existingPoint (remember a ThreadPoint can represent a positive or negative point, as indicated by the isDecrement field). Once that is determined, we decide if we are doing an increment or a decrement. If doing an increment and there is an existing decrement ThreadPoint, we delete that entity and do nothing else. If we are doing a decrement and there is an existing increment ThreadPoint, we delete that entity and do nothing else.

Now, the other thing to notice is that our Thread Entity now has a field called points, which we increment or decrement as appropriate. This field will act as a sort of shortcut in our UI that will allow us to get the current Thread's points total without having to sum all the ThreadPoints for that Thread:

```
    } else {
        await ThreadPoint.create({
            thread,
            isDecrement: !increment,
            user,
        }).save();
        if (increment) {
            thread!.points = Number(thread!.points) + 1;
        } else {
            thread!.points = Number(thread!.points) - 1;
        }
        thread!.lastModifiedOn = new Date();
        thread!.save();
    }
```

Else if we have no existing points at all, we just create a new one that is either an increment or a decrement:

```
message = `Successfully ${
    increment ? "incremented" : "decremented"
} point.`;
});
return message;
};
```

2. Now add `Mutation` to `typeDefs` like this:

```
updateThreadPoint(userId: ID!, threadId: ID!, increment:
Boolean!): String!
```

3. Then, update the `resolver` by adding the `updateThreadPoint` call to the `Mutation` section. Since this is just a wrapper around the repository call that does the actual work, I won't show the code here. Try and see if you can create the `Mutation` yourself without looking at the code.

> **Note**
>
> Most of the resolvers we will use are just wrappers around our Repository calls. This keeps our resolver code separate from our database and Repository calls. So, most of the time, I will not show the resolver code since it is slight and available in the source code.

4. Run the `Mutation` as shown and then check your database:

Figure 15.4 – Run updateThreadPoint

Here, we have the result of our mutation in the Postgres database, using pgAdmin:

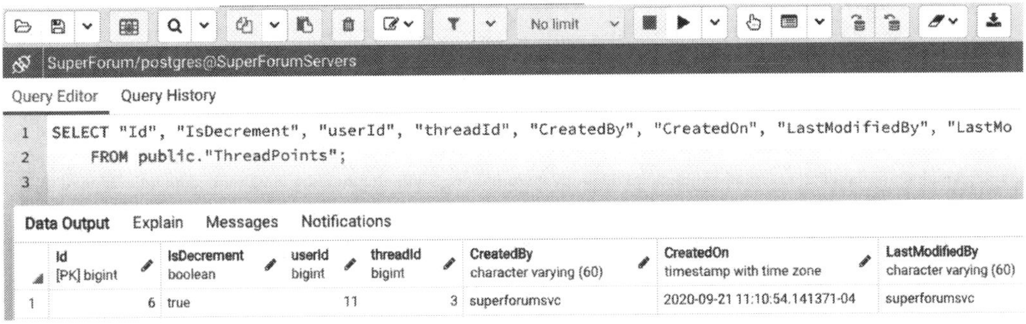

Figure 15.5 – Run the updateThreadPoint database result

So, our record is created successfully, as shown.

Now let's discuss a bit more about this points system that we have and how it works. A *like* points system can allow for both a positive and a negative point, as does our system. However, it must also prevent users from voting more than once. In order to do that, we need to associate each point with both the user that gave it and the Thread or ThreadItem they put it on. This is why we have the ThreadPoint and ThreadPointItem entities.

On a well-trafficked site having many users, adding or removing points at any given time can be a significant load on the server. But worse than this is if we were to have to sum up all of these ThreadPoints or ThreadItemPoints upon each call to get Thread or ThreadItem data. This would be untenable. So for the first issue, we must accept it as part of having a "one vote per user" points system. However, for the summing of points issue, we could attempt several different things in order to improve performance.

The most performant would be to add a caching system, using a secondary service like Redis. However, building a caching system is no trivial matter and well beyond the scope of this book. And we could argue that while our site is just getting started, before it achieves glorious success and billions of dollars, we won't have that kind of traffic. So, as a start, we could try something a little simpler.

So what we are doing instead is adding the points field to our Thread and ThreadItem entities and incrementing the values as calls to add or remove points are made. Not the best solution, but it will do for now. Over time, a caching system or some other mechanism can be built out that is more sophisticated.

The code for ThreadItemPoint is virtually identical. Go ahead and see if you can build the `ThreadItemPointRepo.ts` file yourself. As always, take a look at the code in the source if you get stuck.

In this section, we began integrating our Repository calls with our GraphQL layer. We also fleshed out our Thread and ThreadItem points system. In the next section, we'll continue building out our GraphQL API by integrating our authentication calls.

# Integrating authentication with GraphQL resolvers

Integrating authentication into GraphQL isn't much different from adding any other functionality. In this section, we'll learn how to do that.

Let's now integrate our authentication-related calls. Let's start with the `register` call:

1. You'll recall we already created our `register` call in *Chapter 14, Setting Up Postgres and Repository Layer with TypeORM*. So now, let's add our `typeDefs` and `resolvers`. First, add the `register` call from the source code, to the `typeDefs` file in the `Mutation` section:

2. Now, in our resolvers file, in the `Mutation` section, add the code from our GitHub source code.

   This is again just a wrapper of our repository call so there's not much to explain, but notice we do not return a `User` object; we only return a status message. This is because we want to reduce the chance of any unnecessary information being spilled out. Before we try running it, let's enable our GraphQL playground to accept cookies so we can test it. We need to enable cookies so that our Session State can be saved, which is what allows our calls to check if the User has already logged in.

   In the upper-right corner of the playground, click on the gear icon. Set the `request.credentials` field to `include` as shown, then save it and refresh the screen. We should see this if we run it now:

Figure 15.6 – Register

3. Let's continue with the `login` function. Add the login source code to the `Mutation` section of your `typeDefs` file.

4. Now add the resolver code for `login` from the source code. Our Repository `login` call is checking that the user exists and making sure the password matches. The GraphQL call then takes the `user.id` and sets it to the Session object, `ctx.req.session.userId`, if a successful login happens. Notice also that our resolver does not return the `user` object upon success. We'll create a new function to provide `User` info later.

5. Now let's do the `logout` function. First, add the `typeDefs` entry inside of the `Mutation` section as shown by the source code.

6. Now update the resolvers `Mutation` with the `logout` resolver code from the source. Notice no matter what response comes back from the Repository `logout` call, we `destroy` the `session` using `ctx.req.session?.destroy` and this sets `ctx.req.session?.userId` to `undefined`.

7. Now we need to add one more new call and a new type to our `typeDefs`. Add the function `me` to the `Query` section of the `typeDefs` file, as shown by the source code. Next, underneath the `User` type, add this `union`:

```
union UserResult = User | EntityResult
```

Why do we need these? In our calls to `register` and `login`, we eliminated the returned `User` object because `User` details may or may not be used after these calls and we don't want to unnecessarily expose `User` data. However, there are times when once a `User` is logged in, we may want to see their relevant data. For example, when they access their UserProfile screen. So, we will use this me function to handle that.

8. Now let's add our `UserRepo` call for the me function. Add this function to `UserRepo`:

```
export const me = async (id: string): Promise<UserResult>
=> {
  const user = await User.findOne({
    where: { id },
    relations: ["threads", "threads.threadItems"],
  });
```

First, notice that the user object we find includes any `Threads` and `ThreadItems` that belong to the user. We will use these in our UserProfile screen:

```
if (!user) {
    return {
        messages: ["User not found."],
    };
}
if (!user.confirmed) {
    return {
        messages: ["User has not confirmed their
        registration email yet."],
    };
}
return {
    user: user,
};
};
```

The rest of the function is a lot like the login function.

9.  Now let's create our `resolvers` for the `UserResult` and the me function. At the top of the resolvers `const`, add the UserResult resolver as shown in the code. This is the same as the other Result `union` resolvers – there's nothing new to explain here.

10. In the `Query` section, add the code for the me function from the source code.

    Notice this resolver takes no parameters, as it gets the `userId` from the session. On line 193, it checks the `userId` is in the session. If it is not, it exits early. If the `userId` is in the Session, it uses our `UserRepo` me function to get the currently logged-in `user`. And the rest is basically the same as other functions returning an entity.

11. Let's try running our me resolver. Make sure you've logged in once and have followed the instructions in *Step 3* for the GraphQL playground. If you run me as shown, you should get back relevant data:

Figure 15.7 – Call to the me resolver

As you can see, we use inline fragments again and are able to get back both related Threads and ThreadItems.

In this section, we tied our Repository layer authentication calls to GraphQL and tested their functionality. In the next section, we will finish our application by tying our nearly complete backend to our frontend.

# Creating React client-side Hooks for querying Apollo GraphQL

In this section, we will finish off our application by connecting our React client to our GraphQL backend. We've come a long way and we're almost there.

In order to tie the two parts of our app together, we need to add CORS to our Express server. **CORS** stands for **Cross-Origin Resource Sharing**. It means that our server will be set up to allow a client domain that is not the same as its own domain.

In most server configurations of even modest complexity, the server that hosts the client-side application and the server that provides the API do not exist on the same domain. In general, you will have a proxy of some kind, for example, NGINX, that will accept calls coming from the browser. And that proxy will "redirect" calls as required. We will explain how reverse proxies work in more detail in *Chapter 17, Deploying an Application to AWS*.

> **Note**
>
> A proxy is a stand-in for a service or some services. When a proxy is used, if a client makes a call to a service, they end up accessing the proxy first and not the service directly. The proxy then determines where the client's request should be routed to. A proxy, therefore, provides companies with better control of their service access.

Enabling CORS is also necessary because the React application runs on its own test web server. In our case, it runs on port 3000, while the server runs on port 5000. Although they both use localhost, having different ports effectively means different domains. To update CORS, do this:

1. First, we need to update our `.env` file to have the path to the client development server:

   ```
   CLIENT_URL=http://localhost:3000
   ```

2. Open `index.ts` and add this code immediately after `const app = express();`:

   ```
   app.use(
       cors({
           credentials: true,
           origin: process.env.CLIENT_URL,
       })
   );
   ```

   The `credentials` setting enables the header Access-Control-Allow-Credentials. This allows client JavaScript to receive responses from servers after successfully providing credentials.

3. Also update the Apollo Server so that its own `cors` is disabled. Update this line just before `listen`:

   ```
   apolloServer.applyMiddleware({ app, cors: false });
   ```

   The Apollo Server has its own `cors`, which is enabled by default so we want to disable it.

Now we've installed CORS onto our server. Let's now open our React project in its own VSCode window and install GraphQL to get started integrating with our GraphQL server:

1. After opening the `super-forum-client` folder in its own VSCode window, try running it first to make sure it's working. If you have not done so already, delete the `node_modules` folder and the `package-lock.json` file and run `npm install` once.

2. Now let's install Apollo GraphQL Client. Open your terminal to the root of `super-forum-client` and run this:

```
npm install @apollo/client graphql
```

3. Now we need to configure our client. Open `index.ts` and add this code above `ReactDOM.render`:

```
const client = new ApolloClient({
  uri: 'http://localhost:5000/graphql',
  credentials: "include",
  cache: new InMemoryCache()
});
```

As always, add your imports – pretty self-explanatory. We set the URL of the server, include any credentials needed, and set the `cache` object. Note this means that Apollo caches all our query results.

4. Next update `ReactDOM.render` and have it include the `ApolloProvider`:

```
ReactDOM.render(
  <Provider store={configureStore()}>
    <BrowserRouter>
      <ApolloProvider client={client}>
        <ErrorBoundary>{[<App key="App" />]}</
        ErrorBoundary>
      </ApolloProvider>
    </BrowserRouter>
  </Provider>,
  document.getElementById("root")
);
```

5.  Now let's test that its working by getting ThreadCategories. Open the `src/components/areas/LeftMenu.tsx` file and update it like this:

```
import React, { useEffect, useState } from "react";
import { useWindowDimensions } from "../../hooks/
useWindowDimensions";
import "./LeftMenu.css";
import { gql, useQuery } from "@apollo/client";
```

We've imported some items from the Apollo client. gql allows us to get syntax highlighting and formatting for GraphQL queries. UseQuery is our first GraphQL related client-side Hook. It allows us to do a GraphQL Query, as opposed to doing a Mutation, but it runs immediately. Later, I'll show a Hook that allows lazy loading:

```
const GetAllCategories = gql`
  query getAllCategories {
    getAllCategories {
      id
      name
    }
  }
`;
```

Here is our query. Not much to explain here, but note we get both id and name.

```
const LeftMenu = () => {
  const { loading, error, data } =
  useQuery(GetAllCategories);
```

Our useQuery call returns the properties loading, error, and data. Each Apollo GraphQL Hook returns a different set of relevant properties. We'll see how these particular properties are used in the following code:

```
  const { width } = useWindowDimensions();
  const [categories, setCategories] = useState<JSX.
    Element>(
    <div>Left Menu</div>
  );
  useEffect(() => {
    if (loading) {
      setCategories(<span>Loading ...</span>);
```

In the code just shown, we first check if data is still being loaded by using the `loading` property and providing placeholder text in that case.

```
    } else if (error) {
        setCategories(<span>Error occurred loading
            categories ...</span>);
```

In this error section, we indicate an error occurred during the query run.

```
    } else {
        if (data && data.getAllCategories) {
            const cats = data.getAllCategories.map((cat: any)
                => {
                return <li key={cat.id}>
                <Link to={`/categorythreads/${cat.id}`}>{cat.
                name}</Link>
        </li>;
            });
            setCategories(<ul className="category">{cats}
            </ul>);
        }
```

Finally, if all went well and we got our data, then we display an unordered list of elements representing each ThreadCategory. Notice each `li` element has a unique key identifier. It is always important to have keys when providing an array of similar elements, as it reduces unnecessary renders. Also, each element is a link that shows the user all Threads related to a specific `ThreadCategory`:

```
        }
        // eslint-disable-next-line react-hooks/exhaustive-
            //deps
    }, [data]);
    if (width <= 768) {
        return null;
    }
    return <div className="leftmenu">{categories}</div>;
};
export default LeftMenu;
```

6. Running the app should show this screen in desktop mode. Notice I've clicked on one of the ThreadCategory links that have associated Thread data. But of course, we are currently still using `dataService` to return hardcoded data:

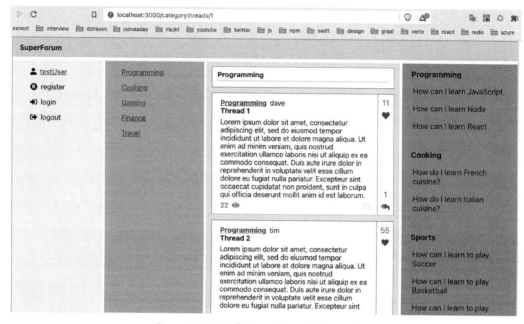

Figure 15.8 – LeftMenu ThreadCategory list

Awesome – we are now connected to our GraphQL server!

# The Main screen

Congratulations – you've come a long way. Now we need to update our Main component so that we return real data from our GraphQL service. Let's create that now:

1. Go to our `super-forum-server` project and open the `typeDefs` file and add the schema entry for the function `getThreadsLatest` just below the `getThreadsByCategoryId` query from the source. Here, we are creating a new resolver, `getThreadsLatest`, that gives us the latest Threads when no specific ThreadCategory is given. When a ThreadCategory is given, we already have the `getThreadsByCategoryId` resolver.

2. Open `ThreadRepo` and add this function:

```
export const getThreadsLatest = async ():
Promise<QueryArrayResult<Thread>> => {
    const threads = await Thread.
```

```
createQueryBuilder("thread")
    .leftJoinAndSelect("thread.category", "category")
    .leftJoinAndSelect("thread.threadItems",
    "threadItems")
    .orderBy("thread.createdOn", "DESC")
    .take(10)
    .getMany();
```

We have a query that includes ThreadCategories and ThreadItems –
leftJoinAndSelect, is ordered by the createdOn field, orderBy, and takes
only up to 10 items (take):

```
if (!threads || threads.length === 0) {
  return {
    messages: ["No threads found."],
  };
}
return {
  entities: threads,
};
};
```

The rest is self-explanatory as it's similar to getThreadsByCategoryId.

Let's also update our getThreadsByCategoryId function to include the
ThreadItems as well:

```
export const getThreadsByCategoryId = async (
  categoryId: string
): Promise<QueryArrayResult<Thread>> => {
  const threads = await Thread.
    createQueryBuilder("thread")
      .where(`thread."categoryId" = :categoryId`, {
        categoryId })
      .leftJoinAndSelect("thread.category", "category")
      .leftJoinAndSelect("thread.threadItems",
        "threadItems")
      .orderBy("thread.createdOn", "DESC")
      .getMany();
  if (!threads || threads.length === 0) {
    return {
```

```
      messages: ["Threads of category not found."],
    };
  }
  return {
    entities: threads,
  };
};
```

It's the same as before only with the additional `leftJoinAndSelect` function.

3.  Open the `resolvers` file and add the `getThreadsLatest` function from the source code at the end of the Query section. This is a wrapper almost identical to the `getThreadsByCategoryId` resolver, except it calls `getThreadsLatest` instead.

4.  Now we need to update our `Main` React component so that it uses our GraphQL resolvers instead of the fake data from our `dataService`. Open `Main` and update the file like this.

The `const GetThreadsByCategoryId` is our first query. As you can see, it uses inline fragments and gets back our Thread data fields:

```
const GetThreadsByCategoryId = gql`
  query getThreadsByCategoryId($categoryId: ID!) {
    getThreadsByCategoryId(categoryId: $categoryId) {
      ... on EntityResult {
        messages
      }
      ... on ThreadArray {
        threads {
          id
          title
          body
          views
          threadItems {
            id
          }
          category {
            id
            name
```

```
            }
          }
        }
      }
    }
`;
```

GetThreadsLatest is basically identical to GetThreadsByCategoryId:

```
const GetThreadsLatest = gql`
  query getThreadsLatest {
    getThreadsLatest {
      ... on EntityResult {
        messages
      }
      ... on ThreadArray {
        threads {
          id
          title
          body
          views
          threadItems {
            id
          }
          category {
            id
            name
          }
        }
      }
    }
  }
`;
```

Now we begin our `Main` component definition with our use of `useLazyQuery` Hooks:

```
const Main = () => {
  const [
    execGetThreadsByCat,
    {
      //error: threadsByCatErr,
      //called: threadsByCatCalled,
      data: threadsByCatData,
    },
  ] = useLazyQuery(GetThreadsByCategoryId);
  const [
    execGetThreadsLatest,
    {
      //error: threadsLatestErr,
      //called: threadsLatestCalled,
      data: threadsLatestData,
    },
  ] = useLazyQuery(GetThreadsLatest);
```

The two Hooks that were shown are now using our queries. Notice these are lazy GraphQL queries. This means they do not run immediately, unlike `useQuery`, and only run when the `execGetThreadsByCat` or `execGetThreadsLatest` calls are made. The `data` property is what contains our query's returned data. Additionally, I have commented out two of the returned properties because we are not using them. However, they are available for use should your call run into errors. `Error` contains information on failures and `called` indicates whether the Hook was called already.

```
  const { categoryId } = useParams();
  const [category, setCategory] = useState<Category |
  undefined>();
  const [threadCards, setThreadCards] =
  useState<Array<JSX.Element> | null>(
    null
  );
```

The previous state objects remain unchanged.

```
useEffect(() => {
  if (categoryId && categoryId > 0) {
    execGetThreadsByCat({
      variables: {
        categoryId,
      },
    });
  } else {
    execGetThreadsLatest();
  }
  // eslint-disable-next-line react-hooks/exhaustive-
  // deps
}, [categoryId]);
```

This `useEffect` was updated to now only execute `execGetThreadsByCat` or `execGetThreadsLatest` as needed. If the `categoryId` parameter is given, `execGetThreadsByCat` should run; if not, the other should run:

```
useEffect(() => {
  if (
    threadsByCatData &&
    threadsByCatData.getThreadsByCategoryId &&
    threadsByCatData.getThreadsByCategoryId.threads
  ) {
    const threads = threadsByCatData.
getThreadsByCategoryId.threads;
    const cards = threads.map((th: any) => {
      return <ThreadCard key={`thread-${th.id}`}
      thread={th} />;
    });
    setCategory(threads[0].category);
    setThreadCards(cards);
  }
}, [threadsByCatData]);
```

In useEffect, threadsByCatData changes cause us to update category and threadCards with data from the getThreadsByCategoryId query.

```
useEffect(() => {
  if (
    threadsLatestData &&
    threadsLatestData.getThreadsLatest &&
    threadsLatestData.getThreadsLatest.threads
  ) {
    const threads = threadsLatestData.getThreadsLatest.
    threads;
    const cards = threads.map((th: any) => {
      return <ThreadCard key={`thread-${th.id}`}
      thread={th} />;
    });
    setCategory(new Category("0", "Latest"));
    setThreadCards(cards);
  }
}, [threadsLatestData]);
```

In useEffect, threadsLatestData changes cause us to update category and threadCards with data from the getThreadsLatest query. Notice when no categoryId is given, we just use a generic "Latest" name for our ThreadCategory.

```
return (
  <main className="content">
    <MainHeader category={category} />
    <div>{threadCards}</div>
  </main>
);
};
export default Main;
```

The rest of the code remains the same as before.

5. Now if we run this for a `categoryId`, we should see this:

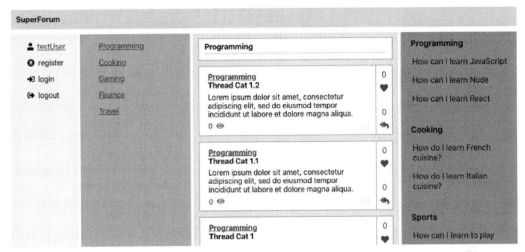

Figure 15.9 – With categoryId

If we run this without a `categoryId`, we should see this:

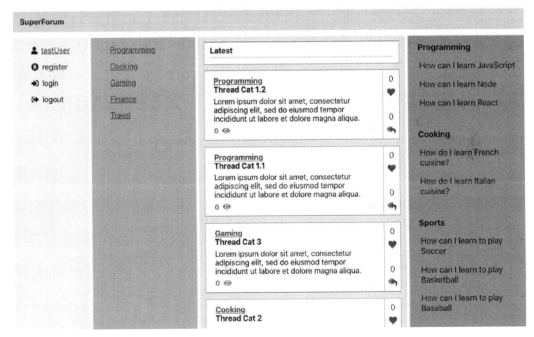

Figure 15.10 – Without categoryId

Good – now we have some actual real data populating on our site screen. Before continuing, let's clean up our styling a bit and get rid of some of these placeholder background colors. I've made minor changes to the `Nav.css` and `Home.css` files. This is what it looks like now:

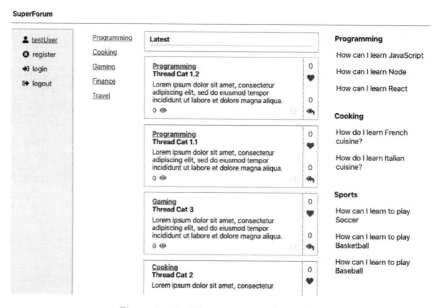

Figure 15.11 – Home screen style update

OK, that's better. Here's one thing to notice on the mobile version of our screen – we have no way for the user to switch to another category, as shown in this screenshot:

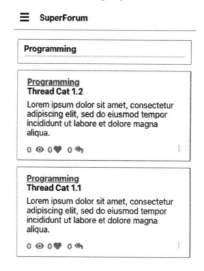

Figure 15.12 – Home screen mobile view

So, let's add a dropdown that will allow the user to switch categories. This dropdown should only appear while in mobile mode. Try and build this control yourself before following along. Hint: use React-DropDown to build the dropdown and replace the category label with the drop-down control. For example, in *Figure 15.12* we see the selected category is **Programming** as shown on the MainHeader control. So then replace that label with the dropdown, but only in mobile mode. Note that we are already using a dropdown in our ThreadCategory route so we should create a component out of it so it can be reused.

If you've given it a try, let's now start building it together so you can compare. Here's the thing I lied a little bit. This is a fairly complex change as it requires two main things. First, we would want to add a new Reducer for ThreadCategories since we know that the list of ThreadCategories is being used in at least two separate components. We also need to componentize the dropdown in the ThreadCategory component so that it can be used in several places. This second piece is fairly involved as the new drop-down component has to be complex enough to receive props from the outside and also send out the selected category whenever it changes:

1. First, let's create our new Reducer. Create a new folder in the store folder called categories. In that folder, create a file called Reducer.ts and add the source code to it. This file is a lot like our User Reducer, except it returns as payload an array of Category objects.

2. Next, we need to add our new Reducer to our AppState's rootReducer like this:

```
export const rootReducer = combineReducers({
    user: UserProfileReducer,
    categories: ThreadCategoriesReducer,
});
```

Our new rootReducer member will be called Categories.

3. Now update the App.tsx component so that upon application load, we immediately get our ThreadCategories and add them to the Redux store.

Here, we are adding the GetAllCategories GraphQL query:

```
const GetAllCategories = gql`
    query getAllCategories {
        getAllCategories {
            id
            name
```

```
      }
    }
  `;
function App() {
  const { data } = useQuery(GetAllCategories);
  const dispatch = useDispatch();
  useEffect(() => {
    dispatch({
      type: UserProfileSetType,
      payload: {
        id: 1,
        userName: "testUser",
      },
    });
    if (data && data.getAllCategories) {
      dispatch({
        type: ThreadCategoriesType,
        payload: data.getAllCategories,
      });
```

Most of this code we've seen before, but this is where we've sent our payload of ThreadCategories to the Redux store:

```
      }
    }, [dispatch, data]);
  const renderHome = (props: any) => <Home {...props} />;
  const renderThread = (props: any) => <Thread {...props}
    />;
  const renderUserProfile = (props: any) => <UserProfile
    {...props} />;
  return (
    <Switch>
      <Route exact={true} path="/" render={renderHome} />
      <Route path="/categorythreads/:categoryId"
        render={renderHome} />
      <Route path="/thread/:id" render={renderThread} />
      <Route path="/userprofile/:id"
        render={renderUserProfile} />
```

```
        </Switch>
    );
}
```

Everything else remains the same. Note you will need to update your imports.

4.  The `LeftMenu` and `ThreadCategory` components will need to have their code for getting ThreadCategories and creating the dropdown removed. But first, let's create our shared control that will do all this. Create a file inside of `src/components` called `CategoryDropDown.tsx` and add this code. Make sure you add any necessary imports:

```
const defaultLabel = "Select a category";
const defaultOption = {
  value: "0",
  label: defaultLabel
};
```

With `defaultOption`, we've created an initial value for our dropdown.

```
class CategoryDropDownProps {
  sendOutSelectedCategory?: (cat: Category) => void;
  navigate?: boolean = false;
  preselectedCategory?: Category;
}
```

`CategoryDropDownProps` will be our parameter type for our `CategoryDropDown` component. `sendOutSelectedCategory` is a function passed by the parent caller that will be used to receive the selected drop-down option by the parent. `Navigate` is a boolean that determines whether the screen will move to a new URL upon selection of a new drop-down option. And `preselectedCategory` allows the parent to force the dropdown to have selected the specified ThreadCategory on load:

```
const CategoryDropDown: FC<CategoryDropDownProps> = ({
  sendOutSelectedCategory,
  navigate,
  preselectedCategory,
}) => {
  const categories = useSelector((state: AppState) =>
    state.categories);
  const [categoryOptions, setCategoryOptions] = useState<
```

```
        Array<string | Option>
    >([defaultOption]);
    const [selectedOption, setSelectedOption] =
    useState<Option>(defaultOption);
    const history = useHistory();
```

Based on our previous learning, the usage of these listed Hooks is pretty obvious. But do notice that we are getting the list of ThreadCategories from our Redux store using `useSelector`.

```
    useEffect(() => {
        if (categories) {
            const catOptions: Array<Option> = categories.
            map((cat: Category) => {
                return {
                    value: cat.id,
                    label: cat.name,
                };
            });
```

Here, we build our array of options to feed to our dropdown later.

```
            setCategoryOptions(catOptions);
```

Here, in `setCategoryOptions`, we are receiving our list of ThreadCategory option elements and setting them so they can be consumed by our dropdown later.

```
            setSelectedOption({
                value: preselectedCategory ? preselectedCategory.
                id : "0",
                label: preselectedCategory ? preselectedCategory.
                name : defaultLabel,
            });
```

Here, we have set our default drop-down selection.

```
        }
    }, [categories, preselectedCategory]);
    const onChangeDropDown = (selected: Option) => {
        setSelectedOption(selected);
        if (sendOutSelectedCategory) {
            sendOutSelectedCategory(
                new Category(selected.value, selected.label?.
```

```
      valueOf().toString() ?? "")
        );
    }
```

In this drop-down change handler here, we are notifying the parent of a selection change.

```
    if (navigate) {
        history.push(`/categorythreads/${selected.value}`);
    }
```

We navigate to the next ThreadCategory route if requested by the parent.

```
    };
    return (
        <DropDown
            className="thread-category-dropdown"
            options={categoryOptions}
            onChange={onChangeDropDown}
            value={selectedOption}
            placeholder=defaultLabel
        />
    );
};
export default CategoryDropDown;
```

And finally, here's our actual JSX, which is pretty self-explanatory.

5.  Now we need to update the `MainHeader.tsx` file like this:

```
interface MainHeaderProps {
    category?: Category;
}
const MainHeader: FC<MainHeaderProps> = ({ category }) =>
{
    const { width } = useWindowDimensions();
```

The only significant change is this `getLabelElement` function, which decides whether the screen is mobile and renders `CategoryDropDown` if it is:

```
const getLabelElement = () => {
    if (width <= 768) {
        return (
```

```
                        <CategoryDropDown navigate={true}
                        preselectedCategory={category} />
            );
        } else {
            return <strong>{category?.name || "Placeholder"}
            </strong>;
        }
    };
    return (
        <div className="main-header">
            <div
                className="title-bar"
                style={{ marginBottom: ".25em", paddingBottom:
                "0" }}
            >
                {getLabelElement()}
```

Here, we use the getLabelElement function.

```
            </div>
        </div>
    );
};
```

The rest of the code is the removal of code mostly, so try and do that yourself. You can, of course, look at the source code if needed. The affected files are ThreadCategory.tsx, LeftMenu.tsx, and Thread.css.

## Authentication-related features

Now let's continue by updating our authentication-related features. Please remember that all your User accounts must have their confirmed field set to true *before* they can log in:

1.  The first thing we want to do is have the user be able to log in. In order to do this and then be able to update our User object in the global Redux store, we're going to refactor our Redux User Reducer.

    First, in the models folder, create a new file called User.ts and add the source code to it. Notice that our User class has a field called threads. This will contain not only the Threads belonging to the user but the ThreadItems of those Threads.

2.  Now let's update our Reducer. Open `store/user/Reducer.ts` and update it by removing the `UserProfilePayload` interface and replacing its references with the new `User` class we just created. Look at the source code if you need to.

3.  Now we can update our `Login` component like this. Update the imports as needed.

    Notice we have imported the Hook `useRefreshReduxMe`. We'll define this Hook in a moment, but first I want to introduce some features of the `useMutation` GraphQL Hook:

    ```
    const LoginMutation = gql`
      mutation Login($userName: String!, $password: String!)
      {
        login(userName: $userName, password: $password)
      }
    `;
    ```

    Here is our login `Mutation`:

    ```
    const Login: FC<ModalProps> = ({ isOpen, onClickToggle })
    => {
      const [execLogin] = useMutation(LoginMutation, {
        refetchQueries: [
          {
            query: Me,
          },
        ],
      });
    ```

    Let me explain this `useMutation` call. The call takes as parameters the Mutation query `LoginMutation` and something called `refetchQueries`. `refetchQueries` forces whatever queries are listed therein to rerun and then caches their values. If we did not use `refetchQueries` and ran the `Me` query again, we would end up getting the last cached version instead of the freshest data. Please note it does not auto-refresh any calls that depend on its queries; we still have to make those calls to get the new data.

The output, `execLogin`, is a function that can be executed later as desired.

```
const [
    { userName, password, resultMsg, isSubmitDisabled },
    dispatch,
] = useReducer(userReducer, {
  userName: "test1",
  password: "Test123!@#",
  resultMsg: "",
  isSubmitDisabled: false,
});
const { execMe, updateMe } = useRefreshReduxMe();
const onChangeUserName = (e: React.
 ChangeEvent<HTMLInputElement>) => {
  dispatch({ type: "userName", payload: e.target.value
  });
  if (!e.target.value)
    allowSubmit(dispatch, "Username cannot be empty",
    true);
  else allowSubmit(dispatch, "", false);
};
const onChangePassword = (e: React.
ChangeEvent<HTMLInputElement>) => {
  dispatch({ type: "password", payload: e.target.value
  });
  if (!e.target.value)
    allowSubmit(dispatch, "Password cannot be empty",
    true);
  else allowSubmit(dispatch, "", false);
};
```

The prior calls are the same as they were previously.

```
const onClickLogin = async (
    e: React.MouseEvent<HTMLButtonElement, MouseEvent>
  ) => {
  e.preventDefault();
  onClickToggle(e);
  const result = await execLogin({
    variables: {
```

```
        userName,
        password,
      },
    });
    execMe();
    updateMe();
  };
```

The `onClickLogin` handler is now calling our `execLogin` function with appropriate parameters. After `execLogin` finishes, it will automatically call our `refetchQueries` list of queries. After that, we make a call to the functions from our Hook, `useRefreshReduxMe`, `execMe`, and `updateMe`. The `execMe` function will get the latest `User` object and `updateMe` will add it into the Redux store. The rest of the code is identical so I will not show it here.

4.  Now let's define our Hook `useRefreshReduxMe`. We want to create this Hook so that our code to set or unset our Redux `User` object can be in this single file. We will be using this Hook from several components. Create a file called `useRefreshReduxMe.ts` in the hooks folder and add the source code.

    From the top, we can see the `Me` const is our query to get user information. The `EntityResult` inline fragment is used to get the string of messages if that's what is coming back. If we get actual user data, then the fields desired are defined by the `User` inline fragment.

    Next, the `UseRefreshReduxMeResult` interface is a return type for our Hook.

    On line 37, we have defined `useLazyQuery` to allow our Hook users to be able to execute the call to the `Me` query at a time of their own choosing.

    Next, we have defined a function, `deleteMe`, to allow users of our Hook to destroy the Redux `User` object at any time. For example, when the user logs off.

    And finally, we have the `updateMe` function to allow the setting of the Redux `User` object. And then we return all of these functions so they can be used by our Hook callers.

5.  Upon app load, we should immediately check if our `User` is logged in and who that is. So, open `App.tsx` and update it like this:

```
function App() {
  const { data: categoriesData } =
  useQuery(GetAllCategories);
  const { execMe, updateMe } = useRefreshReduxMe();
```

Here, we've initialized our useRefreshReduxMe Hook.

```
const dispatch = useDispatch();
useEffect(() => {
    execMe();
}, [execMe]);
```

Here, we call our execMe to get the User data from GraphQL.

```
useEffect(() => {
    updateMe();
}, [updateMe]);
```

And here, we call updateMe to update our Redux User Reducer with the User data if any.

```
useEffect(() => {
    if (categoriesData && categoriesData.
    getAllCategories) {
        dispatch({
            type: ThreadCategoriesType,
            payload: categoriesData.getAllCategories,
        });
    }
}, [dispatch, categoriesData]);
```

I changed our original data field name to categoriesData so it would be clearer what it's for. The rest of the code remains the same.

6.  If you log in now, you'll see that our SideBar userName updates to the logged-in user:

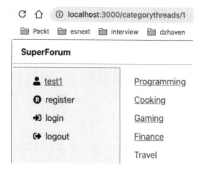

Figure 15.13 – Logged-in user

So, now we can log in, and then show the userName as well.

Awesome, but now let's fix our `SideBar` so that only the appropriate links show at the right time. For example, if the user is logged in, we should not see the **login** or **register** links:

1.  To make sure that the right menus show when the user logs in or out, let's first update our `Logout` component. Make sure imports are up to date:

```
const LogoutMutation = gql`
  mutation logout($userName: String!) {
    logout(userName: $userName)
  }
`;
```

Here's our `logout` mutation.

```
const Logout: FC<ModalProps> = ({ isOpen, onClickToggle
}) => {
  const user = useSelector((state: AppState) => state.
  user);
  const [execLogout] = useMutation(LogoutMutation, {
    refetchQueries: [
      {
        query: Me,
      },
    ],
  });
```

Here, again, we've forced a refresh of our GraphQL cache for the Me query.

```
  const { execMe, deleteMe } = useRefreshReduxMe();
  const onClickLogin = async (
    e: React.MouseEvent<HTMLButtonElement, MouseEvent>
  ) => {
    e.preventDefault();
    onClickToggle(e);
    await execLogout({
      variables: {
        userName: user?.userName ?? "",
      },
```

```
    });
        deleteMe();
    };
```

Again, we've taken our `useRefreshReduxMe` Hook, but here we only call the `deleteMe` function since we're just logging out. The rest of the code remains the same, so I won't show it here.

2.  Now we're going to update the `SideBarMenus` component so that only the appropriate menus show at the right time. Open that file and update it as follows.

In this case, I'll only show the returned JSX as that's the only thing that changed (other than imports):

```
    return (
        <React.Fragment>
            <ul>
                {user ? (
                    <li>
                        <FontAwesomeIcon icon={faUser} />
                        <span className="menu-name">
                            <Link to={`/userprofile/${user?.
                                id}`}>{user?.userName}</Link>
                        </span>
                    </li>
                ) : null}
```

As you can see, we are testing whether the `user` object has a value and then showing our same `userName` UI, else we show nothing.

```
                {user ? null : (
                    <li>
                        <FontAwesomeIcon icon={faRegistered} />
                        <span onClick={onClickToggleRegister}
                            className="menu-name">
                            register
                        </span>
                        <Registration
                            isOpen={showRegister}
                            onClickToggle={onClickToggleRegister}
                        />
```

```
        </li>
    )}
```

In this case, we don't want to show our registration UI if the user does exist so that's what we are doing.

```
{user ? null : (
    <li>
        <FontAwesomeIcon icon={faSignInAlt} />
        <span onClick={onClickToggleLogin}
        className="menu-name">
          login
        </span>
        <Login isOpen={showLogin}
          onClickToggle={onClickToggleLogin} />
    </li>
)}
```

Again, we don't show the login if the `user` object exists already, because that indicates the user had already logged in.

```
{user ? (
    <li>
        <FontAwesomeIcon icon={faSignOutAlt} />
        <span onClick={onClickToggleLogout}
        className="menu-name">
          logout
        </span>
        <Logout isOpen={showLogout}
          onClickToggle={onClickToggleLogout} />
    </li>
) : null}
```

Here, we show the logout UI if the `user` object has a value.

```
    </ul>
  </React.Fragment>
);
```

3.  If you run this code now, when not yet logged in, you'll see this:

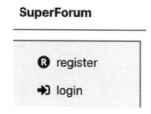

Figure 15.14 – Not logged in SideBarMenus

Now, when logged in, we should see this:

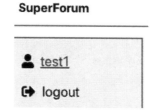

Figure 15.15 – Logged in SideBarMenus

So our sidebar now displays proper links and text. Let's now work on our UserProfile screen.

# The UserProfile screen

Now, since we are in the authentication sections, let's finish our UserProfile screen. We will need to make multiple changes to configure this screen:

1.  First, let's update our GraphQL by adding a field to our `User` type. Update the `typeDefs` file's `User` type by adding this just below the threads field:

    ```
    threadItems: [ThreadItem!]
    ```

    We've added only one new field, `threadItems`. Note that this is different from `threadItems` that's part of the `threads` field, as we are trying to retrieve the ThreadItem entities the user themselves has authored.

2.  We also need to update our User Entity by adding one new field. Update the `User.ts` file by adding this field in it:

    ```
    @OneToMany(() => ThreadItem, (threadItem) =>
    threadItem.user)
    threadItems: ThreadItem[];
    ```

This allows our `User` entity to have associated entities on the ThreadItems entity. Also, make sure you already have the matching field in the `ThreadItem.ts` file, like this:

```
@ManyToOne(() => User, (user) => user.threadItems)
    user: User;
```

3.  Now let's open our UserRepo Repository file and update our me function so that it includes the user's ThreadItems. Update the UserRepo `User.findOne` function like this:

```
relations: ["threads", "threads.threadItems",
    "threadItems", "threadItems.thread"],
```

We've only made a single change, as shown by the highlight, which is to add the `threadItems` and `threadItems.thread` relations.

4.  You'll notice that the UserProfile screen has a change password feature. So let's build that out now. First, we'll need to add a new Mutation to our `typeDefs` file. Add this Mutation to the Mutation section:

```
changePassword(newPassword: String!): String!
```

A pretty self-explanatory Mutation definition.

5.  Now let's implement this function in our UserRepo. Add the `changePassword` function to the end of the UserRepo from the source code.

    Starting at line 125, since the user will be logged in if this call is made, we are expecting the user `id` from the resolver code to be passed in. If it does not exist, then of course we'll error out.

    Then we try and get the `User` object and then run a few checks to make sure the user is valid. And finally, we use `bcrypt` to generate our hashed password.

6.  Now we can create our resolver. Open the `resolvers` file and add the source code for the `changePassword` function into the Mutation section.

    First, on line 389, we check if a valid Session and `userId` in that Session exist, because this is what indicates the user is logged in.

    And lastly, we call our `changePassword` Repository function with the Session `userId` and the given new password.

7. Let's now update our `UserProfile` component. Update the code as follows:

Update the imports as we have imported a couple of new items, `gql` and `useMutation`:

```
const ChangePassword = gql`
    mutation ChangePassword($newPassword: String!) {
        changePassword(newPassword: $newPassword)
    }
`;
```

Here, we have our new Mutation, `ChangePassword`.

```
const UserProfile = () => {
    const [
        { userName, password, passwordConfirm, resultMsg,
        isSubmitDisabled },
        dispatch,
    ] = useReducer(userReducer, {
        userName: "",
        password: "*********",
        passwordConfirm: "*********",
        resultMsg: "",
        isSubmitDisabled: true,
    });
    const user = useSelector((state: AppState) => state.
    user);
    const [threads, setThreads] = useState<JSX.Element |
    undefined>();
    const [threadItems, setThreadItems] = useState<JSX.
    Element | undefined>();
    const [execChangePassword] =
    useMutation(ChangePassword);
```

Here, we've set up our `ChangePassword` Mutation with `useMutation`.

The `useEffect` code shown here is the same as before:

```
useEffect(() => {
    if (user) {
        dispatch({
            type: "userName",
```

```
            payload: user.userName,
      });
      getUserThreads(user.id).then((items) => {
        const threadItemsInThreadList: Array<ThreadItem>
        = [];
        const threadList = items.map((th: Thread) => {
          for (let i = 0; i < th.threadItems.length; i++)
{

            threadItemsInThreadList.push(th.
            threadItems[i]);
          }


          return (
            <li key={`user-th-${th.id}`}>
              <Link to={`/thread/${th.id}`}
              className="userprofile-link">
                {th.title}
              </Link>
            </li>
          );
        });
        setThreads(<ul>{threadList}</ul>);
        const threadItemList = threadItemsInThreadList.
         map((ti: ThreadItem) => (
          <li key={`user-th-${ti.threadId}`}>
            <Link to={`/thread/${ti.threadId}`}
            className="userprofile-link">
              {ti.body}
            </Link>
          </li>
        ));
        setThreadItems(<ul>{threadItemList}</ul>);
      });
    }
  }, [user]);
```

This `onClickChangePassword` function is new. It triggers the `changePassword` call and then updates the UI status message.

```
const onClickChangePassword = async (
  e: React.MouseEvent<HTMLButtonElement, MouseEvent>
) => {
  e.preventDefault();
  const { data: changePasswordData } = await
  execChangePassword({
    variables: {
      newPassword: password,
    },
  });
  dispatch({
    type: "resultMsg",
    payload: changePasswordData ? changePasswordData.
    changePassword : "",
  });
};
return (
  <div className="screen-root-container">
    <div className="thread-nav-container">
      <Nav />
    </div>
    <form className="userprofile-content-container">
      <div>
        <strong>User Profile</strong>
        <label style={{ marginLeft: ".75em"
        }}>{userName}</label>
      </div>
      <div className="userprofile-password">
        <div>
          <PasswordComparison
            dispatch={dispatch}
            password={password}
            passwordConfirm={passwordConfirm}
          />
          <button
```

```
                className="action-btn"
                disabled={isSubmitDisabled}
                onClick={onClickChangePassword}
            >
```

The `onClickChangePassword` handler is set here onto our Change Password button.

```
                Change Password
            </button>
        </div>
        <div style={{ marginTop: ".5em" }}>
            <label>{resultMsg}</label>
        </div>
    </div>
    <div className="userprofile-postings">
        <hr className="thread-section-divider" />
        <div className="userprofile-threads">
            <strong>Threads Posted</strong>
            {threads}
        </div>
        <div className="userprofile-threadIems">
            <strong>ThreadItems Posted</strong>
            {threadItems}
        </div>
    </div>
    </form>
    </div>
    );
};
export default UserProfile;
```

The remaining code is the same.

Now let's show the user's Threads and ThreadItems:

1.  First, we need to update our User model. Add this field to the `User.ts` file:

```
    public threadItems: Array<ThreadItem>
```

2. Now update the Me query inside of the useRefreshReduxMe Hook like this:

```
export const Me = gql`
  query me {
    me {
      ... on EntityResult {
        messages
      }
      ... on User {
        id
        userName
        threads {
          id
          title
        }
        threadItems {
          id
          thread {
            id
          }
          body
        }
      }
    }
  }
`;
```

We've changed the threadItems from getting the threads' threadItems to getting the user's threadItems. We also now get the threadItems' thread.

3. Now, in your UserProfile component, update useEffect like this:

```
useEffect(() => {
  if (user) {
    dispatch({
      type: "userName",
      payload: user.userName,
    });
```

We are now getting our threads from the `user.threads` array, instead of our fake `dataService` call, as shown:

```
const threadList = user.threads?.map((th: Thread)
=> {
  return (
    <li key={`user-th-${th.id}`}>
      <Link to={`/thread/${th.id}`}
        className="userprofile-link">
        {th.title}
      </Link>
    </li>
  );
});
setThreads(
  !user.threadItems || user.threadItems.length ===
    0 ? undefined : (
    <ul>{threadList}</ul>
  )
);
```

We do the same thing for `threadItems` as well. Notice our `Link` to gets updated so that it uses `ti.thread?.id` instead of `ti.threadId`:

```
const threadItemList = user.threadItems?.map((ti:
  ThreadItem) => (
  <li key={`user-ti-${ti.id}`}>
    <Link to={`/thread/${ti.thread?.id}`}
      className="userprofile-link">
      {ti.body.length <= 40 ? ti.body : ti.body.
        substring(0, 40) + " ..."}
```

Here, we had added a tiny bit of extra logic to format long text that might go horizontally off the screen and wrap. Basically, it just means that if the text is longer than 40 characters, we add "..." to it.

```
    </Link>
  </li>
));
setThreadItems(
  !user.threadItems || user.threadItems.length ===
    0 ? undefined : (
```

```
            <ul>{threadItemList}</ul>
        )
    );
} else {
    dispatch({
      type: "userName",
      payload: "",
    });
    setThreads(undefined);
    setThreadItems(undefined);
  }
}, [user]);
```

The remaining code is identical. If you run this, you should see something like the following (again, your data will be different):

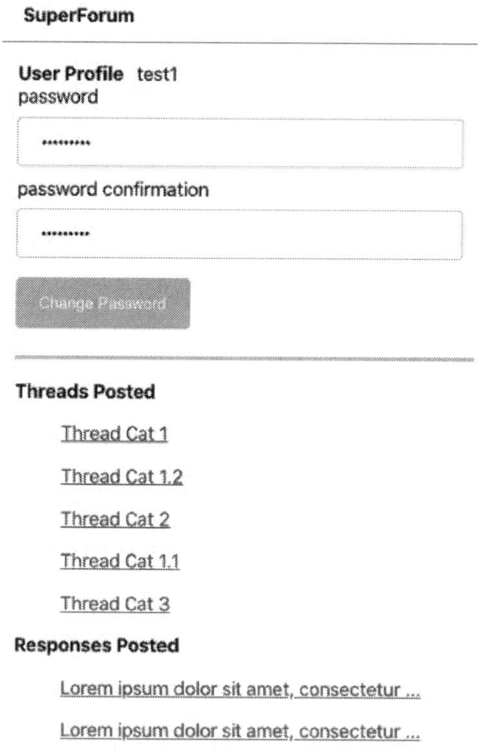

Figure 15.16 – User's Threads and ThreadItems

OK, that's it for our UserProfile. Because this was an enormous amount of material to cover, let's continue our work in the next chapter, *Chapter 16, Adding a GraphQL Schema – Part II.*

# Summary

In this chapter, we have almost completed our application by integrating the frontend and the backend with GraphQL. This was a large and complex chapter so you should feel good about how far you have come.

In the next chapter, *Chapter 16, Adding a GraphQL Schema – Part II*, we will finish coding our application by working on the Thread screen, so that we can view and post Threads, and work on the Points system so that users can see the popularity of individual Threads.

# 16

# Adding a GraphQL Schema – Part II

In this chapter, we're going to continue completing our client and server code. We will complete our Thread screens, which allow us to post new Threads and their responses, and also finish the Points system for the site. Please use the source code from *Chapter 15, Adding a GraphQL Schema – Part I*, to do this.

## Thread route

In this section, we will update our Thread component, which provides our thread route. We're going to be touching on a lot of files as we go through this. Follow these steps:

1.  Open typeDefs and edit the Thread and ThreadItem types. Then, add this field just below views:

    ```
    points: Int!
    ```

2.  Now, open the ThreadRepo file and update the getThreadById function, like this:

    ```
    export const getThreadById = async (
      id: string
    ): Promise<QueryOneResult<Thread>> => {
    ```

```
const thread = await Thread.findOne({
  where: {
    id,
  },
  relations: ["user", "threadItems", "threadItems.
    user", "category"],
});
```

All we did here was add the following `relations` to our `findOne` query:

```
if (!thread) {
  return {
    messages: ["Thread not found."],
  };
}
return {
  entity: thread,
};
};
```

3.  Next, update the `getThreadsByCategoryId` function's call to `Thread.createQueryBuilder`, like this:

```
const threads = await Thread.createQueryBuilder("thread")
  .where(`thread."categoryId" = :categoryId`, {
    categoryId })
  .leftJoinAndSelect("thread.category", "category")
  .leftJoinAndSelect("thread.threadItems",
    "threadItems")
  .leftJoinAndSelect("thread.user", "user")
  .orderBy("thread.createdOn", "DESC")
  .getMany();
```

We've included the relation for the User entity here. The rest of the code for this function remains the same.

4. Now, open the `User.ts` file in your client app and update the `threads` and `threadItems` fields so that they're optional. We need to do this so that we can add a `User` account that has not posted anything yet:

```
public threads?: Array<Thread>,
public threadItems?: Array<ThreadItem>
```

5. Now, open the `models/Thread.ts` and `models/ThreadItem.ts` files in the React client project and replace the `userName` and `userId` fields with a single field user, like this:

```
public user: User,
```

6. We also need to replace the references to the `userName` and `userId` fields in our `DataService.ts` file with a user object. Here, I've placed an object at the top of the file and used it throughout the file to replace those two fields:

```
const user = new User("1", "test1@test.com", "test1");
```

Take a look at the `DataService.ts` file if you need any help, though this should be pretty trivial.

7. Now that we've updated our `User` schema type and our entities, we need to update some queries. In the `Main.tsx` file, update the `GetThreadsByCategoryId` and `GetThreadsLatest` queries, like this:

```
const GetThreadsByCategoryId = gql`
  query getThreadsByCategoryId($categoryId: ID!) {
    getThreadsByCategoryId(categoryId: $categoryId) {
      ... on EntityResult {
        messages
      }
      ... on ThreadArray {
        threads {
          id
          title
          body
          views
          points
          user {
            userName
```

```
        }
        threadItems {
          id
        }
        category {
          id
          name
        }
      }
    }
  }
}
`;
```

For both these queries, we added the `points` and `user` fields, as follows:

```
const GetThreadsLatest = gql`
  query getThreadsLatest {
    getThreadsLatest {
      ... on EntityResult {
        messages
      }
      ... on ThreadArray {
        threads {
          id
          title
          body
          views
          points
          user {
            userName
          }
          threadItems {
            id
          }
          category {
            id
            name
```

```
            }
         }
      }
   }
}
`;
```

8. Now, in our `ThreadCard.tsx` file, find the following JSX:

```
<span className="username-header" style={{ marginLeft:
".5em" }}>
    {thread.userName}
</span>
```

Replace it with the following:

```
<span className="username-header" style={{ marginLeft:
".5em" }}>
    {thread.user.userName}
</span>
```

As you can see, we are now using `user` to get its `userName` field instead of trying to access it directly.

9. Now, we need to make some more changes to our `RichEditor.tsx` file. Note that our Thread screen will be showing user submitted text. So, once a user has submitted what they wish to post, we will make it so that they cannot edit it afterward. We'll do this by making the read-only setting a prop.

   Turn the `RichEditorProps` interface into a class and update it, like this:

```
class RichEditorProps {
    existingBody?: string;
    readOnly?: boolean = false;
}
```

We have made this a class so that a default value of `false` is the normal setting (interfaces don't allow default values). Now, update the parameter list in the `RichEditor` component, like this:

```
const RichEditor: FC<RichEditorProps> = ({ existingBody,
readOnly }) => {
```

We use destructuring to add the `readOnly` field as a parameter. Now, inside the `Editable` component, add it as an attribute, like this:

```
<Editable
        className="editor"
        renderElement={renderElement}
        renderLeaf={renderLeaf}
        placeholder="Enter some rich text…"
        spellCheck
        autoFocus
        onKeyDown={(event) => {
            for (const hotkey in HOTKEYS) {
                if (isHotkey(hotkey, event as any)) {
                    event.preventDefault();
                    const mark = HOTKEYS[hotkey];
                    toggleMark(editor, mark);
                }
            }
        }}
        readOnly={readOnly}
/>
```

As you can see, all we did was append the one `readOnly` prop.

10. Now, open the `src/components/routes/thread/Thread.tsx` file. This file is our main screen for loading the Thread route. Let's update this file.

Here, we're adding a new `GetThreadById` query to get our relevant Thread:

```
const GetThreadById = gql`
  query GetThreadById($id: ID!) {
    getThreadById(id: $id) {
      ... on EntityResult {
        messages
      }
      ... on Thread {
        id
        user {
          userName
        }
```

```
        lastModifiedOn
        title
        body
        points
        category {
            id
            name
        }
        threadItems {
            id
            body
            points
            user {
                userName
            }
        }
    }
}
`;
const Thread = () => {
  const [execGetThreadById, { data: threadData }] =
    useLazyQuery(GetThreadById);
```

Here, we are using our `GetThreadById` query, along with our `useLazyQuery` Hook, and creating an executor function called `execGetThreadById`, which we will run a bit later.

```
  const [thread, setThread] = useState<ThreadModel |
    undefined>();
```

The `thread` state object is what we will be using to populate our UI and share it with other components.

```
  const { id } = useParams();
```

`id` is the URL parameter representing the Thread's `id` value.

```
  const [readOnly, setReadOnly] = useState(false);
```

We will use this `readOnly` state to make our `RichEditor` read-only if we are dealing with an existing Thread record.

```
useEffect(() => {
  if (id && id > 0) {
    console.log("id", id);
    execGetThreadById({
      variables: {
        id,
      },
    });
```

Here, we've run our `execGetThreadById` call by using the parameter given by the URL for the Thread's `id`.

```
  }
}, [id, execGetThreadById]);

useEffect(() => {
  console.log("threadData", threadData);
  if (threadData && threadData.getThreadById) {
    setThread(threadData.getThreadById);
  } else {
    setThread(undefined);
  }
```

Once our `execGetThreadById` call is completed, a `threadData` object is returned. We can use this to set our local `thread` state.

```
}, [threadData]);

return (
  <div className="screen-root-container">
    <div className="thread-nav-container">
      <Nav />
    </div>
    <div className="thread-content-container">
      <div className="thread-content-post-container">
        <ThreadHeader
          userName={thread?.user.userName}
```

Here, we are using the `thread?.user` object to get our `userName` field, instead of `thread?.userName`, which is how we had it set up previously.

```
        lastModifiedOn={thread ? thread.
        lastModifiedOn : new Date()}
        title={thread?.title}
      />
      <ThreadCategory category={thread?.category} />
```

`ThreadCategory` has now been updated so that it will set `CategoryDropDown` to the `Category` option provided. We'll look at this later.

```
      <ThreadTitle title={thread?.title} />
      <ThreadBody body={thread?.body}
      readOnly={readOnly} />
```

Here, we passed the `readOnly` state value to `ThreadBody` since `ThreadBody` uses `RichEditor` internally.

```
      </div>
      <div className="thread-content-points-container">
        <ThreadPointsBar
        points={thread?.points || 0}
        responseCount={
          thread && thread.threadItems && thread.
          threadItems.length
        }
        />
      </div>
    </div>
    <div className="thread-content-response-container">
      <hr className="thread-section-divider" />
      <ThreadResponsesBuilder threadItems={thread?.
      threadItems} readOnly={readOnly} />
```

Here, we passed the `readOnly` state value to `ThreadResponsesBuilder`, which shows our ThreadItem responses.

```
      </div>
    </div>
  );
};
```

The remaining UI is the same as it was previously.

11. Now, let's look at the `ThreadCategory` component. Here's how it looks now:

```
interface ThreadCategoryProps {
    category?: Category;
}
```

We've switched our interface definition so that it takes a `Category` object instead of a string. This allows us to pass it down to our `CategoryDropDown` component:

```
const ThreadCategory: FC<ThreadCategoryProps> = ({
category }) => {
    const sendOutSelectedCategory = (cat: Category) => {
        console.log("selected category", cat);
    };

    return (
        <div className="thread-category-container">
            <strong>{category?.name}</strong>
```

Here, we've used `category?.name` of the `Category` object, whereas previously, we used `categoryName` as the necessary parameter:

```
        <div style={{ marginTop: "1em" }}>
            <CategoryDropDown
                preselectedCategory={category}
```

Here, we've explicitly passed in the `preselectedCategory` prop from our component's `category` prop:

```
                sendOutSelectedCategory={sendOutSelectedCategory}
            />
        </div>
    </div>
    );
};
```

12. Now, update your `ThreadBody` component's call to `RichEditor` by passing the `readOnly` field, like this:

```
interface ThreadBodyProps {
  body?: string;
  readOnly: boolean;
}
```

Here, we've added the `readOnly` field to our props type; that is, `ThreadBodyProps`:

```
const ThreadBody: FC<ThreadBodyProps> = ({ body, readOnly
}) => {
  return (
    <div className="thread-body-container">
      <strong>Body</strong>
      <div className="thread-body-editor">
        <RichEditor existingBody={body}
          readOnly={readOnly} />
      </div>
    </div>
  );
};
```

As you can see, we've passed the `readOnly` prop to our `RichEditor`.

13. Now, let's update the `ThreadResponseBuilder` component, like this:

```
interface ThreadResponsesBuilderProps {
  threadItems?: Array<ThreadItem>;
  readOnly: boolean;
}
```

Again, this is a `readOnly` prop definition. This is because this component uses a `ThreadResponse`, which internally uses `RichEditor`:

```
const ThreadResponsesBuilder:
FC<ThreadResponsesBuilderProps> = ({
  threadItems,
  readOnly,
}) => {
  const [responseElements, setResponseElements] =
  useState<
```

```
      JSX.Element | undefined
   >();
   useEffect(() => {
     if (threadItems) {
       const thResponses = threadItems.map((ti) => {
         return (
           <li key={`thr-${ti.id}`}>
             <ThreadResponse
               body={ti.body}
               userName={ti.user.userName}
```

Here, we've used the Thread's `user` object to get the required `userName`.

```
               lastModifiedOn={ti.createdOn}
               points={ti.points}
               readOnly={readOnly}
```

Here is our `readOnly` field being passed into `ThreadResponse`.

```
             />
           </li>
         );
       });
       setResponseElements(<ul>{thResponses}</ul>);
     }
   }, [threadItems, readOnly]);
   return (
     <div className="thread-body-container">
       <strong style={{ marginBottom: ".75em"
}}>Responses</strong>
       {responseElements}
     </div>
   );
 };
```

The rest of code is the same as it was previously.

Finally, we have our `ThreadResponse` component, which is updated with the `readOnly` prop, like this:

```
interface ThreadResponseProps {
  body?: string;
```

```
    userName?: string;
    lastModifiedOn?: Date;
    points: number;
    readOnly: boolean;
```

Here's the prop definition.

```
}
const ThreadResponse: FC<ThreadResponseProps> = ({
    body,
    userName,
    lastModifiedOn,
    points,
    readOnly,
```

Here, we've used destructuring to pass the readOnly prop in.

```
}) => {
    return (
      <div>
        <div>
          <UserNameAndTime userName={userName}
            lastModifiedOn={lastModifiedOn} />
          <span style={{ marginLeft: "1em" }}>
            <ThreadPointsInline points={points || 0} />
          </span>
        </div>
        <div className="thread-body-editor">
          <RichEditor existingBody={body}
            readOnly={readOnly} />
```

And here, we've passed readOnly into our RichEditor component.

```
        </div>
      </div>
    );
};
```

It's a bit difficult to see since there's no significant visual clue, but you'll notice that on the thread route for any existing Thread, such as http://localhost:5000/thread/1, your editors for your Thread and any responses will all be in read-only mode, which means they can't be edited.

# Points system

Now that we've set everything up so that we can display points, we need a mechanism for setting them. This is what we'll do now. Let's get started:

1. Open the `Thread.tsx` file and take a look at the code. You will find a component called `ThreadPointsBar` near the end of the JSX. This is what shows the vertical bar of points in our `ThreadCard` and our `Thread.tsx` route.

2. We're going to add buttons to allow an increment or decrement of points. We've already built our backend and resolvers, so the work we'll be doing here will just tie that to our client code.

   Inside the `ThreadPointsBar.tsx` file, update the existing JSX, as follows. This is a significant change, so let's break it down:

```
import React, { FC } from "react";
import { FontAwesomeIcon } from "@fortawesome/react-
fontawesome";
import {
  faHeart,
  faReplyAll,
  faChevronDown,
  faChevronUp,
} from "@fortawesome/free-solid-svg-icons";
import { useWindowDimensions } from "../../hooks/
useWindowDimensions";
import { gql, useMutation } from "@apollo/client";

const UpdateThreadPoint = gql`
  mutation UpdateThreadPoint(
    $userId: ID!
    $threadId: ID!
    $increment: Boolean!
  ) {
    updateThreadPoint(
      userId: $userId
      threadId: $threadId
      increment: $increment
    )
```

```
  }
`;
```

First, we have our `updateThreadPoint` mutation.

```
export class ThreadPointsBarProps {
  points: number = 0;
  responseCount?: number;
  userId?: string;
  threadId?: string;
  allowUpdatePoints?: boolean = false;
  refreshThread?: () => void;
}
```

With that, we've converted our `ThreadPointsBarProps` interface into a class
so that we can give some of the fields default values. Notice that, among the fields,
we have a `refreshThread` function, which we'll use to force an update to our
parent Thread so that once we update the points, this will be reflected in our UI.
We'll go through the other fields as we use them. Also, we will no longer be sharing
this prop with our `ThreadPointsInline` component, which I'll show later.

```
const ThreadPointsBar: FC<ThreadPointsBarProps> = ({
  points,
  responseCount,
  userId,
  threadId,
  allowUpdatePoints,
  refreshThread,
}) => {
  const { width } = useWindowDimensions();
  const [execUpdateThreadPoint] =
useMutation(UpdateThreadPoint);
```

Notice that our `useMutation` does not use `refetchQueries` to refresh Apollo Client. Normally, I would use this mechanism, but in testing, I found that the Apollo Client cache, which caches all GraphQL queries by default, was unable to refresh the Thread properly. These sorts of issues happen from time to time for all frameworks. It will be part of your job as a developer to figure out workarounds and solutions to these types of problems. So, instead of relying on `refetchQueries`, we will use our `refreshThread` function, which we can get from our parent, to force a refresh. I will show you the implementation of this function a little later in the `Thread` route component.

```
const onClickIncThreadPoint = async (
  e: React.MouseEvent<SVGSVGElement, MouseEvent>
) => {
  e.preventDefault();

  await execUpdateThreadPoint({
    variables: {
      userId,
      threadId,
      increment: true,
    },
  });
  refreshThread && refreshThread();
};
const onClickDecThreadPoint = async (
  e: React.MouseEvent<SVGSVGElement, MouseEvent>
) => {
  e.preventDefault();

  await execUpdateThreadPoint({
    variables: {
      userId,
      threadId,
      increment: false,
    },
  });
  refreshThread && refreshThread();
};
```

Both these functions, `onClickIncThreadPoint` and `onClickDecThreadPoint`, are executing the `execUpdateThreadPoint` mutation before calling `refreshThread`. The `refreshThread &&  refreshThread()` syntax is one of JavaScript's capabilities that allows you to write less code. This syntax allows you to check that this optional function exists and if it does, execute it.

```
if (width > 768) {
  console.log("ThreadPointsBar points", points);
  return (
    <div className="threadcard-points">
      <div className="threadcard-points-item">
        <div
          className="threadcard-points-item-btn"
          style={{ display: `${allowUpdatePoints ?
            "block" : "none"}` }}
        >
```

Here, we have a small bit of logic that uses the `allowUpdatePoints` prop, which decides whether to show or hide the icon container that allows the user to increment points. We must do the same for the decrement button as well:

```
          <FontAwesomeIcon
            icon={faChevronUp}
            className="point-icon"
            onClick={onClickIncThreadPoint}
          />
        </div>
        {points}
        <div
          className="threadcard-points-item-btn"
          style={{ display: `${allowUpdatePoints ?
            "block" : "none"}` }}
        >
          <FontAwesomeIcon
            icon={faChevronDown}
            className="point-icon"
            onClick={onClickDecThreadPoint}
          />
```

```
            </div>
            <FontAwesomeIcon icon={faHeart}
                className="points-icon" />
```

Here, we've added two new icons, `faChevronUp` and `faChevronDown`. When clicked, they will increment or decrement the points of our Thread.

```
            </div>
            <div className="threadcard-points-item">
                {responseCount}
                <br />
                <FontAwesomeIcon icon={faReplyAll}
                    className="points-icon" />
            </div>
        </div>
    );
  }
  return null;
};
export default ThreadPointsBar;
```

The rest of the code remains the same. However, notice that our CSS has changed slightly. We've updated the existing `threadcard-points-item` class and added a new class called `threadcard-points-item-btn`.

```
.threadcard-points-item {
  display: flex;
  flex-direction: column;
  justify-content: space-between;
  align-items: center;
  color: var(--point-color);
  font-size: var(--sm-med-font-size);
  text-align: center;
}
```

The `threadcard-points-item` class is now a flexbox on a column so that it can show its content vertically.

```
.threadcard-points-item-btn {
  cursor: pointer;
  margin-top: 0.35em;
  margin-bottom: 0.35em;
}
```

The `threadcard-points-item-btn` class converts our icon cursor into a pointer so that when a user hovers over it, the cursor becomes a hand, indicating that it can be clicked.

3.  Now that we've made these changes, we need to update some other relevant components. The first thing we want to do is disable `resultCaching` in our `ApolloClient`. Open the `index.tsx` file and update the `client` object, like this:

```
const client = new ApolloClient({
  uri: "http://localhost:5000/graphql",
  credentials: "include",
  cache: new InMemoryCache({
    resultCaching: false,
  }),
});
```

As the name suggests, this setting is supposed to disable query results from being cached. However, it does not do this on its own – we have to add another setting to our queries.

4.  Update the `Thread.tsx` file. We'll just show the code that has been changed.

First, the `getThreadById` query has been updated slightly:

```
const GetThreadById = gql`
  query GetThreadById($id: ID!) {
    getThreadById(id: $id) {
      ... on EntityResult {
        messages
      }

      ... on Thread {
        id
```

```
        user {
            id
```

We will need this field for our points system later, in order to determine that this user is not trying to increase their own points.

```
            userName
        }
        lastModifiedOn
        title
        body
        points
        category {
            id
            name
        }
        threadItems {
            id
            body
            points
            user {
                id
```

Again, we'll be needing this field to check that a user is not updating their own points.

```
                userName
            }
        }
    }
}
`;
const Thread = () => {
  const [execGetThreadById, { data: threadData }] =
    useLazyQuery(
    GetThreadById,
    { fetchPolicy: "no-cache" }
  );
```

Here, we've added a new option to our query called `fetchPolicy`, which controls the caching policy for our individual call. In this case, we want no caching at all. Again, I had to use `fetchPolicy` and `resultCaching` together to get the desired no-cache effect.

```
const [thread, setThread] = useState<ThreadModel |
  undefined>();
const { id } = useParams();
const [readOnly, setReadOnly] = useState(false);

const refreshThread = () => {
  if (id && id > 0) {
    execGetThreadById({
      variables: {
        id,
      },
    });
  }
};
```

Here, we have defined a function, called `refreshThread`, that calls our `execGetThreadById` executable. This function will be passed to our `ThreadPointBar` component later.

```
useEffect(() => {
  if (id && id > 0) {
    execGetThreadById({
      variables: {
        id,
      },
    });
  }
}, [id, execGetThreadById]);
```

You're probably wondering why we haven't reused `refreshThread` in the first `useEffect` call. To reuse it, we would have to include `refreshThread` in our `useEffect` call list and make an additional call to `useCallback` so that changes to `refreshThread` do not trigger a re-render. The tiny benefit this brings does not justify the extra code:

```
useEffect(() => {
  if (threadData && threadData.getThreadById) {
    setThread(threadData.getThreadById);
    setReadOnly(true);
  } else {
    setThread(undefined);
    setReadOnly(false);
  }
}, [threadData]);


return (
  <div className="screen-root-container">
    <div className="thread-nav-container">
      <Nav />
    </div>
    <div className="thread-content-container">
      <div className="thread-content-post-container">
        <ThreadHeader
          userName={thread?.user.userName}
          lastModifiedOn={thread ? thread.
            lastModifiedOn : new Date()}
          title={thread?.title}
        />
        <ThreadCategory category={thread?.category} />
        <ThreadTitle title={thread?.title} />
        <ThreadBody body={thread?.body}
          readOnly={readOnly} />
      </div>
      <div className="thread-content-points-container">
```

Here, in our `ThreadPointsBar`, we are passing the new props we defined earlier:

```
          <ThreadPointsBar
            points={thread?.points || 0}
            responseCount={
              thread && thread.threadItems && thread.
                threadItems.length
            }
            userId={thread?.user.id || "0"}
            threadId={thread?.id || "0"}
            allowUpdatePoints={true}
            refreshThread={refreshThread}
          />
        </div>
      </div>
      <div className="thread-content-response-container">
        <hr className="thread-section-divider" />
        <ThreadResponsesBuilder
          threadItems={thread?.threadItems}
          readOnly={readOnly}
        />
      </div>
    </div>
  );
};
```

5.  Here's what the Thread route screen now looks like with our new points system
    in place:

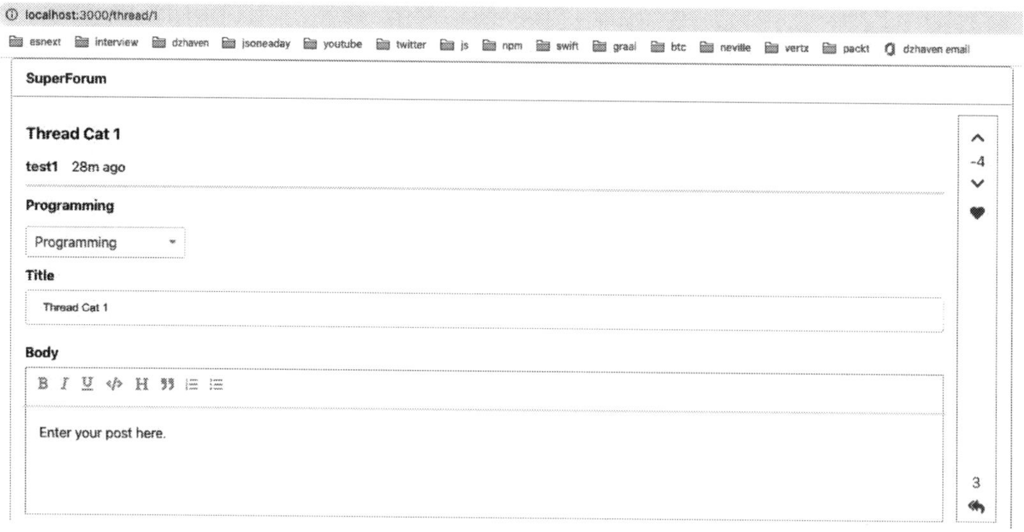

Figure 16.1 – Thread route screen

If you try clicking the points buttons, you'll notice two things. For one, sometimes,
the points change does not immediately show on the screen, despite all the work
we did in eliminating caching as an issue. This is because we have a subtle bug in
our Repository call, which I'll discuss in a bit. The other issue is that our user can
add or remove more than one point at a time. This is another issue in our Styling
layer. We'll revisit these two issues once our client code is complete.

6.  Now, we need to update the points capability for our `ThreadItem` and `Thread`
    responses. We'll start with `ThreadResponsesBuilder`. Update `useEffect`,
    like this:

```
useEffect(() => {
    if (threadItems) {
        const thResponses = threadItems.map((ti) => {
            return (
                <li key={`thr-${ti.id}`}>
                    <ThreadResponse
                        body={ti.body}
                        userName={ti.user.userName}
                        lastModifiedOn={ti.createdOn}
                        points={ti.points}
```

```
        readOnly={readOnly}
        userId={ti?.user.id || "0"}
        threadItemId={ti?.id || "0"}
    />
```

We are now passing the `ThreadReponse` component, which shows the Thread's `ThreadItem`, `userId`, and `threadItemId`. In this component, we have the `ThreadPointsInline` component, which displays the like points for `ThreadItem` or `Thread`, depending on which was passed in, which I'll clarify once we get to that control:

```
        </li>
      );
    });
    setResponseElements(<ul>{thResponses}</ul>);
  }
}, [threadItems, readOnly]);
```

7. Now, the `ThreadResponse` component can be updated. I'm only showing the changed code here.

   First, add the following two fields to the `ThreadResponseProps` interface:

```
userId: string;
threadItemId: string;
```

Now, in the JSX, we can add our `userId` and `threadItemId` fields:

```
return (
  <div>
    <div>
      <UserNameAndTime userName={userName}
        lastModifiedOn={lastModifiedOn} />
      {threadItemId}
      <span style={{ marginLeft: "1em" }}>
        <ThreadPointsInline
          points={points || 0}
          userId={userId}
          threadItemId={threadItemId}
        />
```

Here, we've passed our `userId` and `threadItemId` data to the `ThreadPointsInline` component. Note that this component will display points for either `Threads` or `ThreadItems` eventually. Also, note that I put `threadItemId` in there just so we could distinguish between each `ThreadItem` for now:

```
        </span>
      </div>
      <div className="thread-body-editor">
        <RichEditor existingBody={body}
          readOnly={readOnly} />
      </div>
    </div>
  );
```

8. Now, let's look at the changes we must make to the `ThreadPointsInline` component.

   Add the following import to the list of existing imports:

```
import "./ThreadPointsInline.css";
```

   Take a look at the source code. For the most part, it's a lot like the `ThreadPointsBar` CSS:

```
const UpdateThreadItemPoint = gql`
  mutation UpdateThreadItemPoint(
    $userId: ID!
    $threadItemId: ID!
    $increment: Boolean!
  ) {
    updateThreadItemPoint(
      userId: $userId
      threadItemId: $threadItemId
      increment: $increment
    )
  }
`;
```

Here, we added our `updateThreadItemPoint` mutation definition.

```
class ThreadPointsInlineProps {
  points: number = 0;
  userId?: string;
  threadId?: string;
  threadItemId?: string;
  allowUpdatePoints?: boolean = false;
  refreshThread?: () => void;
}
```

This is now going to be our props list. Notice that we have a field for `threadId`. We will be using this `ThreadPointsInline` control to display our Thread points on mobile screens:

```
const ThreadPointsInline: FC<ThreadPointsInlineProps> =
({
  points,
  userId,
  threadId,
  threadItemId,
  allowUpdatePoints,
  refreshThread,
}) => {
  const [execUpdateThreadItemPoint] =
   useMutation(UpdateThreadItemPoint);
  const onClickIncThreadItemPoint = async (
    e: React.MouseEvent<SVGSVGElement, MouseEvent>
  ) => {
    e.preventDefault();
    await execUpdateThreadItemPoint({
      variables: {
        userId,
        threadItemId,
        increment: true,
      },
    });
    refreshThread && refreshThread();
  };
```

There's nothing particularly special here – both our
onClickIncThreadItemPoint and onClickDecThreadItemPoint calls
are doing similar things to the ThreadPointsBar component in that they call
our update mutation and then refresh the Thread data:

```
const onClickDecThreadItemPoint = async (
    e: React.MouseEvent<SVGSVGElement, MouseEvent>
) => {
    e.preventDefault();
    await execUpdateThreadItemPoint({
        variables: {
            userId,
            threadItemId,
            increment: false,
        },
    });
    refreshThread && refreshThread();
};
```

Now, in our JSX, we will do something similar to our ThreadPointsBar
component and include icons that allow us to increment or decrement the entity
points:

```
return (
    <span className="threadpointsinline-item">
        <div
            className="threadpointsinline-item-btn"
            style={{ display: `${allowUpdatePoints ? "block"
                : "none"}` }}
        >
            <FontAwesomeIcon
                icon={faChevronUp}
                className="point-icon"
                onClick={onClickIncThreadItemPoint}
            />
        </div>
        {points}
        <div
            className="threadpointsinline-item-btn"
```

```
              style={{ display: `${allowUpdatePoints ? "block"
                : "none"}` }}
          >
              <FontAwesomeIcon
                icon={faChevronDown}
                className="point-icon"
                onClick={onClickDecThreadItemPoint}
              />
          </div>
          <div className="threadpointsinline-item-btn">
              <FontAwesomeIcon icon={faHeart}
                className="points-icon" />
          </div>
        </span>
      );
    };

export default ThreadPointsInline;
```

9.  Now, if you load the Thread route screen again, you should see ThreadItems for our Thread. Again, your local data will vary, so please make sure your Thread contains ThreadItem data and their respective points, along with the icon buttons, as shown in the following screenshot:

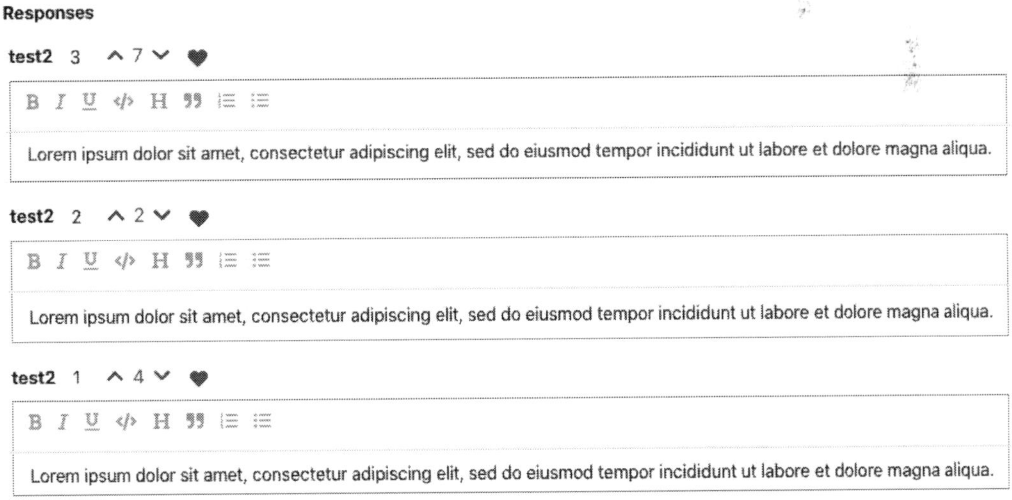

**Responses**

test2   3   ∧ 7 ∨   ♥

    B I U </> H 99 ≔ ≔

    Lorem ipsum dolor sit amet, consectetur adipiscing elit, sed do eiusmod tempor incididunt ut labore et dolore magna aliqua.

test2   2   ∧ 2 ∨   ♥

    B I U </> H 99 ≔ ≔

    Lorem ipsum dolor sit amet, consectetur adipiscing elit, sed do eiusmod tempor incididunt ut labore et dolore magna aliqua.

test2   1   ∧ 4 ∨   ♥

    B I U </> H 99 ≔ ≔

    Lorem ipsum dolor sit amet, consectetur adipiscing elit, sed do eiusmod tempor incididunt ut labore et dolore magna aliqua.

Figure 16.2 – ThreadItem points

Again, if you click the increment and decrement buttons, you should see that we have the same issue that we had with the Thread points. Our points score does not always update, and the user can keep adding or removing points. Let's fix this issue now.

10. Go to your server project, open the `ThreadItemPointRepo.ts` file, find the `updateThreadItemPoint` function, and go to the first call to `threadItem.save()`. Add a prefix to all these calls in the function, like this:

```
await threadItem.save();
```

Can you guess why this will fix the issue we're having? By calling `await` on the `save` call, we are forcing our function to wait until the save completes. Then, when we get our `ThreadItem` data, we are assured that it does indeed contain the newest `points` value. This is one of the tricky sides of using asynchronous code. It's faster, but you have to think about what you're doing; otherwise, you may run into issues like this.

Now, go ahead and update the `updateThreadPoint` function yourself, similar to what we just did with our `updateThreadItemPoint` function. Make sure to update every `save` function.

Now, if you try incrementing or decrementing the points, you should see them update properly.

11. Now, let's fix the issue of users being able to keep adding or removing points. There's actually multiple issues in this code path. Our two resolvers that update points, `updateThreadPoint` and `updateThreadItemPoint`, do not check for user authentication before trying to allow the user to update their points. This is obviously wrong. Additionally, our client-side code is actually passing the `userId` value of `Thread` or `ThreadItem` instead of the currently logged-in user. We can fix both issues together. First, update the `updateThreadPoint` resolver, like this:

```
updateThreadPoint: async (
    obj: any,
    args: { threadId: string; increment: boolean },
    ctx: GqlContext,
    info: any
): Promise<string> => {
```

We no longer take `userId` as a parameter for this resolver. This is because, as shown in the following code, we now check that the user is logged in via the `session.userId` field. Then, when we call our `updateThreadPoint` Repository query, we pass that `session.userId` field in as the `userId` parameter:

```
let result = "";
try {
    if (!ctx.req.session || !ctx.req.session?.userId)
    {
        return "You must be logged in to set likes.";
    }
    result = await updateThreadPoint(
        ctx.req.session!.userId,
        args.threadId,
        args.increment
    );
    return result;
} catch (ex) {
    throw ex;
}
},
```

Make this same change for the `updateThreadItemPoint` resolver, since they are virtually identical calls. Also, don't forget to update our `typeDefs` so that the Mutation signatures for these calls no longer have the `userId` parameter. We'll also need to update the code paths in our client and remove the `userId` parameter there later.

12. Now, add this code to the `updateThreadPoint` Repository call at the top of the implementation:

```
if (!userId || userId === "0") {
    return "User is not authenticated";
}
```

This will prevent any odd values for `userId` getting passed in, and us thinking that the user is authenticated when they are not. Add the same code to the `updateThreadItemPoint` Repository call.

Now, let's fix the client-side code and remove the `userId` parameter. The easiest way to do this is to remove the call from the `ThreadPointsBar` and `ThreadPointsInline` components. If you then save the code, you'll get the compiler telling you where the related calls are via `userId`.

13. Let's start with `ThreadPointsBar`. Update it like this. Remove `userId` from the `UpdateThreadPoint` Mutation parameters. Then, remove it from the props of the component's `ThreadPointsBarProps` type. Next, remove it from the props parameters of `ThreadPointsBar`. Finally, remove `userId` from the calls to `execUpdateThreadPoints`.

14. Next, in the `Thread.tsx` route component, find the call to `ThreadPointsBar` and simply remove the `userId` props. Also, remove the `useSelector` call to get the user reducer as it's no longer being used.

    The `ThreadPointsInline` component also needs the same kind of refactor, but I'll leave that change up to you since it's basically the same type of change we made for `ThreadPointsBar`. Again, try making the change while beginning with the `ThreadPointsInline` component and save your code. The compiler should tell you where the references to `userId` still exist.

    With that, our points should update properly. The points should only update when the user is logged in, and only be able to change by one point, either incremented or decremented. The user should also not be allowed to change the points for their own `Thread` or `ThreadItem`.

Now, let's look at something else. When looking at the `Thread` route component in mobile mode, you will see that our points counts are no longer visible, as shown here:

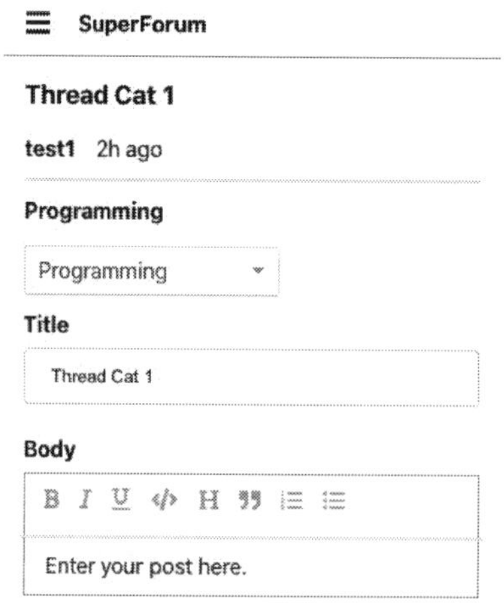

Figure 16.3 – Thread route screen mobile mode

This, of course, is deliberate since there is so little horizontal room. So, let's put our `ThreadPointsInline` component in this mobile screen and update it so that it can work for Threads as well as ThreadItems:

1. Because `ThreadPointsInline` is being refactored to use the `updateThreadPoint` Mutation that `ThreadPointBar` is using, we must move those calls into their own Hook and share them. Create a new file inside the Hooks folder called `useUpdateThreadPoint.ts` and add the respective Git source code to it.

   By doing this, we have simply copied most of the code from the `ThreadPointBar` component into here. Once we've done this, we return the event handlers to be used by our calling component; that is, `onClickIncThreadPoint` and `onClickDecThreadPoint`.

2. Now, let's refactor the `ThreadPointBar` component so that it can use this Hook. Update it like this:

```
import useUpdateThreadPoint from "../../hooks/
useUpdateThreadPoint";
```

Here, we've imported our new Hook and removed the Mutation for `UpdateThreadPoint`:

```
export class ThreadPointsBarProps {
    points: number = 0;
    responseCount?: number;
    threadId?: string;
    allowUpdatePoints?: boolean = false;
    refreshThread?: () => void;
}
const ThreadPointsBar: FC<ThreadPointsBarProps> = ({
    points,
    responseCount,
    threadId,
    allowUpdatePoints,
    refreshThread,
}) => {
    const { width } = useWindowDimensions();
    const { onClickDecThreadPoint, onClickIncThreadPoint }
        = useUpdateThreadPoint(
```

```
        refreshThread,
        threadId
    );
```

Here, we've received the event handlers from our `useUpdateThreadPoint` Hook. The rest of the code is identical.

3.  Now, let's refactor `ThreadPointsInline`, like this:

```
import React, { FC } from "react";
import { FontAwesomeIcon } from "@fortawesome/react-
fontawesome";
import {
  faHeart,
  faChevronDown,
  faChevronUp,
} from "@fortawesome/free-solid-svg-icons";
import { gql, useMutation } from "@apollo/client";
import "./ThreadPointsInline.css";
import useUpdateThreadPoint from "../../hooks/
useUpdateThreadPoint";

const UpdateThreadItemPoint = gql`
  mutation UpdateThreadItemPoint($threadItemId: ID!,
    $increment: Boolean!) {
    updateThreadItemPoint(threadItemId: $threadItemId,
    increment: $increment)
  }
`;
class ThreadPointsInlineProps {
  points: number = 0;
  threadId?: string;
  threadItemId?: string;
  allowUpdatePoints?: boolean = false;
  refreshThread?: () => void;
}

const ThreadPointsInline: FC<ThreadPointsInlineProps> =
({
```

```
    points,
    threadId,
    threadItemId,
    allowUpdatePoints,
    refreshThread,
}) => {
    const [execUpdateThreadItemPoint] =
     useMutation(UpdateThreadItemPoint);
    const { onClickDecThreadPoint, onClickIncThreadPoint }
     = useUpdateThreadPoint(
      refreshThread,
      threadId
    );
```

Here, we've gotten our event handlers from the useUpdateThreadPoint Hook:

```
    const onClickIncThreadItemPoint = async (
      e: React.MouseEvent<SVGSVGElement, MouseEvent>
    ) => {
      e.preventDefault();
      await execUpdateThreadItemPoint({
        variables: {
          threadItemId,
          increment: true,
        },
      });
      refreshThread && refreshThread();
    };
    const onClickDecThreadItemPoint = async (
      e: React.MouseEvent<SVGSVGElement, MouseEvent>
    ) => {
      e.preventDefault();
      await execUpdateThreadItemPoint({
        variables: {
          threadItemId,
          increment: false,
        },
      });
```

```
      refreshThread && refreshThread();
    };

  return (
    <span className="threadpointsinline-item">
      <div
        className="threadpointsinline-item-btn"
        style={{ display: `${allowUpdatePoints ? "block"
          : "none"}` }}
      >
        <FontAwesomeIcon
          icon={faChevronUp}
          className="point-icon"
          onClick={threadId ? onClickIncThreadPoint :
            onClickIncThreadItemPoint}
```

In the following code, there's a tiny bit of logic that decides whether we will update the point of a Thread or ThreadItem:

```
        />
      </div>
      {points}
      <div
        className="threadpointsinline-item-btn"
        style={{ display: `${allowUpdatePoints ? "block"
          : "none"}` }}
      >
        <FontAwesomeIcon
          icon={faChevronDown}
          className="point-icon"
          onClick={threadId ? onClickDecThreadPoint :
            onClickDecThreadItemPoint}
        />
```

We have the same point selection logic here as well:

```
      </div>
      <div className="threadpointsinline-item-btn">
        <FontAwesomeIcon icon={faHeart}
          className="points-icon" />
      </div>
```

```
            </span>
    );
};
export default ThreadPointsInline;
```

Now, if you run the `Thread` route in mobile mode, you'll see this:

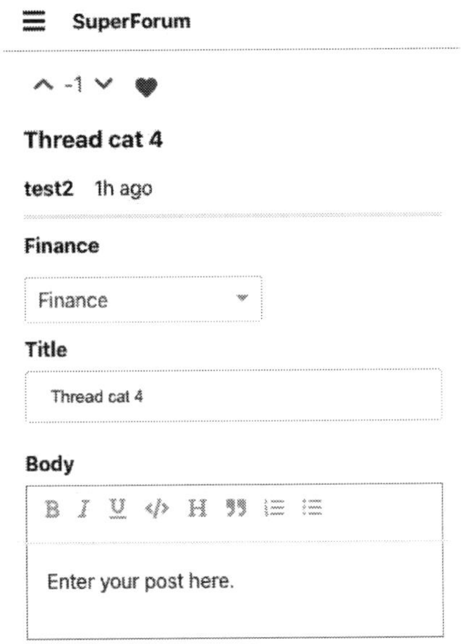

Figure 16.4 – Thread route screen on mobile with our points incrementor

Note that I've made some styling updates to the `ThreadCategory` component so that it can be viewed on the Home route in mobile mode as well.

Now, we can view existing Threads on our screen. However, we also need to be able to add new Threads, as well as ThreadItems. Let's add those features now:

1. First, we need to make a small change to our `createThread` Repository call. Open the `ThreadRepo` file and update the last `return` statement for `createThread`, which looks as follows:

```
    return { messages: ["Thread created successfully."] };
```

Change it so that it looks like this:

```
    return { messages: [thread.id] };
```

Now, if our `createThread` is successful, it will only return the ID. This minimizes payload sizes but gives our client what it needs to know.

2.  Next, we must make another small change to our `Thread` route. Open `App.tsx` and find the route for `Thread`. Update that route like this:

```
<Route path="/thread/:id?" render={renderThread} />
```

This is a very subtle change, but we added a ? immediately after the `id` parameter. This will allow the `Thread` route to load with no parameters, which is what tells the screen that we want to make a new Thread post.

3.  Now, we will add a **Post** button to our Home screen, as shown here:

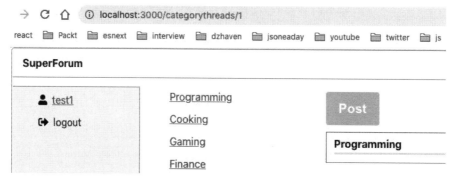

Figure 16.5 – New Post button

Here's the core code update for the `Main.tsx` file:

```
const Main = () => {
  const [
    execGetThreadsByCat,
    {
      //error: threadsByCatErr,
      //called: threadsByCatCalled,
      data: threadsByCatData,
    },
  ] = useLazyQuery(GetThreadsByCategoryId);
  const [
    execGetThreadsLatest,
    {
      //error: threadsLatestErr,
      //called: threadsLatestCalled,
      data: threadsLatestData,
    },
  ] = useLazyQuery(GetThreadsLatest);
```

```
const { categoryId } = useParams();
const [category, setCategory] = useState<Category |
undefined>();
const [threadCards, setThreadCards] =
  useState<Array<JSX.Element> | null>(
  null
);
const history = useHistory();
```

Not much has changed here, but as you can see, we call `useHistory` so that we can modify the URL we are on:

```
useEffect(() => {
  if (categoryId && categoryId > 0) {
    execGetThreadsByCat({
      variables: {
        categoryId,
      },
    });
  } else {
    execGetThreadsLatest();
  }
  // eslint-disable-next-line react-hooks/exhaustive-
  // deps
}, [categoryId]);
useEffect(() => {
  console.log("main threadsByCatData",
    threadsByCatData);
  if (
    threadsByCatData &&
    threadsByCatData.getThreadsByCategoryId &&
    threadsByCatData.getThreadsByCategoryId.threads
  ) {
    const threads = threadsByCatData.
      getThreadsByCategoryId.threads;
    const cards = threads.map((th: any) => {
      return <ThreadCard key={`thread-${th.id}`}
thread={th} />;
    });
```

```
        setCategory(threads[0].category);
        setThreadCards(cards);
      } else {
        setCategory(undefined);
        setThreadCards(null);
      }
    }, [threadsByCatData]);
  useEffect(() => {
    if (
      threadsLatestData &&
      threadsLatestData.getThreadsLatest &&
      threadsLatestData.getThreadsLatest.threads
    ) {
      const threads = threadsLatestData.getThreadsLatest.
        threads;
      const cards = threads.map((th: any) => {
        return <ThreadCard key={`thread-${th.id}`}
          thread={th} />;
      });
      setCategory(new Category("0", "Latest"));
      setThreadCards(cards);
    }
  }, [threadsLatestData]);
  const onClickPostThread = () => {
    history.push("/thread");
  };
```

Here, we have a new handler for the Post button click, which redirects the user to the thread screen without any id. I'll show you why that's important in a bit:

```
  return (
    <main className="content">
      <button className="action-btn"
        onClick={onClickPostThread}>
        Post
      </button>
```

Here, we have our `button` declaration with that handler:

```
        <MainHeader category={category} />
        <div>{threadCards}</div>
    </main>
  );
};
```

The rest of the code is the same as it was previously.

4.  Now, we need to update our `Thread.tsx` component so that when it sees
    we have no `id`, it knows to set itself up so that it can add a new Thread. However,
    in order to do this, we need to update some of its child components. Let's start with
    `RichEditor`. Update this component as follows. I'll only show the code that's been
    changed here:

```
export const getTextFromNodes = (nodes: Node[]) => {
    return nodes.map((n: Node) => Node.string(n)).
    join("\n");
};
```

`getTextFromNodes` is a new helper that will allow the Slate.js format of our
Node array to be translated into a string:

> **Note**
>
> Slate.js allows complex formatting to be performed on a user's text. This
> information is very complex and cannot be saved as simple text. Therefore,
> Slate.js uses objects based upon the Node type at hand to store this formatted
> text. When this data needs to be stored in our database, we will have to
> convert it into text (JSON) first. This is part of the reason we need this
> `getTextFromNodes` function.

```
const HOTKEYS: { [keyName: string]: string } = {
    "mod+b": "bold",
    "mod+i": "italic",
    "mod+u": "underline",
    "mod+`": "code",
};
const initialValue = [
    {
```

```
      type: "paragraph",
      children: [{ text: "" }],
```

InitialValue is now an empty string:

```
    },
  ];
  const LIST_TYPES = ["numbered-list", "bulleted-list"];
  class RichEditorProps {
    existingBody?: string;
    readOnly?: boolean = false;
    sendOutBody?: (body: Node[]) => void;
```

We've added this additional prop so that when our editor has its text updated, that change will go up the component hierarchy to our Thread.tsx component. Thread.tsx needs to know the latest value so that it can send it as a parameter when it tries to create a new Thread. We'll be repeating this *sendOut* pattern in these child components:

```
  }
  const RichEditor: FC<RichEditorProps> = ({
    existingBody,
    readOnly,
    sendOutBody,
  }) => {
    const [value, setValue] =
    useState<Node[]>(initialValue);
    const renderElement = useCallback((props) => <Element
  {...props} />, []);
    const renderLeaf = useCallback((props) => <Leaf {...
    props} />, []);
    const editor = useMemo(() =>
    withHistory(withReact(createEditor())), []);
    useEffect(() => {
      console.log("existingBody", existingBody);
      if (existingBody) {
        setValue(JSON.parse(existingBody));
```

The existingBody prop is the initial value being sent in from the parent component. This value will come in when the Thread.tsx route screen is loaded from an existing Thread. This Thread is, of course, being loaded from our database, which means that the text data will be saved into our database as a string. This is because Postgres does not understand Slate.js' Node types. The side effect of this is that before setValue can receive this data, it must first be parsed in JSON format, which is why you can see setValue(JSON.parse(existingBody)).

```
    }

      // eslint-disable-next-line react-hooks/exhaustive-
      // deps
  }, [existingBody]);
  const onChangeEditorValue = (val: Node[]) => {
    setValue(val);
    sendOutBody && sendOutBody(val);
```

Here, we've set our val from the editor, but also sent it back to the parent component using sendOutBody.

```
  };

  return (
    <Slate editor={editor} value={value}
      onChange={onChangeEditorValue}>
      <Toolbar>
        <MarkButton format="bold" icon="bold" />
        <MarkButton format="italic" icon="italic" />
        <MarkButton format="underline" icon="underlined"
          />
        <MarkButton format="code" icon="code" />
        <BlockButton format="heading-one" icon="header1"
          />
        <BlockButton format="block-quote" icon="in_
          quotes" />
        <BlockButton format="numbered-list" icon="list_
          numbered" />
        <BlockButton format="bulleted-list" icon="list_
          bulleted" />
      </Toolbar>
      <Editable
        className="editor"
```

```
        renderElement={renderElement}
        renderLeaf={renderLeaf}
        placeholder="Enter your post here."
```

The following is a trivial `placeholder` change.

```
        spellCheck
        autoFocus
        onKeyDown={(event) => {
          for (const hotkey in HOTKEYS) {
            if (isHotkey(hotkey, event as any)) {
              event.preventDefault();
              const mark = HOTKEYS[hotkey];
              toggleMark(editor, mark);
            }
          }
        }}
        readOnly={readOnly}
      />
    </Slate>
  );
};
```

5.  Now, we need to update `ThreadCategory` component. I'll only show the code that has been changed here:

```
interface ThreadCategoryProps {
  category?: Category;
  sendOutSelectedCategory: (cat: Category) => void;
```

Here, we have the `sendOutSelectedCategory` function, which allows us to send back a category selection using the `sendOut` method:

```
}
const ThreadCategory: FC<ThreadCategoryProps> = ({
  category,
  sendOutSelectedCategory,
}) => {
```

6.  Next, we'll update our `ThreadTitle` component, like this:

```
import React, { FC, useEffect, useState } from "react";
interface ThreadTitleProps {
  title?: string;
  readOnly: boolean;
```

Now, we want to make our title read-only when we've loaded an existing Thread:

```
  sendOutTitle: (title: string) => void;
```

Once again, here, we have the `sendOut` pattern using `sendOutTitle`:

```
}
const ThreadTitle: FC<ThreadTitleProps> = ({
  title,
  readOnly,
  sendOutTitle,
}) => {
  const [currentTitle, setCurrentTitle] = useState("");
  useEffect(() => {
    setCurrentTitle(title || "");
  }, [title]);

  const onChangeTitle = (e: React.
    ChangeEvent<HTMLInputElement>) => {
    setCurrentTitle(e.target.value);
    sendOutTitle(e.target.value);
```

Here, we've set our title and also sent it out to our component's parent:

```
  };
  return (
    <div className="thread-title-container">
      <strong>Title</strong>
      <div className="field">
        <input
          type="text"
          value={currentTitle}
          onChange={onChangeTitle}
          readOnly={readOnly}
```

Here, we are using our new props:

```
            />
        </div>
    </div>
    );
};
export default ThreadTitle;
```

7.  Now, let's update `ThreadBody`, like this:

```
import React, { FC } from "react";
import RichEditor from "../../editor/RichEditor";
import { Node } from "slate";

interface ThreadBodyProps {
  body?: string;
  readOnly: boolean;
  sendOutBody: (body: Node[]) => void;
```

Again, we need the `sendOut` pattern for the `sendOutBody` function:

```
}

const ThreadBody: FC<ThreadBodyProps> = ({ body,
readOnly, sendOutBody }) => {
  return (
    <div className="thread-body-container">
      <strong>Body</strong>
      <div className="thread-body-editor">
        <RichEditor
          existingBody={body}
          readOnly={readOnly}
          sendOutBody={sendOutBody}
```

Now, we must send the `sendOutBody` function to our `RichEditor` since that control handles body updates:

```
          />
        </div>
      </div>
```

```
  );
};
export default ThreadBody;
```

8. Finally, we have the `Thread.tsx` file. We must make a number of changes here. Let's look at all of them.

You should be able to add the appropriate imports yourself; for example, here, we need the `getTextFromNodes` helper:

```
const GetThreadById = gql`
  query GetThreadById($id: ID!) {
    getThreadById(id: $id) {
      ... on EntityResult {
        messages
      }
      ... on Thread {
        id
        user {
          id
          userName
        }
        lastModifiedOn
        title
        body
        points
        category {
          id
          name
        }
        threadItems {
          id
          body
          points
          user {
            id
            userName
          }
        }
```

```
        }
      }
    }
  }
`;
const CreateThread = gql`
  mutation createThread(
    $userId: ID!
    $categoryId: ID!
    $title: String!
    $body: String!
  ) {
    createThread(
      userId: $userId
      categoryId: $categoryId
      title: $title
      body: $body
    ) {
      messages
    }
  }
`;
```

Here, is our new `CreateThread` mutation:

```
const threadReducer = (state: any, action: any) => {
  switch (action.type) {
    case "userId":
      return { ...state, userId: action.payload };
    case "category":
      return { ...state, category: action.payload };
    case "title":
      return { ...state, title: action.payload };
    case "body":
      return { ...state, body: action.payload };
    case "bodyNode":
      return { ...state, bodyNode: action.payload };
    default:
```

```
        throw new Error("Unknown action type");
    }
};
```

A new reducer also needs to be added; that is, `threadReducer`:

```
const Thread = () => {
  const { width } = useWindowDimensions();
  const [execGetThreadById, { data: threadData }] =
    useLazyQuery(
      GetThreadById,
      { fetchPolicy: "no-cache" }
    );
  const [thread, setThread] = useState<ThreadModel |
    undefined>();
  const { id } = useParams();
  const [readOnly, setReadOnly] = useState(false);
  const user = useSelector((state: AppState) => state.
    user);
```

Here's our `user` object, which only appears if the user is logged in. We will only use this object when we're creating a new Thread:

```
  const [
    { userId, category, title, body, bodyNode },
    threadReducerDispatch,
  ] = useReducer(threadReducer, {
    userId: user ? user.id : "0",
    category: undefined,
    title: "",
    body: "",
    bodyNode: undefined,
  });
```

Here's our reducer. These fields will be used to submit new Threads during creation mode:

```
  const [postMsg, setPostMsg] = useState("");
```

The following code shows the status of our Thread creation attempt:

```
  const [execCreateThread] = useMutation(CreateThread);
```

Here's our actual `CreateThread` Mutation caller, `execCreateThread`:

```
const history = useHistory();
```

We'll be using `useHistory()` to switch to the newly created Thread's route. For example, if the new Thread `id` is 25, then the route will be `"/thread/25"`:

```
const refreshThread = () => {
  if (id && id > 0) {
    execGetThreadById({
      variables: {
        id,
      },
    });
  }
};


useEffect(() => {
  console.log("id");
  if (id && id > 0) {
    execGetThreadById({
      variables: {
        id,
      },
    });
  }
}, [id, execGetThreadById]);


useEffect(() => {
  threadReducerDispatch({
    type: "userId",
    payload: user ? user.id : "0",
  });
}, [user]);
```

Here, we are updating the reducer's `userId`, in case the user has logged in:

```
useEffect(() => {
  if (threadData && threadData.getThreadById) {
    setThread(threadData.getThreadById);
```

```
      setReadOnly(true);
    } else {
      setThread(undefined);
      setReadOnly(false);
    }
  }, [threadData]);
  const receiveSelectedCategory = (cat: Category) => {
    threadReducerDispatch({
      type: "category",
      payload: cat,
    });
  };
```

Here, we have started adding the definitions for our handler functions in the sendOut pattern, which we've been using in our child components. In this case, receiveSelectedCategory receives the newly set ThreadCategory from the CategoryDropDown control:

```
  const receiveTitle = (updatedTitle: string) => {
    threadReducerDispatch({
      type: "title",
      payload: updatedTitle,
    });
  };
  const receiveBody = (body: Node[]) => {
    threadReducerDispatch({
      type: "bodyNode",
      payload: body,
    });
    threadReducerDispatch({
      type: "body",
      payload: getTextFromNodes(body),
    });
  };
```

The `receiveTitle` and `receiveBody` functions also handle updates that are made to `title` and `body` from their respective child components:

```
const onClickPost = async (
    e: React.MouseEvent<HTMLButtonElement, MouseEvent>
) => {
```

The `onClickPost` function handles the **Post** button being clicked and submits a new Thread:

```
e.preventDefault();
if (!userId || userId === "0") {
  setPostMsg("You must be logged in before you can
    post.");
} else if (!category) {
  setPostMsg("Please select a category for your
    post.");
} else if (!title) {
  setPostMsg("Please enter a title.");
} else if (!bodyNode) {
  setPostMsg("Please select a category for your
    post.");
```

The previous if/else statements are validations for the reducer field values, which are used for submitting a new Thread:

```
} else {
  setPostMsg("");
  const newThread = {
    userId,
    categoryId: category?.id,
    title,
    body: JSON.stringify(bodyNode),
```

Note that we are converting the Slate.js array of the Node type into a JSON string, which again is what gets saved into the database:

```
  };
```

This is builds our parameters to our CreateThread mutation:

```
const { data: createThreadMsg } = await
  execCreateThread({
```

```
    variables: newThread,
  });
```

Here, we've executed the Mutation:

```
if (
    createThreadMsg.createThread &&
    createThreadMsg.createThread.messages &&
    !isNaN(createThreadMsg.createThread.messages[0])
) {
    setPostMsg("Thread posted successfully.");
    history.push(`/thread/${createThreadMsg.
      createThread.messages[0]}`);
```

If the Thread creation attempt was successful, then we redirect the user to the newly created Thread route screen, based on its `id`:

```
} else {
    setPostMsg(createThreadMsg.createThread.
      messages[0]);
```

If the attempt fails, we show the user a server error:

```
    }
  }
};
return (
  <div className="screen-root-container">
    <div className="thread-nav-container">
      <Nav />
    </div>
    <div className="thread-content-container">
      <div className="thread-content-post-container">
        {width <= 768 && thread ? (
          <ThreadPointsInline
            points={thread?.points || 0}
            threadId={thread?.id}
            refreshThread={refreshThread}
            allowUpdatePoints={true}
          />
        ) : null}
```

If the screen is being shown on a mobile device and the thread exists, we show this control; otherwise, we don't:

```
<ThreadHeader
    userName={thread ? thread.user.userName :
    user?.userName}
    lastModifiedOn={thread ? thread.
    lastModifiedOn : new Date()}
    title={thread ? thread.title : title}
/>
<ThreadCategory
    category={thread ? thread.category :
    category}
    sendOutSelectedCategory=
    {receiveSelectedCategory}
/>
<ThreadTitle
    title={thread ? thread.title : ""}
    readOnly={thread ? readOnly : false}
    sendOutTitle={receiveTitle}
/>
<ThreadBody
    body={thread ? thread.body : ""}
    readOnly={thread ? readOnly : false}
    sendOutBody={receiveBody}
/>
```

The rest of these child components contain the same logic. If the `thread` object exists, we display a thread. If not, then we go into Thread Post mode:

```
{thread ? null : (
    <>
        <div style={{ marginTop: ".5em" }}>
            <button className="action-btn"
                onClick={onClickPost}>
                Post
            </button>
        </div>
        <strong>{postMsg}</strong>
```

```
            </>
        )}
```

Here is our Thread **Post** button and status message. Again, if our thread object exists, we do not show these, whereas if the thread does, we show them.

The rest of code is identical to what we had previously, so I won't show it here.

9.  Now, if we run the Thread route with no `id`, we get the following screen:

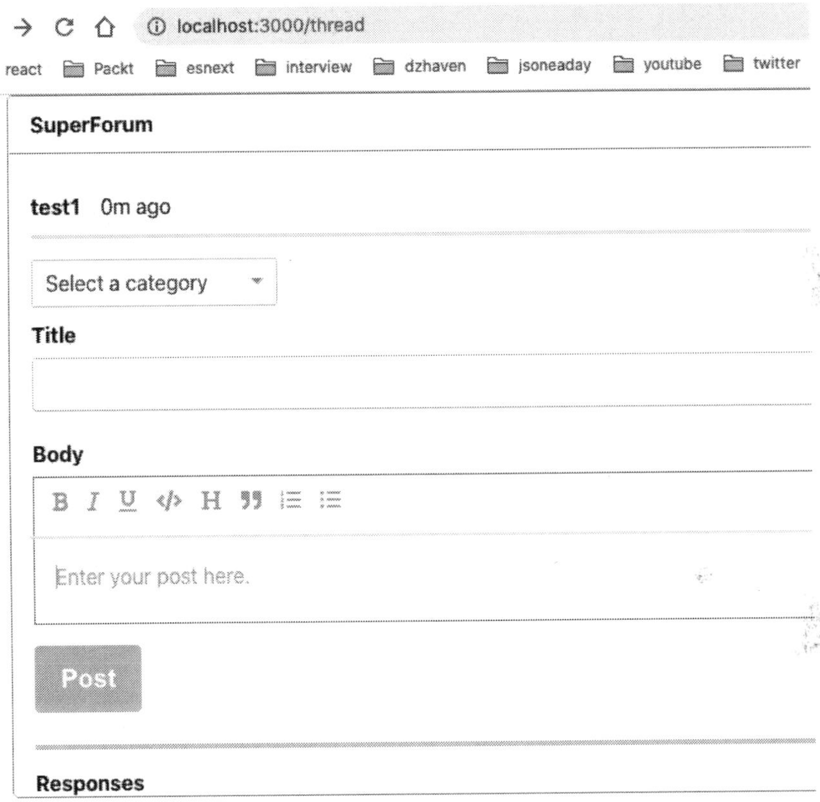

Figure 16.6 – New Thread screen

> **Warning**
>
> Since we are now saving Slate.js Nodes as JSON strings inside the `Body` field of our `Thread` table, before you can test the code, you must purge any existing `Thread` and `ThreadItem` data before you can display it again.

There is an issue here. Since we now have JSON strings in the Body field of our database, when this data comes back, it will look like this on the Home screen:

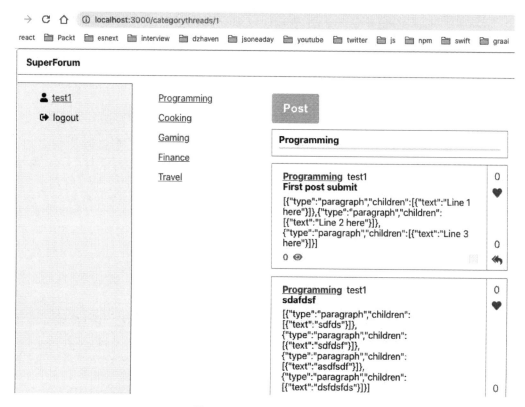

Figure 16.7 – Home screen

Obviously, this is not what we want. Here, we need to update this text so that it's a normal string. Luckily, we can just use our existing RichEditor to display the text and keep all the formatting intact.

10. Update the `RichEditor` component by putting a `readOnly` check on the
Toolbar, like this:

```
{readOnly ? null : (
    <Toolbar>
        <MarkButton format="bold" icon="bold" />
        <MarkButton format="italic" icon="italic" />
        <MarkButton format="underline"
          icon="underlined" />
        <MarkButton format="code" icon="code" />
        <BlockButton format="heading-one"
          icon="header1" />
        <BlockButton format="block-quote" icon="in_
          quotes" />
        <BlockButton format="numbered-list" icon="list_
          numbered" />
        <BlockButton format="bulleted-list" icon="list_
          bulleted" />
    </Toolbar>
)}
```

So, as an example, if we are in `readOnly` mode, this Toolbar does not appear.

11. Update the `ThreadCard` component by replacing the `<div>{thread.body}</div>` line in the JSX with the following:

```
<RichEditor existingBody={thread.body} readOnly={true} />
```

Again, make sure your import of `RichEditor` is also there.

12. You should now see something like this on the Home screen. Your own data will vary from what's being shown here:

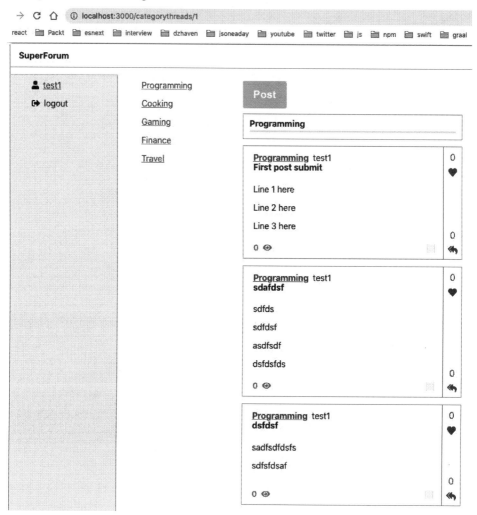

Figure 16.8 – Home screen with body

Note that this will also cause `RichEditor` on our Thread route screen to hide the Toolbar in `readOnly` mode. Now, we just need to allow new `ThreadItem` responses to be made and we're done with this section. We will repurpose the `ThreadResponse` component so that it also allows ThreadItems to be submitted, instead of just being displayed:

1. First, we need to make some minor adjustments to the server side. Open `ThreadItemRepo` and find `createThreadItem`. In the last `return` statement, update it, as follows:

```
return { messages: [`${threadItem.id}`] };
```

Just like what we did with our `createThread` function, we are returning the ThreadItem's `id`.

2. Now, inside `ThreadRepo`, update the call to `findOne`, like this:

```
const thread = await Thread.findOne({
    where: {
        id,
    },
    relations: [
        "user",
        "threadItems",
        "threadItems.user",
        "threadItems.thread",
        "category",
    ],
});
```

We now want to add the parent Thread information so that when we submit a `ThreadItem` response, we can associate it with the correct parent Thread.

3. Now, we need to refactor the `ThreadItem.ts` model in our client-side code so that it takes a `thread` object instead of a `threadId`:

```
public thread: Thread
```

By doing this, we receive the `Thread` object from the query we just updated.

4. Now, update `ThreadResponse`, as shown in the source code. Make sure you have all your imports.

First, you'll see we have our new `CreateThreadItem` Mutation.

In the `ThreadResponseProps` interface, we can see that the `body` prop is the initial value of `RichEditor` before any changes are made. We'll also need to receive the parent `threadId` if we are going to submit a new `ThreadItem`.

After that, we need to get the `user` object from `useSelector`. We're doing this because the current user will be submitting new ThreadItems.

Next, we have `execCreateThreadItem`, which is our Mutation executor for `CreateThreadItem`.

Then, we have our status message, `postMsg`, for when the user attempts to save.

Then, we have the current editing body value, `bodyToSave`, inside `RichEditor`.

Next, `useEffect` is used to initialize our `bodyToSave` value from the passed-in prop `body` so that we have an initial value to start with.

The `onClickPost` function allows us to do some validation checks before we attempt to submit our new `ThreadItem`. Once we've done this, we can submit and refresh our parent Thread.

In the `receiveBody` function, we receive our updated text from our `RichEditor` component. We use this if we are submitting a new `ThreadItem`.

In the returned JSX, we decide not to show `ThreadPointsInline` if we are not in `readOnly` mode. However, if we are in edit mode, we allow the Post button and the status message to be shown.

5.  Now, if we create a few `ThreadItem` posts, we should see something like this:

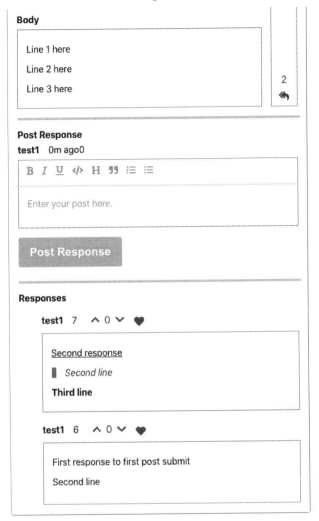

Figure 16.9 – Submitted ThreadItem responses

That's it for the Thread route screen.

We're almost there and you've done a phenomenal job thus far. We've covered so much material and code to get to this stage. You should feel wonderful about your progress. We have one more section to complete and then we're done with our app!

The last item we need to configure is RightMenu. In this menu, we will list up to three of the top ThreadCategories, based on the number of Threads each ThreadCategory has attributed to it. This will involve a longer multi-part query and is a good exercise:

1.  First, we need to add a new type called CategoryThread to the typeDefs file, like this:

```
type CategoryThread {
    threadId: ID!
    categoryId: ID!
    categoryName: String!
    title: String!
    titleCreatedOn: Date!
}
```

Note that titleCreatedOn is only there for checking the sort. We won't use it in our client-side code.

2.  Now, add a new model to our repository folder called CategoryThread.ts and add the following code. Note that this class will not be an Entity in our database. Instead, it will be an aggregation class that will contain fields from multiple entities:

```
export default class CategoryThread {
    constructor(
        public threadId: string,
        public categoryId: string,
        public categoryName: string,
        public title: string,
        public titleCreatedOn: Date
    ) {}
}
```

3.  Now, get the code from the source and create the CategoryThreadRepo.ts file with that code.

    From the top, first, we have made our initial query to get ThreadCategory data from our database using ThreadCategory. createQueryBuilder("threadCategory"). Notice that we have also included our relationship to the Threads table.

Now, we are about to post-process our query to get the results we want. We are not doing this work in our TypeORM query because, for more complex sorting and filtering, TypeORM is sometimes difficult and finicky to work with. Using standard JavaScript will get us what we need more easily.

In the call to `categories.sort`, on line 14, we are doing a descending sort based on the number of Thread records each `ThreadCategory` contains. Then, we take only the first three records of the result.

Then, we take this result and sort the actual Thread records by their `createdOn` timestamp in descending order.

By doing this, we get, at most, three Thread records for each category, ordered by their `createdOn` timestamps.

4.  Now, let's test this using GraphQL Playground:

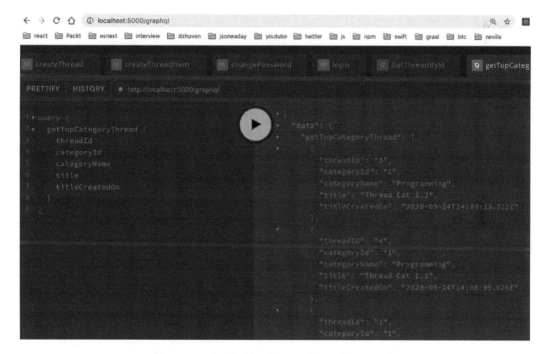

Figure 16.10 – GetTopCategoryThread sort result

As you can see, the sorts and filters are working.

5.  Now, let's finish our client-side code. Open `CategoryThread.ts` and update `category` so that it's now `categoryName`. This will match our server-side model name for this field.

6.  Open `TopCategory.tsx` and update the line shown in the return JSX:

```
<strong>{topCategories[0].category}</strong>
```

Change `category` so that it's now `categoryName`.

7.  Now, open `RightMenu.tsx` and update it from the source code:

After making the necessary imports, we need to define our GraphQL query, `GetTopCategoryThread`, and then use that query on line 20 by calling `useQuery` on it. Here, we're using that query.

Then, on line 26, `useEffect` has been updated to make use of the resulting `categoryThreadData`. The `groupBy` method from `lodash` is grouping our data by `categoryName` so that it's easier to work with. The original code for this was covered in *Chapter 11, What We Will Learn – Online Forum Application*.

Finally, we need to check for mobile width, which returns either `null` or our UI.

8.  Now, if we run our Home screen, we should see our `RightMenu` populated with data:

**Programming**

First post submit

sdafdsf

dsfdsf

**Cooking**

Second cooking post

First cooking post

**Gaming**

First post for gaming

Figure 16.11 – Home screen with popular categories shown

Again, your local data will vary.

With that, we're done! There was a lot of code, and many frameworks and concepts. You've done an amazing job getting through it all. Take a much-deserved break.

In this section, we covered the client-side code of our app and how to glue it to our backend GraphQL server. We had to tweak our styling and make adjustments by refactoring our code. We also had to fix hard-to-find bugs. This is exactly what we'll be doing in real life, so this was great practice.

# Summary

In this final coding chapter, we brought everything together by finishing our code and integrating the frontend React app with the backend GraphQL server. We've learned an enormous amount in this chapter and this book as a whole. You should feel proud of how far you've come.

My suggestion would be, before you move on to the final chapter, to try and make changes to the app. Come up with your own ideas for features and try building them. Ultimately, this is the only way you will really learn.

In the final chapter of this book, *Chapter 17, Deploying an Application to AWS*, we will learn how to deploy our application to Linux and NGINX on the Azure cloud.

# 17
# Deploying an Application to AWS

An application, once finalized, must be deployed before it can be used. We have many options to choose from, including using our own infrastructure. These days, however, most companies prefer to use the services of a cloud provider in order to reduce their IT-related expenditures.

In this chapter, we'll learn about deploying our application to **Amazon Web Services.** (**AWS**) is, of course, the standard when it comes to Cloud providers. We'll be setting up our application services Redis, Postgres, and NGINX on top of a Linux VM.

In this chapter, we're going to cover the following main topics:

- Setting up Ubuntu Linux on AWS Cloud
- Setting up Redis, Postgres, and Node on Ubuntu
- Setting up and deploying our app on NGINX

# Technical requirements

You should now have a solid understanding of web technologies. Although it can take years to become a senior-level developer, you should now feel comfortable with TypeScript, JavaScript, React, Express, and GraphQL. In this chapter, we will once again be using Node and Visual Studio Code.

The GitHub repository is again available at `https://github.com/PacktPublishing/Full-Stack-React-TypeScript-and-Node`. Use the code in the `Chap17` folder.

Let's do some basic setup on your development machine:

1. Create a `Chap17` folder and then copy the `super-forum-server` and `super-forum-client` folders from the source code of the `Chap15` folder.

2. If `node_modules` and `package-lock.json` get copied over, then delete those folders and files.

3. Now, terminal into the `Chap17/super-forum-server` folder and run this command:

   ```
   npm install
   ```

4. Now, terminal into the `Chap17/super-forum-client` folder and run this command:

   ```
   npm install
   ```

# Setting up Ubuntu Linux on AWS Cloud

In this section, we'll learn about selecting and setting up an Ubuntu Linux server on an AWS VM. I'll assume you know how to create an AWS account already. The process is fairly straightforward, as an existing Ubuntu Linux image will already be available to use. Let's start:

1. After we log in, the screenshot shown here will be the current AWS portal. Note that these screens change frequently, so your view may be different:

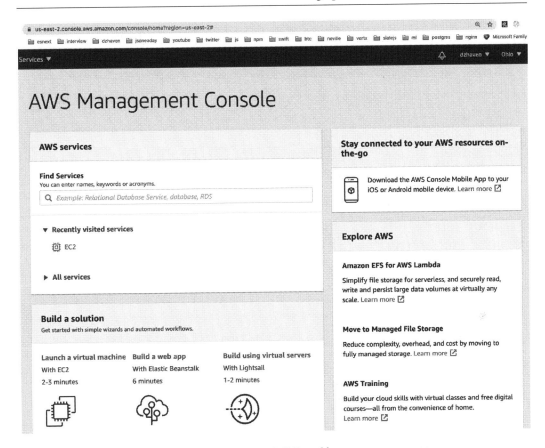

Figure 17.1 – AWS Portal home

2. We can see the **Launch a virtual machine** link. Select it and you will get to this next screen:

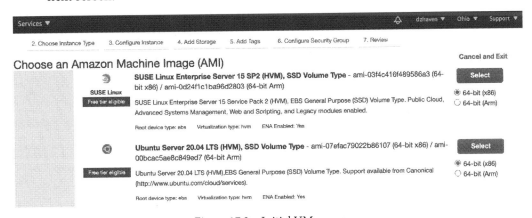

Figure 17.2 – Initial VM screen

Let's select the image for **Ubuntu 20.04 LTS**. This is the latest **Long Term Support** version of Ubuntu.

3.  Once selected, you should see the following screen:

Figure 17.3 – VM instance type selector

I have gone ahead and selected a lower-end image with 1 vCPU and 2 GB of memory. Note that EBS is an AWS-specific performance optimization for storage.

Let's keep things simple by keeping the default settings and select the **Review and Launch** button at the bottom of the screen after making our selection.

4.   Here are the major details of what I have selected:

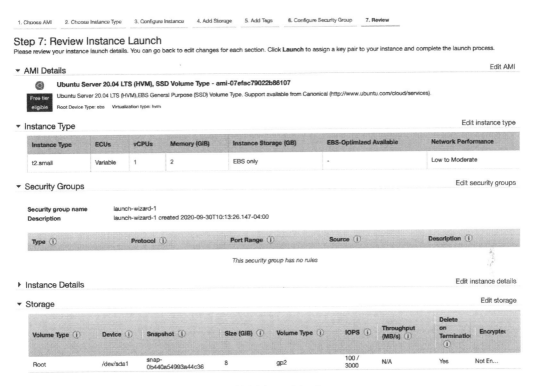

Figure 17.4 – Initial provisioning screen

Now, select the **Launch** button at the bottom to continue.

5.  Next, you will see the following prompt:

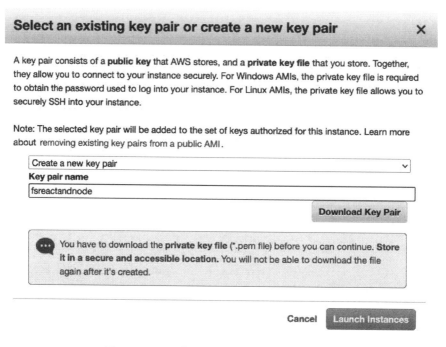

Figure 17.5 – Select an existing key pair dialog

This screen creates a set of encryption keys for use with SSH, one for you and one for AWS, so we can remote terminal into the VM. Download these files and keep them secure. Click the **Launch Instances** button to continue.

> **Warning**
> You must keep your pem file somewhere safe and accessible. You will not be able to download it again.

6.  Once complete, you should see the **Launch Status** screen. Just click on the **View Instances** button at the bottom to continue to the portal:

## Launch Status

How to connect to your instances

Your instances are launching, and it may take a few minutes until they are in the **running** state, when they will be ready for you to use. Usage hours on your new instances will start immediately and continue to accrue until you stop or terminate your instances.

Click **View Instances** to monitor your instances' status. Once your instances are in the **running** state, you can **connect** to them from the Instances screen. Find out how to connect to your instances.

▼ Here are some helpful resources to get you started

- How to connect to your Linux instance
- Learn about AWS Free Usage Tier
- Amazon EC2: User Guide
- Amazon EC2: Discussion Forum

While your instances are launching you can also

- Create status check alarms to be notified when these instances fail status checks. (Additional charges may apply)
- Create and attach additional EBS volumes (Additional charges may apply)
- Manage security groups

View Instances

Figure 17.6 – VM setup complete screen

7.   This will be your VM instance portal:

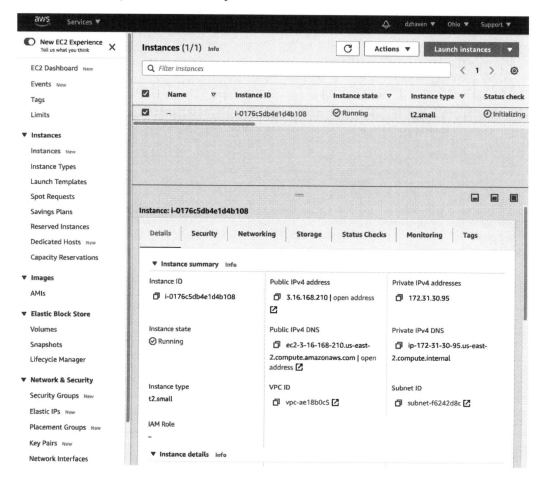

Figure 17.7 – VM portal

8.  Click on **Instance ID** and you will get the **Instance summary** screen:

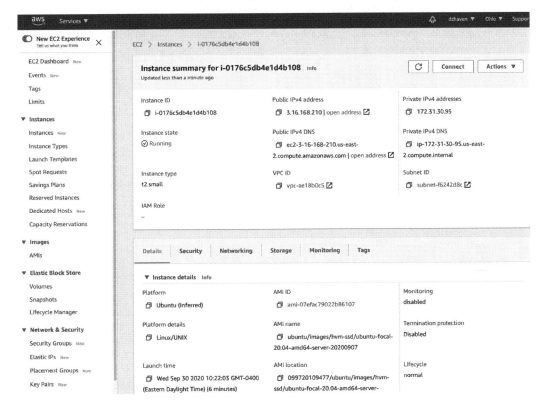

Figure 17.8 – Instance summary

You can see quick facts, such as the running instance state, the public IP address, and the public DNS name.

9. Near the top-right corner of this screen, you will see the **Connect** button. Click it to get the **Connect to instance** screen:

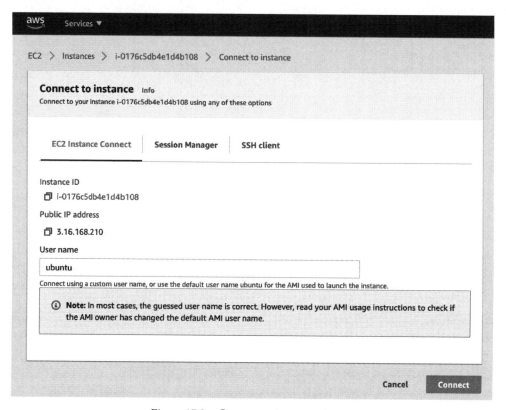

Figure 17.9 – Connect to instance screen

The first tab is **EC2 Instance Connect**, which is a terminal provided for us by AWS. Click the **Connect** button and we will see a terminal to our Ubuntu server inside our browser, as shown here:

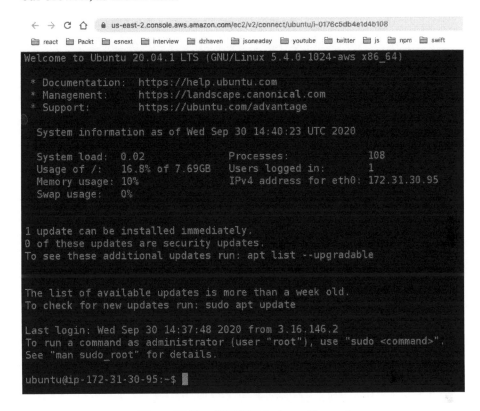

Figure 17.10 – AWS EC2 Instance Connect

This is an optional interface we can use if SSH is not working for some reason. For this demonstration, I will use the SSH interface.

10. Go back to your **Connect to instance** screen and select the third tab, **SSH client**. You should see something like this. Of course, your values will be unique:

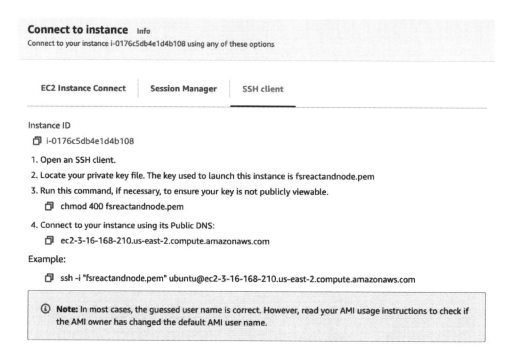

Figure 17.11 – SSH how to instructions

11. Here's a sample of how I ran these instructions on my own terminal:

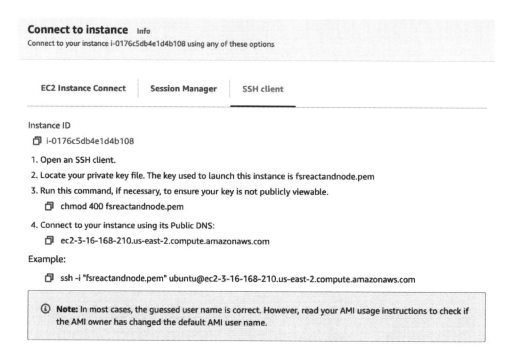

Figure 17.12 – First SSH terminal

First, I changed the permissions of my local pem file as per the AWS instructions. Then, I ran SSH as shown. Note that I used `ubuntu` as the username, your VM should also be the same, and I used `DNS name` for my server.

> **Note**
>
> If this does not work for you, try opening your network inbound rules for SSH to be **Source Anywhere**. If that, too, does not work, you can also revert to using the terminal provided by AWS, as shown previously.

This completes our setup of Ubuntu Linux. Let's install Redis next.

# Setting up Redis, Postgres, and Node on Ubuntu

In this section, we will install our main requirements onto our Linux server. We already covered the setup and configuration of Redis in *Chapter 13, Setting Up a Session State Using Express and Redis*, but let's do it one final time since we will now all have the same underlying OS.

## Setting up Redis

In this section, we will install our Redis server and configure it for our application:

1. On your terminal, log in to the server and run these two commands:

```
sudo apt update
sudo apt install redis-server
```

Apt is a software dependency packaging tool for Linux distributions such as Ubuntu and Debian. Its roughly comparable to NPM. So here, we are updating our `apt` to the latest version and then using it to install Redis.

2. Once the installation is complete, open the `redis.conf` file like this:

```
sudo nano /etc/redis/redis.conf
```

3.  Find the `requirepass` entry, uncomment it, and then add your own password.

> **Warning**
>
> The password in the source code folder's `super-forum-server/dev-config/.env` file for the `REDIS_PASSWORD` variable must match the password you entered in your `redis.conf` file. We will be including the files in the `dev-config` folder later when we do our deployment.

4.  Next, find the `supervised` entry and set it to a value of `systemd`. This allows Ubuntu to control Redis via its `init` system, which uses a command called `systemctl`. Now, save and exit.

5.  Now, let's restart our Redis server to take the new settings:

```
sudo systemctl restart redis.service
```

If we want to stop the service, we can run the following command:

```
sudo systemctl stop redis.service
```

If we want to start the service, we run the following command:

```
sudo systemctl start redis.service
```

6.  If you run this command, it will show whether Redis is running properly:

```
sudo systemctl status redis
```

You should see something like this:

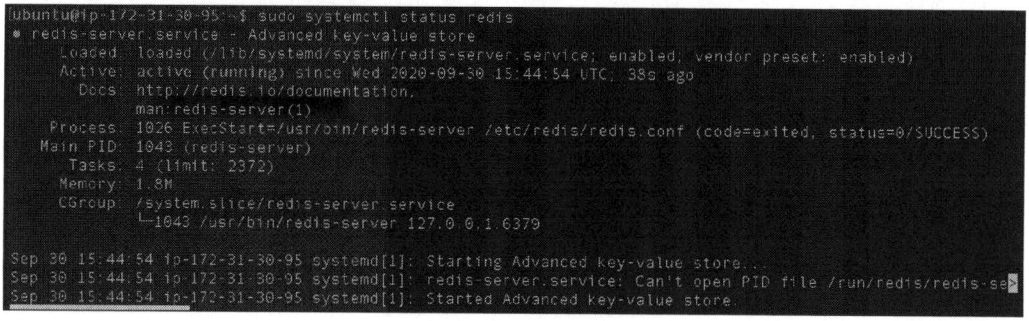

Figure 17.13 – Redis status

In this section, we installed Redis onto our Ubuntu server and turned on the ability to start and stop the server as desired. We will now continue by installing Postgres.

# Setting up Postgres

Now, let's install Postgres for our app:

1.  We'll use `apt` again. Run this command:

    ```
    sudo apt install postgresql
    ```

2.  Let's check that it's working by running the command shown in this screenshot:

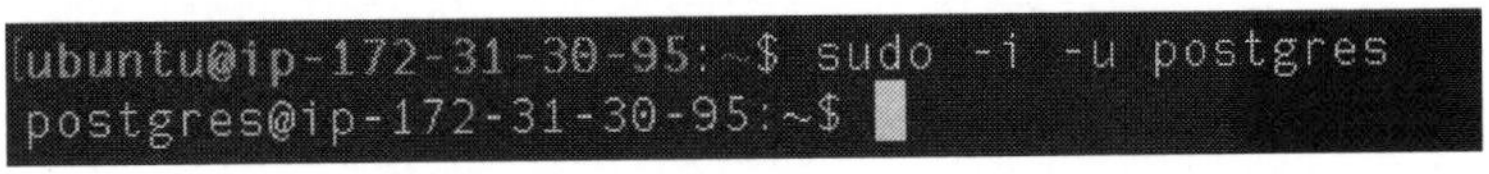

    ```
    ubuntu@ip-172-31-30-95:~$ sudo -i -u postgres
    postgres@ip-172-31-30-95:~$
    ```

    Figure 17.14 – The psql command

    The `postgres` role shown in the command is the global admin account created by default in Postgres. We are basically making our logged-in Linux account act as if it is the `postgres` account temporarily by using `-i` in the command. `-u` indicates which role we are using.

    > **Note**
    >
    > We are not using `pgAdmin` because we get the same capabilities using the `psql` command-line tool, and enabling `pgAdmin` with AWS is cumbersome and difficult.

3.  So, now we are running as the `postgres@<your ip>` user, as was shown in the screenshot. If we were not running as Postgres, we would need to prefix any Postgres commands with `sudo -u postgres`. But since we are running as the role of Postgres, we can just run the command as shown in *Figure 17.13*.

    The `createuser --interactive` command creates a new user based on a series of prompts. Run this command and answer the prompts as shown:

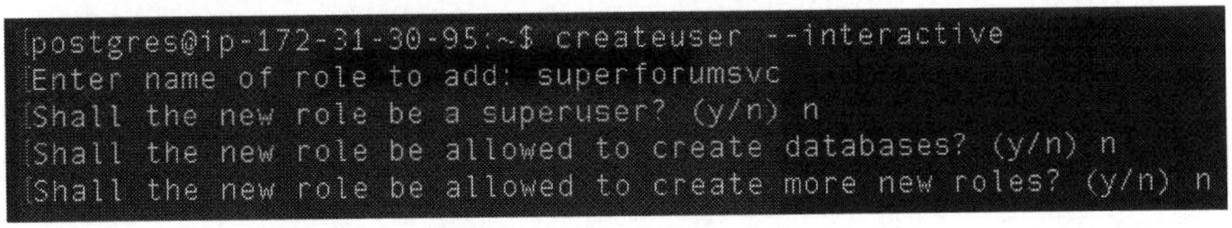

    ```
    postgres@ip-172-31-30-95:~$ createuser --interactive
    Enter name of role to add: superforumsvc
    Shall the new role be a superuser? (y/n) n
    Shall the new role be allowed to create databases? (y/n) n
    Shall the new role be allowed to create more new roles? (y/n) n
    ```

    Figure 17.15 – createuser

    I've set the username to `superforumsvc`.

4. Now, we'll give our new user a password like this:

```
[postgres@ip-172-31-30-95:~$ psql
psql (12.4 (Ubuntu 12.4-0ubuntu0.20.04.1))
Type "help" for help.

[postgres=# alter user superforumsvc with encrypted password
```

Figure 17.16 – Setting a new user password

First, I enable the command-line tool, psql. Then I enter a SQL query to change the superforumsvc user's password.

Note that I cut off the end after the keyword password, which shows what the password is, but it should be in single quotes like this, '<your password>'. Obviously, you'll want to create your own password.

5. Now, let's create the database for the app. First, exit the psql command and then create the database like this:

```
\q
createdb -O superforumsvc SuperForum
```

This command creates the database and makes the superforumsvc role the owner of the new database.

6. Let's now add our ThreadCategory default to our database. In the super-forum-server project, you will find the utils/InsertThreadCategories.txt file. Therein are the Categories we've been using. Of course, you can add your own Categories if you like as well. Here's a sample of my insert attempt for a category:

```
[postgres=# \c SuperForum
You are now connected to database "SuperForum" as user "postgres".
SuperForum=# INSERT INTO ThreadCategories (
Name, Description)
[VALUES ('Programming', '');
ERROR:  relation "threadcategories" does not exist
LINE 1: INSERT INTO ThreadCategories (
                    ^
SuperForum=# INSERT INTO "ThreadCategories" (
Name, Description)
[VALUES ('Programming', '');
ERROR:  column "name" of relation "ThreadCategories" does not exist
LINE 2: Name, Description)
        ^
SuperForum=# INSERT INTO "ThreadCategories" (
["Name", "Description")
VALUES ('Programming', '');
INSERT 0 1
```

Figure 17.17 – Inserting ThreadCategory

As you can see, it fails the first few times. So, let's dig through this. First, you must be on the correct database. So, again use \c to do that. Note that the database name is case-sensitive. Then, make sure your table and field names have double quotes around them. For the `psql` command line, do not use the **public** prefix; this is for pgAdmin only.

That's it for our Postgres setup. Next, let's set up Node.

# Setting up Node

Now, let's install Node:

1. Run the following command:

```
sudo apt install nodejs
```

2. Now, run this to check and you should see the version number of your Node installation:

```
node -v
```

Your node version should be *at least* version 12 or higher. If not, you'll need to run this command:

```
curl -sL https://deb.nodesource.com/setup_12.x | sudo -E bash -
```

And then run this command again:

```
sudo apt install nodejs
```

3. Now, let's install NPM by running the following command:

```
sudo apt install npm
```

4. Now we need to install a way to manage our Node server, that is, to shut it down and autorestart it. So, we will use pm2, which is currently one of the most popular ways of managing Node. Notice we use the -g switch to install it globally:

```
sudo npm install -g pm2
```

In this section, we reviewed how to set up our core service dependencies: Redis, Postgres, and Node. We are now ready to begin setting up the actual server using NGINX.

# Setting up and deploying our app on NGINX

In this section, we will install and configure our app for using NGINX. NGINX is a very popular high-performance web server, reverse proxy, and load balancer. It is respected for its strong performance and also its capabilities to handle different configurations for sites using multiple servers.

We will use it to serve two sites. One will serve our React client, and the other will serve our GraphQL Express server. All of our site traffic will be going to NGINX first and then it will redirect those requests to the appropriate part of our application. Let's start by installing NGINX:

1.  SSH into your server, as shown previously in the *Setting up Ubuntu Linux on AWS Cloud* section and run these commands to install NGINX:

    ```
    sudo apt update
    sudo apt install nginx
    ```

2.  Now that NGINX is installed, let's create a folder to store our server files:

    ```
    sudo mkdir /var/www/superforum
    sudo mkdir /var/www/superforum/server
    ```

    The /var/www directory is the default location for web files, as the name implies.

## Setting up super-forum-server

In this section, we will create the build and deployment process for our server code. It is good to have a standardized process for deployment so that your deployments are consistent and reliable:

1.  Before we can start copying our files, we need to do some basic setup and a build of our server project. Open the super-forum-server project in VSCode. If you look at the package.json file's scripts section, you will see that we have a new script called build. This will compile our server code and package it appropriately for distribution into the dist folder. Now, in order to get this command to work, we will need to install some NPM packages globally first. Run the following command on your developer machine, *not the Ubuntu server*:

    ```
    sudo npm i -g del-cli cpy-cli
    ```

The `del-cli` package is a universal command-line `delete` command. This means that irrespective of whether your development machine is Linux, Mac, or Windows, this command will work the same. Similarly, the `cpy-cli` package allows the universal copying of files and folders. We use these commands so that we can have a single NPM script command that will work the same across all developer operating systems.

Let's explain this script. The build script first deletes the `dist` folder, so that we start afresh each time. It then copies the contents of `dev-config` into `dist` and separately copies the `.env` file into `dist`. And then, finally, it runs the TypeScript compiler.

So, notice we also have a new folder called `dev-config`. This folder will hold configuration-related files that will ultimately be copied into our `dist` folder by the build script. The files in this folder are the `.env` file, for global configuration, the `ormconfig.js` file, for TypeORM configuration, and our `package.json` file.

> **Note**
>
> Your `.env` file in the `dev-config` folder must have the working configuration for *your* server. This includes the passwords you are using, the account names, and the IP addresses. They must all be set correctly according to *your* configurations. If you have trouble getting your server to work, this file is the first place to look.

2.  Unfortunately, there seems to be some sort of bug with the latest Express NPM packages, so we will need to install one more NPM package dependency. Run this command on your development machine:

```
npm i -D @types/express-serve-static-core
```

This dependency is actually already installed when installing `@types/express`, but we are making sure the latest version is now there. If you want to learn more about this bug, refer to this link: `https://github.com/DefinitelyTyped/DefinitelyTyped/issues/47339`.

3.  Note one thing. In the `super-forum-server/src/index.ts` file, I've added a new function, `loadEnv`, near the top of the file. This file will deal with relative path differences of the `.env` file between your development and server environments, using the Node `__dirname` variable.

I've also tweaked the `super-forum-server/dev-config/ormconfig.js` file so that it uses `__dirname` for the path to the TypeORM entities.

> **Warning**
>
> We have enabled the `synchronize` field in `ormconfig.js` to be `true`. This setting is for development deployments only. Do not use this setting in production, since it can trigger unwanted database changes. For production, you should use a pre-made database and then deploy that directly, with the `synchronize` setting set to `false`.

4. OK. Let's now try running our build script. Run this command on your development machine:

```
npm run build
```

Running this should create the `dist` folder, as shown in the following screenshot:

Figure 17.18 – The dist folder

5.  Now, let's try copying our `dist` folder to our server. On the terminal of your development machine, run this command with configurations appropriate to you:

```
scp -i <your pem path> -r <source folder>/*
<username>@<ip>:<dest folder>
```

Note that on Windows, the command will use `pscp`.

Now, when I run this on my machine, I get the following result:

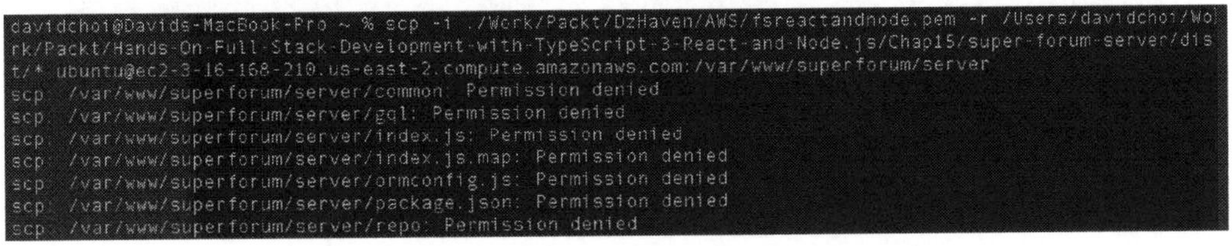

Figure 17.19 – Attempt dist copy failure

So, obviously this failed. This failure is due to a lack of permissions on the destination folder on the Ubuntu server. Let's fix this now.

6.  Log back in to your Ubuntu SSH session and run the following command:

```
sudo chmod -R 777 /var/www/superforum/server
```

This command will open all access temporarily so that we can copy our files. We will close it back up after our copy has happened to reduce security risks.

7.  Now, copy the files by using the same `scp` command from your development terminal. For example, here's my command, run from my developer machine, after opening permissions:

Figure 17.20 – Scp copy

8. Now, check that all the configuration files were copied onto the server by looking in the `server` folder, as follows:

```
ubuntu@ip-172-31-30-95:~$ ls -la /var/www/superforum/server
total 40
drwxrwxrwx 5 root   root   4096 Sep 30 16:54
drwxr-xr-x 3 root   root   4096 Sep 30 16:39 ..
-rw-r--r-- 1 ubuntu ubuntu  411 Sep 30 16:54 .env
drwxr-xr-x 3 ubuntu ubuntu 4096 Sep 30 16:51 common
drwxr-xr-x 2 ubuntu ubuntu 4096 Sep 30 16:51 gql
-rw-r--r-- 1 ubuntu ubuntu 3180 Sep 30 16:51 index.js
-rw-r--r-- 1 ubuntu ubuntu 1921 Sep 30 16:51 index.js.map
-rw-r--r-- 1 ubuntu ubuntu  449 Sep 30 16:51 ormconfig.js
-rw-r--r-- 1 ubuntu ubuntu 1146 Sep 30 16:51 package.json
drwxr-xr-x 2 ubuntu ubuntu 4096 Sep 30 16:52 repo
```

Figure 17.21 – Server folder check

If the `.env` file is missing, you must manually copy it with the following command. Note, this is an issue with Macs, where `.env` files are not visible for some reason:

```
scp -i <your pem path> <your path>/.env
<username><yourserverpath>/.env
```

Again, the precise paths will be different for your machine.

Now, we should close our permissions back up again with this command:

```
sudo chmod -R 755 /var/www/superforum/server
```

This permission gives the owner full access, but gives others only execute and read access.

> **Note**
>
> If we fall down the rabbit hole of security optimizations, we could end up writing another book. Since this will be a development server that will probably be thrown away, let's focus on the main tasks for now. Once you're ready to go live to production with your billion-dollar app, you'll need to exercise some due diligence on security or, better yet, hire someone with at least 10 years' experience.

9. Now, on our SSH terminal session on the Ubuntu server, cd into the `/var/www/superforum/server` folder and then run this command:

```
npm install
```

This will, of course, install all the dependencies for our Node app server.

10. Now, we need to set up our pm2 system so that it will control our Node server. Run this command:

```
pm2 startup
```

This command tells us the specific settings our current user needs in order to configure to use pm2 with systemd and start our Node server when restarting the server. Systemd again is our Ubuntu services controller. After running that command, you should see something similar to this:

```
[PM2] Init System found: systemd
[PM2] To setup the Startup Script, copy/paste the following command:
sudo env PATH=$PATH:/usr/bin /usr/lib/node_modules/pm2/bin/pm2 startup systemd -u ubuntu --hp /home/ubuntu
```

Figure 17.22 – pm2 startup

11. So, copy and paste this command starting at sudo, and then run it on your SSH session of your Ubuntu server. Once run, you should see something like this:

```
ubuntu@ip-172-31-30-95:~$ sudo env PATH=$PATH:/usr/bin /usr/lib/node_modules/pm2/bin/pm2 startup systemd -u ubuntu --hp /home/ubuntu

              --------------

     _/\\\\\\\\\\\\\_____/\\_____/\\_____/\\\\\\\\\\\_
      _\/\\\/////////\\\_\/\\\\\_____/\\\\\\_____/\\\/////////\\\_
       _\/\\_____\/\\\_\/\\\//\\_____/\\\//\\\____\//\\_____\///__
        _\/\\\\\\\\\\\\\/__\/\\\\///\\\_____/\\\/_\/\\\_____\////\\_____
         _\/\\\/////////____\/\\\__\///\\\_/\\\/___\/\\_____\////\\_____
          _\/\\_____\/\\\____\///\\\\\/_____\/\\_____\////\\\___
           _\/\\_____\/\\_____\//\\\/_____\/\\\____/\\_____\//\\\__
            _\/\\_____\/\\_____\///_____\/\\\___\///\\\\\\\\\\\/___
             _\///_____\///_____\///_____\///////////_____

                    Runtime Edition

        PM2 is a Production Process Manager for Node.js applications
                    with a built-in Load Balancer.

                Start and Daemonize any application:
                $ pm2 start app.js

                Load Balance 4 instances of api.js:
                $ pm2 start api.js -i 4

                Monitor in production:
                $ pm2 monitor

                Make pm2 auto-boot at server restart:
                $ pm2 startup

                To go further checkout:
                http://pm2.io/

              --------------

[PM2] Init System found: systemd
Platform systemd
Template
[Unit]
Description=PM2 process manager
Documentation=https://pm2.keymetrics.io/
After=network.target
```

Figure 17.23 – Result of pm2 startup running

12. Next, we want to start our Node server as follows:

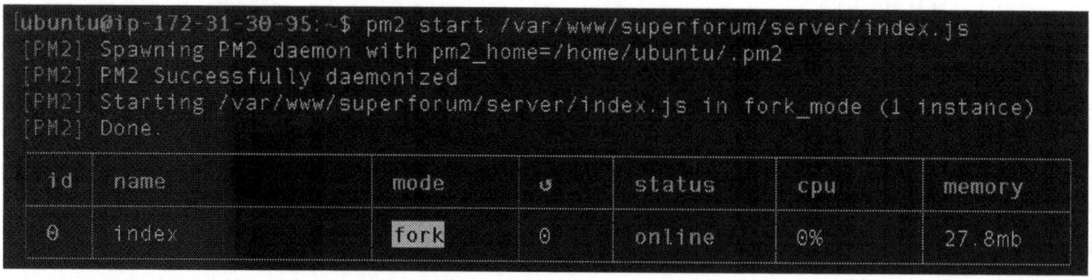

```
[ubuntu@ip-172-31-30-95:~$ pm2 start /var/www/superforum/server/index.js
[PM2] Spawning PM2 daemon with pm2_home=/home/ubuntu/.pm2
[PM2] PM2 Successfully daemonized
[PM2] Starting /var/www/superforum/server/index.js in fork_mode (1 instance)
[PM2] Done.
```

| id | name | mode | ↻ | status | cpu | memory |
|----|------|------|---|--------|-----|--------|
| 0 | index | fork | 0 | online | 0% | 27.8mb |

Figure 17.24 – Node server started

13. We can now save this as part of pm2's startup list by running this command:

```
pm2 save
```

Once run, you should see the following:

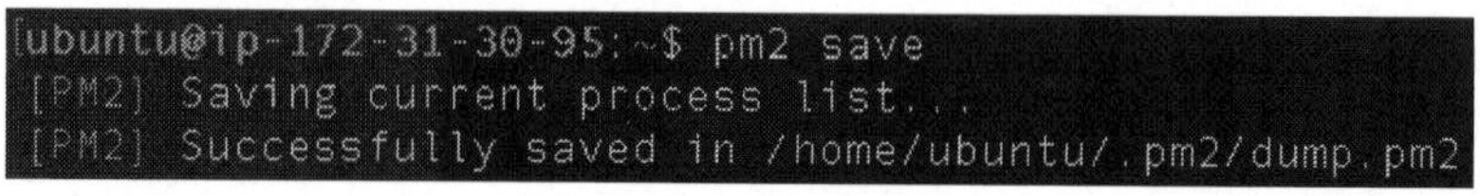

```
[ubuntu@ip-172-31-30-95:~$ pm2 save
[PM2] Saving current process list...
[PM2] Successfully saved in /home/ubuntu/.pm2/dump.pm2
```

Figure 17.25 – pm2 save run

By doing this save operation, our Node server will now start automatically whenever our server is restarted.

In this section, we created a process to build, deploy, and start our Node server. Having configured this setup, we can be sure that it will be repeatable as we update our code in the future.

# Setting up super-forum-client

OK, so now we have to do a similar process for our client-side project. You should have the `super-forum-client` already copied over to your `Chap17` folder, as that's the first thing we did at the start of this chapter:

1. Now, go back to your SSH terminal session on your Ubuntu server and create the folder for the client project like this:

```
sudo mkdir /var/www/superforum/client
```

2. Now, go back to your development terminal in the `super-forum-client` project folder so that we can do the client build and deploy. First, we need to do a minor tweak to our project. You saw that our server project uses an `.env` file for settings. We don't need anything that involved our client project. However, we should be able to at least set the GraphQL server URL as required, depending on the deployment environment. Therefore, perform the following steps:

- Open `index.ts` with VSCode and update the `ApolloClient` code like this:

```
const client = new ApolloClient({
  uri: process.env.REACT_APP_GQL_URL,
  credentials: "include",
  cache: new InMemoryCache({
    resultCaching: false,
  }),
});
```

As you can see, we added an environment variable, called REACT_APP_GQL_URL, just like how we did it on our server. But where is this variable coming from? I'll show that now.

- Open the `package.json` file and look at the scripts section. You should see a new script called `build-dev` that sets the REACT_APP_GQL_URL variable. Feel free to create multiple versions of this script for your own needs with differing variable values.

3. So, now let's run the `build-dev` script:

```
npm run build-dev
```

The build script in the client project is already created for us as part of create-react-app, but we tweaked it by adding the environment variable. Once it completes, you should see this folder called **build**:

Figure 17.26 – The super-forum-client build folder

---

**Note**

Two things to know about React environment variables:

1. The environment variables in React must always start with REACT_APP_. If this prefix is missing, the variable will be ignored.

2. They are inserted into our code at build time and the value gets deployed as part of our client script code. This means users will be able to search the browser scripts and view this data. Therefore, **never** include sensitive information in these environment variables.

---

4.  Now, we just need to open the server's client folder temporarily so that we can do our copy. Run the following command:

```
sudo chmod -R 777 /var/www/superforum/client
```

5.  Now we can deploy our client-side build files. From your development terminal, run this command, with your own proper paths of course:

```
scp -i <your pem path> -r <your path>/*
<username><yourserverpath>
```

The result will look something like this:

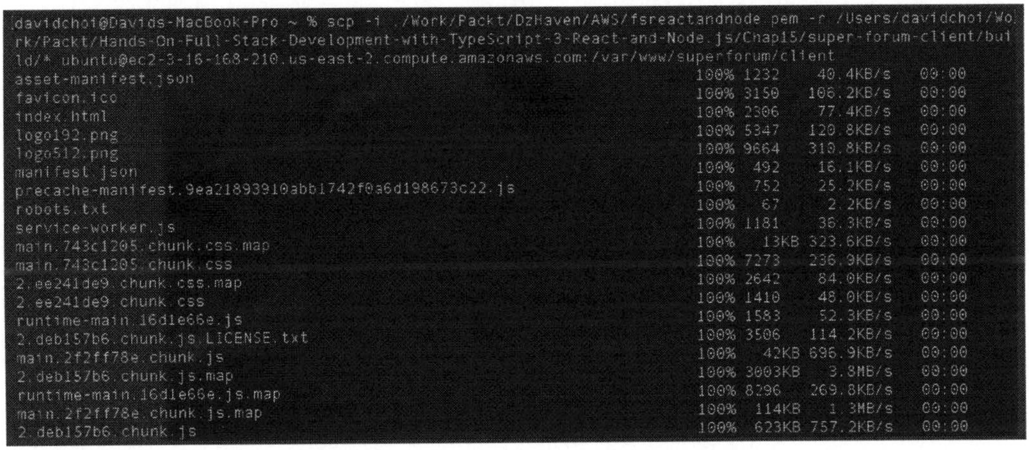

Figure 17.27 – Copying client files to the server

6.  Now, undo the permissions as follows:

```
sudo chmod -R 755 /var/www/superforum/client
```

## Configuring NGINX

All right. We have done a lot of configuring of our server build, so now we can continue by configuring our installed NGINX server:

1.  We need to have NGINX start when starting the system in our Ubuntu server. Run the command shown on your SSH terminal and then authenticate as shown:

```
ubuntu@ip-172-31-30-95:~$ sudo systemctl enable nginx
Synchronizing state of nginx.service with SysV service script with /lib/systemd/systemd-sysv-install.
Executing: /lib/systemd/systemd-sysv-install enable nginx
```

Figure 17.28 – Enabling NGINX start when the system boots

2.  Now, check that NGINX is running with the `status` command shown here:

```
ubuntu@ip-172-31-30-95:~$ sudo systemctl status nginx
● nginx.service - A high performance web server and a reverse proxy server
   Loaded: loaded (/lib/systemd/system/nginx.service; enabled; vendor preset: enabled)
   Active: active (running) since Wed 2020-09-30 16:38:32 UTC; 52min ago
     Docs: man:nginx(8)
 Main PID: 6143 (nginx)
    Tasks: 2 (limit: 2372)
   Memory: 5.0M
   CGroup: /system.slice/nginx.service
           ├─6143 nginx: master process /usr/sbin/nginx -g daemon on; master_process on;
           └─6144 nginx: worker process

Sep 30 16:38:31 ip-172-31-30-95 systemd[1]: Starting A high performance web server and a reverse proxy se
Sep 30 16:38:32 ip-172-31-30-95 systemd[1]: Started A high performance web server and a reverse proxy ser
```

Figure 17.29 – NGINX status

3.  Now, we need to open Port 80 on our AWS VM firewall. Open the browser to the AWS portal and then select **Security Groups**, under the **Network & Security** menu. Then you'll see this:

Figure 17.30 – Security Groups

4. Now, select the non-default group and you'll see the screen shown in the following screenshot. Notice **Inbound rules** near the bottom:

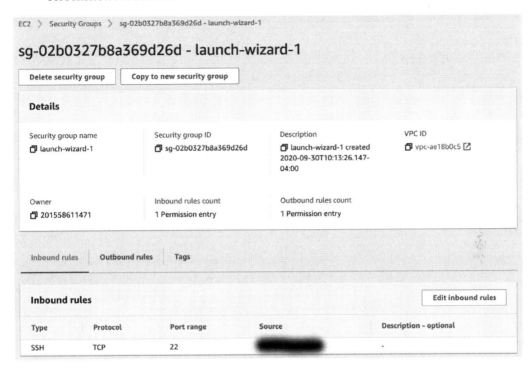

Figure 17.31 – Networking tab; adding an inbound port rule

5. Select the **Edit inbound rules** button and then, on that next screen, click the **Add rule** button.

Once that's selected, you should see this screen shown in *Figure 17.32*. Add the new inbound rule for HTTP, as in the following screenshot:

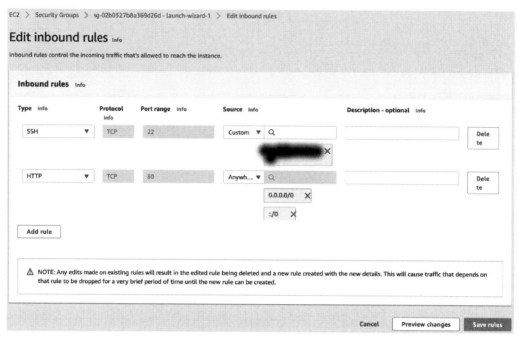

Figure 17.32 – New HTTP inbound rule

By selecting **0.0.0.0/0** as the source, you are allowing any IP addresses, which is what we want. Now, save the rule by clicking the **Save rules** button.

6.  Usually, the local Ubuntu firewall is not enabled. However, if it is enabled, we also need to let traffic through to NGINX on the firewall. If necessary, run the following command:

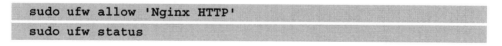

```
sudo ufw allow 'Nginx HTTP'
sudo ufw status
```

Running the preceding command should produce the following result:

Figure 17.33 – Ufw open firewall for NGINX

Now, if we go to our URL with our browser, in my case, it's `ec2-3-16-168-210.us-east-2.compute.amazonaws.com`, yours will be different and again you can find it on your VM instance screen, you should see this:

Figure 17.34 – Default NGINX load screen

7.  So, clearly our NGINX is installed and working. So now we need to make it serve up our site. Note that there appears to be a bug in NGINX for dealing with very long domain names, like the one I received after registering on AWS. Therefore, for our website, we will use the IP address instead.

    NGINX has two options for setting up sites. One allows us to use the configuration file in the `/etc/nginx/conf.d` folder. The other, called Server Blocks, uses the `/etc/nginx/sites-available` folder. We will use the `conf.d` method.

    Run this command:

    ```
    sudo nano /etc/nginx/conf.d/superforum.conf
    ```

8.  Now this is what your file should contain, again with your own folder paths and domain name:

```
GNU nano 4.8
erver {
        listen          80;
        server_name     3.16.168.210;
        root            /var/www/superforum/client;
        index           index.html;

        # super important, needed for refreshes on react app!
        location /{
                try_files $uri $uri/ /index.html;
        }

        location /graphql {
                proxy_pass http://localhost:5000/graphql;
                proxy_http_version 1.1;
                proxy_set_header X-Real-IP $remote_addr;
                proxy_set_header Host         $http_host;
                proxy_set_header Connection "";
                proxy_connect_timeout         300;
                proxy_send_timeout            300;
                proxy_read_timeout            300;
                send_timeout                  300;
        }
}
```

Figure 17.35 – New NGINX conf file

**Here are some things to note:**

Do not forget the concluding semi-colon on each line. Without it, you will get errors.

`server_name` is the domain name or IP address.

`root` is the folder that contains our HTML file.

`location /` is the root of our website.

`location /graphql` is where our GraphQL server lives. We are using `proxy_pass` to redirect calls to `http://<domain or ip>/graphql` to our `http://localhost:5000/graphql` server (our Node server).

`<prefix>_timeout` fields are to prevent Error 503 Gateway Timeout issues, which can sometimes happen with NGINX.

9.   Next, we need to test that our config changes are OK by running the following command:

```
sudo nginx -t
```

You should see this:

```
ubuntu@ip-172-31-30-95:~$ sudo systemctl restart nginx
ubuntu@ip-172-31-30-95:~$ sudo nginx -t
nginx: the configuration file /etc/nginx/nginx.conf syntax is ok
nginx: configuration file /etc/nginx/nginx.conf test is successful
```

Figure 17.36 – NGINX config file status

If there are no errors, we can restart our NGINX server with this command:

```
sudo systemctl restart nginx
```

10.  Let's now see whether our app on the browser comes up. First, let's stop our Node server and restart it without using pm2, so that we can see any errors that might be occurring. Run these commands on your Ubuntu SSH terminal:

```
pm2 stop index
node /var/www/superforum/server/index.js
```

You should see something like this:

```
ubuntu@ip-172-31-30-95:~$ node /var/www/superforum/server/index.js
env path /var/www/superforum/server/common/../.env
client url http://3.16.168.210
Entities path /var/www/superforum/server/repo/**/*.*
Server ready at http://localhost:5000/graphql
```

Figure 17.37 – First run of the Node server

Again, your IP address will be different, and possibly your paths if you changed them. If you see errors instead, go to the troubleshooting section later.

11. Now, open your browser and go to your IP address as given by AWS. Then, click on the **Register** button and let's register a new user, as shown next:

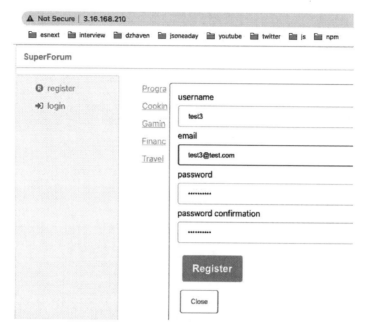

Figure 17.38 – Registering a new user test

Fill in the values as you see fit and click the **Register** button. You should see something like this:

Figure 17.39 – Registration success

12. Now we need to confirm our new user. Run these commands on the Ubuntu SSH terminal:

```
sudo -u postgres psql
\c SuperForum
Update "Users" set "Confirmed" = true;
```

Let's just confirm that all of our users are registered. Once the commands are complete, you should see a confirmation, as follows:

```
ubuntu@ip-172-31-30-95:~$ sudo -u postgres psql
psql (12.4 (Ubuntu 12.4-0ubuntu0.20.04.1))
Type "help" for help.

postgres=# \c SuperForum
You are now connected to database "SuperForum" as user "postgres".
SuperForum=# update "Users" set "Confirmed" = true;
UPDATE 2
```

Figure 17.40 – Confirm registered users

13. Now, let's try and log in with our new user:

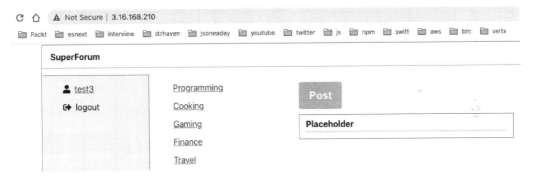

Figure 17.41 – Logged-in test3 user

14. Of course, currently we have no data, so now we'll add one thread post, like this:

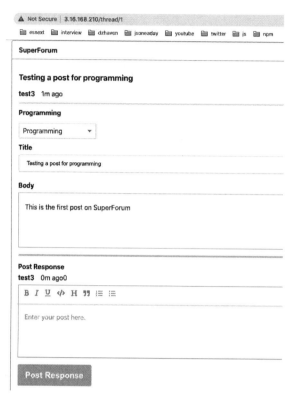

Figure 17.42 – First post

And this is now our home page:

Figure 17.43 – Home screen following the first post

That's it. We're done!

In this section, we finalized our setup of our application using NGINX and all of our other services. Congratulations! You've done a phenomenal job and have gotten through an enormous amount of highly technical material.

# Troubleshooting

Setting up and using cloud services can be a great deal more complex than just using a server on your own network. Here are some basic tips for dealing with issues:

- Any time you update client files, you must restart NGINX.

- Any time you update the server files, you must restart the Node server.

- Always verify that your `.env` settings are correct and match the names you chose during setup; for example, the name of your Postgres database, its username, and password. Also make sure that the path to your `.env` file is correct and is being picked up by the Node server.

- Make sure the `PG_ENTITIES` and `PG_ENTITIES_DIR` variables have the correct paths. For our current app, this would be the following:

  `PG_ENTITIES="/repo/**/*.*"`

  `PG_ENTITIES_DIR="/repo"`

  If these are not set properly, you may get an error, such as `No repository for <Entity Name> was found`.

- If you edit your `.env` file on your server, make sure it is **not** being overwritten during the deploy process. In other words, don't edit your file on the server!

- Always use the `sudo nginx -t` command after updating any `.conf` files for NGINX and then restart the NGINX service once configuration changes are complete. If you do get an error, make sure all of your configuration lines end with a semi-colon.

- If you're making changes in your development environment and testing them there, make sure you have set the `NODE_ENV` environment variable to development. You'll need to set this permanently or else it will disappear on reboot.

- NGINX has a common error of `504 Gateway Timeout`. Make sure your timeout configurations are sufficient. You'll have to play with them.

- Note that very long domain names seem to be an issue in NGINX. For testing purposes, see whether using the IP address works. If it does, and the domain does not, you then know your issue.

# Summary

In this chapter, we cemented our knowledge of web development with React, Node, and GraphQL by finally deploying our application to the cloud. Learning how to deploy our app onto the AWS Cloud is extremely valuable since it is currently the most popular and widely used cloud service. Also, doing this with NGINX was the right move since NGINX is very performant and extremely popular in the Node community.

Thank you so much for joining me on this journey. As a developer, there is always something new to learn and try. But you have taken a huge step by gaining an understanding of some of the most important and key web technologies. You now have all the tools you need in order to create real, full stack, cutting-edge web applications. Again, congratulations!

I wish you continued success.

# Other Books You May Enjoy

If you enjoyed this book, you may be interested in these other books by Packt:

**Node Cookbook - Fourth Edition**

Bethany Griggs

ISBN: 978-1-83855-875-8

- Understand the Node.js asynchronous programming model
- Create simple Node.js applications using modules and web frameworks
- Develop simple web applications using web frameworks such as Fastify and Express
- Discover tips for testing, optimizing, and securing your web applications
- Create and deploy Node.js microservices
- Debug and diagnose issues in your Node.js applications

**Full-Stack React Projects - Second Edition**
Shama Hoque

ISBN: 978-1-83921-541-4

- Extend a basic MERN-based application to build a variety of applications

- Add real-time communication capabilities with Socket.IO

- Implement data visualization features for React applications using Victory

- Develop media streaming applications using MongoDB GridFS

- Improve SEO for your MERN apps by implementing server-side rendering with data

- Implement user authentication and authorization using JSON web tokens

- Set up and use React 360 to develop user interfaces with VR capabilities

- Make your MERN stack applications reliable and scalable with industry best practices

# Leave a review - let other readers know what you think

Please share your thoughts on this book with others by leaving a review on the site that you bought it from. If you purchased the book from Amazon, please leave us an honest review on this book's Amazon page. This is vital so that other potential readers can see and use your unbiased opinion to make purchasing decisions, we can understand what our customers think about our products, and our authors can see your feedback on the title that they have worked with Packt to create. It will only take a few minutes of your time, but is valuable to other potential customers, our authors, and Packt. Thank you!

# Index

Made in the USA
Middletown, DE
16 May 2021